The Ethiopian Revolution
1974–1991

The Ethiopian Revolution
1974 – 1991

*From a Monarchical Autocracy
to a Military Oligarchy*

Teferra Haile-Selassie

**Kegan Paul International
London and New York**

First published in 1997 by
Kegan Paul International
UK: P.O. Box 256, London WC1B 3SW, England
Tel: (0171) 580 5511 Fax: (0171) 436 0899
E-mail: books@keganpau.demon.co.uk
Internet: http://www.demon.co.uk/keganpaul/
USA: 562 West 113th Street, New York, NY 10025, USA
Tel: (212) 666 1000 Fax: (212) 316 3100

Distributed by
John Wiley & Sons Ltd
Southern Cross Trading Estate
1 Oldlands Way, Bognor Regis
West Sussex, PO22 9SA, England
Tel: (01243) 779 777 Fax: (01243) 820 250

Columbia University Press
562 West 113th Street
New York, NY 10025, USA
Tel: (212) 666 1000 Fax: (212) 316 3100

© Teferra Haile-Selassie, 1997

Phototypeset in 10/12pt Baskerville
by Intype London Ltd

Printed in Great Britain by TJ International

ISBN 0–7103–0565–6

British Library Cataloguing in Publication Data
Haile-Selassie, Teferra
The Ethiopian revolution, 1974–1991: from a monarchical autocracy to a military oligarchy
1. Ethiopia — History — 1974–2. Ethiopia — Politics and government – 1974–1991
I. Title
96 3'.071
ISBN 0 7103 0565 6

Library of Congress Cataloging in Publication Data
Haile-Selaisse, Teferra.
    The Ethiopian revolution, 1974–91: from a monarchical autocracy
to a military oligarchy/Teferra Haile-Selassie.
        p. cm.
    Includes bibliographical references and index.
    ISBN 0–7103–0565–6 (alk. paper)
    1. Ethiopia—Politics and government—1974–1991. I. Title.
DT387.95.H33 1997
963.07'1—dc21   96–47529
                                                                     CIP

Dedicated to
my loving and supportive wife, Almaz,
my children, Candy, Yared, Kidist and Hiwot.

Contents

Contents

Contents

Foreword

Ethiopia, the only country in Africa to survive the nineteenth-century European scramble for the continent, has a long, unique, and complex history. This stretches back over three million years to Lucy, or as the Ethiopians call her Dinkenesh, the earliest known ancestor of the human race, to the political turmoil of late twentieth-century Africa.

Though the Ethiopians produced stone inscriptions in ancient times, and began composing royal chronicles on parchment in the early medieval period, the writing of modern style Ethiopian history was until recently the preserve of Europeans and other foreign authors. Foreign scholars made a major contribution towards elucidating many of the complexities of Ethiopia's long historic experience, but often failed to catch the true and authentic spirit of the Ethiopian people. The advent of Ethiopia's own historians – and autobiographical writers – is therefore greatly to be welcomed.

My friend Teferra Haile-Selassie writes partly as a historian, but also, and perhaps more importantly, as a sincere and sensitive observer, who lived through the later historical events which he describes, and indeed played a notable role in several of them. An intellectual product of Ethiopia's post-World War II educational system, he became a patriotic and a hard-working civil servant, and, like so many colleagues of his generation, loyally served a succession of Ethiopian governments: those associated with the names of Emperor Haile Selassie, General Aman Andom, General Teferri Banti, Colonel Mengistu Haile Mariam, and Ato Tesfaye Dinka.

Teferra's book has a double interest. The first chapters reveal how the wide span of Ethiopia's long history is perceived, judged and evaluated by a modern-educated member of the country's present-day generation. The later sections provide perhaps the first insider's view of the workings of the various Ethiopian governments in which he served. Teferra writes, as far as it is possible for anyone to do, fairly and without prejudice. He seeks as far as he can, to show both the good and the bad aspects of pre- and post-revolutionary Ethiopian Government. As the last Ethiopian Ambassador in Britain prior to the coming to power of the EPRDF, he attended the London Conference of 28 May 1991, and his account of that historical important event will be read with special interest and attention.

It is my sincere hope other Ethiopians will follow Teferra's example, by writing further studies of Ethiopia, its history and peoples, and, above all, by recording their memories of the often momentous events which they witnessed, or in which they actually participated.

Richard Pankurst

Preface and Acknowledgement

The purpose of this book is to provide to readers and scholars an objective personal account of the Ethiopian revolution of 1974. As a civil servant who had served for over three decades under the Imperial System and the Military Regime (Dergue), I felt that I could make a modest contribution by presenting as objectively as humanly possible the seventeen years of the Dergue's rule. With the hope to provide the facts to readers and scholars I had endeavoured to reproduce some of the major policies of the Dergue. In producing this work except the first chapter, I mainly depended on my personal experience and notes and whenever possible I had referred to the documents of the government, Commission for Organising the Workers' Party of Ethiopia (COPWE) and Workers' Party of Ethiopia (WPE).

The Dergue in its propaganda activity was effectively using the state-run newspapers, the *Addis Zemen* and *The Ethiopian Herald*. As a result these papers published the Dergue's major decisions and policy declarations including legislation and speeches of the head of the state in their entireties. The papers, the radio and television played a significant role in promoting the policies of the government. Following the formation of the Workers' Party of Ethiopia in 1984 the party organ, *Serto Ader*, a weekly paper, and *Meskerem*, a quarterly Journal of party ideology, became authoritative sources of party and government policies. Other sources which I relied upon to complement my notes, include reports of the Chairman to the Central Committees of COPWE and WPE, annual Revolution Day speeches of the Chairman, the National Revolutionary Democratic Programme of Ethiopia, the Programme of WPE, the President's reports to the National Shengo and other government and party publications.

I am indebted to all my friends who encouraged me to share my experience with those who were not able to have access to a first-hand account of the Ethiopian Revolution, a change that demolished beyond any recognition the socio-economic base of one of the ancient polities in the world. In the absence of memoirs from the main actors in the revolution, the best one could hope for is an account from a civil servant who had served under the system. In this regard, I hope, this work could serve as a modest contribution.

I am deeply indebted to Leila Ingrams who read the first four chapters of the manuscript and made constructive and valuable comments. Her suggestions were used in restructuring some of the chapters. I am also grateful to Rita Pankhurst who despite her heavy commitment found some time to read the first chapter of the manuscript and made useful comments that drew my attention to restructure some of the passages. My special thanks go to Professor Richard Pankhurst, renowned scholar in Ethiopian studies, who sacrificed his holiday in reading the manuscript. His scholarly comments, suggestions and criticisms immensely helped me to reconsider some of the points I had overlooked. His resourceful comments and constructive criticisms have gone a long way in enriching the work and for that I am greatly indebted to him. I also express to him my deepest gratitude for writing a foreword to the book.

I am grateful to Ato Terefe Ras-Work and his wife Weizero Berhane Assfaw whose Christmas gift, a personal computer, facilitated the production of this work and saved me from the trouble of looking for a stenographer. I am also thankful to Amelework and Colin Crowfoot for their moral support and regular hospitality which were useful distractions and indeed stimulated me to be more productive. I also appreciate deeply the support and encouragement that I received from Weizerit Hirut Teferra.

An acknowledgement for the efforts of those who contributed to the production of this work would not be complete without an expression of a profound gratitude to my loving and supportive wife who besides being a valuable source of inspiration and strength, played the roles of an able adviser, critique, an editor and a research assistant. Finally, I would like to express my appreciation to my dear children, Candy, Yared, Kidist and Hiwot, for their understanding and support, which gave me the perseverance that was indispensable for the completion of this book.

Teferra Haile-Selassie

Abbreviations

AALC	African–American Labour Centre
AEPA	All Ethiopia Peasants' Association
AETU	All Ethiopia Trade Unions
AFL-CIO	American Federation of Labour–Congress of Industrial Organisations
EPA	Ethiopian Peasants' Associations
ETU	Ethiopian Trade Unions
CC	Central Committee
Cde.	Comrade
CADU	Chelalo Agricultural Development Unit
CELU	Confederation of Ethiopian Labour Unions
CIA	Central Intelligence Agency
COPWE	Commission for Organising the Workers' Party of Ethiopia
CPSC	Central Planning Supreme Council
Dej.	Dejazmach
EC	Ethiopian Calendar
EDM	Ethiopian Democratic Movement
EDU	Ethiopian Democratic Union
ELF	Eritrean Liberation Front
ELM	Eritrean Liberation Movement
ENSUE	The Ethiopian Students' Union of Europe
EPDM	Ethiopian People's Democratic Movement
EPLF	Eritrean People's Liberation Front
EPRDF	Ethiopian People's Revolutionary Democratic Front
EPRP	Ethiopian People's Revolutionary Party, Amharic acronym, EHAPA

Abbreviations

Fit.	Fitawrari
H.H.	His Highness
ICFTU	International Confederation of Free Trade Unions
ILO	International Labour Organisation
MPP	Minimum Package Programme
NDRPE	National Democratic Revolutionary Programme of Ethiopia
NCCC	National Campaign Co-ordinating Committee
NROC	National Revolutionary Operation Command
OAU	Organisation of African Unity
OLF	Oromo Liberation Front Exporting Countries
OPEC	Organisation of Petroleum Exporting Countries
PDRE	People's Democratic Republic of Ethiopia
PMAC	Provisional Military Administrative Council
PMG	Provisional Military Government
POMOA	Provisional Office for Mass Organisational Affairs
REWA	Revolutionary Ethiopia Women's Association
REYA	Revolutionary Ethiopia Youth Association
RRC	Relief and Rehabilitation Commission
TAE	Teachers' Association of Ethiopia
TPLF	Tigray Peoples' Liberation Front
UDA	Urban Dwellers' Association
WADU	Wollamo Agricultural Development Unit
WPE	Workers' Party of Ethiopia
WSLF	Western Somalia Liberation Front

Glossary of Terms

Abune	Bishop.
Abyotawi Seded	Amharic term for the party of Revolutionary Flame.
Afe Negus	The spokesman of the king; a title given to the Chief Justice.
Ato	The title of a man, Mr.
Awraja	A province or a second level of a regional administrative structure.
Blata	A title given to civilians in government positions.
Dejazmach	A high-ranking title and second to a Ras under the monarchy.
Dergue	The Co-ordinating Committee of the Armed Forces, the Police and the Territorial Army which was formed in 1974. It assumed power by deposing the Emperor Haile Selassie in 1975.
ECHAT	Amharic acronym for a Marxist–Leninist Organisation, the Ethiopian Oppressed People's Movement.
Echege	The highest ecclesiastical office held by an Ethiopian cleric before the Ethiopian Orthodox Church acquired the status of autocephalous.
EMALEDH	Amharic acronym for Union of Marxist Leninist–Organisations of Ethiopia.
Enderassie	A viceroy of the emperor; a governor of a Teklia Gizat, the highest administrative unit under the monarchy.
Fitawrari	A title conferred upon individuals by the crown. It was below Dejazmach.

Geez	The liturgical language of the Ethiopian Orthodox Church.
Hibretesebawinet	Socialism.
Kebele	Urban dwellers' association; a municipal ward; a village.
Kelad	A unit of rural land measurement.
Kine	Poetry.
Kentiba	Mayor.
Lij	A honorific title reserved for a male offspring of the nobility.
MALRED	Amharic acronym for one of the Marxist–Leninist organisations which was a founding member of POMOA.
Mass Organis-ations	A collective term used in reference to peasants' associations, trade unions, urban dwellers' associations, women and youth associations.
MEISON	The Amharic acronym for one of the Marxist-Leninist Organisations, All Ethiopia Socialist Movement.
Neguse	King.
Negeste Negestat	Empress.
Neguse Negest	King of kings; emperor.
Noos Dergue	A sub-committee of the Dergue that was formed in the early stages of the revolution and later was replaced by *Yelewit Hawariat.*
Ras	The highest title that was conferred upon a person in pre-revolution Ethiopia.
Rist	A system of hereditary land ownership.
Shengo	An assembly, a council; a parliament.
Shume	Chief.
Teklia Gizat	The highest administrative division under the monarchy, a governorate-general.
Tsehafe Taezaz	Chancellor; royal scribe; keeper of the Royal Seal.
Waz League	An Amharic name of one of the Marxist–Leninist parties, Labour League.
Weizerit	The title of an unmarried woman or a girl; Miss.
Weizero	Lady; the title of a married woman; Mrs.
Wereda	The smallest administrative unit, a district.
Yelewit Hawariat	Literally apostles of change; representatives of the Dergue who were attached to government institutions at early stages of the revolution.
Zemecha	Campaign.

List of Illustrations

Chapter One
Historical Perspective

History is past politics and politics is present history.

A. K. Freeman (1823–92)

From the Aksumite Period to the End of Zemene Mesafint

The Aksumite royal inscriptions give indications that the kingdom had existed in the era before Christ. Some historians, however, claim that the kingdom was in existence since the sixth century BC. At present, conclusive historical evidence is not available that would establish the exact period of origin of the Aksumite kingdom. Even the most ancient written record, the Prieplus of the Erythrean Sea by a Greek merchant, dates back to the first century AD.[1] Despite paucity of written record on the early period of the Aksumite kingdom, its successor, Ethiopia, is one of the oldest states in history.

According to Ethiopian legend the state existed as a polity for three thousand years. During this period it had its 'Golden and Dark Ages'. The period from the first half of the first millennium AD up to the seventh century was the climax of achievements of spiritual and material culture. The kingdom's military and commercial power of considerable significance and its influence on both sides of the Red Sea coast were unrivalled. Its military expeditions had penetrated into the interior of Southern Arabia. Not only that, some parts of Southern Arabia were under the direct rule of the viceroy of the Aksumite Kingdom. The last viceroy of the Aksumite Kingdom, Abreha, who later rebelled and declared himself ruler of Southern Arabia was an Ethiopian.[2]

1

The Aksumites' encounter was not confined to the Red Sea coast and the Arabian Peninsula; it had developed commercial relations with the then world powers, the Romans and Greeks. Some historians claim that the Aksumite Kingdom's contact with world powers of the time was far deeper than mere commercial transactions. Cultural influence, in particular of the Greeks, had an impact on the Aksumite civilisation. It is claimed by scholars that Greek was spoken in the Aksumite court. Aksumite kings use of Greek on several inscriptions at Aksum are often quoted as evidence to prove the use of Greek as an official language of the kingdom.

The early Aksumite civilisation was not limited to the achievement of material culture. In spiritual culture a great stride was made by the introduction of Christianity during the reign of King Ezana around AD 350. Christianity was introduced by converting Ezana and his close associates. The conversion of the king and his associates by historical accident created a close relationship between the monarchy and the Church. The relationship served the mutual interests of both. The monarchy used the Church to legitimatise its rule and the Church employed the power and influence of the monarchy to spread Christianity.

After the demise of Ezana and until the rise of King Kaleb the Aksumite Kingdom's influence declined, lost its dominions and even its control over the Red Sea route. A struggle for succession among Ezana's sons was one of the major factors that caused the decline of the kingdom. Furthermore the kingdom fell into the hands of a successor without vision and drive. The period from the death of Ezana to a rise of another monarch with vision and drive, Kaleb, took more than a century. A century, in the political life of a state, was long enough to relegate it to insignificance.

Kaleb's accession to the throne in the sixth century (503–33) marked a new era in the revival of the Aksumite Kingdom. It regained its military and commercial influence; lost dominions on both sides of the Red Sea coast were restored. New territories farther into the hinterland of Arabia were conquered. Inscriptions of Aksumite kings, in particular that of Ezana and Kaleb, testify that the Aksumite Kingdom included some parts of Southern Arabia and Nubia.[3] During his reign the Aksumite Kingdom attained prominence in military power, commerce and culture. Christianity was given more importance with the arrival of nine saints from Syria. Establishment of monasteries and translation of religious books into Geez, the liturgical language of the Ethiopian Orthodox Church, gave formidable impetus to spreading the Monophysite Faith. Relations with Alexandria were much closer than ever before. Yet, the Ethiopian

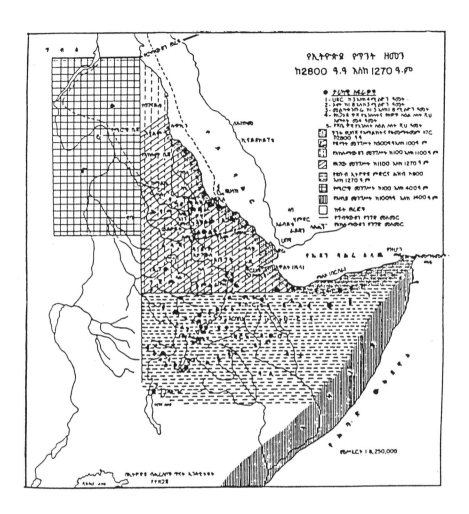

Map 1 Ethiopian map, in Amharic, showing Ancient Ethiopia, ca. 2800
B.C.–1270 A.D.

Church was not autocephalous; it depended on Egypt for an ordination of an Abune (an Egyptian prelate), the head of the Ethiopian Orthodox Church. Church music which is still in use was composed by an Ethiopian cleric, Yared. Literature including *Kine* (poetry) developed tremendously.[4]

The glory of the Aksumite Kingdom began to decline after Kaleb's abdication of his throne in favour of a monastic life. His indifference to appoint a successor was a major factor for the decline in commercial contacts and influence in the world. In the North the Beja tribes rebelled and invaded the region along the Red Sea Coast. Egypt's reluctance to send a new Abune aggravated the precarious internal situation. On the other hand the rise of Islam in the seventh century posed a threat to the Aksumite Kingdom and the Orthodox Faith. Some historians consider, and rightly so, the rise of Islam as a turning point in the history of Ethiopia. Initial contacts of the Aksumite Kingdom with Islamic countries were friendly. Its generosity in extending refuge and succour to the followers of Mohammed when they faced threat of persecution in their country, accounted for his followers holding Aksumites in special esteem.

In the first half of the seventh century the expansion of Islam was fast. Arab armies occupied Palestine, Syria and later on Egypt. This development affected adversely the Aksumite Kingdom's contact with the Roman Empire.[5] From this time on the decline of the Aksumite Kingdom became more visible. In the subsequent period the Red Sea coast, particularly Massawa and the Dahlak islands were lost to the Arabs. The Aksumite Kingdom with the loss of the Red Sea coast, was completely cut off from the rest of the world. However, towards the second half of the ninth century it was able to restore its coastal dominions. By the beginning of the tenth century Massawa, Dahlak and Zeila were under the effective control of the Aksumite Kingdom. At the end of the century another struggle for power ensued: a certain pagan queen, Gudit, possibly from Damot in Gojjam, rose and plundered and almost destroyed the kingdom. Churches were raised and Christians were persecuted. The king, petrified by the havoc, wrote to King George of Nubia, probably to enlist his assistance, that a certain pagan rebel was pillaging his country and enslaving his people and burning churches and chasing him from refuge to refuge. The Christian religion was on the verge of destruction.[6] The king of Aksum implored King George to intercede on his behalf with the Patriarch of Alexandria to expedite the dispatch of an Abune. King George's entreaties were successful. The arrival of an Abune boosted the power of the king of Aksum. At last the pagan queen was defeated and peace was on the horizon.

The rise of Queen Guidit was a symptom of the decay of the Aksumite

Dynasty and a rise of a new one. A steady decline of the Aksumite Kingdom created a favourable climate for the emergence of the Zagwe Dynasty (1100–1275). Its monarchs unlike their predecessors claimed descent from Moses.[7] The throne was usurped from the Aksumites and the political centre of the nation shifted from Aksum to Lasta in the south of the kingdom. Lalibella became the new capital of the nation and remained a political centre for over 175 years.

The Zagwe Dynasty was mainly interested in religious pursuits. It did not share its predecessor's expeditionary zeal and political astuteness. As Abir aptly puts it, *'the Zagwe Dynasty was never interested beyond the boundaries of Lasta.'*[8] Its indifference left the frontiers of the state unguarded. This created a favourable situation for an uncontested claim of the dominions and territories of the state by neighbouring and emerging powers. More-over conditions that favoured the emergence of independent principalities developed.

Among the Zagwe kings Lalibella (1160–1211) was pious and wholly devoted his time and energy to spreading Christianity and constructing exotic Churches. The stone hewn churches in Lasta are products of his creative pursuits. The architectural refinement in the designs of those churches is superb.

In the later part of the 12th century, the Zagwe Dynasty demanded an autocephalous status for the Orthodox Church. For reasons that are not obscure to discern, the Patriarch of Alexandria rejected the request. The Egyptian Government in addition to magnificent gifts of ivory, gold and slaves, enjoyed an indirect control over Ethiopia through the appointment of an Egyptian Abune whose primary loyalty was to his country.[9] The irony was that an Islamic government was influencing the appointment of an Abune to the Ethiopian Orthodox Church.

The Egyptian Abune was not apolitical in the internal affairs of Ethiopia. Given the close relationships of the Church and state in Ethiopia successive Abune's from Alexandria had played decisive roles in anointing kings. A king, in those days, to command the loyalty of his subjects, had to be anointed and blessed by the Abune. The performance of these rituals by the Abune constituted a credible source to legitimise succession to the throne and power. Furthermore the Abune in his capacity as the head of the Church played an important role in the resolution of conflicts between a monarch and a rebellious war-lord. The Abune had a big stake in the temporal life of the nation. Such a key spiritual position was held by a citizen of Egypt, a country which did not conceal its desire to control the source of the Blue Nile. In fact, its successive attempts to occupy

Ethiopia had met humiliating defeat at the hands of the Ethiopians at the battles of Gunda-Gundet in 1875 and 1876 respectively.[10]

An Abune's involvement in the internal affairs of the state had happened on several occasions. Monarchs reacted by taking measures ranging from severing relations to, in extreme cases, detention of an Abune. A case in point is Abune Selama, a Metropolitan prelate, in the second half of the 19th century, during the reign of Emperor Tewodros. The Abune was known for his outrageous court intrigues and meddling in the political affairs of the state. The prelate's plan to have an Egyptian contingent in his palace was disclosed when the Patriarch of Alexandria was paying a visit in Ethiopia. The Patriarch and the Abune jointly submitted a recommendation on the need of an Egyptian contingent to Tewodros. Their submission confirmed Emperor Tewodros's suspicion of their plan to import a foreign legion. Tewodros reacted decisively by placing the prelates under house arrest.[11] This is an incident which shows where the prelate's primary loyalty lay. In the prelates' eyes the interest of Ethiopia had to be subordinated to the political need of Egypt.

The dream of the Zagwe kings, particularly that of King Lalibella to gain autocephalous status for the Ethiopian Orthodox Church, was realised seven hundred years later by Emperor Haile Selassie I in 1949. The remarkable achievement of the late emperor marked the end of the temporal and spiritual influence of Egypt in Ethiopia.

Over 170 years of rule the Zagwe Dynasty was overthrown by King Yekuno Amlak (1270–85) who claimed direct descent from the Solomonic Line. His accession to the throne by force, in keeping with the Ethiopian tradition of transfer of power, is referred to by historians as 'the restoration of the Solomonic Line'. Without conclusive proof to the king's claim, he ought to be considered an impostor who usurped the throne from the last king of the Zagwe Dynasty. Yekuno Amlak ended Ethiopia's self-imposed political isolation of the Zagwe Dynasty. He recovered most of the Aksumite territories and effectively controlled the core regions of the Aksumite Kingdom. The literary renaissance that was begun and flourished during the Zagwe Dynasty reached its climax under the Solomonic Dynasty. Numerous religious works were translated from Coptic and Arabic into Geez. Developments in the production of hagiographies were immense. The Kibre Negest, a narrative on the origin of the Ethiopian kingdom and adulation of the Solomonic Line, was produced parallel to religious works. It was compiled during the reign of King Amde Siyon (about 1314–44) It is '*the foremost creation of Ethiopic literature*'.[12] Valuable works such as *History of the Jews, History of Alexander the Great* and the *Universal History of John of Nikus* were translated into Geez.[13] Around the fourteenth century contemporary chronicles began to appear. The chronicles of King Amde Siyon are well known for their richness in content and precision in recording events.

From the Solomonic Dynasty we shall consider some of the monarchs whose rule had significantly affected the growth and development of the empire.

King Amde Siyon was one of the great kings of the Solomonic Dynasty with foresight and imagination. He was well known for his expeditionary zeal and love for stretching the frontiers of his kingdom in all directions. His well-organised and strong army crowned him with success. The Muslim principalities of Ifat, Hadya, Daoro, Bale, Adale and regions along the Red Sea coast that had broken away from the kingdom were subdued and reincorporated into it.

King Amde Siyon, for the first time in the history of Ethiopia, issued a sort of *modus operandi* for the governance of his kingdom known as *Serate Mengist* (rules for governing). It was an original attempt in defining the powers and prerogatives of the king. The document was an earnest attempt to develop a written constitution. A century later King Amde Siyon's great-great grandson, King Zara Yaqob (1430–68) introduced reforms with far-reaching implications both in temporal and spiritual domains. In administrative innovations he divided his realm into units consisting of provinces and districts and for each of the administrative units appointed governors who were directly accountable to him. Among his governors the Bahre Negash (governor of the maritime province of Bahre Midre which consisted of some of the provinces of Tigray including Shire, Sarea, Akaleguzaye, Hamassen and Bur) was given precedence over other governors.[14]

Zara Yaqob was also interested in ecclesiastical reform. He introduced reforms that facilitated the smooth running of the Church. He built many churches and fortified them with gifts. The following were some of his contributions:

- Broke away from the age-old tradition of one Abune and succeeded in obtaining two Abunes from Alexandria.
- Divided his kingdom into administrative units and dioceses.
- Defined duties of priests in teaching the Gospel and in conducting services in churches.
- Promoted setting up libraries in every church for the use of congregations.
- Issued seven books on the doctrine, laws, rites and customs of the Church.

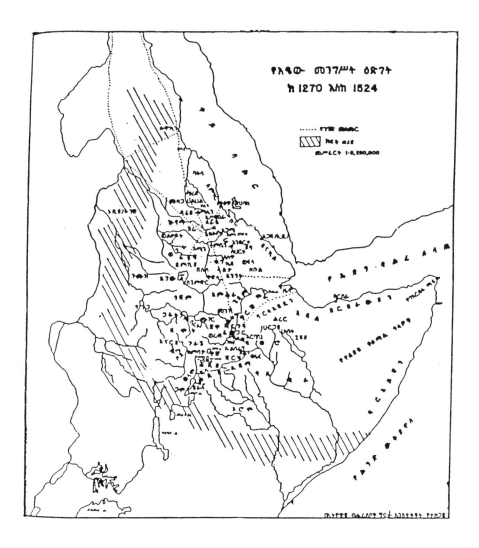

Map 2 Ethiopian map, in Amharic, showing the Medieval Hatse State,
ca. 1270–1524

- Facilitated the reconciliation of the Ethiopian Orthodox Church with the Holy See.
- Decreed abolition of all forms of paganism including offering of animal sacrifices and consultations with witchcrafts.

Zara Yaqob's enthusiasm in regulating the lifestyle of his subjects by rules and directives led to the regimentation of his kingdom. Every Christian was required to wear upon his forehead and arms amulets bearing the names of the Father, Son and Holy Ghost. The sign of the cross was to be affixed on his forehead, hands and even on personal belongings. Church attendance on Sundays was compulsory. Should a Christian fail to follow these prescriptions he would be liable to execution and confiscation of properties.[15]

Zara Yaqob was a monarch of varied talents. He was a great reformer as well as a scholar of repute. *Metsihafe Milade* and *Metsihafe Berhan*, among his scholarly works, are of immense literary value. He also encouraged translation of religious works from alien sources into Geez.[16] The successors of King Zara Yaqob were committed to pursuing his policies and in some cases they enriched them with original contributions. Until the appearance of King Libne Dingle (1508–40) the kingdom was strong and secure. It had the capability and the resources to contain internal rebellion and to repulse any intrusion upon its kingdom. However, his weakness and lack of foresight in strengthening national defence made the kingdom vulnerable to invasion. Turkey occupied Massawa in 1520 and thereafter incited the Moslem subjects of Ethiopia against the kingdom. Turkey's presence in the Red Sea coast transformed the geopolitical map of the area. It systematically pursued an interventionist policy to weaken the Christian kingdom of Ethiopia. It encouraged a religious war against Ethiopia. It further introduced firearms by supplying the Ethiopian Moslems with matchlocks, the advanced weapon of the time, whose possession and use meant an outright victory over those who were armed with traditional means of warfare, spears, swords, bows and arrows.

The threat posed by Turkey had escaped the notice of King Libne Dingle and his ally Portugal. Ethiopia and Portugal were entrenched in exchange of emissaries while the Adale tribes under the leadership of Ahmed El Gazi (Gragn Ahmed as he was known locally) acquired matchlocks and training in the use of arms from the Turks. On the other hand the king, confident in his numerous army, failed to appreciate the scale of the threat that was facing him. His army of 216,000 clashed with Gragn's 12,500 men. The king's army suffered a devastating defeat and he went into hiding with a few of his remaining soldiers.[17] His defeat was a turning point in the history of Ethiopia. The empire that was held by force and the influence of the Orthodox Church was shattered to its core. The state and all of its accomplishments were plundered. Its treasures were looted; churches and monasteries were razed. The cultural and literary legacies that were achieved in a millennium were reduced to ashes. Nine out of ten persons were forced to adopt Islam. The plunder that Gragn Ahmed's rebellion inflicted upon Ethiopia is eloquently summarised by Taddesse Tamrat:

> 'The Muslim occupation of the Christian highland under
> Gragn lasted for a little more than ten years, between
> 1531–43. But the amount of destruction brought in the years
> can only be estimated in terms of centuries.'[18]

The fugitive, King Libne Dingle, solicited the assistance of the Portuguese in 1535 but it took them six years to dispatch a contingent of 400 men. The king was already dead and succeeded by his son Gelawdios when the Portuguese forces arrived in Ethiopia. The delay of the Portuguese assistance gave Gragn ample time to extend his campaign of plunder and destruction right into the heart of the core regions of Ethiopia.

The Ethio-Portuguese forces fought two battles against Gragn's force in 1542. Neither won the day as a victor. The Portuguese force, though much smaller in number than Gragn's army, had an advantage of more matchlocks which decided the outcome of the battles. Gragn, however, having probed the strength of his enemies, retreated to the south-east to solicit more men and matchlocks from his mentor, the Ottoman Empire. The Turks sent him nine hundred matchlock men. Gragn emboldened by the Turkish generous reinforcement engaged the Portuguese contingent and won the battle. The commander of the Portuguese force, Christopher da Gama, the son of the famous explorer Vasco da Gama, was killed and half of his force destroyed. The Portuguese camp and ammunition depot fell to Gragn. The remainder of about 150 men from the Portuguese force regrouped and, reinforced by King Gelawdios's army, made a surprise attack on Gragn's army near Lake Tana and routed it. Gragn fell at the battlefield and his army dispersed and fled; but the Turks resisted and fought until they were overpowered by the Ethio-Portuguese forces. Only forty Turkish soldiers escaped from being slaughtered.[19]

King Gelawdios, after his victory over Gragn, consolidated his power and began his crusade to restore the kingdom of his forefathers that was torn apart by Gragn's rebellion. Moreover he was confronted with the horrendous task of restoring the battered kingdom. Churches and monasteries had to be rebuilt. To restore law and order in a fragmented kingdom, where lawlessness was the order of the day, was a gigantic task. However, Gelawdios did not hesitate to take swift and decisive steps in restoring his kingdom and authority. He re-subdued the frontier provinces of Bale, Daoro and Fatigar that had willingly submitted to Gragn. No sooner had he embarked upon the restoration and reconstruction of his kingdom, he was forced to squander his resources in resisting an Oromo migration from the south.

The Gragn rebellion was a result of the struggle of Christianity and Islam for supremacy. The Portuguese came to the rescue of the Christian kingdom. The Turks instigated a religious war and facilitated its ruthless execution by providing soldiers and matchlocks to Gragn. The Turks' interference in the internal affairs of Ethiopia almost brought the kingdom to the verge of destruction. The Portuguese rescue mission and the determination of the youthful king, Gelawdios, saved Ethiopia from being wiped off the political map of Africa and apostasy. Nevertheless, the Portuguese intervention had its own price. They began to spread Catholicism at the cost of the state religion, the Ethiopian Orthodox Church. They demanded the Roman rite should be enforced throughout the kingdom and the clergy of the Orthodox Church be ordained by a certain Catholic priest, Bermudez. King Gelawdios rejected the proposition. Bermudez then resorted to intrigues that created a misunderstanding that led to a clash between the Ethiopian and the Portuguese forces. The king tactfully resolved the conflict by sending away the Portuguese contingent from the royal court to a distant region, Daoro, from where the Portuguese were chased out when the Oromo migration and invasion engulfed the region.[20]

The failure of Bermudez's intrigue did not deter the Portuguese from resorting to other devious means. By using the Society of Jesus (founded in 1534) the Portuguese set out cunningly to pursue their objectives until they succeeded to convert members of the ruling class in Catholicism. The Jesuits succeeded in converting King Za Dengle (1600–04) to Catholicism. When the king's conversion was discovered, it provoked a rebellion and he paid dearly by losing his life. His successor, Susnyos, made his conversion to Catholicism public and continued vigorously to convert his subjects. His blunt approach to conversion generated a rebellion that ultimately culminated in his forced abdication of the throne in favour of his son, Fasiledus (1632–67). Fasiledus quelled the rebellion by expelling the Jesuit Mission from Ethiopia.[21]

Ethiopia, from the Gragn invasion until the expulsion of the Jesuits,

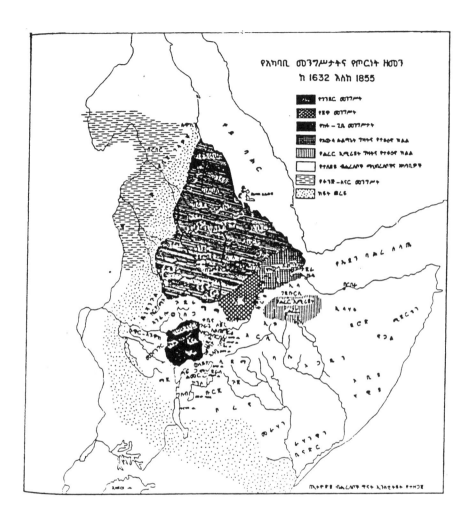

Map 3 Ethiopian map, in Amharic, showing the era of the regional states and warlords, ca. 1632–1855

had been a pawn in the struggle for supremacy among the three religions, the Ethiopian Orthodox Church, Catholicism and Islam. The struggle for religious supremacy, in particular the rebellion of Gragn, paved the way for successive Oromo migrations that lasted from the sixteenth to the nineteenth century.[22] The Oromo people's migration had *contributed immensely* in enriching the cultural and linguistic heritage of Ethiopia. Their positive disposition towards inter-ethnic marriages and cultural assimilation were factors in the formation of a melting pot of Ethiopia. On the other hand, the plunders that were attendant to successive waves of ethnic migrations eroded the strength of the state. The effect of migration coupled with rebellions provoked by religious as well as political motives encouraged the mushrooming of war-lords who rejected the suzerainty of the king over their principalities. The Gonderian kings whose power and influence were in tatters and gradually marginalised, solicited the alliance of the emerging Oromo political force through intermarriages. The Oromo nobility that had established its power-base in Yeju did not hesitate to take advantage of the weakness of the Gonderian rulers. The extent of the influence of the Oromo on the Gonderian court is vividly described by Abir:

> 'In the eighteenth century the emperors began to rely more
> and more upon Galla troops and slowly allowed the Galla
> chiefs to replace the Tigrian and Amhara nobility in their
> courts. Once the court of Solomonic rulers in Gonder
> became dominated by Galla elements whose daughters the
> emperors married, it no longer represented the Christian
> Sematised Ethiopia, and was no longer able to provide the
> link which held the country together.'[23]

The shaken relations of the monarch with the Orthodox Church was further undermined by the influence of the Yeju Oromo in the royal court. The Oromo nobles, although Orthodox Christians, were sympathetic to and in some instances openly advocated Islam. The Orthodox Church had entered into a new phase of doctrinal controversies which were quite often fanned by chiefs to serve their political motives. Doctrinal controversies in the Church, the Gragn rebellion and invasion, the influence of the Jesuits on the monarchy, the non-migratory nature of the court of Gonder that encouraged the kings to indulge in a secluded life of luxury, and the great ethnic migrations weakened the monarchy and created ideal situations for the growth of local war-lords and the breakdown of law and order.

By the second half of the eighteenth century the influence of the king hardly extended beyond the horizon of Gonder. The country was deeply divided. The king in Gonder was reduced to a puppet in the hands of Tigrean regents who were virtually king-makers. Michael Seul of Tigray killed the Gonderian king Yoas and put Yoas's son on the throne.[24] Such was the scale of weakness of the king and the power of a regent. Towards the end of the eighteenth century the Yeju Oromo emerged more powerful than the rest of the regional chiefs and they became regents of the Gonderian kings and virtually ruled Begemidir, Gonder and Yeju. The period of confusion and disorder that lasted for over eighty years (1769–1855) is popularly known as *Zemene Mesafint* (The Era of Princes). It was characterised by the collapse of the central authority and multiplication of principalities. The major contenders for supremacy were the chiefs of Tigray, Begemidir, Yeju, Shewa and Gojjam. However, Ras Ali the Great, the founder of the Yeju nobility, snatched the regency from Ras Michael Seul of Tigray. His dynasty retained the guardianship of the king of kings and the governorship of Begemidir until the appearance of Emperor Tewodros in the second half of the nineteenth century.

The pillars for the unity of the state, the monarchy and the Church, were divided and weakened during the *Zemene Mesafint*. The monarchy lost its influence and credibility for various reasons including the effects of the invasion of Gragn and the apostasy of kings. The Church for its part was torn asunder by town doctrinal controversies pertaining to the nature of Christ. The ecclesiastical schisms which followed the pattern of regional influences of war-lords polarised their relations to an extent where reconciliation was impossible.[25] The Tigreans and others in the north of the empire followed Kara or Tewahido (the Two-Birth Doctrine), the Gojjamis adopted Qebat (Uniction) and the Shewans professed Ye Tsega Lij (the Three-Birth Doctrine).[26] These religious schisms lasted until Emperor Tewodros issued an edict that made Kara or Tewahido as the doctrinal basis of the Ethiopian Orthodox Church.

Ethiopia, during the *Zemene Mesafint*, ceased to exist as one strong polity until the rise of Tewodros. The monarch was reduced to a puppet of a powerful war-lord. One of the kings of this period, Tekle Giorgigs, was dethroned six times[27] between 1789 and 1800. By 1830 the king of kings neither had an army nor revenue commensurate with the lifestyle of a king. His kingdom for all intents and purposes did not extend beyond the four walls of his palace. He lived on minor local income, fines, charity and toll from merchants of Gonder. The Shewan ruler, Sahle-Selassie, declared himself king of Shewa without the consent of the king of kings in Gonder. It was under such chaotic and anarchic con-

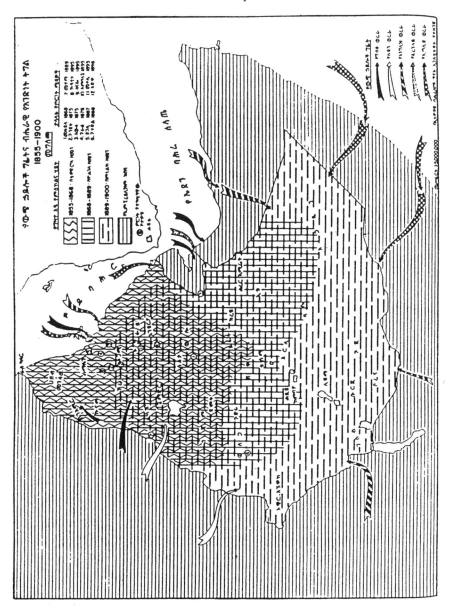

Map 4 Ethiopian map, in Amharic, showing the external challenges and reunification, 1855–1900

15

ditions that the rise of Dejazmach Kassa of Quarra, later Emperor Tewodros, took place.

The Reign of Emperor Tewodros II (1855–68)

The rise of Tewodros was a turning point in the history of Ethiopia. Tewodros, before his accession to the throne, was known under the name Kassa Hailu. Kassa, who rose to the rank of Dejazmach in the Gonderian Court in his youth, was presumed to have exceptional qualities and by the standard of his time, was well-educated and deeply versed in ecclesiastical literature of the Ethiopian Orthodox Church. Some historians claim that he had a working knowledge of Arabic. The basis of this claim might be attributed to his birth in Quarra, a frontier province bordering the Sudan, where he was its governor later on. Indeed his early childhood association and contact with the Arabic-speaking neighbouring community would have afforded him ample opportunity to acquire a working knowledge of Arabic.

Menen, the Queen of Gonder, and her son Ali, governor of Begemidir and Amhara, who was the *de facto* king of kings, were quick to recognise the exceptional leadership qualities of Kassa. They made him governor of the province of Quarra and married him to Ali's daughter, Tewabetch. The queen and Ali cunningly wooed Kassa's loyalty. The political marriage and his promotion to the rank of a Dejazmach neither moderated his loathing for the establishment nor deterred him from pursuing his vision of a united Ethiopia.[28] Personalities like the British consul, Plowden, who were closely associated with him admired him as a person of unusual qualities. Indeed, he must have been endowed with extraordinary qualities of leadership and political acumen to have achieved a meteoric rise in a very short time, and sit on the pinnacle of power. He shattered the myth of the hereditary system of accession to the throne and proved that personal qualities of leadership and foresight buttressed with military strength could constitute an alternative source of legitimacy.

Kassa defeated the powerful regional chiefs one after the other including Ras Ali, the regent of the king of Gonder, in two years (1852–54). At the battle of Gura Amba, November 1852 he defeated Dejazmach Goshu Biru of Gojjam who was sent by Ras Ali to deal a punitive blow to Kassa. The victory of Gura Amba gave a new dimension to the growing popularity of Kassa that became a cause for concern for Ali. The Ras, enraged by the decisive defeat of his trusted vassal, fielded a combined force of Tigray, Begemidir and Amhara under the leadership of his two most trusted Dejazmaches, Biru Aligaz and Belew. The combined army met Kassa's army at Taqussa. After a fierce and bloody battle Biru Aligaz and Belew fell on the battlefield and their forces dispersed and fled. The Taqussa victory boosted Kassa's fame and it emboldened him to engage Ras Ali, his father-in-law, at the battle of Ayshal. The armies of the two protagonists clashed on 29 June 1853 in the bloodiest battle of the *Zemene Mesafint*. Ali, on the verge of losing the battle, fled to Yeju, his power-base, where he died as a fugitive. Kassa's victory at the battle of Ayshal ended the *Zemene Mesafint*.[29]

One of the most powerful chiefs of Tigray and Simen, Wube, who witnessed the disastrous defeat of Ras Ali and Queen Menen, peacefully submitted to Kassa and accepted his overlordship. The truce with Wube gave Kassa a breathing space to consolidate his position in Begemidir and to settle scores with Birru Goshu, a chief of Gojjam, whose father had been slain at the battle of Gura Amba. The battle against Biru gave easy victory to Kassa. After having subdued Gojjam and placing his trusted follower, Ras Engeda, as ruler of Gojjam, Kassa marched to Lasta and defeated Faris Aligaz in July 1854.[30]

Kassa, after two years of successive battles followed by victories, subdued all regional rulers except the king of Shewa, Haile Melekot, whose kingdom enjoyed independence during the *Zemene Mesafint*. Kassa consolidated his power and exercised his authority over the subdued regions by appointing his trusted followers as governors. He also secured the full co-operation of the Ethiopian Orthodox Church by issuing an edict on doctrinal controversies that upheld the official position of Abune Selama, the bishop of the Ethiopian Orthodox Church.[31] The edict had given dividends to both Kassa and the Church. For Kassa it meant a symbolic legitimatising of his planned ascent to the throne. On the other hand for the Church, it meant a consolidation of its influence over the faithful and a hope for ending doctrinal controversies. The doctrinal controversies in the Church were brought to an end by Kassa's edict that proclaimed Tewahido (the Two-Births of Christ) as the sole doctrinal basis of the Ethiopian Orthodox Church. The Echegie, the Ethiopian religious head second to the Egyptian prelate (Abune), was forced to abandon his Sost Lidet doctrine (the Three-Births of Christ) in favour of Tewahido. The humiliation caused to the Echgie by his submission to Tewahido was an outright victory to the Metropolitan Prelate, Abune Selama.

On the other hand, Dejazmach Wube of Tigray, rebelled provoking reprisal from Kassa. He took the initiative and engaged Wube's force at Dresgie in the province of Semen on 9 February 1852. Wube was defeated, captured and imprisoned.[32] The victory in the battle of Dresgie ended the only surviving and powerful challenger in Northern Ethiopia. Kassa, in the midst of euphoria of victory, was anointed and crowned by Abune Selama, King of Kings Tewodros II on 11 February 1855. After his coronation he marched to Shewa, the only remaining regional power of any consequence. In the spring of 1855, Haile Melkot king of Shewa, died of natural causes just before the opening of the battle. His army, after putting up some resistance, was defeated and Shewa was incorporated into the empire of Tewodros.

Tewodros, having accomplished his primary plan of dismantling the establishment by eliminating war-lords who were responsible for the fragmentation of the state, had to face the difficult task of reconstructing a unified polity out of the ruins of rebellious principalities. He executed restoration, reconstruction and reformation tasks with the determination, swiftness and ruthlessness that were characteristic of him.

When Tewodros acceded to the throne, he had effectively commanded the admiration and support of the people. On the other hand his systematic alienation of the nobility from the political life of the state was a major obstacle for the realisation of his vision. Despite the passive resistance from various social groups, Tewodros introduced administrative reforms in the state machinery with far-reaching implications. He divided the empire into smaller administrative units and appointed his followers to administer these new provinces. The administrative reform was supplemented by a system of salary for governors, judges and other state functionaries. The system of payment severed the traditional exploitative link of state functionaries with the peasantry. His tax system waived the exemption privilege of the Church. Along with tax reform he reorganised the Church structure. It was decreed that every church was to be served by two priests and three deacons and provided with adequate land for their subsistence. The excess of land released was redistributed among landless peasants.[33] The Church opposed the reform. Nevertheless he introduced it. The drastic reform in the Church created an unbridgeable rift between Tewodros and the Church leaders. His initial dealing with the Church was businesslike. There was tacit understanding between him and Abune Selama, the Egyptian prelate, to refrain from interfering in one another's domains. The introduction of the reform was a breach of their tacit agreement. The Church retaliated by inciting its followers against Tewodros. The clergy resorted to rumour-mongering. False accusation of apostasy was spread against the emperor.

Tewodros suspected Abune Selama of serving the interest of Egypt. His suspicion was confirmed when the Abune and the Patriarch of Alexandria who was on a visit to Ethiopia in 1856, submitted a letter jointly drafted to Tewodros. The letter was a request to Said Pasha of Egypt to provide an Egyptian garrison for the Abune. To make matters worse the Patriarch signified his keen interest to review Tewodros's army. The Patriarch's interest in military affairs enraged Tewodros. He put both the Patriarch and the Abune under house arrest which led to further deterioration of the relations between the Church and the monarchy. Abune Selama retaliated by excommunicating Tewodros in 1857.

However, Patriarch Kerilos of Alexandria, before he was allowed to leave Ethiopia, lifted the excommunication. From that time on relations continued to deteriorate. The Church and the monarchy which were close allies since the Aksumite period became avowed enemies, one plotting for the downfall of the other. The friction between the Church and the monarchy was exacerbated when Tewodros ordered the arrest and detention of Abune Selama; and razed forty churches in Gonder. Tewodros's excessive use of force in settling his differences with Abune Selama and the uncompromising disposition of the Abune were major factors that frustrated the realisation of his vision of a united Ethiopia. Rubenson on the relations of the Church and monarchy during the reign of Tewodros wrote:

'Tewodros failed to find workable solutions in his relations with the Bishop and the clergy not only deprived him of much needed financial support, but turned the population in general against him. In spite of all shortcomings of her servants, the Church had a strong and unique position in the country. In the predominantly Christian population of the regional kingdoms or chieftaincy that Tewodros set out to unify, the authority of the spokesmen of the Church was more widespread than any other. The Church was the strong unifying element in the society both on the local and national level. It was to the Churches and convents that the sick, infirm, and wounded were brought. They were the haven of refuge for chiefs who had lost against their enemies and had to wait for better days. Although their doctrinal disputes sometimes aggravated a conflict, the clergy usually were the instrument of bringing about any reconciliation that took place. That Tewodros, in spite of all he actually shared with the Church in common views and interests, failed to ally himself with this institution, even at the cost of certain concessions, is probably the single most important cause of his failure to unite Ethiopia.'[34]

Tewodros, as if his provocation of the wrath of the Church and nobility was not enough, intended to compel the Oromos and Moslems to adopt Christianity or face destruction and/or expulsion from the empire.[35] His attitude to the Oromos and the followers of Islam further exacerbated a situation that was volatile and fomented rebellion in the entire country. His confrontation with the Church, Oromos and Moslems earned him the enmity of the people who, when he came to power, admired and supported him.

Tewodros's foreign policy was as progressive as his domestic policies. He had a clear cut policy to introduce Western technology in Ethiopia. Securing the technology of the West, obtaining the support of European powers in the defence of his empire and restoring the lost territories of Ethiopia were the cornerstones of his foreign policy. His close association with John Bell, Consul Plowden of Britain and other Europeans, who were diplomats, missionaries, explorers and traders in the country, had influenced him to adopt a positive outlook towards Europeans. Unfortunately, his positive disposition towards the West neither secured him the technology he was craving for nor gained him a recognition as a head of a sovereign state.

The oversight of the British Foreign Office to act on his letter to Queen Victoria, in which he expressed his desire to send an embassy that would purchase arms and recruit skilled workers, had wounded his pride. Regrettably the oversight of the Foreign Office resulted in the detention of the British consul, Cameron, and a few European missionaries and traders. The detention of the British consul in turn wounded the pride of Great Britain. A plea by Great Britain for the release of its consul and other European prisoners failed to be entertained by Tewodros. Britain's effort to resolve the differences between the two countries proved abortive. Then Great Britain, as a matter of national pride and honour, resorted to military initiative to free the prisoners. The Abyssinian Expedition under the command of General Napier was launched and succeeded in freeing the prisoners. The expedition ended the reign of Tewodros when the mountain fortress of Maqdella was stormed on 10 April 1868. Tewodros, who for the first time in his career faced defeat chose to end his own life rather than tasting the humiliating experience of surrender. Tewodros's foreign policy collapsed as abruptly as his domestic policies did.

Tewodros's domestic position, at the time of the Napier expedition. was shaky since most of the provinces were in rebellion as he himself revealed in one of his notes to Napier. He wrote: '*My countrymen have turned their backs on me and have hated me because I imposed tribute on them and sought to bring them under military discipline.'*[36]

His note shows the extent of his alienation and the weakness of his military strength when the Napier Expeditionary Force confronted him at Meqdella. Rubenson referring to the weakness of Tewodros observed: '*Tewodros has lost his kingdom. It was internal political problems, not the British Army that caused the fall of Tewodros.'*[37]

Tewodros, who had the noblest intentions of creating a united Ethiopia where peace would prevail in place of fratricidal wars that wasted the resources of the nation for generations '*left Ethiopia as divided and disunited as he found it.'*[38] He had dreams to convert weapons into ploughshares and to modernise Ethiopia. His correspondence with European leaders particularly with Queen Victoria reveal his commitment to introduce Western technology in Ethiopia. Sadly, his intentions neither succeeded in mustering European assistance nor rallying the support of his subjects; he was a leader who was misunderstood at home as well as abroad. Despite his shortcomings he had succeeded in sowing the idea of a united Ethiopia, the need for administrative reform, creating a standing army, developing infrastructure and a host of other progressive ideas. His ideas and visions constituted the very building blocks of the policies of his successors.

The Reign of Emperor Yohannis IV (1872–89)

The defeat of Tewodros and his tragic death at the battle of Maqdella plunged the country into another struggle for succession. Three rivals who coveted the throne were Wag Shume Gobeze of Lasta. Dejazmach Kassa Mircha of Tigray. and King Menilek of Shewa. Soon after the death of Tewodros and the withdrawal of the British expeditionary force Gobeze crowned himself Tekle Giorgis, king of kings of Ethiopia in 1868.

Ras Adale Tessema of Gojjam, a brother-in-law of Tekle Giorgis, recognised the overlordship of the emperor, Kassa Mircha who was also a brother-in-law of Tekle Giorgis, did not allow his ambition for the throne to be thwarted by a political marriage. On the other hand, Menilek who had already begun to exhibit his claim to the throne by using the designation of Neguse Negest (king of kings or emperor), reluctantly humbled himself to the suzerainty of Tekle Giorgis. The emperor, by cajoling and making concessions to his rivals, managed to hang on to the throne without any meaningful power, until he was defeated and overthrown by Kassa Mircha at the battle of Assam in July 1871.[39] Despite the numerical superiority of Tekle Giorgis's army that was in the ratio of 5:1 to Kassa's army, victory went to the latter whose forces were well armed by the Napier Expeditionary Force. Kassa was given firearms and ammunition as a reward for his co-operation in facilitating the Napier Expedition. After the defeat of Tekle Giorgis, Kassa wasted no time in consolidating his power in the core regions of the north. Six months from the day of his victory, he was crowned by the bishop of the Ethiopian Orthodox Church, as king of kings, in the throne name of Yohannis IV in Aksum in 1872.[40]

Yohannis's accession to the throne, unfortunately, coincided with the era of the scramble for Africa and the rise of Muhammed Ahmed, the Mahdi of the Sudan. His reign, unlike that of his predecessor, was preoccupied in defending the territorial integrity of the country against colonial powers, in particular Italy. The presence of an aggressive and an expansionist neighbour in the north of his empire, Egypt, which in the 1880s was replaced by a fanatic religious movement, Mahdism, made his task of governance difficult. He was underestimated as lacking drive for reform and political sensitivity but proved otherwise in defending the interest of his empire with puritanical zeal[41]. He had even succeeded in restoring the Bogus region in the present Eritrea from Egypt in exchange for rescuing an Egyptian garrison from the Sudan where it had been put under siege by the Mahdists.

In the domestic scene his ingenuity in applying proper balance in the use of power, persuasion and administrative devolution, released his resources, which otherwise would have been committed to subdue rebellious governors and for containing intruders like the Egyptians, Italians and Mahdists. His policy, in particular that related to a united Ethiopia, was a logical continuation of Emperor Tewodros's vision of Ethiopia; but his approach in the realisation of this vision was different from that of his predecessor. He was sensitive to the needs of the nobility and the Church which enabled him to win, if not their loyalty, at least their crucial support. By devolving power to regional chiefs, he succeeded in humbling them into submission where his predecessor, Emperor Tewodros, miserably failed to do so. To neutralise the rebellious dispositions of regional chiefs in particular that of King Menilek of Shewa, he made Ras Adale, the ruler of Gojjam, king – the highest title that was exclusively enjoyed by the hereditary rulers of Shewa.

Ras Adale assumed the throne name of Teklehayimanot. He was further favoured by an addition to his kingdom Keffa, one of the richest provinces in the south. The favour that Emperor Yohannis extended to him offended Menilek, as it was intended to do and even put the kings at loggerheads with each other. Yohannis who was threatened by Menilek's ambition for usurping the throne never hesitated to put the latter under strict scrutiny. Yohannis took it upon himself to incite close family members of Menilek including his wife Weizero Bafena, who was covetous of the Shewan throne, against Menilek[42]. Yohannis's plan to isolate Menilek came to the fore when the armies of the latter and Teklehayimanot's clashed at the battle of Embabo in 1882. Teklehayimanot was defeated and taken prisoner along with his sons. It was the angry intervention of Yohannis that forced Menilek to release the prisoners. Menilek was not spared a reprimand of his suzerain for taking a punitive measure against the king of Gojjam without even caring to notify the emperor.[43]

Yohannis conducted his relation with Menilek with great patience and tact. Their initial relationships were not smooth. Menilek, even after Yohannis's coronation as king of kings, kept using the title of Neguse Negest (king of kings) until he was forced to renounce it in 1878. From 1872–78 Yohannis was preoccupied with Egypt's belligerence and as such did not show serious concern for the threat posed by Menilek. When Yohannis's successive victories over Egyptian forces at the battles of Gundet (1875) and Gura (1876) gave him a breathing space he turned his full attention to the domestic scene and settled scores with Menilek. He marched to Shewa and Menilek, on his part, mobilised his army for a final showdown with the emperor in 1878. The intervention of the Church averted a bloody war between Yohannis and his vassal. The two rivals signed the Liche Agreement in 1878 when Menilek renounced his title of Neguse Negest and accepted the suzerainty of Yohannis. Yohannis reciprocated by recognising Menilek as king of Shewa. The reconciliation led to the marriage of Yohannis's son, Ras Araya, to Menilek's daughter, Weizero Zewditu, who in 1916 upon the deposition of Lij Iyasu, became empress of Ethiopia. The political marriage was a symbolic expression of the sincerity of the contracting parties to the Liche Agreement. It ended the feud and induced a semblance of peace in the country. After the agreement, Emperor Yohannis devoted most of his time and resources in defending the empire from external intrusions while Menilek spent his energy in expanding his kingdom to the east, west and south of Shewa.

In the spiritual domain, the doctrinal controversies that divided the Church, which Tewodros had attempted to resolve by decree, still persisted and revived after his death. Yohannis, who had realised that a divided Church was a threat to his power and the unity of his empire, gave priority to the resolution of the doctrinal controversies whose origin might be traced to the seventh century. He, unlike his predecessor, resolved the controversies by convening an ecclesiastical council at Borumeda. Under his chairmanship the Ethiopian Orthodox Church debated the controversies and reached a decision by consensus that upheld Tewahido (the Two Births of Christ) as the official interpretation of the nature of Christ in the Ethiopian Orthodox Church. The adherents of other interpretations were required to renounce or face expropriation of properties and even execution.[44]

The Liche Agreement and the Council of Borumeda were significant achievements that enhanced Yohannis's efforts in consolidating his empire. Dejazmach Zewde Gebre-Selassie, a great-great-grandson of the emperor summarised the contribution of his ancestor:

'Yohannis shared the aspirations of earlier rulers of Ethiopia, but he succeeded where they failed. The weak and disunited country he inherited became in his hands a powerful and united empire, and his death in battle was a tragedy for Ethiopia.'[45]

Yohannis's perpetual worry was the hostile neighbour, Egypt, under Khadive Ismail. Egypt's defeat in two successive battles in the 1870s did not have restraining effects on her belligerence. When the Ottoman Empire withdrew from the Red Sea coast, Egypt filled the void created by the withdrawal of the Turks. It occupied Massawa on the Red Sea coast and its forces penetrated deep into the interior of Ethiopia and captured Harar. Yohannis's plea for restraint and a negotiated settlement of their differences was ignored by Egypt. The Red Sea littoral and Harar remained under the occupation of Egypt until 1882 when the British occupied Egypt. Egypt's influence in the Red Sea, as a result of the British occupation and the rise of the Mahdi, faded away and eventually it withdrew its forces from Harar, Massawa and other Red Sea possessions. The siege of the Egyptian garrison, in the Sudan by Mahdists, compelled Egypt to seek the friendship and assistance of Ethiopia. Egypt and Great Britain, to avert annihilation of the Egyptian garrison in the Sudan, signed the Hewett Treaty with Ethiopia in 1884. The treaty was named after Rear-Admiral Sir William Hewett, Commander-in-Chief of Her Majesty's ship of war in the East Indies, who signed the treaty on behalf of Her Majesty Queen Victoria.

The treaty aimed at resolving the differences between Egypt and Ethiopia and establishing an everlasting peace between them. The treaty[46] covered the following items:
– Free transit of goods through Massawa to and from Ethiopia;

- The restoration of Bogus, the North and North-eastern part of present day Eritrea;
- Withdrawal of the troops of Egypt from Kessala, Amedib and Sanhit in the Sudan border;
- Extradition of criminals;
- Appointment of an Abune (bishop) for Ethiopia by the Patriarch of Alexandria and
- Submission of future disputes between Ethiopia and Egypt to Great Britain for settlement.

The Ethiopian Government fulfilled its share of the treaty by rescuing the Egyptian garrisons from Mahdists and provided them safe passage to the port of Massawa on the Red Sea coast. On the other hand, Great Britain, which was in control of the port of Massawa, contrary to the spirit and intent of the treaty, allowed it to be occupied by Italy. Great Britain's failure to carry out its obligation, provoked the wrath of one of its diplomats, Mr A. B. Wylde, the British consul in Aden. Censuring his government's conduct he wrote:

> 'From the north he ought to have been safe if our treaty
> with him went for anything. Look at our behaviour to
> Yohannis from any point of view and it will not show one ray
> of honesty, and to my mind, it is one of our worst bits of
> business out of the many we have been guilty of in Africa,
> and no wonder our position diplomatically is such a bad
> one with the rulers of the country at present. England made
> use of King Yohannis as long as he was of any service, and
> then threw him over to the tender mercies of Italy, who went
> to Massawa under our auspices with the intention of taking
> territory that belonged to our ally, and to allow them to
> destroy and break all of the promises England had solemnly
> made to King Yohannis after he faithfully carried out his part
> of the agreement. The fact is not known to the British
> public, and I wish it were not for our credits sake; but
> unfortunately it is, and it reads like one of the vilest bits of
> treachery that has been perpetrated in Africa or in India in
> the eighteenth century.'[47]

Indeed the British took advantage of Yohannis's goodwill and inexperience in international relations.

Egypt ceased to be a menacing neighbour ever since it withdrew its garrison from the Sudan but the vacuum it left was filled in by uncompromising religious fanatics, the Mahdists. They were more hostile to the Ethiopians than the Egyptians. They, in their adventure of Jihad (Islamic holy war against infidels), penetrated deep into the Ethiopian plateau as far as the city of Gonder and razed it in 1888[48]. Yohannis's north-western flank was exposed to the Mahdists that demanded no less than the conversion of himself and his subjects to Islam for an exchange of peace. On the north along the Red Sea coast Italy, at the invitation of Britain to frustrate France's colonial ambition in Ethiopia, had secured a foothold in Massawa and had become a constant source of irritation and incursion. This was an unfortunate time for Ethiopia, because of the opening of the Suez Canal, the importance of the Red Sea increased and colonial powers competed to control it. From this time on Ethiopia remained the coveted prey of colonialism.[49] Italy's presence in Massawa posed a fresh threat to the territorial integrity of Ethiopia. Italy wasted no time in expanding its occupation of Ethiopian territories. She occupied Zulla to the south of Massawa and the villages of Sahati and Wai.[50] Ras Alula Ingdah, the Governor of the maritime province, repeatedly requested General Carlo Gene, commander of the Italian garrison in Massawa, to withdraw his forces from Ethiopian territories and refrain from future encroachment. The Italian general, however, ignored Alula's warning and kept on pushing in towards the mainland until the two forces clashed 20 kilometres from Massawa at Dogali in 1887. An Italian force of 500 men was annihilated by Alula's army. Less than a dozen Italian soldiers escaped Alula's punitive measure.[51]

The Italians, humiliated at the battle of Dogali, abandoned Sahati and Wai, and retreated to Massawa. The victory of the Ethiopians restrained the expansion of Italy into the interior of Ethiopia until Yohannis foolishly removed Ras Alula and replaced him by Fitawrari Dahab who had a record of defecting to the Egyptians, Mahdists and the Italians. Yohannis marched to settle scores with the Mahdists without making adequate arrangements for the defence of his maritime province. Moreover the local tribal chiefs' alliance with Italy was also a contributory factor for the unchallenged incursion of Italy into the Eritrean plateau.

Yohannis, with his maritime province undefended marched to the Sudan border and his army clashed with the Mahdists' force at Mettema. It was a fierce battle where the Ethiopians had dominated the scene and the Mahdists were retreating when a stray bullet fatally wounded Yohannis and claimed his life. When the news of Yohannis's death reached the Mahdists' camp, they regrouped their forces and charged against the Ethiopian forces that were shocked by the death of their emperor. The Ethiopians began to retreat and finally fled in the face of the Mahdists' counter-offensive.[52] The Mahdists succeeded in capturing the corpse of the emperor from the Ethiopians and severed the head from the body and presented their trophy to the Mahdi in Khartoum.

Yohannis inherited a divided and a weak Ethiopia, but at his tragic death he left to his successor, Emperor Menilek II, a united and much larger and prosperous empire. He should, more than anything else, be remembered for sacrificing his life in the defence of his country.

The Reign of Emperor Menilek II (1889–1913)

The death Yohannis at the battle of Mettema opened the way to the throne for Menilek's succession. Ras Araya Selassie, the only son of Emperor Yohannis and the son-in-law of Menilek, died without leaving an heir in 1887. The untimely death of the heir apparent enabled Menilek to realise his dream for the throne. Some scholars claim that Yohannis and Menilek had an understanding in the event of Ras Araya's death without an heir, the throne would go to Menilek. However the Liche Agreement did not make any reference to succession. The private meetings of the two monarchs before the conclusion of the agreement might have encouraged such speculation.

Yohannis, among the siblings of his three brothers at his death bed, chose Ras Mengesha to succeed him. The other two nephews of Yohannis, Dejazmach Meshesha Maru and Dejazmach Bogale Ali, contested Yohannis's choice. The struggle for succession among the three cousins made conditions favourable for Menilek to seize the throne and crown himself as Niguse Negest of Ethiopia. The Tigrain army which was battered and dispersed at the battle of Mettema did not pose any threat to Menilek. Moreover, the forces of the three contenders were no match for Menilek's huge and well-armed army.

Ras Mengesha, one of the contenders for the throne, who had felt that the throne had been usurped from him, declared his non-allegiance to Menilek and formed an alliance with the Italian governor of the colony of Eritrea, General Antonio Baldissera. The Italians who had been labouring to incite local chiefs against Menilek seized the opportunity and used it to their own advantage. The friendship struck between Mengesha and the governor of the Italian colony of Eritrea reached its climax when they signed a convention on 6 December 1891. The vow of solidarity consisted of three articles whereby the contracting parties affirmed their friendship to stand against a common enemy. The Italians recognised Mengesha as the legitimate heir to the throne and he reciprocated by acknowledging Italy's sovereignty in the occupied territory. Both parties entered into obligation not to do anything that might adversely affect the interests of the other. The final provisions of the pact affirmed the friendship between the Tigrains and the Italians[53]. The coded message of the vow of solidarity was that the Italians would support Mengesha should he choose to reclaim the throne from Menilek. In case of any aggression by Menilek the Italians would stand by Mengesha and vice versa. The Italians had also extracted from Mengesha his recognition of their sovereignty. The sovereignty provision of the covenant was shrouded in vagueness to conceal Italy's ambition to occupy the whole of Ethiopia.

Mengesha and the Italians staged a joint military manoeuvre on either side of the River Mereb. It was a demonstration of force to scare Menilek. The alliance between Mengesha and the Italians was short-lived. Mengesha compromised the interest of his country by allowing the Italians to extend their *de facto* border to the bank of the River Mereb which later on became the *de jure* border between Ethiopia and the Italian colony of Eritrea.

Menilek's accession to the throne was not challenged by King Tekle Hayimanot of Gojjam or King Michael of Wollo. Both of them submitted to his overlordship.

Menilek's association with Tewodros from his early age to late adolescence had inspired him to develop his own conviction in matters pertaining to the governance of a state. Furthermore his association with Tewodros had taught him a lesson that excessive use of force in the governance of a state alienates a ruler from his people and even generates rebellion. It must have been from this negative experience that he had developed an approach based on love and respect in his dealings with his associates and vassals. His generous and forgiving gesture towards the vanquished had earned him their absolute loyalty as demonstrated by King Teklehayimanot of Gojjam and King Tonna of Wolayta. Menilek had definitely drawn lessons from the mistakes of his predecessors. His style of government was in many respects different from the styles of his predecessors.

Even though Emperor Yohannis had avoided the harshness of Emperor Tewodros concerning religion, he had a fanatic attitude that was not inherently different from the stance of his predecessor. Proselytising of Moslems was central to his domestic policy. He was intolerant of Islam. Moslems were not allowed to hold public offices unless they were converted to the Ethiopian Orthodox Faith. The council of Borumeda required all Moslems holding public offices either to adopt the Orthodox Faith and remain in office or face dismissal.[54] On the other hand Menilek had a liberal policy. He appointed Moslems as well as followers of other

faiths to public offices. Menilek, upon the restoration of the kingdom of
Shewa, had a clear policy for the governance of his kingdom. He had an
appreciation for the need of a standing army, a sound economic base to
sustain his kingdom and to restore the ancient kingdom of Ethiopia.
According to him, the kingdom stretched in the north to the confluence
of the White and the Blue Niles, in the south as far down to lake Nayassa
and in the east it included the Red Sea littoral.[55] This was the first attempt
of an Ethiopian monarch to define the frontiers of his empire.

One of the first steps that Menilek took after the restoration of the
kingdom of Shewa, was to employ foreigners as well as national agents
for the procuring of firearms. He opened up his kingdom for foreign
missionaries, explorers and traders. He had even engaged a French citizen
for training his army in the use of firearms and modern warfare. He had
benefited from his contact in establishing diplomatic relations with colonial powers and acquiring weapons in a relatively very short time. He
consolidated his rule in his ancestral power-base Shewa. He was fortunate
in commanding the loyalty and respect of the Shewan nobility and the
common people that were his reliable assets in his accession to the throne
of Ethiopia.

Shewa had developed a system of hereditary succession that had protected it from being torn apart by rival war-lords. It, ever since the time
of Negaassie Kirstos Werede Qal, the founder of the Shewan dynasty,
except for a short period during the reign of Emperor Tewodros, was
ruled by a hereditary chief. The hereditary system had been a source of
stability, peace and prosperity for Shewa. It enjoyed an independent
system of self administration. The kingdom of Shewa sprang in the district
of Menz in the latter part of the seventeen century and in a span of eight
generations grew in its size tremendously.

Shale-Selassie (1813–47), one of the most popular rulers of Shewa,
declared himself king of Shewa, without the consent of the king in
Gonder. Since then a Shewan ruler used the title of Neguse (king) instead
of the designation of Merdazmach (a title conferred upon a person of a
noble birth). When Menilek came to power he had behind him a tradition of seven generations.[56] Moreover, his childhood association with
Emperor Tewodros had sharpened his outlook. Having built an army that
was not matched by the forces of other rulers whose armaments consisted
of lances, spears, and in some cases matchlocks with inferior fire power,
subdued them one after the other. He had the capability to mobilise a
force of 130,000–196,000 for war in the 1880s.[57] Naturally, such an inun-
dating military power was not effectively challenged by ill-armed forces
of rival rulers. The only one who had superior force to Menilek was

Emperor Yohannis IV who had forced Menilek to a position of a reluctant vassal.

A Shewan king normally carried out two to three campaigns in a year. Menilek's' first campaign was to Wollo to have a secured frontier in the north of his kingdom and at the same time to display his interest in the throne of Ethiopia. It took him eight years (1868–76) of tough campaigns to bring the entire province of Wollo under his rule.[58] The struggle for the throne between Wag Shume Gobeze (Emperor of Ethiopia 1868–72) and Dejazmach Kassa Mircha (Emperor Yohannis IV) and preoccupation of the latter with an Egyptian threat of invasion encouraged Menilek to launch his campaign to incorporate Wollo into his kingdom of Shewa.

Menilek, having secured his Northern frontier, extended his campaign to the south, south-west and south-east of Shewa. The incorporation of those regions into his kingdom laid the groundwork for the final conquest of Harargie that was left to an Amir when the Egyptian garrison pulled out in 1885. However the restoration of the medieval empire of Ethiopia reached its climax by the re-conquest of the Ogaden in 1891. All the aforementioned regions except the Ogaden were restored when Menilek was king of Shewa. The Kingdom of Shewa that Menilek inherited had been enlarged several times by 1889.[59]

When Menilek became Emperor of Ethiopia he had completed a good portion of the restoration of the medieval territories and the unification of Ethiopia. The vision of Tewodros was realised by Menilek who excelled both his predecessors in statecraft and diplomacy. He did not feel safe until the frontiers of his empire were defined and sealed by international treaties, with the colonial powers of the region, when the policy of the scramble for Africa was systematically executed. He had realised that to enter into any international treaty with Great Britain, France and Italy, who had colonial territories adjoining Ethiopia, he ought to have his country recognised as an independent and sovereign state. In an era of the scramble for Africa, he set for himself such an ambitious aim which was next to impossible. However, his skill in diplomacy and shrewdness helped him in safeguarding the interest of his country. The question of the recognition of Ethiopia by the colonial powers as an independent and sovereign state was acquired by his skill in blending the art of diplomacy with the use of force in resisting colonial expansion. The recognition of sovereignty of Ethiopia, that his predecessors failed to extract from the colonial powers, was the result of his victory over Italy, at the battle of Adwa in 1896. The vanquished and belligerent state, Italy, was forced to recognise Ethiopia as an independent and sovereign

30

state. The other colonial powers who witnessed Italy's humiliation at the hand of Menilek followed suit. The key to the delimitation of the boundaries of Ethiopia with the colonial possessions of Italy, France and Great Britain, was the victory of Adwa. The importance of the Adwa victory had been dealt with in depth by many scholars and there is no need to repeat their arguments here. Reference to it is made to show its relevance in defining the frontiers of Ethiopia by international treaties. Menilek succeeded in securing defined frontiers for Ethiopia.

Menilek signed the following treaties[60] with the three major colonial powers in Africa:

1. Treaty between Ethiopia and Italy, relative to frontiers between Ethiopia and Eritrea 26 October 1896;
2. Convention between Ethiopia and France, relative to frontiers between Ethiopia and French Somaliland of Djibouti, 20 March 1897;
3. Treaty between Ethiopia and Great Britain, relative to frontiers between Ethiopia and British Protectorate on the Somali Coast, 14 May 1897;
4. Treaty between Ethiopia and Great Britain, relative to the frontiers of Ethiopia and the Sudan, 15 May 1902;
5. Treaty between Ethiopia, Great Britain and Italy, relative to the frontiers of Ethiopia and the Sudan; Eritrea and the Sudan, 15 May 1902.
6. Ethiopia and Great Britain, relative to frontiers between Ethiopia and British East Africa, 6 December 1907;
7. Convention between Ethiopia and Italy, relative to frontiers between Ethiopia and Eritrea (Dankil Coast), 16 May 1908;
8. Ethiopia and Italy (Convention and Additional Act), relative to frontiers between Ethiopia and Italian Somaliland (Benadir), 16 May 1908.

These treaties were the result of Menilek's able leadership and his victory at the battle of Adwa, 1896. The invincibility of the colonial powers was shattered and Ethiopia won international recognition as sovereign state with defined borders.[61]

Ethiopian chiefs who aspired for the throne made contacts and struck friendship with foreign powers. Yohannis IV struck friendship with Great Britain and even collaborated with the Napier Expeditionary Force that defeated Emperor Tewodros. The donation of arms and ammunition by Napier gave him a decisive edge in defeating Neguse Negest Tekle Giorgis. From an earlier time Sabagadis, Michael Suel and Wube of Tigray and

King Sahle-Selassie of Shewa had made contacts with foreign countries, mainly to acquire arms and ammunition.

Menilek who never concealed his ambition for the Ethiopian throne, had an appreciation for contacts with foreign powers with a knowledge of reciprocal demands that were antecedent to them. His contacts were more diversified than his predecessors'. He made contacts with France, Russia, Italy, Great Britain, Egypt and others. However, it was with Italy and France that he struck close friendships. The Italians being aware of his ambition for the Ethiopian throne, openly demonstrated their friendship to him which contributed in straining his relationship with Emperor Yohannis. The treaties of 1883 and 1887 on Friendship, Commerce and Alliance between Shewa and Italy were clear demonstrations of Italy's determination to create a rift in the relationships between Menilek and Yohannis.

The friendship of Italy and Menilek continued even after the latter became emperor of Ethiopia. Their relationship culminated in signing the Treaty of Wichale, 1889. It was drafted by the Italian consul, Count Antonelli. Menilek who was handicapped by the lack of a legal adviser, counted on the friendship of the consul in considering the treaty. The court interpreter Ato Yoseph's shortcoming in the mastery of the Italian language was public knowledge. The treaty is a classic example of an international agreement that was conceived in deception and fraud. Italy was the culprit. The Amharic version of the article reads: '*The Emperor of Ethiopia, for all matters that he wants from European kings, could communicate with the assistance of the Italian Government.*'[62] The Italian version of the article which required of the Ethiopian Government to conduct all its negotiation of affairs with European countries through the Italian government states: '*His Majesty the King of Ethiopia consents to avail himself of the Italian Government for any negotiations (or for all the business) which he may enter into with all other Powers and Governments.*'[63] The Amharic and the Italian versions are significantly different from each other. The Amharic version is optional while the Italian is obligatory.

The Amharic version of the article was drafted in line with 1883 Treaty between Shewa and Italy that stated: '*It shall be in the power of His Majesty the King of Shewa to avail himself of the Italian Consular Authority or of the Royal Commissioner in Aseb for all letters or communications which he may wish to have forwarded to the governments in Europe where such authorities are accredited.*'[64]

The Ethiopian Government could not have possibly wished to enter into a treaty that was basically different from the Shewan treaty of 1883 in using the good offices of the Italian Government. Rubenson unequivocally revealed the dubious intention of the drafter of the treaty, Count Antonelli:

> 'Since the option concept was well established by the consistent use of the Italian phrase sera infacolta in treaty drafts intended for Yohannis and Menilik from as early as 1879, and verbal similarities, moreover, prove that Antonelli had the 1883 treaty in front of him when he prepared the 1888 draft, the changes must be assumed to have been deliberate. As important as the change from option to obligation, was the shift from a "postman" function to that of a foreign policy guardian. The aim was to control Ethiopia's relations, in other words, do away with Ethiopia's external sovereignty, and it was only logical that the Italian Government attempted to use the clause, Article XVII of the treaty signed on May, as basis for proclaiming a protectorate over Ethiopia.'[65]

When the Ethiopian Government discovered the fraudulent intent of the Italian Government, it unilaterally annulled the treaty that triggered the battle of Adwa in 1896. After the defeat of Italy in the battle of Adwa, Ethiopia and Italy replaced the Treaty of Wichale by a new treaty that was signed in Addis Ababa on 26 October 1896. The new treaty included provisions on the recognition of Ethiopia as a sovereign and independent state, non-cession of any territory by Italy to any other power. The non-cession provision required of Italy not to cede Eritrea or any part thereof to another power if it decides to withdraw from Eritrea. It was further stipulated that Eritrea would revert to Ethiopia.[66]

The treaty of 26 October 1896 induced other European countries to revise their recognition of Italy's alleged protectorate status over Ethiopia. Except Russia and France which expressed their reservations on Italy's claim of protectorate over Ethiopia, other Europeans accepted Italy's claim based on the Treaty of Wichale, 1889. Turkey, because of its claim of the port of Massawa on the Red Sea coast, rejected Italy's claim. Ultimately, it was Ethiopia's decisive victory at the battle of Adwa that changed the attitude of European countries and compelled them to accept Ethiopia as an independent and sovereign state.

We shall now consider the domestic policies of Menilek. Twenty years of an uninterrupted reign over Shewa had stood him in good stead to avoid repeating the mistakes of his predecessors. He, unlike his prede-cessors, had a unique opportunity to experiment with his policies on

Shewa, before his accession to the throne of Ethiopia. The Shewan style of government, by the standard of that time, was progressive. He gave due recognition to personal achievements and merits. Persons who distinguished themselves by their deeds attracted Menilek's attention. Personalities of humble origins and captives as Fitawrari Habte Giorgis. (Defence minister) and Dejazmach Balcha Safo (Governor) were promoted to key positions. Furthermore religious and ethnic tolerance was a distinctive feature of Menilek's style of government; persons from all faiths were given opportunities to develop their talents. On the other hand, his predecessors, both Tewodros and Yohannis had exhibited excessive intolerance to the followers of faiths other than the Ethiopian Orthodox Religion. The Christian dimension of Ethiopia and ethnicity were not given outrageous prominence during the reign of Menilek, who had already developed a tradition of religious and ethnic tolerance in his twenty years of rule of a multi-denominational and a multi-ethnic kingdom of Shewa. Another quality of Menilek was his magnanimity to the vanquished. For instance, Tonna, the King of Wolayta, who fought against Menilek, after his defeat, was pardoned and reinstated to his previous position. Such gesture of magnanimity characterised Menilek's style of government. Invariably the local administration of subdued provinces were left to the local hereditary chiefs. His tact in administration of his empire generated in his subjects a sense of identity. Darkwah, concerning the tactfulness of the Shewan rulers particularly that of Menilek, observed: '*Under Menilik the governor of Yefat was the son of Walsma Mohammed called Abagz Walsma. A careful scrutiny of the governors and shumes (chiefs) of the eastern block of the kingdom reveals that nearly all of them were Moslems.*'[67]

Menilek, upon his accession to the throne, extended the Shewan system of administration to the rest of his empire. On the efficiency of the Shewan style of government Darkwah remarked:

'The administrative machinery of Shewa was probably the
most efficient in the whole empire. It was a monarchical
absolutism that worked through a hierarchy of officials. Its
smooth running and therefore efficiency, especially in the
provinces depended on faithful and devoted officials. The
devotions of officials as well as the co-operation of the
ordinary citizens were readily forthcoming because the
subjects of the kingdom had so much to benefit from
the regime. After March 1889 the Shewan system was
extended to cover the whole empire and the efficiency of

the system was one of the potent factors which made
Shewanisation of the Empire.'[68]

The significant aspect of Menilek's style of government was sensitivity to
the needs of citizens, involving them in decision through consultation
and basing individual merits and achievements as factors for a successful
career. Darkwah in elaborating Menilek's style of government noted:

> 'The career of Gobena illustrates an important principle
> which was basic to the structure of the administration; that
> in Shewa, race, birth, or religion was in itself neither a
> passport nor a barrier to a position of importance and
> confidence. The absence of caste meant that every individual
> inhabitant could rise to an eminent position in the
> society.'[69]

Menilek, having consolidated his position both in the domestic and the
international fronts, embarked upon modernisation. The task of modernisation was vulnerable to forces which were opposed to changes in
traditional values. The opposition to his effort of modernisation came
even from persons who were very close to him, including Empress Taytu,
his wife, and Ras Mekonnen, Governor of Harargie and Menilek's confi-
dant. A case in point is the construction of the Franco-Ethiopian Railway
Line, where the queen and Ras Mekonnen objected to its construction
for they felt that opening up an access to the sea would make the state
vulnerable to invasion.[70]

The introduction of modern education met resistance too. The resistance was articulated by the nobles who genuinely felt that their children
would be converted to an alien religion. In 1906 a proclamation which
compelled parents to send their six-year-old children to modern schools
was issued. In other fields, despite resistance from conservatives, he continued in introducing postal, telephone, telegraphic, banking, health,
transportation and other services. His blueprint for modernisation was
executed with ease and patience.

A modern system of government, for the first time in the country's
history, was introduced. A cabinet system of government with defined
attributions was in place.[71] These were indeed modest attempts; but ideas
for change were implanted. The cabinet consisted of seven ministers
appointed by the emperor. Ethiopia's relations with European powers
were defined by diplomatic and consular norms. European powers,

including Great Britain, France, Italy and Russia, appointed permanent representatives to the Court of Menilek.

Menilek, during his long years of reign, restored and unified most of the medieval territories of Ethiopia and introduced administrative and social reforms of far-reaching implications. He injected into the nation the idea of modernity; above all enhanced the prestige of Ethiopia as an independent and sovereign state in the midst of European '*scramble for Africa*'. His reign was marked with peace, stability and prosperity.

Succession to Menilek

Menilek, at his death bed in 1909, chose his grandson, Lij Iyasu, who was sixteen years of age, to succeed him. From the day of Menilek's incapacity until he was succeeded by Lij Iyasu his grandson, Queen Taytu, Menilek's consort, had virtually assumed power in the name of the ailing emperor. She made a number of appointments to high offices that provoked the wrath of the nobility. However, after the death of the emperor, the queen was banished to Entoto, on the outskirts of Addis Ababa. She was effectively alienated from court politics and intrigues and died while she was in banishment.

Lij Iyasu under the regency of Ras Tessema Nadew assumed power in 1911. In his three years of reign, he succeeded in injuring the sensitivities of the nobility and the Church by his close association with Moslems and his alleged conversion to Islam. He was deposed by the nobility with the concurrence of the Church and replaced by Weizero Zewditu, Menilek's daughter, and Ras Teferri Mekonnen (the future Emperor Haile Selassie) as her regent and Crown prince.

Neguse Michael of Wollo, the father of Iyasu, who was enraged by the deposition of his son, marched to Addis Ababa with a force of 80,000 men. The government's force of 12,000 clashed with the Wolloye force at Segale, a plain some 120 kilometres to the North of Addis Ababa. It was a bloody battle. The government force, after suffering a number of reverses, won the battle and Neguse Michael was captured. The defeat of the Neguse Michael abruptly ended the Wolloye ambition for the Ethiopian throne.

Zewditu was a stopgap monarch. She was an ordinary lady who was neither graced with the talents of state craft nor the political acumen of her stepmother, Queen Taytu, who was the inspiring and driving force behind the important decisions of Menilek including the abrogation of the treaty of Wichale. Zewditu by contrast was a lady of modest educational background but a personification of the ideals of conservatism as opposed to her regent and heir. Crowning Zewditu and appointing Teferri Mekonnen as regent and Crown prince were compromises between the traditional and progressive elements of society. The progressive forces who were led by the regent and heir consolidated their power and influence, and demanded the title of king for the regent and heir. Empress Zewditu whose supporters had dwindled due to natural attrition and repression by the progressive forces, succumbed to their demands, that led to the crowing of Ras Teferri Mekonnen as king in 1928.[72]

The coronation of Teferri as king was to make his succession to the throne legitimate, if the empress was incapacitated. Two years from the coronation of the regent, Zewditu's death facilitated the succession of Neguse Teferri as Haile Selassie I Emperor of Ethiopia, Elect of God and Conquering Lion of the Tribe of Judas, on 30 October 1930.

The First Part of the Reign of Emperor Haile Selassie I (1930–35)

Haile Selassie, having consolidated his grip on the throne, began his crusade to continue modernising the country whose sound foundation was laid for him by Menilek. He introduced modest social reforms in education and the abolition of slavery. The landmark in his innovative adventures was the proclamation of the 1931 Constitution. The constitution, the first of its kind in the history of Ethiopia, was an imitation of the Japanese constitution of 1889. A good portion of this historic document dealt with the powers and prerogatives of the emperor and the succession to the throne. It also timidly attempted to introduce a bicameral parliament where the members of the Senate were chosen by the emperor and members of the Chamber of Deputies were elected by indirect means from those who owned immovable property. His subjects had neither the right to elect nor to be elected. At any rate, the constitution could be regarded as an important departure towards a constitutional rule in a society where the rights and duties of the people were determined by the whims of an emperor.

Haile Selassie was inspired by his European tour that took him to Great Britain, France, Italy, Sweden, and a number of other countries when he was yet a regent in 1924. After his return he was intent to introduce some aspects of Western civilisation that impressed him. His outlook was broadened by his exposure to the international community of nations. He broke thousands of years of his country's isolation by his determination to associate Ethiopia with prestigious institutions of that period such as the

League of Nations and the International Labour Organisation in 1919 and 1923 respectively.

The Italian Occupation of Ethiopia (1935–41)

Italy's attempts to occupy Ethiopia had, in the past, been successfully repulsed by the Ethiopians at the battles of Dogali and Adwa. In the battle of Dogali an Italian garrison of some 500 men was annihilated by Ras Alula Ingda, Governor of Tigray including most parts of present day Eritrea. This humiliating defeat was exacerbated when nine years later in the battle of Adwa, 1896, Menilek's army defeated Italy's 17,000–18,000 strong force under the command of General Oreste Barateri, governor of the colony of Eritrea. The casualties including the killed, wounded and captured, accounted for over 50% of Italy's colonial army engaged in the battle. General Barateri with his remaining force fled in disarray to Eritrea.[73] The defeat of Italy was a disaster without parallel in European colonial adventures.

The turn of events in Europe, particularly the threat from Nazi Germany's aggression prompted Great Britain and France to adopt a policy of appeasement towards Italy to alienate that country from Germany. Italy took advantage of Britain's and France's anxieties and pressed them to ignore the Tripartite Treaty of 1906 regarding the maintenance of the independence and integrity of Ethiopia. Italy,[74] having obtained the tacit agreement of Britain and France, parties to the treaty, in invading Ethiopia, began preparing for occupation and stepped up its diplomatic offensive against Ethiopia. France that had very much felt the threat of Nazi Germany, did not hesitate to cave in to Italy's colonial ambition in Ethiopia. The Mussolini–Laval agreement of 1935, was a shift of policy on the territorial integrity and independence of Ethiopia. An Italian author wrote:

> 'Scholars agree that in spite of the ambiguous language of
> the "free hand" Laval handed over Ethiopia as a price he was
> willing to pay for an *entente* with Italy. Laval did not care
> much about Ethiopia, as far as he was concerned, it was a
> purely African matter.'[75]

On the other hand Britain initially was reluctant, not on the grounds of principle that Italy's aggression should not be rewarded but saw it from its colonial interest perspective. Britain also came forward with a proposal to give Ethiopia the port of Zeila[76] on the Red Sea coast in exchange for which Ethiopia was to cede the Ogaden region to Italy. Anthony Eden was sent to Rome to sound the proposal to the Italian Government. Before it was formally submitted to both parties Mussolini rejected it on 24 June 1935. As the threat of aggression by Nazi Germany became more a reality than a possibility, Britain and France grew more desperate in befriending Italy. At last they worked out a plan that ceded more than half of Ethiopia to Italy and the remaining part to be Italy's protectorate with an access to the port of Aseb. Before the plan was formally submitted to Italy and Ethiopia a leak to the press generated heated debate in the House of Commons and Sir Samuel Hoare was forced to resign. Since the plan was drawn up in secret consultation with Italy she was prepared to accept, but Ethiopia rejected it.[77]

The plan was an instrument of treachery whereby the independence of a member state of the League of Nations was compromised to buy the friendship of an aggressor. As events later on proved, the policy of appeasement failed and Italy joined the Axis.

The Hoare–Laval Plan was an abdication of obligation of the Three Powers Treaty of 1906 concerning the territorial integrity and independence of Ethiopia by the parties to the treaty. The plan gave to Italy the green light to invade Ethiopia. Italy, having obtained the assurances of its colonial allies, unleashed its war of aggression against Ethiopia on 3 October 1935. The League of Nations that was dominated by Britain and France failed to take sufficient measures within the spirit of its convention to deter the invasion of Ethiopia that was left to fend for her defence. Italy, to avoid the risk of running another humiliating experience in its invasion of Ethiopia, used modern weaponry including mustard gas in violation of the Gas Protocol of 1925. The war was between two nations of unequal military powers; one had the advantage of modern technology and the other, had nothing except the patriotism of its people to guard jealously their independence with obsolete arms. In this connection Alberto Sbacchi observed:

'The Italian army owed its victory to their superior weaponry, and the employment – for the first time in a colonial war – of aerial bombardment and gas. The Ethiopians, with their aristocratic leadership not only lacked sophisticated armaments but fought a conventional war of pitched battle with frontal assault, using mostly horse-mounted soldiers armed with a sword or a spear, reminiscent of medieval war strategy.'[78]

Haile Selassie lost the war and fled to Jerusalem and later moved to Great Britain where he remained with his family in exile until July 1940. A few days after the flight of the emperor the Italians entered the capital city, Addis Ababa, in the spring of 1936 bringing the independence of one of the oldest nations to a sad end.

Following the occupation of Addis Ababa, Italy annexed Ethiopia and merged it with its colonies of Eritrea and Somaliland. The new territory was christened *Africa Orientale Italiana* (Italian East Africa). The enlarged colony was governed by a viceroy who was accountable to the Ministry for Africa in Rome. The Ethiopian territories were reorganised on ethnic lines. Tigray and Danakel regions were incorporated into Eritrea and the Ogaden region was merged with Italian Somaliland. The rest of Ethiopia was also divided on ethnic lines into four regions: Amhara, Harar, Oromo-Sidamo and Shewa. An Italian governor, who exercised autonomy in internal administration subject to the overall supervision of the viceroy was appointed for each region.

The first viceroy was General Pietro Badoligio who led the victorious fascist army to Addis Ababa from the north. After a few weeks as viceroy, he was, on grounds of poor health, replaced by General Rodolf Graziani, the Commander-in-Chief of the Southern Front of the Italian Colonial Army. Graziani's rule was marked by terror and extreme cruelty that resulted in antagonising the people who, initially, were not opposed to Italian rule. His rule of terror, particularly the massacre of unarmed civilians in Addis Ababa, monks, nuns, and clergies of the monastery of Debre Libanos following an attempt on his life in February 1937, was a contributory factor in strengthening resistance movements. Since prolonging the viceroy's tenure of office meant an alienation of the Ethiopian people from the colonial administration and eroding Italy's influence in Ethiopia, Rome replaced him by the Duke of Aosta.[79]

Although the Duke's approach to the administration of the colony was more humane than his predecessor's, it was during his time that racist legislations came in a big way. However his more sophisticated style of governance had a great impact in defusing the hatred and the militant attitude that were generated by Graziani's rule of terror. He headed an elaborate administrative structure that was responsible for military, administrative and developmental affairs of the colony. At the apex of the organisation was the Ministry for Africa in Rome that controlled all major decisions. The viceroy, whose administrative seat was in Addis Ababa, had under him a four-tier structure consisting of Governorate-Generals (Amhara, Oromo-Sidamo, Harar, Eritrea, Somalia, and Shewa and Addis Ababa), Commissions, Residences and Vice Residences.[80]

The colonial administration was manned by Italians who were not prepared for the task. The viceroy commented that 50% were unqualified and 25% were thieves.[81] The inadequacies of the colonial officials, the cumbersome organisation and the impractical regional boundaries hindered the implementation of Italian colonial policies.

The Italian occupation of Ethiopia, despite its atrocities, had some significant inputs in changing the attitude of the Ethiopian society towards the adoption of Western civilisation. The introduction of Western values shook the fabric of the Ethiopian society which created a more conducive climate for any attempt to modernise the country. The introduction of the idea of entrepreneurship in commerce and industry, modern system of transportation, and even the top-heavy colonial administration had invaluable impact on the conservative mode of life that was prevalent in Ethiopia before the Italian occupation. Furthermore, influences of traditional institutions in particular of the nobility and chieftaincy were undermined by Italy's colonial policy. By 1941 a good number of the nobles who were threats to Haile Selassie's power had disappeared from politics by natural attrition and Italy's scorched-earth policy which virtually destroyed the nobility as well as its power-base. After the restoration of independence, those nobles and chiefs who collaborated with Italy were disgraced and lost their social position of influence and were not of any consequence to pose serious challenges to the emperor. The concurrence of events made conditions favourable for the emperor to resume his modernisation that was interrupted for five years by the Italian occupation.

The Second Part of the Reign of Emperor Haile Selassie I (1941–74)

The joint force of the British Army and the Ethiopian patriots defeated and expelled Italy from Ethiopia in 1941. After the defeat of Italy, Haile Selassie and the British authorities had to consider the question, who would be in charge of the administration of the country? Despite Sir Anthony Eden's declaration in the House of Commons Britain's commitment to help in re-establishing an independent Ethiopia and restoring Emperor Haile Selassie, some of the British commanders considered Ethiopia as an ex-enemy territory and held the view that it should be administered by the British until a peace treaty was signed with Italy. On the other hand Haile Selassie claimed that since he had not renounced his sovereignty following his defeat at the battle of Mai Ceu, 1936, he had the right to resume his rule that was interrupted by the Italian occupation.[82] Those differences coupled with the opinion of certain

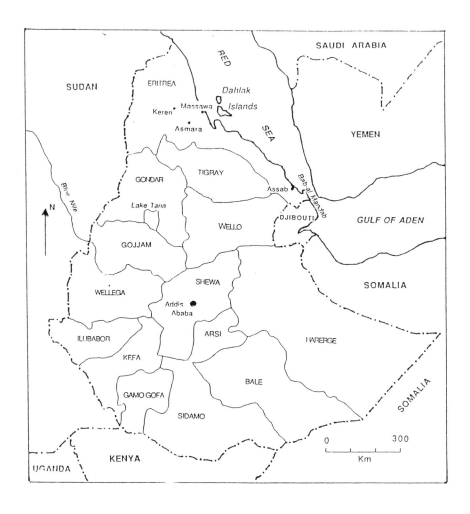

Map 5 Administrative divisions of Ethiopia, 1952–86

British officials that Ethiopia should, at least for a short period, be under British protectorate, prompted the emperor to take symbolic steps that would demonstrate to the British his assertion of sovereignty. His first act of defiance of a British rule was to appoint unilaterally seven ministers.[83] The emperor's action provoked a protest from the local British commanders. The emperor, conscious of his vulnerability, climbed down by stating that the ministers were appointed to assist the British Military Force in running the administration of the country. The British authorities reluctantly entertained the explanation of the emperor. However he felt that unless Britain's declaration to restore the independence of Ethiopia was guaranteed by some form of an Anglo-Ethiopian agreement, it could not be taken for granted. He formally requested the British Government for an Anglo-Ethiopian agreement, that among other things, would contain provisions on financial aid, recruiting expatriate advisers, rendering assistance in establishing an army, a police force and courts. His request was entertained by the British Government. After a long protracted negotiation, the Anglo-Ethiopian Agreement of 1942 was concluded and signed. The agreement reflected mainly the issues that were of importance to the British Government. The coercive branches of the state machinery – the army, the police force and from the court system the High Court, were placed under the control of the British. Moreover the Ethiopian side was put under an obligation to obtain in advance the consent of the British Government, should it decide to recruit foreign nationals as advisers and seek to take any action in any part of the country that would entail military operation. Furthermore, the agreement, which was not better than a formal acceptance of British protectorate over Ethiopia, placed the Ogaden region, the city of Dire Dawa and the Franco-Ethiopian Railway Line, under the British Government. Britain, on the other hand, entered into an obligation to advance a four-year subvention of £3,250,000 and train a standing army and a police force at her own expense and in return retained the post of the Commander of the Police Force.[84] The agreement which reduced the status of Ethiopia to a protectorate remained in force until it was replaced by another agreement.

In keeping with the provisions of the agreement, the Ethiopian side annulled it by serving three months' notice to Britain and also submitted a new draft that would replace it. It was then replaced by the Anglo-Ethiopian Agreement of 1944. The new agreement[85], among other things, covered the right of the Ethiopian Government to recruit advisers without seeking the approval of Britain (article 3): placing the British Military Mission under the Ethiopian Government (article 6); reverting the city of Dire Dawa and the Franco-Ethiopian Railway Line to Ethiopia (article 5); restoring a small part of the Ogaden to Ethiopia (article 7) and retaining the occupation of Haud region from the Ogaden by Britain (article 7).

Although the 1944 agreement gave the Ethiopian Government a wider latitude of freedom of action, it fell short of restoring full sovereignty to Ethiopia. The Ogaden issue that had strained the relations of the two countries was finally settled by the Anglo-Ethiopian Agreement of 1954. This agreement, amongst other things, provided for the restoration of the Haud, the reserved area, to Ethiopia and the withdrawal of the British Military Mission from Ethiopia.[86] It took over ten years for the Ethiopian Government to restore the pre-1935 territories and frontiers of Ethiopia.

The British indeed dominated Ethiopia from 1941–44 and played a significant role in the restoration and reconstruction of Ethiopia. Britain's financial aid and assistance in training an army and a police force, re-introducing modern education were genuine contributions. The other positive aspect of the Anglo-Ethiopian relations was its indirect effect in motivating the Ethiopian Government to see the need of diversifying its external relations. Ethiopia expanded its diplomatic interaction with other countries like the United States, which was still emerging from the cocoon of its isolationist policy to assume a new leadership role in the postwar politics. The Ethiopian Government invited the United States Government to participate in development programmes. It responded positively to the request of Ethiopia, considering its interest in the strategic location of Ethiopia in the Horn of Africa. The wheel of collaboration began to grind. The United States involved itself in concrete terms by assisting in establishing a civil airline (1946) and advancing silver for minting coins and a stabilisation loan.[87] Eventually, the sporadic co-operation resulted in the conclusion of the Ethio-United States of America Treaty of Amity and Economic Assistance in 1953. After the signing of the treaty the British influence in Ethiopia gradually faded away and was fully replaced by the United States. Ethiopia remained a faithful partner of the United States until Emperor Haile Selassie was overthrown by a military junta in 1974.

The first phase of the emperor's reign was largely devoted to acquisition and consolidation of power; it did not give him a breathing space for carrying out modernisation programmes. Much of his time and energy was committed to keeping an acceptable balance between conservative and progressive elements of society. The nobility and the Church who represented conservatism did not allow him to continue forcefully with his programme of modernisation. However, because of the Italian occupation the forces of conservatism, in particular the nobility, was weakened and uprooted from its power-base. Moreover, the impact of the Italian occupation on the socio-economic consciousness of the ordinary person was a positive element for the introduction of a modern system of administration. When Haile Selassie triumphantly entered his capital city conditions were more favourable than they were before 1935 for reinstating his plan of modernisation. Since the country was torn apart by war, the reconstruction work awaiting for him was horrendous. It ranged from the maintenance of law and order to the re-establishment of the government machinery with the necessary legislations, policies and directives. The state structure including administrative set-up, the army, the police, the judicial system, education, health, etc., had to be started from scratch. The key to these programmes of reconstruction was a steady revenue and trained manpower that the country was severely starved of.

The government, to guarantee a steady flow of revenue for the bureaucracy, issued a rural land tax law, Proclamation No. 8 of 1942. The proclamation classified rural land into cultivated, semi-cultivated and uncultivated lands. Annual tax rates, on a Gasha (forty hectares) of cultivated land, semi-cultivated and cultivated lands, were fixed at Birr 15, 10 and 5 respectively. Since the proclamation along with tax rates injected the need for land measurement the northern Teklai Gizats (Governorate-Generals) Begemdir, Gojjam, Tigray where the land tenure system was communal, revolted against the implementation of the proclamation. The fear of those regions that resisted the enforcement of the proclamation was genuine because when the Kelad (a system of land measurement) was introduced excess land was expropriated. The rebellion was pacified by another proclamation (No. 70 of 1944) that excluded all those regions where communal ownership of land was in practice from the application of the 1941 proclamation. In fact the proclamations shifted the tax burden to peasants where communal ownership was not in practice. The Church was also exempted from paying taxes on its large amount of land. The Church, as a big landowner, and those regions of communal land ownership resisted and blocked any attempt by the government to correct the inequity in the rural land tax.

Tax on income, before 1935, was unknown. After the restoration of independence the number of wage earners relatively increased. Salaries and wages began to be paid entirely in cash contrary to practices before 1935. The change in the system of payment in the public sector and the appearance of wage-earning class-constituted sufficient ground for

45

introducing an income tax. Hence, Proclamation No. 6 of 1944 was issued.

A structure of government with a cabinet system was in place. The cabinet had an advisory role to the emperor. The political map of the country was redrawn consisting of Teklai Gizat, Awraja (a province), Werreda (district), and Mikitle Werreda (sub-district) which was abolished later on. The court structure followed the administrative subdivisions. An army, a police force and an air force were established with assistance of the British and the Swedes. While the British focused on the army and the police force, the Swedes contributed in the establishment of the Imperial Ethiopian Air Force which was one of the best in Africa, and the Imperial Body Guard, an elite core which gave a good account of itself in the Korean war in the 1950s.

To attract badly needed foreign investment, an investment proclamation that provided incentives such as tax holidays, tax exemption on imported capital goods, repatriation of profit and other incentives, was issued. The government's role in joint ventures was defined as well.

The bureaucracy, including the armed forces, exacerbated the shortage of trained manpower. To meet the growing need for trained personnel schools, vocational training centres, and other institutions were established with the assistance of friendly countries. During this phase of reconstruction, education was accorded high priority. The emperor had a strong conviction that the key to his modernisation was the development of a sound educational system. As a mark of his commitment to education the cabinet portfolio of education was held by himself.

The few schools that were established before 1935 were closed by the Italians. Like all other government services, the education system had to be rebuilt from scratch. By 1974 when the emperor was deposed, excluding mission, church, foreign community and private schools, there were 3,196 primary and 631 secondary schools with enrolments of 644,998 and 166,116 pupils respectively. The overall enrolment including mission, church, foreign community and private schools was 1,123,752. Out of this 9,889 accounted for students' enrolment in the Addis Ababa and Asmera universities.[88] The efforts of local institutions were supplemented by bi-lateral and multi-lateral overseas education grants and technical co-operation programmes. Given the immensity of problems of reconstruction and the shortage of resources, the achievements of Haile Selassie's government particularly in the field of education deserve due recognition. Of course one could argue that given 33 years of stability and peace access to education could have been extended to the bulk of the population.

Access to health care showed considerable growth in comparison with the services that were rendered before 1935. The number of hospitals and beds rose from very few in the pre-war period to 84 and 8,623 respectively in 1974. The service was supplemented by 1,000 clinics spread all over the country. Although the growth of health service compared with service prior to 1935 was remarkable, the demand was not met. For a population of 30 million the doctor/patient ratio was 1:100,000[89] which was low even by the standards of developing countries.

Simultaneously with developments of social services steps were taken to introduce banking, insurance, transport, communication, etc. Ironically, in the economic sector significant measures were not taken to change the quality of life of the peasants who constituted the backbone of the nation's economy. The efforts that were directed to introduce the peasantry to the use of improved implements, fertilisers, insecticides, improved seeds and other inputs, were not carried beyond pilot projects that were more of showpieces than anything else. The means of production of the peasant were allowed to remain in their primitive stages. The peasant was in too distressed a condition to be able to meet the revenue demand of the burgeoning bureaucracy. Due to his very low productive capacity a peasant was unable to meet all his obligations, including tax, a share of a landlord and development levy imposed by an unscrupulous governor.

The industrial sector was given better attention than the agricultural sector. Legislation that provided incentives to domestic and foreign investors was issued. It was a positive industrial policy designed to attract external as well as domestic investments. On the eve of the revolution the number of manufacturing establishments, in the public and private sectors, was about 430 employing over 60,000 workers.[90] When undertakings with five or more workers were considered, the industrial labour force was estimated at 300,000. However, the total number of wage earners including those in the public service and the armed forces was approximately 400,000–500,000.[91] The labour force showed a considerable growth when compared with the number of wage earners before 1935, which was almost non-existent.

The imperial regime did not do enough to improve the lot of the peasantry by reforming the land tenure system. In fact it was given a modern veneer as consequence of which the peasantry was subjected to a more refined mode of exploitation. The emperor, soon after the restoration of his empire, relying on his royal prerogative distributed state lands and enemy properties to his retainers, patriots, and to the members of the royal family. The example of venality he set spread through the length and breadth of the country. Loyal retainers and patriots were, without regard to their competence, appointed in key positions in the bureaucracy as a reward for their loyalty to him. Especially provincial administration remained the exclusive fief of retainers. The Enderassies (governors) with the exception of a few, were despots who never had any regard of basic human rights. They adhered to laws and regulations in as much as they served their interests. Detention, summary dismissal from employment and expulsion of citizens from a Teklai Gizat without recourse to due process of the law, were rules rather than exceptions. As one went farther from the capital nepotism, corruption and venality were common features of provincial administrations. The Addis Ababa government of Prime Minister Aklilu Habtewolde's influence and directives did not have any impact farther than the fringes of Addis Ababa. The Enderassies were by law accountable to the minister of Interior but it never worked out as it was intended by the legislature. By-passing the minister or even the Prime Minister to deal directly with the emperor was a norm of the Enderassies; the emperor never discouraged such administrative irregularities. He invariably encouraged it to create a tug of war between the cabinet and the provincial administration. The Enderassies behaved as if they were minor emperors in their respective Teklai Gizats. The provincial administration of the imperial regime was a government within a government.

As if the liberal use of state properties and services for personal use was not enough, most of the Enderassies levied development charges allegedly for local development programmes. Neither the programmes nor the rate of the levies were approved by the central government. The amounts collected were enormous; but a portion of them went to prestigious projects like a life-size statue of the emperor at Finote Selam, a tiny town in Gojjam, where potable water was in dire need. However, a good portion of the so-called development levy found its way to the coffers of provincial administrators. The central government's effort to rationalise the use of development levies was flouted by opposition from quarters where vested interests were threatened. Development levy, landlord's crop-sharing system, fragmentation and mismanagement of land, and evictions of tenants from farms without any compensation, made the lives of peasants miserable.

The spread of modern education, the development of a modern bureaucracy, qualitative changes in the officer core of the armed forces, and the growth of a working class required a fresh approach to the system of government. Students demanded changes in the land tenure system and liberal political system. The working class demanded better conditions of work and payments. The emperor's pampered Body Guards challenged his style of government when they staged the abortive *coup d'état* of 1960. Despite the shock from the coup the emperor failed to institute timely changes that would respond to popular demands. The Revised Constitution of 1955 was a marked improvement on the 1931 Constitution; but it failed to address the main concerns of the politically conscious and vocal sector of the society. The people of Ethiopia had great faith in the emperor hoping that he would change their country into a democracy, where there would be enough room for everybody including the monarchy, but his love for power and unwillingness to share it with his subjects, caused his downfall.

NOTES

1 John Markakis, Anatomy of a Traditional Polity, Oxford, 1974, p. 13; Donald Levine, Greater Ethiopia, Chicago, 1974, p. 7, Stuart Munro-Hay, Aksum: An African Civilisation of Late Antiquity, Edinburgh, Edinburgh University Press, 1991, p. 69.
2 Sergew Habte-Selassie, Ancient and Medieval History of Ethiopia to 1270, Addis Ababa, 1972, p. 160; Stuart Munro-Hay, Aksum: An African Civilisation of Late Antiquity, Edinburgh, Edinburgh University Press, 1991, p. 159.
3 Sergew Habte-Selassie, op. cit., p. 124; Munro-Hay, op. cit., pp. 226–230.
4 Sergew Habte-Selassie, op. cit., p. 174.
5 A. Jones and Elizabeth Monroe, A History of Abyssinia, New York, 1969, p. 44.
6 Jones and Monroe, op. cit., p. 47.
7 Jones and Monroe, op. cit., p. 48.
8 M. Abir, The Era of the Princes, London, Longmans, 1968, p. xix.
9 Jones and Monroe, op. cit. p. 50.
10 Sven Rubenson, The Survival of Ethiopian Independence, London, 1976, pp. 322–328.
11 Tekle Tsadiq Mekuria, Atse Tewodros Ena Ye Ethiopia Andnet, Addis Ababa, 1981 (Ethiopian Calendar), pp. 210–221.
12 Levine, op. cit., pp. 92–100.
13 Jones and Monroe, op. cit., p. 54.
14 Taddesse Tamrat, Church and State in Ethiopia, London, 1972, p. 261.
15 Jones and Monroe, op. cit., p. 56.
16 Dr Fikre Tolossa, The Amhara Contribution to the Civilisation of Ethiopia, Ethiopia Review, April 1993, pp. 82–87.
17 Tekle Tsadiq Mekuria, Ye Gragn Ahmed Werera, Addis Ababa, 1966 (in Ethiopian Calendar), pp. 279–284.
18 Taddesse Tamrat, op. cit., p. 301.
19 Jones and Monroe, op. cit., p. 85.

20 Jones and Monroe, op. cit., p. 85; Richard Pankhurst, Economic History of Ethiopia: 1800–1935, Haile Selassie University Press, Addis Ababa, 1968, p. 9.
21 Marcus, op. cit., p. 15.
22 Abir. op. cit., p. xii.
23 ibid., p. xxiii.
24 Jones and Monroe, op. cit., p. 123.
25 Abir, op. cit., p. 38.
26 Bahru Zewde, A History of Modern Ethiopia, 1855–1974, London, Athens (Ohio University Press) and Addis Ababa, 1991, p. 14.
27 Sven Rubenson, King of Kings Tewodros of Ethiopia, Addis Ababa, 1966, p. 132.
28 Tekle Tsadiq Mekuria, Atse Tewodros Ena Ye Ethiopia Andnet, 1981, p. 71.
29 Sven Rubenson, The Survival of Ethiopian Independence, p. 136.
30 Bahru Zewde, op. cit., p. 32.
31 Abir, op. cit., p. 141.
32 ibid., 142.
33 Sven Rubenson, King of Kings Tewodros of Ethiopia, 1966, pp. 66–70.
34 ibid., p. 72.
35 Jones and Monroe, op. cit. p. 131.
36 Sven Rubenson, King of Kings Tewodros of Ethiopia, 1966, pp. 66–70.
37 Sven Rubenson, The Survival of Ethiopian Independence, 1976, p. 272.
38 Sven Rubenson, King of Kings Tewodros of Ethiopia, p. 89.
39 Bahru Zewde, op. cit., p. 43.
40 ibid., pp. 42–43; Harold G. Marcus, The Life and Times of Menilek II: Ethiopia 1844–1913, New Jersey, ed. 1995, pp. 31–32.
41 Marcus, op. cit., p. 121.
42 R. H. Kofi Darkwah, Shewa, Menilek and the Ethiopian Empire, London, 1975, p. 84.
43 Bahru Zewde, op. cit., pp. 44–46.
44 ibid., pp. 45–48.
45 Zewde Gebre-Selassie, A Political Biography of Yohannis IV, London, 1975, p. 256.
46 E. Hartslet, The Map of Africa by Treaty, London, 1967, Volume II pp. 422–423.
47 Earnest Work, Ethiopia: A Pawn in European Diplomacy, New York 1935, p. 74.
48 Marcus, op. cit., p. 82.
49 ibid. p. 75.
50 Richard Pankhurst, Taddesse Beyene and Taddesse Tamrat, The Centenary of Dogali, Addis Ababa & Asmara, 1987, p. 126.
51 David Mathew, The Study of a Polity, London, 1947, p. 218.
52 Marcus, op. cit., p. 22.
53 Pawlos Gnogno, Atse Menilik, Addis Ababa, 1984 (EC). p. 108.
54 Bahru Zewde, op. cit., pp. 48–49; Tekle Tsadiq Mekuria, Atse Yohannis Ena Ye

Ethiopia Andnet, Addis Ababa, Kuraz Publishing Agency, 1982 (EC), pp. 197–201.

55 Pawlos Gnogno, op. cit., pp. 106–107.
56 Darkwah, op. cit., p. 211.
57 ibid., p. 87.
58 ibid. p. 181.
59 ibid. p. 108.
60 Hertslet, op. cit., No. 95 to 259.
61 Pierre Petrides, The Boundary Question between Ethiopia and Somalia, New Delhi, 1983, p. 17.
62 The Amharic Translation of Article XVII of the Treaty of Wichale is the author's. For the Amharic version see Pawlos Gnogno, op. cit., p. 140.
63 Harold G. Marcus, The Life and Times of Menilek II: Ethiopia 1844–1913, p. 114.
64 Hertslet, op. cit. No. 95 to 259.
65 Sven Rubenson, The Survival of Ethiopian Independence, p. 385.
66 Hertslet, op. cit., p. 459.
67 Darkwah, op. cit., p. 136.
68 ibid., p. 140.
69 ibid., p. 135.
70 Pawlos Gnogno, op. cit., p. 251.
71 ibid., pp. 259–268.
72 Bahru Zewde, op. cit., p. 135.
73 Harold G. Marcus, The Life and Times of Menilek II: Ethiopia 1844–1913, p. 173.
74 Heartslet, op. cit p. 440.
75 Alberto Sbacchi, Ethiopia Under Mussolini, London, 1985, p. 11.
76 Public Records Office. Sir Birton's Telegram No. 210 from Addis Ababa to the Foreign Office. FO/371/19124, London; Report on Abyssinia, FO/371/19160, 11 September 1935, p. 6.
77 FO/371/19124; Eden, Anthony (Sir), Facing the Dictators, Boston: Houghton Mifflin 1962, pp. 291–311; Samuel Hoare (Sir), Ourselves and the World Peace, National Union of Conservative Associations Facts and Leaflets. No. 3363–3486, London, 1935, p. 10; Josee Laval, The Unpublished Diary of Pierre Laval, London, The Falcon Press Ltd. 1948, p. 31.
78 Sbacchi, op. cit., p. 26.
79 ibid., pp. 48–50.
80 ibid., pp. 85–87.
81 ibid., p. 83.
82 V. H. Norberg, The Swedes in Haile Selassie's Ethiopia 1924–1952, Uppsala, 1977, pp. 50–51; Public Records Office, FO/371/27518, Memorandum by the Secretary of State for War to the War Cabinet on administration of Ethiopia, London, 14 May 1941. The memorandum summarising British policy on the administration of Ethiopia states:

1. *His Majesty's Government would welcome the reappearance of an independent Ethiopian State, but in the meantime the conduct of military operation requires that the Emperor should abide strictly by the advice of the British authorities.*

2. *Ethiopia is temporarily under British guidance and control, pending the decision of the Peace Conference, His Majesty's Government are technically in the position of an Occupying Power.*

3. *In areas notified by the Commander-in-Chief as areas occupied by the British Military Forces, and these may change from time to time as the military situation demands, the political and administrative executive of the Commander-in-Chief will be the Deputy Chief Political Officer. Departmental control and administrative supervision on behalf of the War Office and His Majesty's Government will be exercised through the Chief Political Officer, thus such areas will be under British administration.*

4. *When the Commander-in-Chief, Middle East, considers military occupation of an area may be dispensed with, such an area will be placed under the authority of the Emperor, it being understood that should the situation demand the Commander-in-Chief may require any such area to revert to purely British administration. In administering these areas on behalf of the Occupying Power the Emperor must accept British guidance and control on pain of loss of our support. That guidance and control will be exercised through the Deputy Chief Political Officer and his staff at the centre and by political missions attached to the Emperor's Officials in the provinces. Legislations in these areas will be in the name of the Emperor but must be acceptable to the Deputy Chief Political Officer.*

5. *Although as stated above in paragraph 4 the Emperor will administer on behalf of the Occupying Power, it is important that his authority in the eyes of his own people should not be undermined.*

6. *Communications between the Emperor and His Majesty's Government will be sent through the Deputy Chief Political Officer of the General Officer Commanding who will transmit to the Commander-in-Chief through the Political Officer.'*

83 Harold G. Marcus, Ethiopia, Great Britain and the United States 1941–1974, London, 1983, p. 9.

84 Harold G. Marcus, Ethiopia, Great Britain, and the United States 1941–1974, p. 12; Norberg, op. cit., pp. 50–52; Public Records Office, FO 371/35634, Memorandum of the Chancellor of the Exchequer to the War Cabinet London, 6 December 1943.

85 Norberg, op. cit., pp. 53–54.

86 Norberg, op. cit., p. 54; John H. Spencer, Ethiopia At Bay: a Personal Account of the Haile Selassie Years, Algonac., Michigan, 1984, p. 102.

87 Harlod G. Marcus, Ethiopia, Great Britain, and the United States 1941–1974, p. 25.

88 Facts and Figures, Central Statistical Office, Addis Ababa, 1987, pp. 105–107; Ethiopia: Statistical Abstract, Central Statistical Office. Addis Ababa, 1982, p. 250.

89 Facts and Figures, Central Statistical Office, Addis Ababa, 1987, p. 110.
90 ibid., p. 51.
91 ibid., pp. 51–70.

Chapter Two

The Price of Modernisation

It is also axiomatic that change begets change, that each step
forward leads logically and inexorably to the next, and the
next. Once unleashed, the forces of history cannot be contained or restrained and he is naive indeed who says 'thus far
will I go and no more farther'.

Emperor Haile Selassie I

Institutional Changes

The effects of Haile Selassie's modernisation began to show in every facet
of social interaction. The pillars of the Ethiopian polity, the monarchy,
the Church and the nobility, gradually lost their influence in the wake
of structural change in the society. After the Second World War, Ethiopia's
age-old curtain of isolation was lifted. It opened up its doors to Western
civilisation and values and did not hesitate to embrace them indiscriminately. The spread of modern education, a more liberal contact with the
external world and the wind of change that was irreversibly affecting
the political map of Africa had their corresponding inputs in influencing the Ethiopian scene. The emperor was actively involved in the
decolonisation process of Africa. He was respected and held in very high
esteem by African as well as Western leaders as an elder statesman. He
had immensely contributed in defusing the regional groupings of new
independent African states, a factor which was leading to the polarisation
of relations among states into the Monrovia and Casablanca blocs by
proposing the formation of the Organisation of African Unity (OAU).

Addis Ababa was chosen as the permanent seat for the headquarters of the OAU due to his prestige and Ethiopia's long history of independence. As Africa's elder statesman he played a vital role in resolving conflicts among member states of the OAU. His international role, no doubt, had earned for Ethiopia more prestige and respect.

On the domestic scene, however, things were not as encouraging as in the international field. Haile Selassie's government was a collection of loyalist individuals without any common political or ideological bond. Its major preoccupation was routine state functions. The government lacked vision and a sense of direction. It was not answerable to the people, a fact which made it insensitive to the growing demand and needs of the populace in general and the politically conscious segment of the population in particular. Indeed the introduction of a modern bureaucracy and the rule of law, the establishment of a modern army, a police force and access to modern education had systematically weakened and undermined its feudal base. Under feudalism, the combination of the monarchy, the Church and the nobility was the *raison d'être* of the state but the emperor's experiment in modernisation indirectly weakened and eroded the partnership of these traditional institutions.

The Church played a decisive role in the spiritual and temporal life of society. The monarchy relied on the support and blessing of the Church for its rule. The Church was the sole institution which had the means to influence the attitudes and beliefs of its followers through its numerous churches which are invariably found wherever human settlement, save nomadic areas, existed. In the pre-restoration period (1941), no other institution had a network comparable to the Ethiopian Orthodox Church at the grass-root level. The Church commanded prestige and respect in society. Its prominent role in the society graced it with extensive power of influence. However, the appearance of modern education, the spread of missionary activities by other Christian denominations and the introduction of a modern state structure and administration weakened its role. The Church was, no more as it used to be, the only source of influence in the community. Modern schools with their better qualified teachers and facilities took over education. Missionary schools with their incentive of medical services to the community attracted the Church's congregation. The spread of education created new values and aspirations in society which the Church was not prepared to accommodate. It, however, remained impervious to any change and failed to meet the spiritual needs of the enlightened and educated middle class. The failure of the Church to cope with changing circumstances was a visible symptom of its diminished role in shaping the life of its congregation.

Even though it retained its privileged position at state level, its influence in society was diminished. The emerging reality, in post-war Ethiopia, was the secular nature of the state, where members of one denomination and/or ethnic origin were not allowed to dominate the affairs of the state. In articulating the secular nature of his government, the emperor in one of his public utterances said, ' ... *religion is personal but a state is common.*'[1]

This statement was a declaration that the Church had to abandon its temporal role in the affairs of the state and confine itself to its spiritual role. The change of attitude regarding the role of the Church coupled with the effects of modern education and the Church's failure to keep abreast with changing circumstances weakened its traditional role in society.

The nobility had already lost its traditional power-base and influence after the Italian occupation of Ethiopia in 1935. Moreover, the introduction of a centralised government and the creation of a standing army had ended regional political influences of the nobility. The Italian occupation, in this respect, had produced an unexpected benefit by abolishing the traditional power-base of the nobility. Many of the nobles fell at the battlefield fighting gallantly and the survivors were hunted down and executed by the fascist invader; those who wilfully submitted to Italian authorities were stripped of their power and influence. After the restoration of independence, the emperor had no intention of reviving the influence of the nobility which had been a threat to his power. Although the nobles had lost their traditional role, they were absorbed in the new state structure as governors, positions which were their exclusive fiefs until the overthrow of the regime in 1974.

The traditional alliances of the monarchy, the Church and the nobility were replaced by a modern bureaucracy and a standing army. It was through a gradual process of change that Haile Selassie weakened the institutions which were the backbone of his power and influence.

The bureaucracy and the army which were constituted on a new set of values had aspirations incompatible with blind loyalty to the crown. The emperor failed to foresee that the loyalty of these new forces could not be taken for granted. As more and more educated and enlightened individuals joined the new state structure a set of new demands and expectations began to grow. The regime's failure to introduce timely reforms that would respond to the new realities, fomented dissatisfaction. The officers of the Imperial Body Guard, the Public Security, the Police Force and some civilian elites in the Civil Service became, not only aware of the inadequacies of the political system they were serving, but resolved to replace it with a more democratic form of government. The Imperial Body Guard whose loyalty to the crown was beyond suspicion staged the 1960 abortive coup while the emperor was on a state visit to Brazil. The declared objective of the plotters of the coup was to introduce a system of government under a constitutional monarchy. The coup failed mainly due to insufficient planning, the loyalty of the army to the crown and lack of visible popular support. It was the first expression of resentment of the enlightened sector of society, since the restoration of independence in 1941. The coup awakened society particularly the elites and students from their political slumber.

The university students in Addis Ababa demonstrated in support of the coup. From that time on, students remained the vocal critic of the regime and demanded a change in the socio-economic system of the state. Their contact and interaction with scholarship students from the newly independent African countries, in the Addis Ababa University, and the change in the composition of the university's staff in favour of overseas educated nationals had a significant input in changing the campus student politics into a systematic challenge to the policies of the regime. The slogan, '*land to the tiller*', became a painful reminder to government of the injustices that the peasantry had to endure for centuries. Moreover, the sixties were years of student radicalism all over the world and Ethiopian students shared this radicalism.

Another factor which triggered student radicalism in Ethiopia, was the Peace Corps Programme of President J. F. Kennedy's Administration whereby young men and women were sent in several thousands to developing countries to preach the gospel of Western values and to contain the spread of communism: '*By the mid-1960s Ethiopia had the largest Peace Corps contingent in the world.*'[2] Over two thousand volunteers were placed in schools as teachers all over the country. Soon the student radicalism of the Addis Ababa University spread in the secondary schools like a contagious disease engulfing high school pupils. The presence of Peace Corps volunteers had invariably drawn the attention of their pupils to the shortcomings of the government and the backward level of the socio-economic development of the country. The student population which lacked political consciousness in the fifties and early sixties drastically changed in outlook and political maturity in the 1970s. The contact with student unions in other countries and overseas Ethiopian students' associations had contributed in broadening their views and enabled them to articulate their demands. The challenge posed by the students became a nuisance to the government. Instead of instituting changes that might have a soothing effect on student uprising, the government resorted to repressive measures to contain students' riots. Some students were expelled from the university and others imprisoned; their publication and union were banned.

The emperor, even after an attempt of the overthrow of his government, failed to admit the defects of the administration. He dismissed the coup as an attempt of misguided individuals for personal ambition and lust for power. Marcus commented that the coup *'would not cause the slightest deviation from the path of progress he had initiated for his country. He was convinced that the programmes he had initiated were those best calculated to secure achievement and progress . . . and he was determined to use them with all the vigour and energy at his disposal. There would be no change of government and the government's programmes.'*[3]

The bureaucracy was changed qualitatively when an increasing number of educated persons joined its ranks. The new breed of bureaucrats did not inherit the sycophantic loyalty of their fathers to the crown. In the army, the officers' corp as well as the rank and file had changed in composition. Junior officers who were trained in national military academies grew in number. Most of the officers had been in the United States for further training under the Ethio–US Mutual Defense Agreement of 1953. The American Military Assistance Advisory Group's (MAAG) training programme had also a significant impact in changing the outlook of officers. The combined effect of the internal and overseas training had produced a sizeable number of officers who were able to differentiate between loyalty to the crown and to the people. The army's loyalty to the crown was not a matter to be taken for granted in the 1970s.

The post-coup government was not different in its policies and programmes from its predecessor. The government still remained a one-man show without any meaningful devolution of power to the local level. All decisions, be it economic or political, had to have the advance approval of the emperor. His uncompromising desire to control every aspect of the government, perpetuated inefficiency and indecision at every level of administration. Lockot commenting on the style of government of the emperor wrote: *'Haile Selassie retained his independent judgement, and developed a superior performing technique to achieve balance without letting any players join in. Up till his death, he remained the solo virtuoso.'*[4]

The Economy

Ethiopia's economy is largely dependent on agriculture. More than 85% of the population's means of livelihood is agriculture. The country with its immense agricultural potential, climatic variations and water resources could, according to the International Bank of Reconstruction and Development, sustain a population of 310 million. Unfortunately, on account of feudalism and lack of sound development policies the potential of the country is not realised. People of Ethiopia still are victims of endemic natural and man-made disasters which are invariably followed by famine.

The agricultural potential of the country and its rich manpower resources were not rationally developed, mainly because of the imperial government's lack of political will and resolve to introduce agrarian reform. Minor reforms, such as the abolishing of Gult (a system of land ownership whereby land was given for services rendered to the state; tenants shared their produce with the landlord and provide corvee labour) was not a solution for the basic problem of the land tenure system that stifled agricultural development.

The landed aristocracy, the Church and the Balabats (hereditary chiefs who commanded a degree of social status in the community and invariably owned one-third of the land in their locality) were not in favour of any drastic land reform that might jeopardise their interest in land. Attempts in land reform by the imperial government faced vehement opposition from those with vested interests, including the members of parliament, who were themselves landowners. The land tenure system was very complex, but at the time of the revolution there were two major systems. The Northern provinces of Tigray, Begemidir, Gojjam, Wollo and Northern Shewa had a communal system of land ownership. Anybody who could establish his ancestral link had the right to share the communal land. In regions where the communal system of land ownership was practised, the problem of tenancy was marginal, affecting 15–25% of the population. In the other parts of the country the prevailing land tenure system was private ownership of land where the problem of tenancy was very extensive, affecting 80–85% of the farmers. The remaining 15–20% accounted for owner-farmers and farmers with other contractual arrangements. Agrarian reform was a precondition for releasing the potential of the peasants who constituted more than 85% of the total population of about 31 million. The government had, in spite of the need for reform in the tenancy and land tenure system, adopted a planned development strategy. A National Economic Council, with the objective to set economic priorities, was established in 1954. From 1957–73 three five-year plans were adopted. In the First Five-Year Plan (1957–62) the emphasis was on the development of infrastructure, commercial agriculture, skilled and semi-skilled manpower for the manufacturing sector.[5] The total investment over the plan period reached 835 million Ethiopian Birr. Sixty per cent of this fund went to the develop-

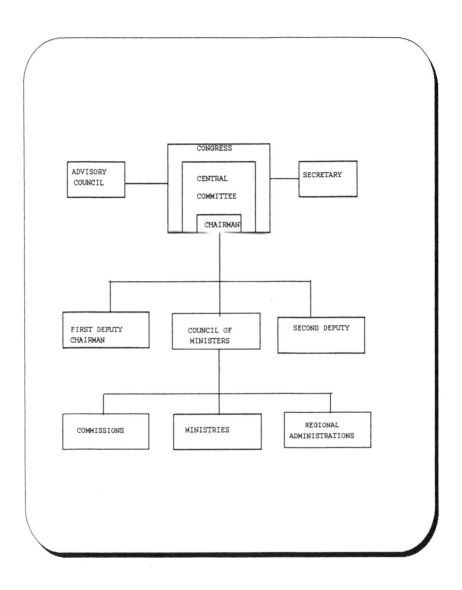

Chart 1
Organisation chart of PMAC and PMG, 1974

ment of transport and communications, while the social sector was allotted 5% of the planned allocation of 8.5%. The plan performance was below target due to the inability of the bureaucracy to execute the plan and other constraints. However, to keep the tempo of planned development alive, a second Five-Year Plan (1963–67) followed giving priorities to industry and commercial agriculture. The investment allocation for the plan was 2,000 million Birr. The plan had met similar constraints with its predecessor. The bureaucracy's incapacity and lack of co-ordination between the technical departments were the major constraints for the under fulfilment of the plan.[6]

The Third Five-Year Plan, which drew lessons from the first and second plans, covered the periods 1969–73. This plan recognised for the first time the core problems of the country in its development strategy. It gave emphasis to the expansion of education and rendering agricultural extension service to farmers for improving their productive capacities. The total investment earmarked for the plan was 2,865 million Ethiopian dollars. The amount allotted for education was 12.4% as against 1.8% in the Second Five-Year Plan.[7] The plan largely depended on the utilisation of external assistance. During the plan period, external assistance accounted for 23% of the total investment, thus showing dependency rather than self-reliance which was the intrinsic objective of the plan.

The First and Second Five-Year plans ignored the development of peasant agriculture. Even the third Five-Year Plan, which recognised the need for changing the peasant sector, allocated only 1% of the plan's projected expenditure.[8] A meagre amount was earmarked for the peasant sector which accounted for 87% of the gross domestic product. The major problems, in the three plan periods, land tenure and tenancy were not tackled, even though there were pious declarations in the plans to tackle them. Instead of major agricultural reform, pilot projects which aimed at exposing the farmers to the use of modern agricultural technology, inputs (fertiliser, pesticides, hybrid seeds, improved implements, etc.), credit and marketing facilities were introduced. The pilot projects were funded from bilateral and multilateral sources. The first pilot-project, the Chilalo Agricultural Development Unit (CADU), whose major financier was the Swedish Government, was launched in a district reasonably suitable for crop as well as livestock production, in the province of Chilalo, Governorate-General of Arusi. The project succeeded in improving the productive capacity of the farmers in the pilot area. However, the prospectus induced landlords to embark upon commercial agriculture which resulted in the mass eviction of tenants without compensation and encouraged the extraction of higher rents by landlords.

The financiers, having realised the counter-productive nature of the project, indicated the need for a land reform for its success which was ignored. Other projects which were launched in co-operation with the World Bank did not bring about significant changes in the quality of life of the peasants. The government, having realised that the projects which had depended heavily on financial assistance from external source could not be extended to cover other regions with domestic resources, launched a pilot project less costly and covering many districts. The Minimum Package Programme (MPP), as the project was called, had as its objective to enable peasants to produce more by providing them inputs, mainly extension services and credit.[9] The programme, under the circumstances, was the best that one could have hoped for without altering the land tenure system. The MPP was a major agricultural strategy in the Third Five-Year Plan for increasing the productive capacity of peasant cultivators. The project was launched in 1971 and lasted until the PMAC introduced the most radical agrarian reform, in the Third World, in 1975.

The industrial sector, in comparison with the agricultural sector recorded a fast rate of expansion between 1950–65, the total foreign capital investment reaching 350 million Birr.[10] The government's generous investment code which provided incentives to foreign capital investment, failed to attract investors. Edmund Keller in summarising the starvation of foreign capital in the pre-revolution period commented:

> 'Despite intense efforts to attract foreign capital to stimulate the modernisation of the industrial sector of the economy, growth between 1950 and 1970 was slow. The total amount of foreign investment in Ethiopia over this period was small even by African standards. In the early 1950s the average annual inflow of foreign capital was approximately E$12 million. By the end of the 1960s, this average had risen to E$25 million per annum. This is not an indication that foreign capital was inconsequential to economic development. In fact, in the decade before the Ethiopian revolution, foreign capital (public as well as private) accounted for 30–60% of all development expenditure. What these meagre figures do indicate is the small size of the manufacturing sector.'[11]

Haile Selassie's government was also much starved for development aid compared with other sub-Sahara African countries. The aid funnelled to the government from Western countries, despite the regime's loyalty to the West, was very meagre indeed. The aid to the regime considering its long years of association with the West hardly exceeded a per capita assistance of US$5 per person which compared unfavourably with Somalia which had a per capita assistance per person of US$20. Even the United States, which had acquired a communication base in Ethiopia, was not generous in its development assistance. The US economic assistance from 1953–75 was a meagre US$350 million in the form of technical assistance, capital goods and food aid.[12]

The reluctance of the regime to introduce agrarian reform coupled with meagre aid and insufficient capital in-flow failed to generate appreciable economic growth. The level of economic performance and access to social services was below the standard of the UN. The country, with a GDP of 3,939.5 million Birr, and a per capital income of less than 207 Birr (US$100), illiteracy rate of 93% and 15–20% of the population having access to health facilities, was classified as one of the 25 least developed countries of the world.[13]

The Working Class

Along with the growth of the bureaucracy and the army, the economic sector grew and provided employment opportunity for a wage-earning class, a newcomer in the Ethiopian social structure. Workers were not allowed to form unions. In the Ethiopian reality of the time trade unions were identified with strikes and other work-stoppages which were normally regarded as serious offences against the establishment. Workers were underpaid and their conditions of employment were horrifying. Labour laws did not exist until the promulgation of the Labour Relations Decree in 1964. Workers were denied the right to organise themselves in the defence of their rights. However, the Labour Relations Decree of 1964, with the sympathetic support of some enlightened bureaucrats in the ministries of Commerce and Industry, National Community Development and pressure from the International Labour Organisation (ILO), was issued.

The legislation, among other things, contained provisions on the determination of labour disputes and conditions of work; collective agreements, workers' and employers' rights to organise associations. On the basis of this legislation, trade unions and employers' associations were formed in the private sector while the workers of state-owned undertakings as banks, telecommunication, light and power, were denied the exercise of such rights. The workers in the private sector organised themselves into company-based unions which were affiliated to a notional body, the Confederation of Ethiopian Labour Unions (CELU). The formation of CELU was a very significant departure in the history of the Ethiopian trade union movement. It, soon after its formation, affiliated itself with the International Confederation of Free Trade Unions (ICFTU). Its affiliation with ICFTU, its regular participation in the annual conferences of the ILO, the co-operation programmes it had with the African American Labour Centre (AALC) and contacts with other regional workers' organisations transformed the level of consciousness of its members. The workers through their organisations managed to redress many of the injustices of the past by collective bargaining and where bargaining failed by resorting to legal redress. The master–servant relationship was broken to the dislike of employers who were used to unilateral determination of conditions of labour and arbitrary cancellation of employment contracts. A tripartite Labour Relations Board, to mediate, conciliate and adjudicate labour disputes, was established. The members of the board were two representatives of government and one each from the national level of workers' and employers' organisations. The representations in the board were in line with the accepted norms of the ILO for the settlement of industrial disputes.[14]

CELU lacked enlightened leadership. As a result of this constraint its contribution did not go beyond fighting for the interests of its members. Unlike its counterparts in ex-colonial Africa, it was not politically conscious enough to demand for any change in the system of government nor shared the views of the student movement nor demanded the extension of the rights its members enjoyed to the workers in state-owned undertakings. As a newcomer to the trade union movement, it was studying the basics of trade unionism and how well to protect the interests of its members against unscrupulous employers who did not imagine sitting at the same table with the representative of workers to bargain collectively on conditions of work. A good portion of CELU's formative years was spent on struggling for recognition by employers on one hand and on the other educating the rank and file on the benefit of trade unions. Scraping from the minds of the workers the master-servant relationship was a gigantic task by itself. With positive help and encouragement from the enlightened, dedicated and young employees of the Department of Labour, the teething problems of CELU were contained within reasonable bounds. Trade union rivalries which were instigated by employers to discourage membership to trade unions compounded CELU's problems. Victimisation of workers for their involvement in trade union activities, in violation of the law, was quite common. Nevertheless, the Department of Labour and the Labour Relations Board had put their weight in the defence of the workers' rights against the naked excesses of unscrupulous employers. Employers who had enjoyed a free hand in unilateral determination of conditions of employment, for nearly half a century, had to fight for the continuation of a system of industrial relations without workers' participation and governments regulatory power. Incidents where employers instigated strikes were quite numerous and many workers had fallen into the trap and lost their jobs. The labour law made it absolutely impossible to go on strike without exhausting the dispute settlement machinery. Even after the machinery had been exhausted, strikes and lockouts had to remain in abeyance until a cooling-off period of sixty days had elapsed. The laborious legal provision for the settlement of disputes was a subtle way of prohibiting any work-stoppages including strikes. Before the lapse of the cooling-off period, the dispute would have been referred to the Industrial Relations Board whose decision was final except on a point of law when the Supreme Court intervened. The consequence of an illegal work-stoppage was the loss of employment. Unscrupulous employers had exploited the loophole in the law by instigating a strike and then resorting to summary dismissal of employees who had participated in industrial reaction. The Labour Relations Board, on the grounds of public policy, had on a number of occasions made decisions which discouraged mass dismissal of workers.

In pre-revolution Ethiopia, wages of industrial workers were low. The average monthly wage in the textile industry was 26–30 Birr while in plantation the daily wage ranged between seventy-five cents and one Birr. Industrial safety and health in many workplaces were substandard. Conditions of work, in many instances, were detrimental to the health and welfare of workers. Against all odds the Department of Labour had done a remarkable job in issuing minimum labour standards which were complemented by collective agreements to rectify a situation that was a result of half a century of neglect.

CELU, with a membership of about 150,000 workers, had struggled to be a force that had to be reckoned with. In its ten years of existence up to the eruption of the 1974 revolution, it did not, however, overcome its teething problems, let alone be a political force of any consequence.

In the fifties and sixties the United States followed a policy of actively associating itself with trade union movements in African countries. In highlighting Washington's desire to control the African Trade Union movement Vice-President Nixon addressing the Congress on his extended trip in Africa in 1957 stated; '*It is of vital importance that the American Government should closely follow what goes on in the trade union sphere and that American consular and diplomatic representatives should get to know the trade union leaders of these countries intimately.*'[15] Nixon's strategy of intimacy with union leaders was translated into action in Ethiopia when CELU was formed in the middle of the sixties. No sooner than it was formed, the African American Labour Centre appointed advisers and associated itself with labour education programme of CELU.[16]

The Intelligentsia

The intelligentsia of pre-revolution Ethiopia was sizeable and relatively a privileged class. It comprised teachers, public service employees, managerial and professional staff in the public and the private sectors of the economy; the officers' corp of the army and the police force as well. It was a class without a common political view. It ran the state machinery and the economy. It was part and parcel of the establishment. Members of the intelligentsia were, by Ethiopian standards, well paid and enjoyed the fruits of secure careers. The intelligentsia was a class which was not prepared to sacrifice its privileges by participating in political activities which might displease the regime. However, many of its members, in private, were critical of the government and even supported any democratic change but were too timid to take any concrete steps to express what they stood for. They supported change as long as the necessary sacrifices were made by others. It was an egocentric class without any commitment to society. Its members enjoyed all the benefits of society without any obligation. Individuals, who in their student days were radical, were tamed and concentrated on the furtherance of their private interests and careers when they joined the bureaucracy. Education was the most reliable route to success. Anyone with higher education, ambition and hardworking could be successful in the bureaucracy. Social status and family background were not barriers to success; individual achievements were highly regarded, more often than not, generously rewarded.

As a result of this a culture where individuals shunned teamwork had developed. The feudal tradition which had been skilfully developed and refined by the monarchy had its influences on the intelligentsia. Due to this cultural influence on the members and their privileged positions in the society, they were rather indifferent either to form or join any organised body that seemed to pursue political objectives. This is not intended to discredit those individuals who were vocal in underscoring the need for change. They were few and quite often labelled as mavericks or idealists who were out of touch with the realities of the society. The members of the intelligentsia who had the moral obligation to be advocates and initiators of peaceful change failed to act in unison. It must be conceded that the emperor was sensitive to any criticism of the establishment. Under such circumstances, nobody dared to suggest to him that his style of government was not adequate to meet the growing demands of the people; and those who revealed their support for democratic change fell prey to his displeasure. Individuals who expressed their liberal views paid dearly by either losing their positions or, if lucky, being banished to a remote and underdeveloped province as administrators.

The emperor, in spite of his stubbornness to heed to suggestion for reform, was aware of the need for social, economic and political changes. For instance, in one of his annual Coronation Day addresses to the Parliament, on 2 November 1966, he summarised the goals of his government in the following impressive words:

'What we seek is a new and different way of life. We seek a way of life in which all men will be treated as responsible human beings, able to participate fully in the political affairs of their government; a way of life in which ignorance and poverty, if not abolished, are at least the exception and are actively combated; a way of life in which the blessings and benefits of the modern world can be enjoyed by all without the total sacrifice of all that was good and beneficial in the old Ethiopia. We are from and of the people, and our desires derive from and are theirs. Can this be achieved from one dusk to the next dawn, by the waving of a magic wand, by slogans and imperial declarations? Can this be imposed on our people, or be achieved solely by legislation? We believe not. All that we can do is provide a means for the development of procedures which, if all goes well, will enable an increased measure and degree of what we seek for our nation to be accomplished.'[17]

The declaration might have been a genuine expression of the emperor's feeling towards the gradual involvement of the people in the political, social and economic life of the state. However, the statement was deliberately vague on the modality of associating the people with the political life of the nation. In an absolute monarchy, where the affairs of the state were determined by one man, there was no opportunity for involving the people in the affairs of state. The fact that he was from the people did not necessarily reflect identity of desires and aspirations. Such a wrong sense of identification of his desires with that of the people made him, perhaps, reluctant to introduce a change in the system of his government.

His public utterances were progressive and meant only for international consumption. The people wanted sharing state power which was bound to diminish the role of the monarchy which he jealously guarded against any intrusion. Had he been true to his public utterances he would have changed the course of history for the better.

Lack of a political culture was and still is an issue closely related with the intelligentsia. Ethiopia had neither acquired nor developed a political culture whereby different shades of views are freely expressed and opposition is tolerated. It had built up a culture of submission to the mighty. In elucidating this aspect of Ethiopian political culture Margery Perham wrote: '*Ethiopia has been a country where the strong have always preyed upon the weak.*'[18]

The choice for the weak was and still is under the guise of democracy either to submit or to perish. In the Ethiopian political tradition opposition was not tolerated. Those persons who held views opposed to those in power were considered as mortal enemies and faced, if lucky, detention or else liquidation. The accepted mode of expression of one's dissatisfaction with the system was and, surprisingly still is, to take up arms and go to the woods for a final showdown. A glance at the transfer of power from the end of the *Zemene Mesafint* to the present, illustrates the relevance of the use of force and resort to violence in the transfer of power. Haile Selassie was no exception. Like his predecessors he did not entertain a democratic mechanism for organised opposition. As a result of this cultural influence of intolerance, Ethiopians are not as fortunate as other Africans to develop a political culture where those in opposition are allowed to express their views freely, or form and join political organisations. Lack of political culture and particularly intolerance to constructive and democratic opposition are probably the price that Ethiopians had to pay for their long history of independence.

The fear of reprisal from the regime due to the cultural realities of the country, might have hindered the intelligentsia from taking the initiative to organise itself into political bodies. The lack of political organisations was probably one of the factors responsible for the lack of political consciousness at grass-root level. Except for the privileged few, the bulk of the population was apolitical. The miserably low level of political consciousness emboldened past leaders to assume a paternalistic style of government.

The Peasantry

The peasant was, and still is, the backbone of the Ethiopian economy. Until the appearance of industrialisation, in the last half century, the peasant was the only productive force of the society. The monarchy, the nobility, and the clergy depended on his efforts. His primary duty was to labour relentlessly to feed the unproductive segment of society. He, in return, was not rewarded for his services. The government which depended on the fruit of his labour did not do enough to provide him with basic amenities needed to sustain a decent quality of life. While the style and quality of life of the unproductive segment of the society improved, the peasant's condition deteriorated. The burgeoning bureaucracy continued to sap whatever the peasant was able to produce. Lack of access to modern agricultural technology coupled with cyclical droughts put him in a very difficult position where he was unable to meet his tax obligation to the state and to deliver the share of the landlord.

Moreover, enterprising landlords began evicting peasants and became farmers with the use of modern agricultural technology and credit advanced to them from state-owned banks at low interest rate. For example the introduction of mechanised farming in the Governorate-Generals of Arsi, Bale and in other provincial administrations was responsible for the eviction of thousands of farmers. The government was a passive onlooker of the eviction of farmers *en masse*. It failed to take any significant steps in providing means of livelihood to those who were evicted from their ancestral farms.

The pre-revolution peasant was an individual who laboured to meet his obligations to the state and the landlord. In return, he did not get the services to which he was entitled, as of right. As a result of natural disaster, when he failed to meet his basic requirements, he was left to his own devices. His choice was either to remain on his farm and perish, which many did, or migrate to urban settlements to join the army of the unemployed. Famine and epidemics were the distinctive features of the Ethiopian peasant since time immemorial. The peasant considered natural calamities as God's wrath on mortals for their failure to follow his divine wishes. This fatalistic attitude towards natural calamities had relieved the government from its obligation in taking steps that would have contained the effects of natural calamities before they blew up. Fatalistic explanations for these occurrences of natural calamities gave way in the seventies to scientific explanations which made it incumbent upon the government to take concrete steps to contain the effects of these predictable disasters. Government, however, failed to take proper action. A government which was fully aware of its responsibilities to the people in times of distress and natural calamities, not only failed to take proper action, and was not even prepared to admit the presence of famine in the northern provinces, particularly in Wollo.

Ethnicity

Ethiopia is a multi-ethnic polity which is inhabited by not less than eighty ethnic groups. Each has its own language, culture and custom. The dominant ethnic groups are the Amharas, Oromos and Tigreans. Of the three major ethnic groups the Oromos are numerically dominant. However, they were less dominant than the Amharas and the Tigreans in the political life of the state until the *Zemene Mesafint* when they were associated with the politics of the state through intermarriages and political alliances. The distinct characteristics of the Ethiopian ruling class was its ethnic intermarriages which had helped to defuse, to a certain extent, ethnic polarisation.

The monarchy adopted Amharic as the language of the court and for the transaction of the affairs of the state. Even in the court of Emperor Yohannis IV whose mother tongue was Tigrigna, Amharic was the official language. Amharic has been the official language of Ethiopia for over seven hundred years. During these long years it developed immensely by borrowing words from the other languages. While the adoption of a national language was a sound policy, the monarchy's callous disregard to the languages and cultures of non-Amhara ethnic groups, was an error of judgement and lack of foresight. The development of a national language and local vernaculars are not necessarily contradictory. The development of other languages could have been undertaken in conjunction with the development of a national language.

In pre-revolution Ethiopia, all ethnic groups had suffered under the repressive and exploitive arms of feudalism. Amharas, Oromos, Tigrians, Somalis, Afars, Guragis, etc., were victims of the system. It would be absolutely absurd and unfair to ascribe the evils of the system to one ethnic group on the grounds of wrong presumption that it had dominated the governance of the state – a view, quite often, expressed by misinformed scholars and insurgent organisations. Paul Henze commenting on the absurdities of such allegation wrote:

'There are obviously both positive and negative features in
Ethiopia's past. I am puzzled by many of the partisan views
and much of the conventional wisdom I hear about Ethiopia.

If the state is simply an Amhara conspiracy against the rest
of the people who inhabit it, why have the inhabitants of
Wag, Gaynt, Smyen, Manz, Jiru, Gojam, Bulga, *Merhabete*
and *Yefat*,[19] remained at such a low level of economic and
political development? . . . If the vast southern regions brought
into the empire by Menilek II suffered such deep alienation
from it, why have they generated so little resistance to the
Marxist regime? If Northerners find Amhara and Oromo so
unappealing, why have so many Eritreans and Tigreans
migrated southward, and why did they continue to take
advantage of opportunities to participate in government,
professions and trade throughout the country.'[20]

In spite of all its shortcomings, Haile Selassie's government had never
pursued ethnocentrism as a policy of the state. Emperor Haile Selassie,
declaring the policy of the state in respect to ethnicity and race relations,
stated:

'Above all, Ethiopia is dedicated to the principle of the
equality of all men, irrespective of differences in race,
colour or creed. As we do not practise or permit
discrimination within our nation, so we oppose it wherever
it is found. As we guarantee the right to worship as he
chooses, so we denounce the policy which sets man against
man on issues of religion. As we extend the hand of universal
brotherhood to all, without regard to race or colour so we
condemn any social or political order which distinguishes
among God's children on the most spacious of grounds.'[21]

To accuse Haile Selassie's government of ethnocentrism, as some ethni-
cally based movements do, is a travesty of truth for gaining political
advantages. Haile Selassie's government, regardless of its failings in socio-
economic developments, to its credit, provided a semblance of stability
for almost half a century. Except in the remote corners of Eritrea and
the Ogaden, stability and peace reigned in the rest of the country. The
resistance movements in Eritrea and the Ogaden were the only organised
oppositions to Haile Selassie's government. The movements, in both
regions, had their origins in their colonial past.

71

The Problem in Eritrea

Eritrea is the name given to the regions which colonial Italy seized from Ethiopia from 1869 to 1890 to create a colony in the Horn of Africa. The territory stretches along the Red Sea coast. It is a natural sea outlet of the Ethiopian mainland. Most of the territory was part of Ethiopia until the creation of the Italian colony of Eritrea in 1890. The colony was, after 51 years of colonial rule, lost to Italy in 1941. It was under British Military Administration for ten years until it was federated with Ethiopia by the decision of the United Nations. Britain encouraged the formation of political parties of varied persuasions promoting political views ranging from union with Ethiopia to independence.

Britain, being the administering power of the enemy territory had the advantage of influencing events in Eritrea to her side than the other interested parties, Ethiopia, Egypt and Italy. Since Britain had the desire to incorporate that part of Eritrea bordering its condominium of the Sudan, it had encouraged the Moslem population to seek integration with the Sudan. Italy on the other hand advocated for independence to the territory. Ethiopia argued strongly that Eritrea had to be restored to her. However, due to conflicting claims, the disposal of Eritrea was subordinated to the geopolitical interests of the Western powers which culminated into federating Eritrea with Ethiopia. The federal solution was a negation of the wishes of the majority of the people which was union with Ethiopia.[22] Ultimately the federal solution was reluctantly accepted by Ethiopia and the majority of the Eritrean people. The federal arrangement lasted for ten years until the Eritrean Assembly by a unanimous vote abolished it, and opted for complete union with Ethiopia[23] on 15 November 1962. Eritrea then became the fourteenth province of Ethiopia.

The dissolution of the federation exacerbated a situation which was volatile. Certain Arab countries took the integration with Ethiopia as an outright annexation and stepped up their support to disgruntled individuals who were already living in exile and had formed the first liberation organisation which aimed at an independent Eritrea, in the 1950s.[24] The group which styled itself as the Eritrean Liberation Movement (ELM), after the dissolution of the federation stepped up its political activities, mainly in Arab countries. Other individuals who fled the country after the dissolution of the federation formed another movement, the Eritrean Liberation Front, (ELF) whose declared objective was to sever Eritrea from Ethiopia by armed struggle. The front was an organisation of Moslems who had identified themselves with the Arabs.[25] This sectarian front held an inimical posture towards the Christian highlanders of Eritrea. The front had the support and assistance of certain Arab governments. Its ambition was to create a Moslem Eritrean state which would be associated with the Arab League. As events later on proved, the front was accorded an observer's status in the Arab League.

The ELM and ELF did not succeed to co-operate for the furtherance of their common goal, the independence of Eritrea. Their views on an independent Eritrea were incongruous. Finally, they settled their differences by resorting to force. In 1965 a conflict broke between the two fronts and the ELM was severely beaten to the point of ceasing to operate as an effective armed front.[26] The ELF emerged as the sole organisation for carrying out armed struggle in Eritrea.

It divided Eritrea for the purpose of military operations into five military zonal commands. For one of the zonal commands, a Christian from the highlands was to create a semblance of non-sectarian front, put in charge without any effective representation in the Moslem-dominated leadership of the ELF. The ELF was rife with internal feuds, tribal and religious rivalries and in some cases these negative feelings resulted in the massacre of the Christian members of the fronts' Eritrean Liberation Army (ELA). The tribal and religious feuds reached a level where splinter groups, the Popular Liberation Front (Simharites), the Obeletes (Barka) and the Issayas group (the Christian Highlanders), appeared in the early 1970s.[27]

The groups formed alliance under a common front which later on emerged as the armed wing of Osman Sabbe. The General Secretariate of Osman Sabbe in the Middle East handled the political affairs of the alliance.[28] The alliance, as events later on proved, constituted the nucleus for the Eritrean People's Liberation Front (EPLF) which emerged as the powerful movement by annihilating the armed wing of the ELF. The rivalry between the leaders Isayas Afeworki and Osman Sabbe, reached a point where they could not co-operate and work together. Sabbe broke away to form the Eritrean Liberation Front–Popular Liberation Force (ELF–PLF).[29] Formation of alliances and breaking away were main features of the liberation fronts; a process which had led to the emergence of fronts with ideologies ranging from radical Marxism to reactionary capitalism. However, the ELF and the EPLF were, among the various fronts, well-organised both in politics and the armed struggle. The ELF started as a sectarian front and ended up as a movement with Marxist persuasion which was a concern to the West, particularly to the United States which was, from the Kagnew Communication Base in Asmera, jealously guarding against the spread of communism in the Horn of

Africa. On the other hand, the EPLF was very cautious, at its initial stage of formation, towards any particular political ideology that would have been prejudicial to its interest. It had adopted a pragmatic approach to adjust its political ideology to the dictate of circumstances. It posed as a Marxist front to get the support of the Eastern Bloc.[30]

Prior to the 1974 Ethiopian revolution, the West, particularly the United States, was not disposed to support the causes of the Eritrean fronts, even though it had conducted secret meetings with Isayas Afeworki, the leader of the EPLF, in the late sixties.[31] According to political observers, the meeting took place because of Washington's concern regarding the influence of communism in the liberation movements particularly ELF's Marxist leaning was worrying to Washington. However, the meeting did not result in Washington's endorsement of EPLF's stance but left the door open for future contacts.

The EPLF, on the other hand, was convinced that the United States was totally committed to Haile Selassie's government and had begun to associate itself with the communist bloc and other forces. The EPLF's association with the communist bloc was not motivated by ideological identity; it was a pragmatic strategy to obtain weapons and political support from socialist countries. Tesfatsion Medhane revealing EPLF's opportunism, with respect to political ideologies, wrote: '*The ELPF flaunted different images about itself. It professed different and opposing ideologies to suit the interests of various groups whose favours it sought.*'[32] Tesfatsion's assertion is confirmed by Teklai Gebre Mariam, who was a member of EPLF's Central Committee and Deputy Chief of its security system, in his declaration: '*Besides, one cannot tell what its (EPLF's) guiding philosophy is; sometimes it pretends to be Marxist-Leninist, at other times a confirmed Maoist, and still other times drops these mantles and stands with Arab reaction. What then is the real EPLF?*'[33]

The statements of these two Eritreans, one who was a member of the ELF and the other a member of the Central Committee of the EPLF, were proved to be true when Ethiopia shifted its alliance to the socialist bloc causing cessation of assistance and support from the bloc, the fronts conveniently changed alliance to the West.

The Problem of the Ogaden Region

The Ogaden region of Ethiopia is a vast expanse of desert and savannah bordering the Somali Republic. The region is quite suitable for pastoral mode of life. It is inhabited by Somali-speaking Ethiopians. Its rich grassland generously hosted Somali herdsmen who crossed the border in

74

search of better grazing pasture and water for their herds since time immemorial. The migratory habit of the Somali nomads from the Republic of Somalia was acknowledged in the treaties Ethiopia signed with the ex-colonial powers, Great Britain and Italy. The Ogaden was coveted by Italy ever since it acquired the ex-Italian colony of Somaliland.

The Italo-Ethiopian Boundary Convention of 1908 which delimited the boundaries between Ethiopia and the former Italian Somaliland was signed and ratified by both governments. Nevertheless, Italy never resisted the temptation to annex the Ogaden. The territory is richer in resources than the ex-Italian possession; it has rich pasture and water in its numerous wells, the two most precious commodities in a desert where the annual precipitation is not sufficient to sustain luxuriant vegetation. The two major rivers the Wabi Shebele and the Juba, the only sources of water supply to the Republic of Somalia, spring from the highlands of Ethiopia and flow there for several hundreds of kilometres before they cross into the Republic of Somalia in their long journey to the Indian Ocean. Italy, who had realised the relative economic advantages of the Ogaden, was waiting for an opportune time to annex and incorporate it into its colonial possession. Italy's dream was realised when it occupied Ethiopia in flagrant violation of the covenant of the League of Nations, in 1936. Italy, after its successful occupation of Ethiopia did not take any time to incorporate the Ogaden into its colonial possession of the ex-Italian Somaliland. The Italian colonial greed had begotten the irredentism of its successor state, the Republic of Somalia. After the Second World War, Italy lost both Ethiopia and its colony of Somaliland. Ethiopia with the assistance of Great Britain gained its independence while Italian Somaliland was placed under British military rule. Britain was reluctant to restore the Ogaden to Ethiopia. The Ogaden, the ex-Italian colony of Somaliland, the British Protectorate of Somali along the Red Sea Coast and the Northern Frontier District of Kenya, by historical accident, fell under British rule during the Second World War. Britain came with a bizarre scheme of carving out a new nation under the collective name of Greater Somalia. Britain's plan for the region was submitted to the Big Four (US, USSR, France and Great Britain) by Ernest Bevin, British Foreign Secretary. The proposal which envisaged a British trusteeship over the new territory was rejected by the three powers.[34]

The rejection of the proposal, however, did not restrain Britain from pursuing its design through the Somali Youth Club which later on transformed itself into the Somali Youth League in 1945. The main objective of the League was to arouse the Somalis, including the Ethiopian citizens of the Ogaden, through its office in Jijiga in the Ogaden. The Youth

League, which assumed power at the independence of Somalia in 1960, made the creation of Greater Somalia the cornerstone of its domestic and foreign policies. It went a step farther to include the ex-French Territory of the Afars and the Isas and the Northern Frontier District of Kenya. Article Seven of the Constitution of the defunct Republic of Somaliland clearly made irredentism the official policy of the state. The constitutional provision was in flagrant defiance of Article One of the Trusteeship Agreement of the United Nations which stated that the boundary of the future independent state of Somalia *'would be those already fixed by international agreement.'*[35] The international agreement which had been referred to in the Trusteeship Agreement was the 1908 Italo-Ethiopian Boundary Agreement. Moreover, the founding fathers of the Organisation of African Unity (OAU), which anticipated a chaotic situation in Africa should re-drawing of its map be resorted to, at the Second Conference of the OAU in Cairo, made this declaration: *'Solemnly declare that all member states pledge themselves to respect the borders existing on their achievement of national independence.'*[36] Nevertheless, the government of the then Republic of Somalia, ignoring the decision of the UN and the OAU continued pursuing to realise its dream of *Greater Somalia.*

Barely a year had elapsed after Somalia's existence as an independent state when it unleashed its first war of irredentism against Ethiopia in 1961 and another in 1964. In both engagements the Somali forces were defeated by the Ethiopian army.

The 1961 conflict broke out just after the 1960 coup attempt to overthrow Emperor Haile Selassie. Somalia's attack on Ethiopia was an error of judgement. The Ethiopian force, not only defeated and chased away the invading force of Somalia out of Ethiopian territory but followed it in hot pursuit beyond the Ethiopian border deep into Somali territory. The commander of the Ethiopian force in the Ogaden, General Aman Michael Andom, the first chairman of the PMC, was reprimanded for defying the headquarter's order to restrain his force from crossing the international border. The general's move could have given Ethiopia a better bargaining edge when the Somali Government demanded the withdrawal of the Ethiopian force from its territory. Ethiopia could have been in a much better position to require Somalia to renounce her claim on Ethiopian territory. Unfortunately, the opportunity was wasted when the leadership caved in to vanity which Edmund Keller brilliantly summarised: *'An important aspect of the emperor's style of leadership is image management. He wanted to be seen as a consummate statesman, a benevolent and progressive autocrat and a moderniser.'*[37] Somalia realised that her military strength was not a match for Ethiopia's and that resort to force in settling her dispute with Ethiopia relegated her into an aggressor, changed her strategy and began to invest her resources on a Western Somalia Liberation Front (WSLF), whose formation she instigated in the 1960s. The front was a puppet movement of the defunct Moqadishu government and was committed to the *Greater Somalia* dream.

The WSLF from its headquarters in Moqadishu while conducting its war of propaganda was engaged in intermittent guerrilla activity. The Somalia Government with the WSLF as a cover mounted guerrilla activity in the Ogaden, Bale and Sidamo regions of Ethiopia. The WSLF was nothing other than a regular Somalia force operating in disguise. The Haile Selassie government effectively contained the guerrilla activities instigated by the Somalia Government. However, after the 1974 revolution, the guerrilla activity was intensified and finally culminated into the invasion of Ethiopia by the Somalia regular army in 1977.

External Relations

Haile Selassie's government performance cannot be complete without a glance at his foreign policies. He had been influenced in his early childhood by his French tutor, who enabled him to develop a taste for Western Civilisation. His role models were Napoleon and Frederick the Great. Machaevelli had also his share of influence in shaping his political outlook. When he was appointed as Crown prince and regent in 1916, he had already identified his political associates in the West. His extended tour to France, Italy, Germany, Great Britain and Sweden was an overt demonstration of his appreciation of Western civilisation and values. In those days he had no choice for a political ally other than the major colonial powers. America was pursuing an isolationist policy and Russia was under social transformation. Besides, he had no reason to seek a close association with Russia that had abolished a monarchical system of government for which he was preparing himself.

Before 1935 the cornerstone of Haile Selassie's foreign policy was to have Ethiopia accepted as an independent state in the international community of nations. [He was of the view that weak nations, including Ethiopia's security, could be guaranteed by being a member of the League of Nations whose covenant was constructed upon the lofty concept of collective security.] To secure membership in the League of Nations, he had to satisfy that his country respected human rights by taking steps to abolish slavery gradually against the opposition of the nobility. The coveted membership to the League was obtained in 1923. The tenet of Haile Selassie's foreign policy was shaken when Italy, one of the member states who had supported Ethiopia's admission to the League, invaded his country in violation of the covenant of the League. The other members of the League, in gross indifference to their obligation in the covenant to take concerted action against an aggressor, allowed the invasion of Ethiopia by Fascist Italy. The failure of the League to live up to its ideals tragically ended the pre-war foreign policy of Emperor Haile Selassie.

After the restoration of independence in 1941, he had again made collective security the principle of his foreign policy. Ethiopia became one of the founding members of the United Nations in 1948. Haile Selassie, having learnt the bitter lesson of history while in exile in Britain, decided to have a great power as a patron. Among the post-war powers the most natural choice was the United States. Even though diplomatic relations with the United States date back to the early 1900s, they had not developed to the level that Haile Selassie would have liked. He began courting the United States in 1943 when Britain was still in effective control of the Horn including Ethiopia. The management of Ethiopian Airlines and a concession for oil exploration in the Ogaden were given to American Companies, Trans World Air Lines and Sinclair, respectively. His approach, in doing so, was double edged; on one hand he made his strong feelings on the restoration of Ogaden clear to Britain; on the other, his plan to give the United States a stake in Ethiopia began to unfold. The British influence in Ethiopia gradually waned while the American interest gathered momentum.

The United States, which had assumed global interest in the post-war period, was using discreetly Radio Marina, an ex-Italian facility in Asmara, since 1942.[38] America used the facility to communicate with its bases elsewhere. The station served as a link to world-wide American communication from Virginia in the United States to Morocco in North Africa and the Philippines in the Pacific. The Americans expanded the facilities of Radio Marina and finally converted it into a permanent communication base. The base was of vital importance to the US which made its unhampered use imperative. In the American view, unhampered use of the facility could have been guaranteed only if Eritrea remained under the control of Britain or any other nation friendly to the interest of the United States. According to the American assessment of the time Eritrea was not capable to govern itself on the grounds of economic, political and administrative considerations. The American verdict on Eritrea reads:

'Eritrea is neither socially, politically, administratively, nor economically qualified for independence, nor will it be for some time. An independent regime will be unable to

maintain law and order against internal ravages of border
marauders, or to prevent a move for secession and union
with Ethiopia – which would not be unlikely by the people
of the central plateau. If attacked from outside, it would be
unable to maintain its territorial integrity without external
aid.'[39]

Independence was an unpalatable solution for Eritrea because the United
States believed that an independent Eritrea might end up as a surrogate
of an unfriendly power. This assumption was a vital component of the
United States' policy for the Red Sea region.

Ethiopia which claimed Eritrea on historical, cultural, economic and
political considerations petitioned the United Nations for the reversion
of Eritrea to Ethiopia. Its claim was not fully supported by the US until
it proved its allegiance to the West by contributing a contingent of troops
to the Korean war. Its modest gesture of good will and loyalty to the West
had induced the US to change its previous stance of ceding to Ethiopia
the port of Aseb and the adjoining territory, inhabited by the Danakil
tribes. The US and the other Western powers, who were satisfied with
Ethiopia's loyalty to the West, were instrumental in the UN's decision to
federate Eritrea with Ethiopia. Marcus summarising the gratitude of the
Western powers to Ethiopia for its participation in the Korean War wrote:

'The gesture yielded favourable comments in July 1950, at a
meeting of American, British and Italian officials, who
agreed that a satisfied Ethiopia might play an important role
in the defence of the Middle East. It became obvious to all an
Eritrean–Ethiopian federation offered the perfect
compromise: the Solomonic crown could hold sovereignty;
the colony would remain intact, assuaging the feelings of the
Moslems and others who wish to remain separate from
Ethiopia; and Rome could argue that Italy's achievement in
Africa would retain its integrity and the settlers would
remain insulated from Addis Ababa's direct control.
Washington applied pressure on the emperor, who
acquiesced because the United States has made the proposal
and the emperor has great faith in the United States'
judgement.'[40]

After the disposal of Eritrea was settled, Ethiopia and the United States concluded two treaties in 1951 and 1953 which constituted the basic documents for the relation of the two countries until 1974.

Egypt fell into the hands of a radical leader (Gamal Abdel Nasser) in 1952 whose persistent demand for the withdrawal of British and French interests from the Suez Canal increased American anxiety and triggered a much deepened involvement in Ethiopia. The 1951 and 1953 treaties formalised the use of Radio Marina that was later on christened as Kagnew Communication Base. The treaties, besides the unhampered use of the base, provided for the use of the defence facilities of the Ethiopian Government.[41]

The Kagnew Communication Base which quartered over 3,000 of the 6,000 US military personnel in Ethiopia served for tracking satellites, monitoring communication and allowing the US access to the Red Sea.[42] The United States was strategically placed to monitor developments in the Horn, the Red Sea and the Middle East, until the use of the base became irrelevant due to the development of satellite communication systems and the shift of American policy to have a dominant presence in the Indian Ocean from its new base at Diego Garcia. In the 1950s, the US had uncontested presence in the Horn.

In the 1960s when Somalia attained its independence, it declared irredentism as the tenet of its domestic and foreign policies. Its constitution provided for the annexation of territories, inhabited by Somali-speaking people, from Ethiopia, Kenya, and the ex-French colony of Djibouti. The irredentist policy of the Republic of Somalia was a concern to Ethiopia while the US was apprehensive of Somalia's desperation to seek a patron who would subscribe to its dream of *Greater Somalia.* Although the Somali Government, at the time of its independence, was Western-oriented, the US and its allies did not entertain its request for military assistance in excess of its legitimate defence needs. However, ' . . . *the United States, Italy and West Germany jointly offered Somalia a modest military aid package for the training and equipping of a 6,000-man army, adequate for maintaining internal security but not for fighting a war of expansion.*'[43] The offer was considered not to disturb the status quo in the balance of power in the Horn which was in favour of Ethiopia as a result of a well-trained and equipped 18,000-man army. Somalia rejected the Western offer for training and equipping a 6,000-man army in favour of a Russian aid package for setting up a 10,000-man army.[44] This was a prelude to the USSR's presence in the Horn which later on developed into a deeper relationship after a military take-over, embracing socialism as a political ideology, in 1969. The US became wary of developments in the Horn. The Ethiopian Government, which felt the need for a larger defence force because of USSR's involvement, implored the US to step up its military assistance. The dangerous development in the Horn made it incumbent upon the US to step up its military aid to Ethiopia. The defence treaties of the 1950s were revised to provide for more military assistance in training and equipping a 40,000-man army comprising of four divisions. The assistance enabled Ethiopia to maintain its military advantage over Somalia until the balance of power was tilted in favour of Somalia in the 1970s.

The US, in a quarter of a century of association with Ethiopia, provided military assistance worth US$280 million and trained about 3,978 military personnel at a cost of US$28 million.[45] The military assistance was considered generous but failed to match the USSR's to Somalia that was estimated at US $1,000 million.[46] The excessive military assistance to Somalia changed the balance of power in the Horn, in the latter part of the 1970s, in favour of Somalia as demonstrated by its unprovoked invasion of Ethiopia in 1977.

Nothing makes more clear the meagreness of the American assistance to Ethiopia than Marcus's comment which states: *'Yet, the data reveal that neither the US Government nor the American capitalism eagerly poured millions into bastion Ethiopia, either to make it into a militarily significant factor or to transform its economy'.*[47]

The United States assistance to Ethiopia was not confined to military aid. Under the Point Four Programme development assistance worth US$350 million was made available until 1975. The US development assistance mainly concentrated on education, health and agriculture. The most worthy programmes financed by the US development assistance were: the Gonder Public Health College, the Alemaya Agricultural College, Jimma Agricultural School, Asmara Midwife and Nursing Training School, Empress Menen Handicrafts School in Addis Ababa, Rural Vocational and Industrial Arts in provincial centres, Commerce Development Centre, Crop Development Centres, Locust Control, Animal Disease Control, Malaria Control, Coffee Research and a programme for providing scholarships abroad. Even though the development assistance of the US was practical and useful, it failed to meet the huge requirement of the Ethiopian Government, and it persistently requested the US Government to increase the level of its assistance. The Ethiopian Prime Minister, Ato Aklilu Habtewolde, in one of his memos to Washington pointing out the insufficiency of US assistance to Ethiopia wrote: *'Ethiopia must ask itself again, just what place does Ethiopia actually hold in the eyes of the US?'*[48] On another occasion the Prime Minister told the American Ambassador to Ethiopia his serious concern about the co-operation of the two governments: '*Ethiopia, he said took the relationship with the United States seriously, but he was not certain that America reciprocated.*'[49] Still on another occasion, in 1959, when the Ethiopian economy was in bad shape the Prime Minister '*grumbled that Washington has not provided really useful help to Ethiopia.*'[50]

Marcus commenting on the *raison d'être* of the Ethio-United States relationship during the reign of Emperor Haile Selassie wrote: '*American devotion to Ethiopia stemmed not from a perceived military need, but from a practical geopolitics, whereas Ethiopia courted the United States as a hedge against invasion, incursion and insolvency.*'[51] Both Haile Selassie and the United States have benefited from their relations. For Haile Selassie, the relationship enabled him to suppress internal dissension and deter external invasion. Above all, the country enjoyed an uninterrupted stability and peace for over a quarter of a century. It helped to boost the emperor's image as an elder statesman. For the United States, at least in the short-run, the relations helped it to protect the West's interest in the Red Sea and the Arabian Gulf by providing a dominant presence in the Horn to the exclusion of the USSR, particularly in the 1950s and 1960s. The relationship was also a contributory factor in containing the spread of communism in the Horn for more than a quarter of a century. Nevertheless, as events in the 1970s proved, the Ethio-United States solidarity was short-sighted.

The United States did not exert sufficient pressure on Haile Selassie to democratise his government. Such a step would have ensured both the US's geopolitical interest in the Horn and the continuation of Haile Selassie's dynasty. Moreover, the US could have been spared its humiliation on being requested to withdraw unceremoniously from Ethiopia. Fred Halliday in assessing the quarter of a century of Ethio-American relations made the following thought-provoking observations:

> 'It was of utmost importance that the US, which was in a position to influence events in Ethiopia to a considerable extent, succeeded so little: the short-term price of sustaining the imperial state without reform was the suffering visited upon Ethiopia in the 1972–3 famine. The long-run result was the 1974 revolution, and the change in Ethiopia's alignment.'[52]

Although the major political and economic partner of Ethiopia was the US, Haile Selassie cultivated a sound relationship with other Western countries. His government received technical assistance, grants and loans from the Western as well as Eastern bloc. Next to the British the Swedes played useful roles in education and health and particularly in the training of the Imperial Ethiopian Air Force and the Imperial Body Guard from 1943–52. Swedish military assistance was replaced by American military aid but the Swedes continued participating in development programmes. Ethio-Swedish relations date back to the 1930s when the emperor had liberally used them as advisers. This trend, of involving the Swedes in the post-war period, continued. The Swedes were favoured for their genuine assistance without any political strings attached.

Haile Selassie's external relations with the West had been very successful indeed. He had gained its trust and confidence which bolstered his image as one of the most seasoned statesmen of the world. His sound foreign policy and its careful execution had earned for Ethiopia respect and prestige. In Africa he was held with great esteem as the founder of the OAU and the elder statesman of Africa. Peter Shewab, illustrating the wisdom of Haile Selassie in the execution of his foreign policy, wrote: *'Haile Selassie was masterful in neutralising support for his opponents in Eritrea and Somalia. The failure of the military junta that overthrew the emperor to successfully continue this policy lends credence to the argument that Haile Selassie's influence over other world leaders was large.'*[53] Had Haile Selassie applied an iota of his wisdom in the execution of his foreign policy to reform his domestic policies, he could have changed the course of history for the benefit of Ethiopia and its people.

NOTES

1 H. W. Lockot. The Mission, London, 1989, pp. 133–166.
2 Paul Henze, The United States and the Horn of Africa: History and Current Prospectas, a Paper Presented to the Conference on International Relations in the Horn of Africa, Cairo, 27–30 May 1990.
3 Marcus, op. cit., p. 159.
4 Lockot, op. cit., p. 55.
5 Keller, op. cit., p. 99.
6 ibid., p. 99.
7 ibid., p. 100, Imperial Ethiopian Government, Third-Five Year Development Plan, Addis Ababa, 1968, p. 47.
8 Kaplan and Nelson, op. cit., p. 147.
9 ibid., p. 147.
10 Keller, op. cit., p. 107.

11 ibid., p. 109.
12 Bender, Gerald and Others, African Crisis Area and US Foreign Policy, Berkeley and London, 1985, p. 180.
13 Central Statistical Office, Peoples Democratic Republic of Ethiopia, Facts and Figures, pp. 43–45; The Propaganda and Culture Committee, A Decade of Revolutionary Transformation 1974–1984, Addis Ababa 1984, p. 7.
14 The author was a senior officer of the Department of Labour in the Ministry of National Community Development.
15 Ellen, Locks, Ray, Wolf and Others, The Dirty Work: CIA in Africa, London 1982, p. 71.
16 '*CIA helped to establish the African American Labour Centre (AALC) in 1964. In many ways the AALC was meant to supersede the post war role of the International Confederation of Free Trade Unions (ICFTU) and ensure Washington's control of labour activities in Africa.*' Ibid. p. 73.
17 Lockot, op. cit., pp. 136–137.
18 Margery Perham, The Government of Ethiopia, London: Faber & Faber, 1948, p. 372.
19 Underlined provinces are added by the author.
20 Paul Henze, Address to a Symposium sponsored by Eritrean for Peace and Democracy, Crystal City, Arlington, Virginia, 10 March 1990. Paul Henz had served as an American diplomat in Ethiopia. Currently he is resident consultant at the Rand Corporation, Washington DC.
21 Lockot, op. cit., p. 137.
22 United Nations, Report of the United Nations Commission for Eritrea, General Assembly Records: Fifth Session, Supplement No. 8 (A/1285). Lake Success, New York, 1950, pp. 211–224.
23 Dr Menasse Haile, Legality of Secessions: The Case of Eritrea, *International Law Review*, vol. 8. No. 2, New York, Fall 1994, p. 487.
24 Tesfatsion Madhane, Eritrea: Dynamics of a National Question, B. R. Gruner, Amsterdam, 1986, p. 27.
25 ibid., p. 28.
26 ibid., pp. 29–50.
27 ibid., p. 30.
28 ibid., p. 30.
29 ibid., pp. 38–42.
30 ibid., p. 41.
31 ibid., pp. 39–42.
32 ibid., p. 71.
33 ibid., p. 71.
34 Marcus, op. cit., p. 69.
35 Petrides, op. cit., p. 56.
36 ibid., p. 4.
37 Edmund Keller, Revolutionary Ethiopia, Bloomington and Indianapolis, Indiana University Press, 1988, p. 2.

38 Marcus, op. cit., pp. 82–83.
39 ibid., p. 85. As extracted from the US National Archives, State Department, Office of Intelligence Research, Division of Research for the Near East and Africa, Intelligence Report, N. 5311 (25 July 1950).
40 ibid., p. 85.
41 See Schwab, op. cit., pp. 91–92; Marina Ottaway, Superpower Competition and Regional Conflicts in the Horn of Africa, in R. Craig Nation and Mark V. Kauppi, ed., The Soviet Impact in Africa, Lexington, Massachusetts, Toronto, 1984, p. 71; Marcus, op. cit., pp. 82–89.
42 Schwab, op. cit., p. 93.
43 Marina Ottaway, op. cit., p. 171.
44 ibid., p. 173.
45 Gerald J. Bender and Others, African Crisis Area and USA Foreign Policy, University of California Press, Berkeley and London, 1985, p. 180.
46 Ottaway, op. cit., p. 175.
47 Marcus, op. cit., p. 90.
48 ibid., p. 93.
49 ibid., p. 112.
50 ibid., p. 112.
51 ibid., p. 114.
52 Halliday, op. cit., p. 218.
53 Schwab, op. cit., p. 100.

Chapter Three

From an Absolute Monarchy to a Military Dictatorship

January–September 1974

As a new desire arises or as old desires grow stronger in various groups, or as environmental conditions change, and as institutions fail to change a relative disequilibrium may arise, and what we call a revolution breaks out.

Crane Britain

Mutiny and Urban Revolt

The pre-revolution Ethiopia's reality totally confirms the situation described in the quotation. A new class came into being following the emperor's intensive effort in modernisation of the nation since the restoration of the empire in 1941. The intelligentsia and the working class had constantly demanded, though not openly, the fulfilment of their economic and political aspirations. The intelligentsia as represented by university students, the working class and the men-in-uniform shared common misgivings against the *ancien régime*. As already pointed out in Chapter Two, students were the most vocal and organised critics of the government. The military had neither shown its discontent with the political system nor had it taken any action that might be interpreted as disloyalty to the crown. Its record of loyalty was beyond any doubt, save the 1960 abortive coup of the Imperial Body Guard and the Public Security. Those involved in it paid dearly for their misadventure. The officers who had participated in the coup were court-martialled and incarcerated in prison receiving terms ranging from three to ten years while the only surviving leader of the *putsch* General Mengistu Newaye, commander of the Imperial Body Guard, was sentenced to death. Those whose innocence was doubtful were transferred to the Army. The restructuring and the overhauling of the Body Guard and the Public Security made the chances for another revolt or mutiny remote until two disgruntled contingents of the Fourth Army Division in the town of Negale and Dolo in the Governorate-General of Sidamo mutinied on 12 January 1974. The mutineers detained their officers and demanded that the emperor should send his envoy to listen to their petitions and give decisions on the spot. Requesting the emperor to send an envoy was by the standard of the time disrespect to the person of the emperor and that would have invariably provoked a stern disciplinary action against the offender. The emperor sent, instead of a special envoy, the commander of the Ground Force, Lieutenant-General Dresse Dubale, accompanied by other officers to meet the mutineers whereupon his arrival at the camp he was detained. The general was subjected to an ordeal of drinking unpotable water that was the regular source of water for the mutineers. He was also invited to their ration of dried bread that could hardly be eaten unless it was moistened with some tea or broth. The mutineers' mistreatment of their commanding officer was to make him appreciate the appalling conditions in the camp which they had endured so long.

The emperor, who was saddened by the action of the mutineers, sent as his personal envoy Major-General Abera Wolde Mariam, the commander of the Air Force, to deliver his message to the Negale mutineers. The imperial message was an assurance that their demands for improved living conditions in the camps, increase in salaries, pension and other monetary benefits would be favourably considered and that they should release the Commander of the Ground Force and other officers. The mutineers complied with the royal request and order was restored in the two camps. However, the manner in which the mutiny was resolved set a bad precedent. It also revealed the government's lack of resolve and determination in dealing with breaches of discipline. The concessions made to the mutineers without running the risk of reprisal triggered similar actions in the different units and contingents. The government was naive to believe that appeasement would restore discipline to the army.

The failure of the policy of appeasement was in evidence when the Ethiopian Teachers' Association with a membership of about 18,000 went on strike demanding salary increases and suspension of the Education Sector Review, an education policy jointly produced by the government and the World Bank to replace the existing education system, on 18 February 1974. The demands of the teachers unlike that of the Negale mutineers were not parochial. Their demands cut across the society. Their additional demands, among other things, included the introduction of a national minimum wage, pay increase to industrial workers and civil servants, introduction of a pension scheme for industrial workers, revision of labour laws, more restriction on work permits to foreign nationals, granting the right to form trade unions to employees of public-owned undertakings, imposition of price control regulations, etc. The teachers by including grievances affecting other segments of society, succeeded in marshaling the support and sympathy of a wider sector of the community.

At this particular juncture, it would be in order to make a digression to explain the purpose and scope of the Education Sector Review for it was one of the major factors that contributed in discrediting Prime Minister Aklilu Habtewolde's government.

The Education Sector Review recommended three education strategies for replacing the existing academic-orientated system. The alternative strategy which was adopted by the government for implementation was a work-orientated 4–4–4 school system. The first level of education of the recommended system consisted of 'a minimum formation education' of four years duration which could, as and when resources of the country permitted, be accessed by all school age children[1]. It would be followed by four years of education for a selected number of pupils from the first level education and further followed by four years secondary education for a selected number of pupils from the second level education. Those who would successfully complete secondary education would be eligible for tertiary level education. The Education Sector Review Report in comparing the recommended system to existing system of education stated: *'The present system at all levels is structured primarily to provide ongoing education. By contrast the recommended system is intended to provide a self-contained programme at each level that would be terminated for most students.'*[2] The report further in elaborating its recommendation pointed out that most of the pupils at the completion of four years of primary education *'would enter the work-force and participate in non-formal education (adult education) with a minority entering secondary-level schools.'*[3] It further proposed the reduction of qualification of teachers for primary schools from 10+1 to 8+1, thereby reducing the cost for an elementary schoolteacher from 41,240 Birr to 22,700 Birr.[4] It was also recommended in the report to make students bear a large share of the cost of their education. According to the report by 1990–2000 a major portion of the cost of higher education would be transferred to the students. It assumed that students could cover their cost of instruction by student loans and part-time work.[5] While the nation's economy was showing signs of saturation in absorbing even graduates, to assume availability of part-time jobs for students was an unrealistic proposition.

Proposals to limit the bulk of children of the nation to functional literacy and introduce a payment system for higher education were direct blows to the aspirations of students for higher education. Ethiopians enjoyed, without distinction, free education from primary to university. Without this opportunity few Ethiopians could have afforded to cover the cost of the education for their children. The attempt to introduce a system of payment for higher education and changing the education system of the country, without taking into consideration the general mood of the nation, was a political blunder by a regime whose fate was hanging by a thread.

The Education Sector Review was probably conceived with good intentions to provide education that was in harmony with the economy of the country and functional as well. Political consideration should have been allowed to override economic and other considerations in tampering with a sensitive issue that invariably affected the entire society. The proposals of the Sector Review were time bombs. The teachers, who discerned the sensitivity of the issue, capitalised on them to advance their parochial interests that were left unsatisfied for years. A system, that was allegedly designed to condemn the children of the 'have nots' to inherit the misfortune of their parents, aroused the indignation of the citizens who gave their support and sympathy to the teachers' cause.

The disgruntled teachers struck and demonstrated demanding the suspension of the Education Sector Review and the immediate adjustment of other grievances. The university students joined the demonstration to underscore their opposition to the Sector Review. To make matters even worse for the beleaguered government the taxi drivers of Addis Ababa withheld their services and joined the demonstration for a totally different reason.

Following the increase on oil price by OPEC, the government raised the local cost of petrol by fifty per cent – a very significant increase. The taxi drivers who were devastated by the price rise on petrol demanded a downward revision of the price and would suspend their services until such time their demands were met. The price rise was made before the Negale mutiny, but the delayed reaction of the taxi drivers coincided with the teachers' strikes and demonstrations in mid-February. Until this day evidence that would establish a collusion between the teachers, students and taxi drivers is not available. On the other hand to dismiss the incident as purely coincidental would be foolish.

Demonstrations and strikes were illegal during the *ancien régime* but the government failed to take any action to restrain the teachers, students and taxi drivers. The government, as it did with the mutiny in Negale, chose to capitulate rather than face confrontation. The emperor, on an unprecedented scale, addressed the nation calling for calm and tried to exonerate his government from the economic problems of the country by putting the blame on the world economic situation. He announced the suspension of the Sector Review and assured the teachers that their demand for a salary increase and adjustment would be resolved within a month. He also appealed to them to call off their strike. The teachers, who had expected immediate redress to their grievance, ignored the appeal of the emperor and continued with their strike. On the other hand, the taxi drivers settled with a downward revision of ten cents on the price of a litre of petrol.

The following excerpt from the nationwide address of the emperor shows his conciliatory gesture to defuse any impeding uprising:

'1. The Education Sector Review, conducted at great efforts by scholars and experts from Ethiopia, friendly countries and international organisations, was designed to develop and expand the Ethiopian educational system; so that education for which We have always given priority will spread rapidly throughout the country and in a way that it will be more relevant and meaningful to the daily life of our people while taking account of the social and cultural norms of our society. We have, however, ordered as announced before, the postponement of the implementation of the study until the goals and purposes of the Education Sector Review are fully explained to Our people and until the necessary organisational framework and machinery for its implementation are completed.

2. As regards the request submitted by teachers to the Ministry of Education, We have ordered a study into the salary scale of teachers taking into consideration the salary in other sectors as well as the economic resources of the country. We have been greatly saddened by the interruption of their activities while the study is being conducted and they were informed that a decision on their request would soon be made. Furthermore, the Ethiopian Teachers' Association had advised all of its

members that a decision would be given to their request within a month and that they, in the meantime, should continue their normal duties.

3. The increase in price on important goods and fuel is the cause of the general world economic crisis and as such its control is beyond individual countries. The increased price of fuel and the resultant high cost of living have disrupted the general world economic stability, and each country is striving to solve the crisis within its own means and resources. On Our part, We had ordered that a detailed study be conducted to solve this problem taking into account first its effects on the cost of living of Our people. Based on this study, We have ordered that the price of fuel, so vital to the smooth functioning of the economy, should be reduced as much as possible, although this will entail a decrease in the revenue of the government, and thus a modification and streamlining of its programmes of work and postponement of the implementation of some of its programmes.

4. We have ordered a price control on those goods essential to the basic needs of Our people whether these goods are locally produced or imported. This measure will ensure fair prices commensurate with the standard of living of the people but without adversely affecting the producer. The implementation of such a measure will create confidence between consumers and producers. Everyone, therefore should co-operate to guarantee its success.'⁶

However, the emperor's statement did not succeed in defusing revolts that were caused by years of neglect. The Negale mutiny created a chain-reaction in the armed forces. The Second Division in Asmera, a force consisting of a third of the Ground Force of the nation, mutinied on 26 February, arrested the commander, other senior officers, the mayor of the city and other senior officials of the Municipality of Asmera and took over the radio station of the city. The Division announced its rejection of the salary increase that was made following the demands of the Negale Mutiny. The major demands of the Division were:

– Freedom to form political parties:

–   Democratic election of provincial administrators;
–   Enforcement of price control regulation;
–   Land reform;
–   Bringing to justice officials who embezzled state funds and squandered state property;
–   Salary and wage increases to the Army, Police, Civil Service and industrial workers in line with the rise in the cost of living;
–   Establish a joint committee composed of representatives of the government and the army to follow up the satisfactory resolution of the demands.

The government again capitulated to the demands of the armed forces by making fresh salary increases and by improving other monetary benefits to the Army and the Police. The monthly salary of a private was revised bringing the basic salary to 112 Birr with a ceiling of 150 Birr. The pension of a private was also increased by 30 Birr raising the monthly minimum pension benefit to 50 Birr and in the case of a private who was pensioned due to an accident, in the course of duty, the minimum was raised to 85 Birr. Professional allowances of a private and non-commissioned officer were increased by 20 Birr. For the family of a private or non-commissioned officer who happened to be killed in the course of duty for six months full salary and thereafter a minimum of 50 Birr to be paid monthly. These monetary benefits were made effective from 1 March 1974. The armed forces and the Police who were satisfied with the government for settling their grievances thanked the emperor by making representation to the Imperial Court. On the morning of 26 February a representative of the Police thanked His Imperial Majesty for his generosity in adjusting their grievances to the satisfaction of the Police Force. In the afternoon of the same day a spokesman of the Army, warrant officer Kebede Haile, expressing the gratitude of the men-in-uniform said: '*We representatives of the Armed Forces are standing in full attention before Your Imperial Majesty today to demonstrate our loyalty to you.*'[7] Replying to the representative of the Armed Forces His Imperial Majesty said: '*. . . as Commander-in-Chief of the Armed Forces, We direct and order you to carry out your sacred duties in collaboration with the rest of the nation so that our country can surmount the great problems facing her today. And should you have any grievance, you should report to Us, as you have done in the past, while performing your duties.*'[8]

As it could be discerned from the list of demands, the petition of the men-in-uniform affected practically all sectors of the society. The diversity of the petition was an outright signal shown to the government that the

92

loyalty of the army could not be taken for granted as it used to be. The government was being required to make significant political and economic concessions. Moreover, the demand for a joint follow-up committee was another indication that the government was not trusted to make any significant change that would adversely affect its interest.

The Cabinet Resigns

The emperor, as usual, assured the representatives that their grievances would be considered and adjusted. Following the intervention of the emperor, surprisingly Prime Minister Aklilu's cabinet resigned on 27 February. According to the statement the Prime Minister gave to the later Inquiry Commission he said that Ato Getahun Tessema, Dr Tesfaye Gebre Egze and Ato Mulatu Debebe, Ministers of Interior, Information and National Community Development respectively, had conspired against him by calling a cabinet resignation.[9] Therefore, the initiative for resignation was taken by the Prime Minister. The resignation of the cabinet was a miscalculated political error. In a polity where there was no tradition of an elected government resignation did not make any sense. Even for argument's sake if one assumes that the resignation of the cabinet was instigated by the emperor, it fails to meet the demand for an elected form of government. The resignation was an exercise in futility. Since the resignation of the cabinet was not a pressing issue at that particular time, taking necessary legal steps, allowing the formation of political parties, committing the cabinet to a timetable for holding an election and formal transfer of power to the winning party, could have served as plausible options. Such tactical options would have disarmed those who were advocating some form of change, in the political system, without proposing a credible replacement for the *ancien régime*. Under the circumstances such a step towards democratisation would have been entertained as a practical step in changing the system of government. The resignation of the cabinet, coupled with the capitulation of the government in the face of demands from certain units of the Armed Forces, revealed the government's inability and weakness to control or manipulate the events that took place since the Negale mutiny in January to an attempted *coup d'état* by some units of the Second Division in the latter part of February 1974. The resignation of the cabinet was the end of a government largely composed of persons of humble origins.

The Emperor Appoints a New Prime Minister

The emperor, the ultimate umpire of the cabinet's musical chair, in accepting the resignation and the subsequent appointment of the new Prime Minister said: '*We have accepted the resignation of Our ministers as of February 27, 1974 and in accordance with Order No. 44 of 1966 concerning the appointment of Our Prime Minister, We have appointed Lij Endalkatchew Mekonnen as Prime Minister and Lieutenant-General Abiye Abebe as Minister of Defence.*'[10]

On the same day the Commander of the Ground Forces Lieutenant-General Dressie Dubale was replaced by Lieutenant-General Wolde Selassie Bereka.

Endalkatchew who had held various cabinet posts in Prime Minister Aklilu's cabinet was the son of Ethiopia's first Prime Minister, Bitweded Mekonnen Endalkatchew, who was married to the emperor's niece. Endalkatchew was ambitious and had shown charismatic leadership in the cabinet and diplomatic posts he had held. He was an unsuccessful candidate for the United Nations' Secretary-General. His hopes for the most-important post in the world being dashed he had turned his full attention to the post of Prime Minister, a post he coveted for a long time. His dream was realised when he was appointed Prime Minister on 1 March 1974. The day after his appointment, in a press interview, articulating the style of his government he said that he would '*listen to the heartbeats of all segments of the population and head a credible government that would effectively serve the needs of the people at large.*'[11]

He chose the members of his cabinet, in conformity with his press statement, on the basis of talent, experience and youthfulness. The Prime Minister and other cabinet members took the oath of office in the presence of the emperor on 5 March 1974. The cross section of the cabinet was representative of the nobility, the educated class and conservative elements from the older generation. The nobility, in comparison to the composition of Prime Minister Aklilu's cabinet, had gained more seats. The full cabinet members were:[12]

1. Lij Endalkatchew Mekonnen, Prime Minister.
2. Lieutenant-General Abiye Abebe, Minister of Defence.
3. Lij Michael Imru, Minister of Commerce and Industry.
4. Dej. Zewde Gebre Selassie, Minister of Interior.
5. Lieutenant-General Assefa Ayene, Minister of Telecommunications and Posts.

6. Ato Belete Gebre Tsadiq, Minister of Land Reform and Administration.
7. Dej. Kebede Tessema, Minister of the Imperial Court.
8. Ato Ahadu Sabure, Minister of Information.
9. Dej. Tesfa Yohanis Berhe, Minister of Mines.
10. Ato Getatchew Bekele, Minister of Public Works and Water Resources
Development.
11. Ato Mellion Neqniq, Minister of National Community Development.
12. Ato Terefe Taddesse, Minister of Education.
13. Ato Minassie Haile, Minister of Foreign Affairs.
14. Ato Tekalign Gedamu, Minister of Planning and Development.
15. Ato Belatchew Aserat, Minister of Justice.
16. Ato Bulcha Demekssa, Minister of Agriculture.
17. Dr Jemal Abdirkadir, Minister of Public Health.
18. Ato Mohammed Abdurhaman, Minister in the Prime Minister's
Office.
19. Ato Kifle Wodajo, Minister in the Prime Minister's Office.

The soldiers, having satisfied most of their demands, went back to their
barracks but the civilian population continued with demonstrations and
strikes invariably accompanied by violence and disturbance of public
order.

Prime Minister Endalkatchew, in the meantime, vigorously appealed to
the public for calm and a breathing space to enable him to concentrate
on the problems that were bedevilling the nation. On the other hand,
he, to consolidate his power and to win the army to his side, constituted
a co-ordinating committee of the Armed Forces and the Police chaired
by Colonel Alem Zewde Tessema, commander of the Airborne Brigade.
The committee's task was presumably to enforce law and order in an
otherwise volatile situation that was heading towards anarchy. The out-
going cabinet was suspected of making conditions more difficult for the
new cabinet. Under this pretext the co-ordinating committee arrested
the ex-Prime Minister Aklilu Habtewolde and eighteen other cabinet
ministers and detained them in a military camp at Goffa Sefer in the
southern part of Addis Ababa on the 27 of April 1974. Given the close
relationship Colonel Alem Zewde Tessema enjoyed with Endalkatchew,
one may be inclined to believe that the detention of the ministers was
instigated by Endalkatchew.

The new Prime Minister in his nationwide maiden speech outlining
the policy of his government stressed that the primary preoccupation
would be to enforce law and order that was deteriorating at a faster pace

than could be anticipated. To restore law and order he took the following measures:

- enforcement of law and order were placed under the joint responsibility of the Armed Forces and the Police;
- the Armed Forces and the Police were brought under the command of the Minister of Defence;
- dusk to dawn curfew in Addis Ababa was imposed.

However, his strategy for the enforcement of law and order failed to yield the desired result. The civilian population continued with demonstrations and strikes until the situation reached a point where it was absolutely impossible to continue with normal functions of the state as outlined in the Prime Minister's speech.

Government–CELU Agreement

CELU, which was an indifferent spectator to the mutinies of the armed forces, strikes and demonstrations of the teachers, students, and taxi drivers woke up from its slumber with a list of demands. It threatened that failure to meet its demands for salaries and wages increase, pension coverage, insurance, suspension of Education Sector Review, tax exemptions for workers' provident funds, revision of labour laws, etc., would provoke a general strike. The government refused to capitulate to the threat of CELU, thereby risking a general strike which paralysed the entire nation particularly the capital city from 7–11 March 1974. The strike was called off after the government and CELU signed an agreement. The details of the provisions of the agreement[13] were:

- 'Council of Ministers will present to Parliament within one month draft bills revising the present provisions governing strikes and dismissal from jobs without adequate reasons.
- Instructions have been given to the concerned department to give the necessary guidelines and instructions to all employers to provide salary adjustments to all employees, in accordance with the labour relations laws, to meet the rising cost of living taking into consideration the financial positions of each employer. Those employers who cannot grant salary adjustment within the guideline will have to do so within two months starting from March 11.
- Regulations of minimum wages, which the government has

96

accepted in principle, will be studied within two months by the legally established Labour Relations Board, with a view to implement the study.

– Strict control will be taken against all those representatives of management who are believed to hamper good labour relations.

– Regulations will be issued within three months to enable representatives of labour and other consumers throughout the country to participate in price control of which the government has already taken concrete measures such as assigning controllers and others.

– The implementation of the Education Sector Review, which was designed to expand and develop education throughout the country, has been postponed until its benefits are fully understood by the people. It will be reviewed thoroughly by a study group consisting of teachers and scholars from various organisations before it is implemented.

– Decision on the demands of teachers will be given by March 19 after a study by the concerned officials and teachers.

– Legal provision governing immunity from taxes of the provident fund, to management and labour contributed, will be issued within a month.

– Draft laws on labour pension schemes, similar to those governing civil servants, will be presented to Parliament within six months, and regulations governing disability pay will be studied and issued within three months.

– The nature of contractual word will be examined so that if the nature of the job calls for a permanent employee, employers should have such employees on a permanent basis. If the nature of the job is of a limited period, the present hiring system will be maintained. However, if the duration of the job is of one or more years, draft laws on such jobs will be presented to Parliament, together with draft laws governing strikes and dismissal from jobs, to provide compensation to employees.

– Regulation to curtail conflict of interest of company board members selected from the civil service and the judiciary now under preparation will be issued as soon as possible to regulate such conflict of interest.

– Regulations to enable the Advisory Labour Board of which

labour is a member, will be issued soon strictly to control the employment of foreigners while competent Ethiopians are available.

- The government will take all necessary measures, on a priority basis, to create job opportunities.
- The question of free education will be studied with the Education Sector Review. In the meantime, the Ministry of Education has been ordered to give free instructions so that all government schools will not charge any registration fees at the beginning of each year, nor any other fees except those agreed upon by parent associations and those legally proclaimed.
- Regulations concerning publication of newspapers will be issued in the future. Until then the Confederation of Ethiopian Labour Unions will publish its newspaper, '*The Voice of Labour*', within the present system of review, but it will be given priority for it contains educational articles.
- All employees of government agencies, whose rights and interests have not been covered by the civil service regulations of 1954 Ethiopian Calendar and subsequent regulations, have been granted the right to form unions in accordance with Proclamation No. 210/1956, Article 21.
- No action of any kind shall be taken against union members because of the general strike that has been staged by the Confederation of Ethiopian Labour Unions. There shall be no cuts in salary or other allowances of union members as a result of the general strike without the decision of the Labour Relations Board.[14]

The agreement was a victory for both the government and CELU. For the government it ended the four-day strike that almost paralysed the nation; for CELU, even though it did not bring any immediate material gain, it was a morale victory to persuade the government to make official commitment to issue laws governing pension, insurance, workman's compensation, and minimum wage within a period not exceeding three months. The agreement also boosted the image of CELU as a powerful force with which any government had to contend with.

Employers' Federation Challenges Government–CELU Agreement

On the other hand, the Employers' Federation of Ethiopia, the major organisation whose interest was affected adversely by strikes and other related actions, was absolutely ignored by both the government and trade unions. The agreement made between the government and CELU on wages and other conditions of work was concluded without involving the Employers' Federation of Ethiopia. It was not consulted on the impact that the agreement would have on the national economy in general and on the members of the Federation in particular. On this account the Federation submitted a petition to the Labour Relations Board requesting it to declare the general strike of 8–11 March 1974 illegal and the agreement null and void. The board tactfully avoided nullifying the agreement but gave its verdict on the illegality of the strike which was called in violation of the Labour Relations Proclamation No. 210/1964. The Proclamation prohibited the staging of strikes without fully exhausting grievance settlement procedures and before the expiry of the statutory requirement of a cooling-off period of sixty days. The declaration of the strike as an illegal work-stoppage would have entitled employers, who were directly affected by the strike, to terminate employment contracts of those workers who participated in the general strike. The Board, being aware of the volatile political situation, ruled against the exercise of their right to summary dismissal of employees who took part in the illegal strike or any other activity that might have been considered prejudicial to an employment contract. The decision of the Board did not secure any advantage to the Employers' Federation other than having the satisfaction of the strike declared illegal and relieving its members from any obligation to pay wages for the duration of the strike. However, CELU condemned the decision of the Board as illegal and categorically declared its rejection with a threat to stage another strike. It then resorted to inciting isolated strikes and slow-downs to the point of disrupting the carrying out of normal activities in the capital.

More Strikes, Demonstrations and Purges

The accord signed with CELU did not restrain individual unions and unorganised workers from staging strikes. The employees of the Civil Aviation went on strike on 11 March, bringing the service of Ethiopian Airlines to a standstill. By this time the demands of workers became stereotyped. The Civil Aviation workers' demands were improvement on conditions of work, wages, salaries and certain issues which were peculiar to their industry. Strikes spread to manufacturing and other sectors of industry. On 13 March, the Tobacco Monopoly's workers submitted an eleven-point petition on conditions of work, including a demand for the removal of the chairman of the board of directors of the company, Ato Taddesse Yacob, who had already resigned from his cabinet post, an action that had disqualified him from the membership in the board of directors of the company. On the 16 March the series of strikes and demonstrations compelled the government to issue public notices prohibiting strikes, demonstrations and distributing leaflets that instigated public disturbance.

Towards the end of March the demands of employees of the public service and state-owned undertakings changed in content focusing on other demands for the sacking of department heads and senior executives. The shift of demand from the cry for improvement in salaries, wages and other conditions of work to dismissal of managerial level staff did not wholly meet the disapproval of the new Prime Minister, for it provided an excuse to sack those officials and executives whom the new leadership were not inclined to retain in service. The new brand of demand that enjoyed the tacit approval of the leadership spread from the capital to the provincial cities of Jimma in Keffa, Metu in Illubabor, Assella in Arsi and Arbaminch in Gamu Goffa, Governorate-Generals.

Demonstrations in those four cities were marked by police brutality against the demonstrators. The Chamber of Deputies, which was standing on the sidelines to the events in the country, demanded a public inquiry on the Police Force's handling of demonstrations in the four cities. The government went farther than the request of the deputies by dismissing unpopular Enderassies. The Enderassies of Sidamo, Arsi, were sacked on 8 April and they were followed by the dismissal of the Enderassies of Shewa and Keffa on 16 April. By the end of Spring of 1974 the remaining Enderassies were removed one after the other and replaced by new ones.

In Addis Ababa, the demand for the removal of senior officials and executives continued unabated resulting in the dismissal of senior officials of the ministries of Finance, Agriculture, Justice, Health, etc. The government invariably met the demands of employees in this regard. The demand for sacking senior officials reached its climax when four thousand employees of the Municipality of Addis Ababa went on strike demanding, among other things, the resignation of the Lord Mayor, Dr Haile Giorgis. The strike ended after two weeks when the government succumbed to the demands of the strikers by dismissing the Mayor on 11 April 1974.[15] Ato Mulugetta SinGiorgis, Deputy Mayor, was made Acting Mayor.

The demand for sacking executives of state-owned industries resulted in a mass dismissal of experienced managerial staff. For instance, the Franco-Ethiopian Railway Company Workers' Union called off a strike that lasted for over five weeks upon the government's acceptance of the dismissal of thirteen executives, including the general manager. The strike of the General Transport Company's Workers, which brought life in the capital to a standstill was called off when ten top executives including the general manager were dismissed. The firing of executives continued in the Telecommunications Board, Ethiopian Light and Power Authority, Ethiopian Coffee Board, Imperial Highway Authority, Addis Ababa Water and Sewerage Authority and Commercial Bank of Ethiopia. By the end of May the sacking exercise was more or less accomplished and demonstrations and strikes were scaled down.

A parallel development was taking place in the military too. Removal of senior officers of the Armed Forces and the Police was also swiftly carried out simultaneously with the sacking of officials and executives in the state administration and state-owned enterprises. By the end of May, commanders of the Armed Forces and the Police, including divisional commanders were replaced. The dismissal of senior officials and officers both in the army and the civilian sector was so frequent it was difficult to keep record of the extraordinary phenomenon that was siphoning away the experienced manpower of the nation.

Even religious institutions were not spared dancing to the tune of the circumstances obtaining at that particular moment. The clerics of the Ethiopian Orthodox Church demonstrated against the Patriarchate demanding for better conditions of work. The Islamic community in the capital city also went to the streets for religious equality. An estimated 100,000 people including sympathetic Christians and 3,000 students participated in the demonstration staged by the Moslem community, on 20 April 1974.

The strife that began to ravage the nation in February was a symptom of the people's craving for a political transformation of the state. In April, the men-in-uniform became more demanding. The Third Division of the army and the Police Force in Harargie Governorate-General captured the radio station of the city of Harar and demanded the dismissal of the commander of the Division, General Haile Bykedagn, and the commissioner of the Ethiopian Police Force, Lieutenant-General Yilma Shebeshi, on 1 April 1974. The commander of the Third Division resigned the next day. The Police commissioner was removed from his command and appointed as Enderassie of Bale in the last week of April.[16]

Towards the end of April the Co-ordinating Committee of the Armed

Forces, Police and the Territorial Army came out of its barracks again and rounded up about 25 senior civilian and military officials, including the members of the old cabinet who had been released from the first round of detention. The Co-ordinating Committee made representation to the emperor to explain to him the need of the second round of detention of officials and at the same time pledged the loyalty of the army to the emperor and the new cabinet. After the second bout of arrest and detention of officials and tactical performance of rituals of pledging loyalty to the emperor, the army retired to its barracks, on 29 April 1974. For the whole of May until mid-June the Armed Forces and the Police concentrated on enforcing law and order.

The new cabinet, emboldened by the pledge of loyalty of the Co-ordinating Committee of the Armed Forces, Police and the Territorial Army, took steps to stop strikes and demonstrations. It issued public notices prohibiting strikes and demonstrations on 30 April and 3 May respectively. However, the public notices did not restrain strikers and demonstrators from illegal actions.

Creation of a Committee and High Security Commission

Endalkatchew, in his brief tenure of office, created a committee and then a commission presumably to enforce law and order. The committee, which was chaired by Lieutenant-Colonel Alem Zewde Tessema, Commander of the elite Airborne Brigade and a henchman of Endalkatchew, did not achieve much except in detaining the ex-Prime Minister and other members of the old cabinet whom Endalkatchew considered threats to his position. The committee's conduct soon became a liability to his political goals and he had to replace it by a 25-man High National Security Commission. The commission which was composed of hand-picked members from the Armed Forces, Police and the Territorial Army and chaired by the Minister of Defence, like its predecessor, failed to contain the deterioration in law and order. In fact, it was considered by junior officers in the army as a divisive organisation, created to sow the seeds of discord among the different units of the armed forces.

The commission was given sweeping powers to detain those who disturbed public peace and order, to hear petition of employees and/or organisations and dispose them in a manner it deemed fit. The power of the commission duplicated the attributions of existing ministries. The commission was a state within a state. It exercised its powers, in parallel, with other institutions, particularly with the ministries of National Community Development which was responsible for all labour matters and

Justice which had a final say on the decisions of the Labour Relations Board, on points of law. The creation of the commission inadvertently changed the venue of labour disputes from the Ministry of National Community Development and the Labour Relations Board to the commission. The enthusiasm of the commission in settling labour disputes rather than promoting industrial peace exacerbated an already confused and fluid situation. The commission, by entertaining labour disputes, put itself into an impossible position. The encounter of the commission and the industrial labour force invariably led to violence, arrests and detentions. The first such encounter of the commission which ended in a total disaster was its attempt to settle a 25-point demand of the Telecommunications Board's employees. The employees of the Board, among other things, demanded the dismissal of the entire management staff. The commission rejected the demand and instructed the representatives of the employees to convey properly the basis for the decision of the commission in rejecting their demand to all employees of the Board. The employees' representatives, in an attempt to explain the decision of the commission, allegedly misrepresented it with a malicious intent. The representatives' action was regarded as a breach of confidence that provoked the commission to round up 24 alleged ring leaders. Other overtures of the commission in resolving labour disputes were also unsatisfactory. Anyhow, the commission during its short life span, did not come nearer to the *raison d'être* of its establishment. It was dissolved and replaced by a Co-ordinating Committee of the Armed Forces, Police and the Territorial Army when the latter decided to play a more prominent role, towards the end of June 1974.

An Inquiry Commission

On the other hand, one of the popular demands of the army, as well as the organised segments of the society, was a full investigation into the alleged corruption of the former government officials. The new Prime Minister constituted a seven-man Inquiry Commission that would investigate whether the former officials had unlawfully enriched themselves or squandered public funds or property. The Prime Minister chose seven wise men and submitted their names for the approval of the emperor. The emperor while approving the appointment instructed the Prime Minister to widen the scope of investigation to include the incumbents as well. With this pertinent amendment to the terms of reference of the Inquiry Commission the following gentlemen were appointed as members of the commission:[17]

103

1. Ato Hiruye Tadesse.
2. Ato Abebe Benti
3. Ato Mewael Mebratu
4. At Bililign Mandefro
5. Fitawrari Tadesse Marcos
6. Colonel Haile Mariam Aredo
7. Major Shemilis Metaferia

The commission, having realised the need for an enabling legislation, submitted a draft law describing its powers and functions to the government. The cabinet referred the draft to Parliament. Parliament made significant changes to the bill particularly in empowering the commission to investigate administrative and judicial malpractices. In the procedure of the appointment of members of the commission an element of institutional representation was injected and the membership of the commission raised from seven to fifteen members. The institutional distribution of the fifteen members was:

– six selected by the Chamber of Deputies from the public;
– six from the six units of the Armed Forces (the Army, Police, Air Force, Navy, Territorial Army and Imperial Body Guard);
– one from the Ethiopian Teachers' Association;
– one from the University Teachers' Association; and
– one from the employees of the Auditor General's Office.

Upon the enactment of Proclamation No. 326/1974 the original seven members of the commission were relieved of their duties and replaced by the following members:[18]

1. Professor Mesfin Wolde Mariam
2. Dr Bereket-Ab Habteselassie
3. Dr Jehad Aba Quoya
4. Ato Mawael Mebratu
5. Ato Assefa Liben
6. Ato Zenebe Haile
7. Ato Hussen Ismael from the Ethiopian Teachers' Association
8. Dr Mekonnen Woldeamlak from the University Teachers' Association
9. Ato Getatchew Desta from the Auditor General's Office
10. Commander Lemma Guttema from the Navy
11. Lieutenant-Colonel Negash Michael from the Police Force

12. Major Alemayehu Seyoum from the Imperial Body Guard
13. Major Admassu Negash from the Armed Forces
14. Captain Mitiku Demissie from the Air Force
15. Captain Selame Hiruy from the Territorial Army

Members of the Co-ordinating Committee of the Armed Forces, Police and Territorial Army met the members of the Inquiry Commission to exchange views on the work of the commission, on 15 July. A representative of the Co-ordinating Committee stressed that the function of the commission was to investigate whether the former and present government officials squandered public funds or were involved in administrative and judicial malpractices harmful to the country. A representative of the Co-ordinating Committee reminding the members of the commission of the importance the Armed Forces attached to the investigation said: *'It is the duty of the armed forces to ensure that the officials are thoroughly investigated and brought to a court of law.'*[19] The representative of the committee in further reminding the members of the commission of the seriousness of their responsibilities reiterated: *'These officials who are responsible for the present sordid state of the affairs of Ethiopia and for the lives of more than 100,000 Ethiopians, are allowed to go free to re-establish the feudal system of government which prevailed until recently, and thereby plunge the country into greater disaster.'*[20]

In his concluding remarks the representative of the Co-ordinating Committee assured the members of the commission that the committee would give them its full support in order to facilitate the work of the commission and in the meantime informed them that eighty-six officials including the 25 ministers and other senior officials who were already remanded in custody were arrested as of 18 July 1974. The members of the commission, however, did not hesitate to inform the representatives of the Co-ordinating Committee that the investigation would take much longer than had been anticipated by the committee.[21]

The commission began to function when it elected Professor Mesfin Wolde Mariam and Major Mersha Admassu as chairman and deputy chairman respectively, on 18 July 1974.[22] A preliminary report of the commission on the 1973/74 famine in Wollo was not disclosed until 20 October 1974. The Co-ordinating Committee which was not prepared to wait until the commission wound up its investigation, in flagrant defiance of civilised behaviour and without court trial summarily executed sixty persons.

105

A Constitution Drafting Conference

Another significant step that Endalkatchew had taken immediately after his appointment was to set up a constitution-drafting conference. The emperor, in one of his nationwide addresses, announced that he had instructed the Prime Minister to convene a constitutional conference to revise the 1955 Revised Constitution. According to the imperial declaration, the major issues[23] were:

1. Defining and clarifying the institutional relationship between the different branches of the Imperial Ethiopian Government.
2. Making the Prime Minister responsible to the Parliament.
3. Guaranteeing further the rights of the people.
4. Organising and streamlining the procedure and administration of justice to speed up due process of law.
5. Safeguarding the resources and the wealth of the nation.

These directives did not give to the conference a free-hand in revising the constitution. At any rate, towards the end of March a list of members of the conference, presumably representing a cross-section of the society, was made public. The twenty-nine men and one woman members[24] of the conference were:

1. Bitweded Assfaw Wolde Michael
2. Ato Yilma Deressa
3. Dejazmach Girmachew Tekle-Hawariat
4. Blata Tirfe Shumiye
5. Afengus Kitaw Yetateku
6. Dr Goytom Petros
7. Afenegus Taddesse Mengesha
8. Blata Matias Helete-work
9. Ato Tekle Tsadiq Mekuria
10. Weizerit Yodit Imru
11. Ato Assefa Liben
12. Dr Aklilu Habte
13. Ato Amanuel Amde Michael
14. Kegnazmach Abdulaziz Sheik Mohammed
15. Ato Teferra Degfe
16. Melake Selam Tekle-Berhane Wolde Yesus
17. Haji Mohammed Sani
18. Ato Worku Teferra

19. Haji Yusuf Abdurhaman
20. Fitawrari Gebre-Hiwot Welde Hawariate
21. Fitawrari Hadad Karar
22. Dr Abraham Demoz
23. Ato Berhanu Wakoya
24. Ato Fiseha Bayeh
25. Ato Fiseha-Tsion Teke
26. Dr Haile Wolde Michael
27. Ato Negash Gebre Mariam
28. Ato Abebe Retta
29. Ato Addis Alemayehu
30. Major Abebe Desta

The members of the conference could be classified under the following broad headings:

Ex-ministers, civil servants and a general	10
Judges	6
Academics	4
Representatives of the Ethiopian Orthodox Church	2
Representatives of Islam	2
Others (workers, military, media, business, etc.)	6
Total	30

The distribution of members was skewed in favour of ex-ministers, judges and academics which constituted 67%. Surprisingly four of the ex-minsters were members of Prime Minister Aklilu's cabinet.

The conference, at its first meeting, elected Ato Tekle Tsadiq Mekuria as its chairman, Ato Amanuel Amde Michael as deputy chairman, Ato Worku Teferra and Dr Abraham Demoz as reporters, in the first week of April.[25]

The emperor, subsequent to the appointment of members of the conference, directed Parliament to amend Article 131 of the Revised Constitution which required two parliamentary sessions for amending the constitution to one session. Article 131 as amended read: *'The constitution may be amended by an identical joint resolution adopted by three-fourths of the members of each chamber in one session of Parliament and proclaimed with the approval and authority of the emperor.'*[26] Furthermore, to facilitate the

107

consideration of a Revised Constitution the emperor cancelled the summer recess of the Parliament which normally began at the end of June and lasted to 2 November.

The Constitutional Conference, working under great stress, completed its assignment and submitted copies of the draft to the Prime Minister and the Co-ordinating Committee of the Armed Forces, Police and the Territorial Army, on 6 August 1974. The Co-ordinating Committee by that time was not keen to press for the promulgation of a revised constitution. On the other hand Endalkatchew's cabinet was bogged down with the restoration of law and order, it did not produce its cabinet policy until the first week of April. The cabinet's policy was the first attempt of an Ethiopian Government to disclose its programme to the people. It covered issues ranging from enforcement of law and order to broad strategies in economic, social and political developments. The following is a text of the policy statement of the new cabinet:

Policy Statement of the New Council of Ministers

Introduction

At various times in our history the people and leaders of Ethiopia have with courage and determination, overcome grave challenges and have passed on to succeeding generations a country renowned and respected for its unity and independence. Ethiopia faces today one such challenge. This challenge is the result of long-standing and cumulative problems which culminated in the crisis leading to the resignation of the Council of Ministers on 27 February 1974.

It is incumbent on all of us that we should realise that our country faces at present serious difficulties. National Security is one of them. Unless we are vigilant the continuation of the present situation may weaken our positions on our sea coasts and borders. Another obvious concern is the serious financial difficulty. To provide sufficient services and to implement development programmes, the Government requires more funds than are available at present. The drought affecting different parts of our country has inflicted heavy and frightening damages.

Those of us who have been asked to assume responsibility have accepted the call with great humility and with full knowledge that the present national crisis will require of each of us no less than our full commitment to serve our people and to search unsparingly for solutions to our country's manifold problems.

We have also answered the call of duty with the understanding that the present constitution will be amended and that our task consists of facilitating the necessary change in the interim period.

With the above considerations in mind, we set forth below the principles guiding the direction and actions of the Council of Ministers. Specific section for this transitional period will be announced subsequently as necessary by the appropriate ministries and agencies of the government.

Pledges by the Council Members

All of us, as members of the Council of Ministers who are entrusted with high responsibility, shall, to the best of our ability, strive to discharge our duties with honesty, diligence and a sense of justice, and without regard to personal consequences. We shall, at all times, endeavour to put Ethiopia's interest above our individual interests. In the discharge of our official duties, we shall refrain from making decisions when such decisions appear to conflict with our interests. As a token of our good faith, we shall register with a Government agency (soon to be designated) all our properties together with an explanation of the manner in which we have come to acquire them, as well as other additional properties we may acquire while in Government service.

A Commission of Inquiry has been established in order to investigate former and present ministers of the Government with the view to ascertaining whether they have misappropriated Government funds or have unlawfully enriched themselves. Since the primary purpose of the Commission's investigation is to establish confidence in Government by separating the guilty from the innocent and by bringing the guilty before a court of law, the Council of Ministers will give the Commission its fullest support in order to enable it to discharge its responsibility.

Priority Measures

As a matter of high priority, the Government will devote its full attention to the present fiscal difficulty and the drought problem. On the fiscal front, new action will be initiated in addition to those already undertaken. With regard to the drought, a comprehensive plan will be elaborated in order to tackle more effectively all the attendant problems.

With a view to instituting a constitutional monarchy, the Government will assist the Constitutional Commission in all its requirements so that its study of constitutional reform will be completed and that the result of its work submitted to Parliament.

Political and Administrative Matters

The Government's policy with regard to political matters will be guided by the following objectives: The strengthening of the country's unity; the safeguarding of its borders; the enriching of its cultural heritage a united people handed to us; the strengthening of the country's diverse traditions as pillars of national culture; the further consolidation of Ethiopian nationalism and cultural heritage without regard to ethnic affiliation, religion or sex.

With a view to encouraging the people to plan for and participate in the administration and social life of their localities, the Government will explore and institute various modalities which will make such participation possible.

Rights and Obligations

In order to safeguard the honour and independence of the people of Ethiopia which our forefathers have kept intact and in order also to uplift the spiritual and material well-being of our people by extending to the full enjoyment of those fundamental human and legal rights provided for in the present Constitution, particularly the rights of conscience, speech, and peaceful assembly, the Government shall endeavour to consolidate firmly the enjoyment of those rights.

Administration

The Government will undertake the necessary study and will implement measures to improve the efficiency of the administration, so as to avoid duplication as well as eliminate waste of human and material resources.

Proper safeguards will be implemented to ensure that all Government officials shall discharge their responsibilities with honesty, justice and diligence. With that in view, a law will be passed requiring all Government officials and employees to register at the time of employment with a Government agency all their properties, as well as all such additional properties they may acquire while in Government service.

Since Government agencies are instituted to provide service to the public, a special office shall be established to handle grievances of citizens who feel that they have not received the services to which they are entitled and that these agencies have violated their fundamental legal rights. This office will be headed by a person who, by virtue of the fact that he is not involved in the day-to-day struggle of political life, is capable of obtaining the confidence of the people, and who, at the same time, is competent and experienced.

Line of Administrative Responsibility

In order to ensure that the proper line of administrative responsibility is respected and that provincial Governors and the police will carry out their duties in accordance with the law, the Minister of Interior will exercise proper control as provided by law over the actions of Governors and those responsible for public security.

Administration of Justice

The Government will undertake the necessary measures to improve the administration of justice and to obtain full respect for and observance of the laws of the country. Steps will be taken to reduce wasteful litigation, to reform the court system and to ensure full implementation of the laws of the country.

Education

Educational goals shall be more effectively oriented to national objectives and will be employed to accelerate the pace of development. To the extent the resources of the Government allow, full effort will be made to extend to our people, academic, professional and vocational education on an equitable basis.

Economic and Social Development

Development Objectives

The economic and social development policy of the Government will be derived from the following long-term objectives:

Accelerating the Pace of Development

Although Ethiopia's human and natural resources are adequate to enable the country to attain prosperity in the long run, the country finds itself today in a state of severe underdevelopment. In order to meet the additional needs which an increasing population imposes, as well as to liberate our people from the clutches of poverty, the pace of development in every sector of the national economy will have to be stepped up considerably.

Closing the Wide Income Disparities

So as to enable a spirit of harmony, peace and co-operation to prevail in the Ethiopian nation, which we all regard as one large family, the Government will pursue a policy which will aim at reducing the wide disparities in standards of living.

Partnership between Government and People

As development is a national responsibility, calling for the full contribution of the people, the Government will endeavour to ensure that the people will take an active part in all development efforts.

Self Reliance

Despite the fact that Ethiopia requires assistance from friendly countries and international institutions, it is necessary that her development policies should aim at increasing self-reliance.

Land Reform

Land reform is one of the major instruments to achieve long-term economic and social development objectives set forth above.

In order to accelerate the pace of development and to raise the standard of living of the vast majority of the people, far-reaching and purposeful reforms in the land tenure system are required.

The traditional land tenure system has severely constrained agricultural productivity. In areas where tenancy prevails, deprived of adequate compensation, the tenant farmer does not have the incentive to produce adequately. In some other areas land holdings have become excessively fragmented and uneconomical as a result of successive inheritance. In

112

areas with a long history of settlement, the problem is one of deforestation, soil erosion, and in some instances, over population. The areas inhabited by nomads present yet another category of problems where land tenure and livestock development require special attention.

In order therefore to improve the condition of 90% of the population which is engaged in agriculture, appropriate actions will be taken to implement the following measures of land reform:

Distribution of Land

Recognising that it is only when the tenant farmer becomes the owner of his land that he acquires the necessary incentive to produce more and contribute to his full capacity to the development of his country the Government will initiate a policy of enabling the tenant farmer and those who may wish to derive their living by working on the land to acquire their own farms.

With that end in view, the Government will immediately undertake the following actions:

(i) Except for land designated for collective and public use, Government land grants will henceforth be made only to those who shall make their livelihood by working on the land.
(ii) Holdings in excess of what is considered to be reasonable limit of the owner's capacity to develop will be taken over by the Government and will be distributed to those who will make their living by working on the land. With due regard to relevant ecological conditions, maximum land holdings and the appropriate modalities for compensation will be determined by law.

Landlord–tenant Relationships

Recognising the need to regulate on an equitable basis the relationships between the tenant and landlord while the specific measures envisaged above are being implemented, a draft law, conforming the spirit and the purposes of the present policy statement, will be prepared and submitted to Parliament to replace or amend, as appropriate, existing legislation on landlord–tenant relationships.

113

Holdings

In areas where communal and individual land holding prevail (commonly referred to as Erest areas), the problem being one of excessive fragmentation into uneconomic units, soil erosion and lack of modern techniques of agricultural production, special measures will be undertaken with the view to increasing the farmer's productive capacity.

Nomadic Lands

In order to enable the nomadic population to benefit from and participate fully in all development activities, priority will be given to their interest when development projects are prepared and implemented.

Special effort will also be made to teach the nomadic population modern methods of animal husbandry and to introduce them to other agricultural activities.

Protection of Forests and Soil

Not realising that our forests help to protect our soils from being eroded by rain and wind, and our rivers and springs from drying up, our people have throughout the years denuded the country's forest resources in order to meet their daily requirements.

A programme of afforestation and soil protection will consequently be established as a matter of priority.

With a view to implementing the provision of Article 103 of the Revised Constitution, which stipulates that our forests are held in trust by the Government for succeeding generations, immediate steps will be taken to return to public ownership forest lands which have been given to individuals.

Mineral Resources

The Government undertakes to intensify prospecting for mineral resources, so as to realise fully the country's potential and to give impetus to its development.

Taxation

The tax system imposes on the people difficulties both with regard to its equitability and collection. As taxes are an important instrument for development, the Government undertakes to improve equitability by broadening the tax base to reach those who have the capacity to pay more and by making it more progressive and improving the system of collection.

Employment

In order to reduce unemployment and make labour a significant factor contributing to the country's development, the Government will pursue a policy which will increase employment in agriculture, commerce and industry. The Government will provide credit and other supporting services to those who may have the skills but lack capital and other facilities to be employed productively.

Price Control

A system of price control will be instituted in order to provide the people a steadily growing standard of living by ensuring that any rise in their incomes would not be adversely affected by rises in consumer prices. At the same time, due regard will be paid to the interest of producers so as to enable them to receive equitable returns for their efforts.

Recognising the role that marketing organisations play in stabilising consumer prices, the Government will undertake a thorough study and will create appropriate marketing organisations with the requisite means.

Public Health

Health plays an important role in improving the quality of life and the economic and social well-being of the people. With this in view, the Government will give priority to eradicating those diseases which are deeply rooted in ignorance and poverty.

Rural Development

In order to distribute the benefits of development equally, the Government will pursue a policy of reorienting development programmes in the fields of education, health, agriculture, etc., from urban to rural areas where the vast majority of the population resides and where the benefits of development have not yet reached. In addition, appropriate small- and medium-scale rural industries will be established.

To introduce new agricultural methods and to give the widest possible impact to the present 'Minimum Package Programme', the Government will assign priority to the construction of rural feeder roads.

Water Resources

To alleviate the present shortage of water for human consumption and agricultural uses, the Government will, in co-operation with the people, undertake a stepped-up programme of well drilling and water conservation in rural localities.

Settlement

Due to a history of long settlement, over-population and soil erosion, the land in certain areas of the country has become impoverished, and can no longer provide adequate yields to the farmers even for their subsistence. There is also wide unemployment and under-employment. In order thus to solve this complex problem the Government will undertake appropriate settlement schemes.

Popular Participation in Development

To benefit fully from ideas and plans emanating from the people, as well as from their direct contributions, the Government will give full encouragement to the people in order to enable them to participate in all phases of the development effort. To this end, the Government will undertake administrative reforms at the local level so as to share responsibility for development with the people directly concerned.

Self Reliance

If Ethiopia is to attain in the long run the development objectives set forth above, something more than a steadfast pursuit of those objectives is required. The creativity, the patriotism and the national consciousness of its people will have to be brought to bear on the entire development effort. The country will also have to depend more on its resources and relatively less on external assistance.

Foreign Capital

As has already been explained, development involves the participation and partnership of all. With this in view, the Government will encourage the participation in the country's development efforts of foreign investors, who, while seeking to benefit themselves, will also bring benefit to the country. The Government will endeavour to make sure that such investors are welcome by our people and that they will operate on the basis of mutual confidence.

Foreign Policy

The Government's foreign policy will be guided by the objectives of safeguarding Ethiopia's independence and territorial integrity, the strengthening of international peace and security, and the promotion of global co-operation in all fields of human endeavour. To these ends, the Government will give full support to the realisation of the objectives of the charters of the United Nations and the Organisation of African Unity.

The Government will strengthen relations and co-operation with all friendly countries. With African countries, in particular it will seek through the Organisation of African Unity, to consolidate further the unity of the brotherly African peoples and their common interest.

By reason of history, geography and economic conditions Ethiopia's interest and aspirations are intimately tied with those of the developing countries. In recognition of this, the Government, will actively participate in the councils of developing countries as well as in conferences of non-aligned countries in promoting the collective interests of developing countries.

To strengthen Ethiopia's desire to live in peace with all her neighbours, the Government will pursue an active policy of neighbourly co-operation in economic and trade matters, air, land and maritime communications. Ethiopia's boundaries having been fixed by international agreements, the Government will conduct its relations on the basis of recognition of these boundaries in accordance with the existing international agreements.

Conclusion

As members of the Council, we have in the foregoing seen fit to set forth the principles that will guide the actions of the Government. Notwithstanding the transitional nature of our responsibilities, we have felt that our commitments and convictions should be made a matter of public record and that they should guide our actions. We wish to express the conviction that the confidence, co-operation and support of our people

117

will be with us. It is incumbent on every Ethiopian that he approaches his daily tasks with a keen awareness of the implications of his actions so as not to allow the present difficulty to develop into a crisis. If an attitude of irresponsibility prevails, we might not only lose irretrievably the opportunity that this challenge presents, but we might find ourselves in a situation the consequence of which will be tragic. Such an outcome should be avoided at all costs, lest we find ourselves to be unequal to the legacy of honour, unity and independence that our great forefathers have handed to us.

Let us therefore work together in a new spirit for the everlasting unity, peace and prosperity of our people. Let us not allow time to overtake us, nor let the opportunity of the challenge slip from our hands. Let us not allow personal conveniences to weaken our resolve. Let the vision of our ultimate objective guide our actions. May the Almighty be always with us.' [27]

The above policy was conceived on the assumption of a continuation of a market economy and a reformed constitutional monarchy, where the chief executive of the government, the Prime Minister, would be accountable to a parliament. However, the enforcement of law and order sapped the energy and time of the cabinet that could have been used for the implementation of its policy. Moreover, a genuine support was not forthcoming from the Co-ordinating Committee, except empty pledges of support to the new cabinet.

The policy statement provided the basic tenets for the motto of *Ethiopia Tikdem* of 1 November 1974 which by this time was upgraded as a philosophy. Ideas such as putting the common interest above individual interests, equality of opportunities to all citizens irrespective of religion or sex, safeguarding the territorial integrity of the country and the unity of the nation, self-reliance, government and people partnership in development efforts, co-operation with other countries on the basis of mutual respect and equality, etc., were copied from the policy statement to *Ethiopia Tikdem.*

Co-ordinating Committee Steps up Arrests of Officials

Beginning on 29 June 1974, the Co-ordinating Committee of the Armed Forces, Police and the Territorial Army stepped up its arrest of officials of the central government including Enderassies (Governor-Generals), provincial administrators, judges and senior military and police officers. Arrests and detentions became the orders of the day. The Co-ordinating

Committee would simply announce, through the media, the list of names of those officials who were wanted for detention, ordering them to report within a specified time at a specified detention place. The announcement would warn that failure to report by the specified time at the specified place, would result in the confiscation of the properties of those who failed to turn themselves in. Many officials gave themselves up either by walking or driving to the headquarters of the Fourth Army Division. The only senior official who rejected the edict of the Co-ordinating Committee was Dejazmach Tsehayu Enqo Selassie, the Enderassie of Keffa. He remained at large for over two months at his birthplace, Merhabete, a province in Northern Shewa some two hundred kilometres farther to the north of the capital city. He was overpowered by a security force and killed while resisting arrest in the first week of September 1974.

In those awful days, awaiting for daily notice requiring to give oneself up to the authorities was an agonising ordeal to the wanted persons and their families. The lists of persons who gave themselves up, killed while resisting arrest and those who were wanted for detention were routinely published in the daily newspapers. The cabinet was regularly informed by the Co-ordinating Committee of the names and the number of officials who were detained. On one of the briefing sessions the cabinet was told that the widespread arrests were made to ensure the smooth running of its activities.

In tandem with the arrests, the Co-ordinating Committee submitted to the emperor the following fresh demands.[28]

1. That all political prisoners be granted amnesty by His Imperial Majesty, except those who had been charged with crimes against the unity of the country and welfare of the nation.
2. That all Ethiopians living in exile for various reasons be allowed to return home.
3. That the parliament should remain in session to consider the constitution under revision and
4. That the Armed Forces' committee be allowed to maintain contacts with officials of the government.

The emperor gave the following decisions[29] which were transmitted through the appropriate channel to the Co-ordinating Committee:

1. Political prisoners' cases be reviewed urgently with a view to granting them amnesty.
2. General amnesty be granted to all Ethiopians living in exile abroad.

3. Parliament be in session during its summer recess.
4. Permission to make direct contact with the government officials be granted to the Co-ordinating Committee.

The Co-ordinating Committee gradually began to take independent action in defining and popularising the motto of *Ethiopia Tikdem.* The principles embodied in the motto according to a press release issued by the Co-ordinating Committee on 9 July 1974, were:

1. To be loyal the Emperor;
2. To uphold the Crown of His Imperial Majesty;
3. To ensure the smooth-running of the cabinet by removing obstacles from within and outside the cabinet;
4. To strive for the rapid development and progress of Ethiopia;
5. To expedite the drafting of a constitution and ensure its implementation when adopted;
6. To improve laws governing conditions of work in the interest of industrial workers and farmers on the basis of equality;
7. To impress upon the people the dignity of labour and the value of hard work in a spirit of unity, equality and brotherhood among Ethiopians;
8. To maintain contact and co-operation with the new Council of Ministers;
9. To ensure the eradication of negative social practices and customs that hinder development and progress;
10. To modernise the existing provincial administration;
11. To appeal to the international community to step up its donation to victims of famine in the country;
12. To assure international tourists that the door is open to them to visit any part of Ethiopia without anxiety;
13. To appeal to all friendly countries to continue their development assistance and co-operation and reassure them that the military is committed to national development and progress;
14. To reassure the public that only those who had abused their official position and unlawfully enriched themselves with public funds and property would be arrested, others should have no fear of arrest and detention;
15. To achieve the military's objectives without any bloodshed.

The press release was prompted by the need to reassure domestic as well as the international audience that the military was for peaceful change, without any bloodshed. The military's pledge of loyalty to the emperor and its commitment to guarantee the continuation of the monarchy was intended to dispel rumours that the military was preparing itself for overthrowing the government and to assume full power for itself. Subsequent to the issuing of the press release a misleading modifier was added to the motto which read as *Aleminim Dem Ethiopia Tikdem* (without any bloodshedding let Ethiopia advance). With hindsight, one could be certain that the Co-ordinating Committee was in the business of engaging itself in deceptive and subtle means to prepare the ground for a complete military take-over of the government.

Formation of the Dergue

The behaviour of the commission prematurely provoked the Armed Forces to play a more active role in harnessing the political upheaval to their favour. To this end, the army formally constituted a Dergue, a Co-ordinating Committee of the Armed Forces, the Police and the Territorial Army, on 21 June 1974. At the founding meeting of the committee two protagonists. Majors Mengistu Haile Mariam of the Third Army Division and Atenafu Abate of the Fourth Army Division were elected as first and second chairmen respectively. Major Gebreyes Woldehanna who lost his life in an air accident in 1990 was elected as secretary of the committee. Upon the emergence of the Co-ordinating Committee of the Armed Forces, Police, and the Territorial Army which after deposition of the emperor was known under the Geez word Dergue (committee or council). Endalkatchew was left with no alternative other than to dissolve his High National Security Commission. The formation of the Co-ordinating Committee was a turning point in giving a sense of direction and purpose to the spontaneous uprising that was much in evidence since the beginning of February 1974.

The Co-ordinating Committee, which was seeking to have a say in the running of the government, requested the emperor to grant it permission to work in close collaboration with the new cabinet. The emperor who, due to advancing age, was being used as a rubber stamp by both the new Prime Minister and the Co-ordinating Committee, granted the request. Then the cabinet and the Co-ordinating Committee as a first step for their collaboration constituted a joint committee. This marriage of convenience between the cabinet and the Co-ordinating Committee soon proved to be a sham when the latter withdrew from the joint committee and began to assert itself by taking action independent of the government.

Even after the withdrawal of the Co-ordinating Committee, Endalkat-

121

chew was optimistic of developments and the course of events taking place in the country. Nothing more clearly demonstrates his cautious optimism than a statement made by him in a nationwide radio and television interview, on 17 June 1974, four days before the formation of the Co-ordinating Committee. In assessing the situation in the country from February to June of that year he commented:

'I should say that we are prisoners of law and order. We cannot get out of it. But the people are expecting too much. They say why has this or that not be done? The means employed to achieve it by way of peaceful demonstration or strike is rather confusing. However, I should say that we have come across some of the crucial problems. The country now is entering the stability stage. Some of the remnants of these problems are still prevalent. And when I say primarily what we can do and problems have been resolved I cannot fully say so. But I hope that things are assuming the right track and all will be well in time to come.'[30]

The optimism of the Prime Minister was shattered when the true intention of the Co-ordinating Committee revealed itself in July. The partnership with the new Cabinet and the Armed Forces' pledge of loyalty and support to the cabinet went asunder when the Co-ordinating Committee forced Endalkatchew to resign and arrested his minister of defence, Lieutenant-General Abiye Abebe. Subsequently Endalkatchew was replaced by Lij Michael Imru, the son of Ras Imru Haile Selassie, a cousin of the emperor who was held in high esteem for his liberal views by most Ethiopians and indeed by the Co-ordinating Committee as well. Ras Imru was the only aristocrat who was not detained by the Co-ordinating Committee and continued to enjoy the respect of the armed forces until his death from natural causes.

The Dergue Proposes a New Prime Minister

The Co-ordinating Committee, in the presence of His Majesty the Emperor, explaining the necessities of removal of Prime Minister Endalkatchew and the cabinet reshuffle observed:

'As his Excellency Lij Endalkatchew the out-going Prime Minister has sided with his former colleagues and close

relations, now under detention could not subscribe to the
views and objectives of the committee as outlined in the
motto (*Ethiopia Tikdem*). Further, he had been not only an
obstacle for a smooth transition but also had attempted to
create a division among the armed forces. The committee
therefore requests Your Imperial Majesty that Lij
Endalkatchew be relieved of his post.'[31]

The spokesman, continuing his submission to the emperor, explained
that the Co-ordinating Committee had contacted a number of persons
including Ato Hadis Alemayehu, a senator and an author of good repute,
but he declined to accept the post of the premiership. The spokesman
in proposing a new Prime Minister said: '*The Committee which firmly believes
that the administration of the country shoud be headed by a civilian, humbly
requests Your Imperial Majesty to appoint His Excellency Lij Michael Imru as the
next Prime Minister.*'[32] The emperor, who by this time had virtually lost his
power, and had no choice other than to acquiesce the request of the
Armed Forces.

Lij Michael Imru, the new Prime Minister, in his acceptance speech on
a nationwide address said that his government would concentrate its
efforts on narrowing the gap between the rich and the poor; retain
most of the members of Endalkatchew's cabinet; reinforce the Relief and
Rehabilitation Commission; call the nation to rally behind the reform
efforts; review the constitution that was being drafted and expedite its
submission to the emperor and subsequently to Parliament; work closely
with the Co-ordinating Committee of the Armed Forces, Police and the
Territorial Army.[33]

Persons with good reputation were promoted to high government posts
while incumbents were either pensioned or laid off without pay or
detained on the flimsiest of accusations, mostly at the instigation of the
Co-ordinating Committee.

As of 3 August 1974, the following was the List of Lij Michael Imru's
Cabinet:[34]

1. Lij Michael Imru, Prime Minister;
2. Dej. Zewde Gebre-Selassie, Deputy Prime Minister and Foreign
   Minister;
3. Lieutenant-General Aman Michael Andom, Defence Minister and
   Chief of Staff of the Armed Forces;
4. Ato Getatchew Bekele, Minister of Public Works and Water Resources
   Development;

5. Dej. Kebede Tessema, Minister of Imperial Palace;
6. Dej. Tesfa Yohannis Berhe, Minister of Mines;
7. Ato Tekle Tsadiq Mekuria, Minister of Education;
8. Ato Mellion Neqniq, Minister of National Community Development;
9. Ato Belete Gebre Tsadiq, Minister of Land Reform and Administration;
10. Ato Belatchew Asrat, Minister of Justice;
11. Ato Tekalgn Gedamu, Minister of Telecommunications and Posts;
12. Ato Mohammed Abdurhaman, Minister of Commerce and Industry;
13. Colonel Belatchew Jemaneh, Minister of Interior;
14. Ato Negash Desta, Minister of Finance;
15. Ato Berhanu Wakoya, Minister of Planning and Development;
16. Dr Jemal Abdurkadir, Minister of Public Health;
17. Dr Dagnatchew Yergu, Minister of Agriculture;
18. Fitawrari Demissie Teferra, Minister in the Prime Minister's Office.

The Co-ordinating Committee, after the removal of Prime Minister Endalkatchew, became more involved in the decision-making process of the government. Power gradually shifted from the crown and the cabinet to the Co-ordinating Committee. Endalkatchew, along with other high-ranking civilian and military officials, was arrested, thereby depriving the emperor of his most trusted retainers and close associates. The emperor was effectively isolated and was made easy prey to the Co-ordinating Committee's predatory instincts. On 2 August, the Co-ordinating Committee began in earnest its campaign of vilification against the emperor and his government.

A Campaign of Vilification Against the Emperor

Cases of corruption involving embezzlement and misappropriation of public funds and properties were continuously presented by the media and blown out of proportion and some of the charges were concocted to discredit the crown and the person of the emperor. The business interests of the emperor were cited as abuse of public property for his own private use. The St George Beer Factory and the General Transport Company were adduced as evidence to prove the emperor's unlawful enrichment with public funds and properties. In mid-August the Co-ordinating Committee probably felt it had done the groundwork in discrediting the emperor and his government began to take drastic actions. The institutions by which imperial will was expressed were dismantled. The first institution that faced the Co-ordinating Committee's onslaught was the Ministry of Pen, an institution that served as a private secretariat of the emperor. It was the most important institution by which imperial will was expressed and exercised. It was a very powerful institution for it issued imperial orders, decrees and edicts on matters ranging from granting of titles, awards, funds, land or any other state property, to make appointments in important and key posts of the empire. All letters of appointment to senior government posts that were not within the competence of the Civil Service were issued by the Ministry of Pen. The Ministry was brought under the control of the Co-ordinating Committee, thereby depriving the emperor of the means to take any action independently. Nevertheless, the Ministry of Pen, two days after it was controlled by the Co-ordinating Committee, was dissolved along with the Crown Council, a body consisting mainly of aristocrats and noted personalities to advise the crown, and the Chilot, a court of the highest order whereby the emperor alone dispensed justice in a manner he deemed fit. The Chilot, although it was outside the court system of the empire, reviewed decisions of the regular courts when an appeal was, more often than not, made by individuals. There was no limit to its jurisdiction. The dissolution of these institutions, under the pretext of administrative reform, was used as a feeler to detect the mood and reaction of the public. There was neither protest nor any other adverse reaction to the dissolution of those institutions. The indifference of the public to the act of undermining the crown encouraged the Co-ordinating Committee to go on in executing its plan to confiscate the properties of the emperor and other members of the royal family. Still the confiscation of royal properties did not provoke any reaction or disapproval from the public.

The successive steps taken by the Co-ordinating Committee whether designed or coincidental, were executed with caution. To recapitulate, the following is a sequence of the steps taken by the Co-ordinating Committee:

- abolished the High National Security Commission;
- created the Dergue, a Co-ordinating Committee, on 21 June 1974;
- arrested and detained ministers, other senior civilian and military officers;
- removed Prime Minister Endalkatchew;
- appointed a new Prime Minister and other cabinet ministers more amenable to carry out its wishes;
- made campaigns of vilification against the emperor, aristocrats and certain officials of the government;
- dissolved institutions whereby imperial will was expressed; and

– confiscated properties of the emperor, other members of the royal family and those who refused to give themselves up to the armed forces.

These logical steps led to the deposition of the emperor without much ado. However much the sequences of actions seem to be logical they were not results of a blueprint charted out well in advance by the Co-ordinating Committee. The steps taken by the Co-ordinating Committee were dictates of events and the general mood of the people for a change in the system of government. The Co-ordinating Committee deserves credit for its judicious and cautious execution of the dictates of events. The most popular phrase of the junta, '*the Dergue acts in response to the mood of the people*', aptly describes the Co-ordinating Committee's response to popular demands.

The Co-ordinating Committee, from the end of August until the overthrow of the emperor on 12 September 1974, stepped up its propaganda of vilification against the person of the emperor. His domestic business interests, particularly the St George Beer Factory and its subsidiary the Metta Abbo Beer Brewery, the General Transport Company and the Haile Selassie Prize Trust and real estates were cited repeatedly as examples of gross misappropriation of state property for his own private use. A statement issued by the Co-ordinating Committee disclosed that from the breweries the emperor received an annual dividend of more than 15 million Birr.[35] The statement further revealed that the royal properties were confiscated and put under a National Resources Development Company that was formed to administer expropriated properties. The statement went on to assert that the emperor hoarded billions of dollars that were robbed from the people in foreign banks. The statement added that the emperor refused to repatriate the money so that it could be used to alleviate the plight of the victims of famine. The statement concluded that the economic problem of the country was primarily due to the flight of capital caused by the emperor, the royal family and others who were in positions of power and influence. Under these circumstances, the people were told to tighten their belts and work hard to contain the economic crisis. The emperor's domestic business interests and deposits in foreign banks were exaggerated to justify his impending deposition. On the eve of the Ethiopian New Year, the Teachers' Association of Ethiopia at its general meeting passed a strongly worded resolution. The resolution condemned the emperor's refusal to repatriate the money he allegedly hoarded in foreign banks. The resolution further requested the

Co-ordinating Committee to court martial the emperor and arrest other members of the royal family.

The Dergue Deposes the Emperor and Assumes Power

The spread of malicious rumours against the emperor, the royal family and persons in high government office successfully eroded the myth that the monarchy was a symbol of Ethiopia's unity and tarnished the emperor's reputation in the eyes of people. The Co-ordinating Committee, after having systematically built up hostility against the emperor, issued Proclamation No. 1 of 1974 that deposed him. It was read to the emperor by Major Debella Dinsa, a member of the Co-ordinating Committee, on the Ethiopian New Year, 12 September 1974. The proclamation ended the reign of the 250th emperor of the Solomonic Dynasty.

The proclamation deposed the emperor, suspended the Revised Constitution of 1955, dissolved Parliament, established a Provisional Military Government, guaranteed continuation of a constitutional monarchy, recognised the succession of the Crown prince as the next king, promised a new constitution, prohibited the right to strike and stage demonstrations, declared any opposition to the philosophy of *Ethiopia Tikdem* illegal. It further enabled the Co-ordinating Committee to assume the power of the government. The Proclamation was tactfully drafted to convey a message that the Co-ordinating Committee was not against the monarchy as an institution but its mission was to relieve the people from the reign of a corrupt despot and government. Consistent with the committee's propaganda of vilification against the emperor the proclamation gave the following justifications for dethroning him:

'Although the people of Ethiopia have looked, in good faith, upon the crown as a symbol of their unity, Haile Selassie I, who has ruled the country for more than 50 years ever since he assumed power as a Crown Prince, has abused the authority, dignity and honours of office for the personal benefit and interest of himself, his immediate family and retainers. As a consequence he has led the country into its present inextricable situation. Moreover, as he has progressed in age, being 82 years old, he cannot shoulder the high responsibilites of his office.'[36]

The proclamation was carefully drawn-up to guarantee a smooth transfer of power from the emperor and his government to the military junta. It

127

brought to successful fruition a creeping coup. However, it failed to make a provision for a head of state for the interim period between the deposition of the emperor and the coronation of the Crown prince who was convalescing from a stroke in Switzerland. No one with a sane mind would have expected the Crown prince to return for his coronation to Ethiopia while his father, the emperor, the other members of the royal family including his daughter and under-age children of the royal family were indiscriminately imprisoned. If there was anyone to be put behind bars next to the emperor, the Crown prince would have been the undisputed victim. As the governor of the drought-stricken Governorate-General of Wollo where thousands of people died, he did absolutely nothing to come to the rescue of the victims of famine. Moreover, Wollo was one of the most maladministered Governorates-General of the empire. He had governed Wollo ever since his father became emperor of Ethiopia in 1930. During this long period or five development decades his contribution, if any, to improve the quality of life in his administration was irrelevant. The famine in Wollo was partly the result of mismanagement of the province. He made a wise decision in deferring his return to the country for his coronation. Fortunately the carrots of the Provisional Military Government of Ethiopia (PMG) failed to lure him into a trap.

The PMG, being certain that the Crown prince would not accept its invitation, issued Proclamation No. 2, 13 September 1974 that enabled the Co-ordinating Committee of the Armed Forces, Police and the Territorial Army to assume an acting head of state's role under a new designation, the Provisional Military Administrative Council (PMAC or Dergue). The Dergue remained as acting head of state until the monarchy was abolished by Proclamation No. 27, 17 March 1975.

Along with Proclamation No. 2 of 1974 the PMG issued directives instructing all officials of government, including those in the diplomatic service, to continue their normal duties in line with the philosophy of *Ethiopia Tikdem*. The PMG further declared its foreign policy and international obligations were based on the following principles that Ethiopia would

– be strictly non-aligned;
– adhere to the charters of the United Nations and the Organisation of African Unity and would respect all international obligations on the basis of mutual respect and equality;
– do everything in its power to help people in colonial territories in the world in general and Africa in particular, to gain their independence;

128

– maintain and further strengthen existing friendly ties with all friendly governments in the world; particularly the African countries and especially maintain friendly relations with the Sudan and Egypt – the two countries that benefit from the River Nile and also maintain the friendly ties with Ethiopia's close neighbours, Kenya and Somalia.

The foreign policy of the PMG was identical with the emperor's foreign policy. It was a sign of wisdom on the part of the PMG to endorse the foreign policy of the defunct government whose judicious execution had earned political dividends to the country.

Along with the declaration of both domestic and foreign policies of the PMG, a cabinet reshuffle was made. In the fresh redistribution of cabinet portfolios the Defence Minister and Chief of Staff of the Armed Forces, Lieutenant-General Aman Michael Andom, was appointed as chairman of the Provisional Military Administrative Council (Dergue) and the Council of Ministers retaining his former posts. The Prime Minister, Lij Michael Imru was appointed as Minister of Information and subsequently was transferred to the Office of the Chairman of the Council of Ministers as a political adviser. Dej. Zewde Gebre-Selassie, when the post of deputy Prime Minister was abolished, retained his post as Foreign Minister. The cabinet reshuffle, except the Prime Minister and Deputy Prime Minister, did not affect other members of Lij Michael's cabinet.

With changes in the structure of government effected, the PMG announced its objectives. The objectives were nothing other than redefining the philosophy of *Ethiopia Tikdem* considering recent political developments that brought the Dergue to the helm of political power. The objectives[37] as of 12 September were:

1. To ensure equality among Ethiopians;
2. To abolish divisions along the lines of tribal or religious affiliations;
3. To remove traditional beliefs and administrative practices that hinder development and national unity;
4. To reform the judiciary;
5. To launch a national health campaign;
6. To decree a land reform legislation;
7. To launch a national literacy campaign and to provide free education to all Ethiopians;
8. To safeguard the fundamental rights of Ethiopians;
9. To cleanse the society from immoral practices;
10. To promote feelings of nationalism and patriotism;

11. To inculcate in the people that mutual trust, good faith, co-operation and equality are the prerequisites for unity and progress;
12. To promote the dignity of labour;
13. To encourage the expansion of indigenous industries and the promotion of local products;
14. To preserve and protect the cultural heritage of the country;
15. To issue a broad national policy for development.

Public Support for the Dergue

The measures taken by the Co-ordinating Committee had massive support. The support from the people was genuine. The downtrodden people of Ethiopia saw a ray of hope towards a brighter future in the military take-over. Popular demonstrations following the deposition of the emperor, in most cases, were spontaneous. On the other hand the support given and messages of congratulations to the Co-ordinating Committee from organised sectors were opportunistic gestures. The first organised body that welcomed the deposition of the emperor was the Teachers' Association of Ethiopia (TAE) that had a long-drawn-out dispute on salaries and other benefits with the government. The support of TAE was a forgone conclusion since it had urged the deposition of the emperor and arrest of the members of the royal family, even before his deposition.

Another organisation that was quick in giving its support was the Patriotic Association. It accused the emperor of cowardice at the time of the Italian invasion for fleeing into exile. It claimed that he was unfit to govern the people of Ethiopia and his deposition was long overdue.[38]

The Ethiopian Orthodox Church was not an indifferent spectator either. His Holiness the Patriarch of the Ethiopian Orthodox Church in a written message expressed his full support to the PMG and congratulated it for its accomplishments.[39] The most baffling thing was the support of the Church. The Church, which had enjoyed a privileged status since the introduction of Christianity to Ethiopia, had the audacity to join others in sending hypocritical messages of congratulation. Emperors of Ethiopia, including Emperor Haile Selassie, had been very generous to the Church. In fact, it was the generosity and support of the monarchs of Ethiopia that helped in facilitating the evangelisation of the country. Particularly Emperor Haile Selassie had, where others before him failed, succeeded to make the Church autocephalous. It was because of his strong faith that he liberated the Church from centuries of Egyptian religious domination. On this count alone the Church, in his hour of sadness, at least, should have given him spiritual and moral support instead of attempting to win the favour of the new regime. The Church as a religious institution should have remained neutral.

The Moslem community in the capital also expressed its appreciation by sending a deputation to the Chairman of the Dergue. The Imam of the Grand Mosque, speaking on behalf of the Ethiopian Moslems, said that Ethiopian Moslems all over Ethiopia were delighted with the peaceful change and that the Moslem Community fully supported the action taken by the PMAC and its objectives.[40]

Provincial governors and other heads of government institutions followed suit by declaring their support for the Dergue, and their readiness to implement its objective.[41]

The University Teachers' Association and the Ethiopian Students' Union did not send messages of support or express opposition as the Confederation of Ethiopian Labour Unions (CELU) did. CELU outrightly opposed the military take-over on the grounds that it would lead to a military dictatorship. It further made its stance clear by demanding that the military junta should hand over power to a civilian provisional government. To rally support for its resistance to the military's sinister design to assume power permanently, it distributed leaflets. The opposition of CELU to a military government was a major factor leading to the deterioration of the already strained relations between the military junta and CELU. The PMG, in its desperate damage limitation exercise, issued a statement labelling the leaders of CELU as agents of imperialism and partners of the defunct government and appealed to the rank and file of the membership to elect new leaders to replace the agents of imperialism.[42] The stern action against the leadership prompted two members of CELU, the Franco-Ethiopian Railway Workers' Union and the Metehara Plantation Workers' Union to dissociate themselves from CELU's opposition to a military government. The unions went to the extent of condemning CELU's stance and pledged themselves to co-operate with the PMG.

National Advisory Shengo

To defuse the rumour that the military was not prepared to hand over power to a civilian government and to win the support of the people, the PMG created a Shengo (National Advisory Committee) whose members were civilians. The members were drawn from institutions by election. The fifty-two seats in the Shengo were distributed in the following manner:

131

- Sixteen members representing government institutions mainly in Addis Ababa;
- Fourteen members one from each of the 14 Tekliagizat (Governorates-General);
- Two members from religious institutions representing Christians and Moslems;
- Three members from the Confederation of Ethiopian Labour Unions;
- Two members from the University Teachers' Association;
- Two members from the Ethiopian Teachers' Association;
- Two members from the farmers' co-operatives of Chillalo Agricultural Development Unit (CADU);
- Two members from Wollamo Agricultural Development Unit (WADU);
- One member from the Central Statistical Office;
- One member from the Institute of Public Administration;
- One member from the Central Personnel Agency;
- One member from the Pension Commission;
- One member from the Office of the Auditor-General.

The membership of the Shengo was reasonably representative of a wide cross-section of the community. The omission of the business community, with hindsight would seem to have been deliberate.

The Shengo was an advisory body to the military government. Its major functions were to recommend:[43]

- guidelines for the Ethiopian people to choose the type of government they want;
- a draft constitution in line with the philosophy of *Ethiopia Tikdem* and
- a reform, based on studies, of the political, economic and social system of the country.

The Shengo considered bills and proposals from government departments and submitted its recommendations to the Dergue. It acted as a parliament without power to legislate. Its presence was an immense political support to the Dergue and its policies. The members of the Shengo and their constituents identified themselves with the Dergue. The association with the Dergue gave them a sense of participation in shaping the destiny of the country. After a short period of political honeymoon with the Dergue, the members realised that the Shengo did not go far enough to provide popular participation in the affairs of state.

Opposition to the Rule of the Dergue

The labour unions intensified strikes and other work stoppages under various pretexts that were accompanied more often than not, with violence against employers and the officers of the Department of Labour. Abuses and assaults on government officers, employers and or their representatives were carried out in the presence of police officers who turned a blind eye to the excesses of violent workers. The attitude of the police officers was in accord with the prevailing mood of the Dergue to condone, in some instances workers' excesses. Advice of the Department of Labour offered to the Dergue on discouraging workers from resorting to strikes that were accompanied by violence was ignored. The Social Committee of the Dergue, responsible for labour relations, was of the opinion that workers should be allowed to ventilate their pent-up emotions built up by exploitation and neglect. By the time the Dergue took over government in early September 1974, the industrial relations of the country were undermined to a point of no return. Involving labour unions in the Shengo did not help in reversing the deterioration of industrial relations. The Dergue realised that other corrective measures had to be taken. The workers were disillusioned by the Dergue's campaign for popularity and stepped up industrial unrest even after the Dergue's take-over of government. Eventually the Dergue was compelled to take drastic steps in prohibiting strikes and demonstrations, and imposing a curfew. Despite draconian measures taken by the Dergue to contain strikes, demonstrations and other disturbances, lawlessness continued unabated. The Dergue resorted to force in breaking up demonstrations and strikes. As a result many lives were lost and several people seriously hurt. The use of excessive force by the Dergue led to a further deterioration of its relations with unions particularly with CELU.

CELU, that did not come to terms with the rule of the Dergue, called an extraordinary meeting of its members convened from 15–17 September 1974. The meeting passed a resolution demanding the stepping down of the Dergue and its replacement by a representative civilian provisional government and the reinstatement of the right to strike and demonstrate, freedom of expression and other basic rights. The resolution brought the Dergue and CELU into confrontation. The Dergue ordered CELU to withdraw its resolution or face the consequences of failing to comply with the order. CELU defiantly refused to retract its resolution, thereby provoking the Dergue to arrest and detain its President, Beyene Solomon, Vice-President Gideye Gebre, and Secretary-General Fiseha Tsion Teke. CELU retaliated by calling a general strike to take place on 25 September 1974. The Dergue frantically lobbied the members of CELU and in some cases resorted to intimidation of union leaders which resulted in the fizzling out of the threat of a general strike. The struggle between the Dergue and CELU, the former with all resources and the military might of the state, the latter with only the good will of its impoverished members, was naturally resolved in favour of the Dergue. From that time on the labour unions remained subservient to the Dergue.

Subduing CELU did not mark the end to the Dergue's opposition. University students, who were nightmares to the *ancien régime*, were not prepared to accept a military dictatorship. The University Students' Union at its meeting from 15–18 September 1974 endorsed CELU's resolution. Moreover it rejected the Dergue's decision to send all university students, teachers and senior secondary school pupils to the countryside to propagate the philosophy of *Ethiopia Tikdem* under a National Campaign for Development Through Co-operation. After the meeting the students staged an unauthorised demonstration. Fortunately, the Dergue restrained its security forces from taking action to disperse the demonstrators and the demonstration was over without any unpleasant incident. However, the students adamantly continued to confront the Dergue by staging another unauthorised demonstration on 11 October 1974. This time the students of the Almaya Agricultural College in Harargie Governorate-General joined the demonstration. Demonstrations particularly in the capital were violent, and the security men used force to disperse the demonstrators, resulting in several arrests.

Underground leftist organisations expressed their resentment and opposition to the Dergue in clandestine leaflets that advocated replacing the Dergue by a provisional people's government. The demand for such a government was advanced mainly by a clandestine underground leftist organisation, the Ethiopian People's Revolutionary Party (EPRP) that had to a considerable extent infiltrated students', teachers' and workers' organisations. The University Students' Union and CELU's adoption at their meetings, the popular slogan of the EPRP, 'People's Provisional Government', was a fairly reasonable indication to the extent of its influence on them.

Opposition to the Dergue's rule was not limited to underground movements, students' and workers' organisations. Within the armed forces, opposition to the Dergue was also building up. Certain units of the Imperial Body Guard, the Army Aviation and Army Engineering mutinied. The Dergue brutally crushed the mutiny, thereby ending dissension and splits within the armed forces. The ring leaders who survived the storming of their camps were arrested and the Imperial Body Guard was absorbed in the Ground Force and many of its officers and men were dispatched to garrison the port of Aseb, on the Red Sea coast.

Ethiopia Tikdem *Redefined*

The Dergue was on one side, frantically taking measures to suppress civilian as well as military opposition. On the other hand it was mounting a systematic propaganda against the *ancien régime* and bracing itself for a take-over of government. Parallel to the policy of the civilian government, it was engaged in developing a policy framework of its own. Its policy began as a slogan, *Ethiopia Tikdem,* and then gradually redefined and upgraded it to a philosophy on 10 July 1974. After the deposition of the emperor, in September, a need for redefining and elaborating the philosophy of *Ethiopia Tikdem* arose. As would be expected, components such as loyalty to the emperor and the crown were dropped from the meaning of *Ethiopia Tikdem.* The most substantive and coherent definition of the philosophy of *Ethiopia Tikdem* was one issued on 1 November 1974. The basic principles enunciated in the philosophy were:

'When we say *Ethiopia Tikdem,* we mean that the interest of the many must be given precedence over the interest of the few.
    When we say *Ethiopia Tikdem,* we mean Ethiopians given equal opportunity for progress linked with the world community and particularly with neighbouring countries in brotherhood and mutual respect work for the common good while ensuring their freedom by being vigilant to strike back at aggressors.
    When we say *Ethiopia Tikdem,* we mean Ethiopians of all ethnic affiliations share and share alike the fruits of universal education so that they will be able to work together and benefit in common.
    When we say *Ethiopia Tikdem,* we mean for Ethiopians to be able to work together and benefit together, every citizen should have an equal privilege to medical and health care in order to enhance physical and mental well-being.
    When we say *Ethiopia Tikdem,* we mean let us move ahead by supplanting moral degeneration by moral rejuvenation.
    When we say *Ethiopia Tikdem* we mean a government of the people, by the people, for the people.

135

> *Ethiopia Tikdem* means that justice should be done to all fairly.
>
> *Ethiopia Tikdem* means that transportation, which acts as the basis of the nation's developmental process should be set up so as to serve the entire needs of the country.
>
> *Ethiopia Tikdem* means that both rural and urban areas should abide by the principle of interdependence, realising each other's strong and weak points so as to initiate an overall development of the country.
>
> *Ethiopia Tikdem* means that land, which is the common home and property of all the living, should be placed under control so that the whole Ethiopian population can exploit it for the common use.
>
> *Ethiopia Tikdem* means developing awareness of the values of our cultural heritages, line them up, protect and preserve them for posterity.'[44]

From the elaboration on the meaning of *Ethiopia Tikdem* one would notice the influence of the tenets of the French Revolution, equality, freedom and brotherhood; the human rights declaration of the United Nations that all are born free and equal. The philosophy of *Ethiopia Tikdem* was a declaration of universal ideas and as such fell short of being a political and socio-economic development programme of the government. At the time of its declaration, the Co-ordinatinating Committee was in desperate search for an idea that was appealing and non-controversial as well. From this point of view, the slogan *Ethiopia Tikdem* was a good choice. It had created a favourable impression on the people. The flexibility of the motto was another useful dimension. It meant different things at different times to different people, even to the Dergue. The Dergue defined, redefined and further elaborated it to accommodate the circumstances of the time. In July it was conceived as a motto, in August it was upgraded to a philosophy, in September it was christened as Ethiopian Socialism, and finally when the Dergue became the ideological freak of the leftist organisations, it became lost in the sea of scientific socialism.

After the take-over of the government, the military junta's priority was to explain to the people the philosophy of *Ethiopia Tikdem* rather than formulating development policies. The primary task of the chairman of the Dergue, Lieutenant-General Aman Michael Andom, was to address employees of government institutions and public rallies. His effort was supplemented by other members of the Dergue who travelled across the length and breadth of the empire to explain the philosophy and role of the military in the transformation of the political situation in the country. The public addresses of the chairman were widely publicised. He was provided with ample opportunities to address government employees, trade union members, units of the Armed Forces in and around the capital, Eritrea and Harargie; and visited drought-stricken regions of the Ogaden. His addresses and visits were well received by the people and the army. He made two trips to Eritrea, once as defence minister and second time as chairman of the Dergue. The first trip lasted over ten days from the end of August to the first half of September. He inspected military units, met and exchanged views on the problems in Eritrea with elders in Asmara, Keren, Adi Keyih, Mandeferra and Massawa. Upon his return to the capital he gave an extensive press interview on his tour and his initial recommendation for peacefully resolving the conflict. His recommendations[45] to the government were:

1. To reform the system of administration.
2. To remove all obstacles that impeded social progress.
3. To reform the judiciary system and abolish any unlawful investigations which were carried out in the past.
4. To discuss ways for quick amnesty of political prisoners.
5. To allow the return of exiles and make arrangement for their settlement.
6. To seek ways that would enable students and others to go abroad freely.
7. To promote foreign investment with a view to expand the economy of Eritrea and create employment opportunities for the people.
8. To facilitate the reopening of industrial establishments which had interrupted their operations due to problems in Eritrea and implement all those pending economic development projects.

From his field trip the general was convinced that administrative and judicial reforms supported with economic development and employment opportunities would create a conducive climate for the peaceful resolution of the conflict. The rebels, who were demanding independence, failed to consider his recommendations to avail themselves of the new opportunity created by the political transformation in the entire country. On the second leg of his tour in Eritrea, he addressed a huge public rally in Asmara. On his address he appealed to the Eritrean people not to squander the opportunity for peace that was created by the change in Ethiopia. He stressed the military government's commitment to the unity of Ethiopia and to create a conducive situation for the development of a democratic form of government. He authorised the elders to convey to the rebels the positive disposition of government to settle amicably the conflict in Eritrea. His effort was not reciprocated by the rebels.

Competition for Leadership of the Dergue

The frequent tours and public addresses of the general portrayed him as an undisputed popular leader of the change that was in the making – a development which was loathed by other aspirants for leadership, particularly the First Vice-Chairman of the Dergue, Major Mengistu Haile Mariam. The members of the Dergue who felt threatened by the popularity of the general were engaged in conspiratorial intrigues which led to the deterioration of normal working relationships between the chairman and the members of the Dergue. By mid-November the general confined himself in his home, thus giving an excuse for his enemies to demand his dismissal from the chairmanship of the Dergue.

During the general's absence from office, Major Mengistu Haile Mariam, until then an unknown quantity, made himself public by addressing units of the Armed Forces, Police and the Territorial Army in and around the capital, starting on 16 November 1974. His speeches mainly concentrated on explanations of the meaning of the philosophy of *Ethiopia Tikdem*, the achievements of the Dergue in preparing the people for a change, and its unsuccessful attempt to resolve the problem in Eritrea by peaceful means due to the intransigence of the rebels. His address to the Armed Forces and the Police Force was an exercise in public relations in introducing himself as a potential leader of the Dergue. His public appearance was a step taken to brace himself for the leadership of the Dergue by overthrowing the incumbent chairman.

Four days after Mengistu's first public appearance, the Dergue issued a statement on the dismissal of Lieutenant-General Aman Michael Andom from the chairmanship of the Dergue, on 23 November. The following is a summary of the reasons[46] for his dismissal:

1. Showing the tendency of a dictatorial leader in his action.
2. Failing to inform the Council of important decisions affecting the general welfare of the country, especially the set-up of its defence; taking unilateral action in engaging the service of a foreign military adviser.
3. Abusing his authority by failing to attend meetings of the Council.
4. Refusing to relinquish the post he had held concurrently – Chief of Staff and Defence Minister.

5. Making unattainable promises to the Armed Forces in advancing his own popularity.
6. Attempting to sow the seeds of discord between the Armed Forces and the Council by trying to communicate secretly with different units of the Armed Forces.
7. Refusing to explain the actions he had taken to the Council.

The charges against the general were dubbed acts of conspiracy to take over power from the Dergue. As it was customary with the Dergue to issue amendments to or elaborations on previously made statements, a polished version of the charges against the general was given after he was killed in a shoot-out resisting arrest on 27 November 1975. The revised charges[47] were:

1. Working against the philosophy of *Ethiopia Tikdem* by making unilateral decisions contrary to the popular movement.
2. Plotting against the popular movement of the people and the Armed Forces and trying to undermine it in order to consolidate his power in collaboration with his few accomplices, thus breaking the oath of office he took to alleviate the plight of the subjugated masses.
3. Attempting to create division between the rearguards of the Armed Forces and the members of the Council.
4. Trying to divide members of the Council.
5. Absenting himself from his office for eight days.

The revised charges, although identical in content to the previous charges, put emphasis on acts of conspiracy to reverse the movement and to usurp power from the Dergue. Reading between the lines one notices that the general had made headway in marshalling sufficient support from the Armed Forces to pose as a threat to the Dergue. The Dergue's statement which stated that the general had become a security risk confirms the extent of the general's influence in the Armed Forces. The difference between the Dergue and the general was nothing other than a struggle for power. A difference over major policy issues as the unity of the country, particularly the handling of the problem in Eritrea, were not mentioned in the charges other than the vague accusation that the general acted contrary to *Ethiopia Tikdem*. Moreover General Aman's speech when he visited Eritrea shows that he fully subscribed to the philosophy of *Ethiopia Tikdem*. He said; *'Few individuals, some sections of the society or tribal groups will not decide the future of Ethiopia. The unity of Ethiopia is sacred.'*[48] The unity of Ethiopia was one of the cardinal points in the philosophy of *Ethiopia Tikdem* that the general unequivocally declared. Besides his record on the unity of the country had withstood the test of time. He proved himself as commander of the Third Division when Somalia attempted to invade Ethiopia in the early sixties. It was under his able leadership that the invading army of Somalia was defeated and humiliated. On the status of Eritrea he observed: *'The unity of Ethiopia and Eritrea is eternal'*[49]. As certain quarters assume the difference among General Aman and certain members of the Dergue, usually referred to as radicals, was neither on the resolution of the problem in Eritrea nor maintaining the unity of the country. The struggle was purely motivated by a desire of some members of the Dergue to assume power. The goals of those power-hungry individuals within the Dergue were to get rid of a chairman who had shown an immense capacity of leadership contrary to the expectations of those elements within the Dergue who wanted a puppet chairman. The Dergue had made a wrong choice in electing the general, for he was not the sort of person who would have fitted that role. The general was tremendously assertive and was not the type of officer who would entertain any order from junior and non-commissioned officers. Besides holding concurrently four key posts – Chief of Staff of the Armed Forces, Minister of Defence, Chairman of the Council of Ministers and Chairman of the Provisional Military Administration Council (PMAC or Dergue) made him extremely powerful. The power and influence he enjoyed from these very important offices added to his assertiveness, independence of mind and confidence in making independent decisions, shattered the Dergue's hope for a puppet leader. General Aman was a formidable and charismatic leader. Had time been on his side he probably could have changed the course of the Ethiopian Revolution. Unfortunately, after three and a half months of dynamic leadership he was prematurely killed in a shoot-out with the Dergue's security guards.

Another version of his demise was that he committed suicide when he had run out of ammunition. This version seems to be quite plausible and compatible with the personality of General Aman. He, being an officer with self-confidence and an air of arrogance, would have opted to end his life at his own hand rather than surrender to junior and non-commissioned officers who disregarded the cardinal principles of an army – discipline and respect for a chain of command, principles which the general cherished dearly. In underscoring these principles at a commissioning ceremony at the Harar Military Academy he said: *'However mighty an army be, its structure just and scientific, its weaponry up to date, it nevertheless can be defeated, as history attests, if it lacks discipline and orderly chain of command.'*[50]

On the day General Aman was killed the Dergue executed two Dergue members and fifty-seven former officials including a grandson of the emperor, and two ex-prime ministers. The statement issued after the execution of the officials, gave this explanation:

> 'The Council (Dergue) also found it necessary to execute
> former civilian and military officials on whose account
> repeated plots have been made that might engulf the country
> into a blood bath. This decision was imperative to save the
> lives of innocent people that had suffered for so long in
> the past. Hence the Council ordered the execution of those
> found guilty of maladministration, hindering fair
> administration of justice, selling secret documents of the
> country to foreign agents and attempting to disrupt the
> present Ethiopian popular movement.'[51]

The Dergue by summarily executing those accused of administrative and judicial malpractices broke its promise to the people for a fair trial by a court, after a thorough investigation by the Inquiry Commission had been conducted. The Dergue's execution of the officials was a heinous crime committed in a state of desperation. Contrary to the justification given for the execution of the officials, their guilt was not established by the Inquiry Commission that was by law empowered to make a thorough investigation into the alleged administrative and judicial malpractices of the officials. The summary execution of the accused was carried out while the Inquiry Commission was conducting its investigation. Moreover, none of the officials had a power-base that would, as alleged, plunge the country into a civil war. The Dergue's act of desperation was a response to General Aman's growing popularity and influence in the army. The only dividend that the Dergue gained from the summary execution was creation of a deeper bond among its members for having soaked their hands in the blood of sixty souls.

To portray a semblance of a thorough investigation and fair trial the crimes of the victims were presented to the people in four categories consisting of gross abuse of authority, plots to incite civil war, breach of oath of office, and attempts to create divisions among the various units of the armed forces. The absence of any distinction between categories one and two, for instance, reveals the arbitrariness of the classification. The names[52] of the sixty officials were listed in four categories as follows:

141

Category One: Gross Abuse of Power

1. Tsafe Taezaz Aklilu HabteWolde (Prime Minister)
2. H. H. Ras Asrate Kassa (Crown Councillor)
3. Lij Endalkatchew Mekonnen (Prime Minister)
4. Ras Mesfin Seleshi (Enderassie)
5. Lieutenant-Cololonel Tamirat Yegezu (Enderassie)
6. Ato Akale Work HabteWolde (Minister)
7. Dr Tesfaye Gebre-Egzy (Minister)
8. Ato Mulatu Debebe (Minister)
9. Ato Abebe Retta (Minister)
10. Dej. Solomon Abraha (Enderassie)
11. Dej. Legessie Bezu (Enderassie)
12. Dej. Sahlu Defaye (Enderassie)
13. Dej. Worku Wolde Amanuel (Enderassie)
14. Dej. Kifle Ergetu (Senator)
15. Dej. Worku Enqu Selassie (Enderassie)
16. Dej. Amero Abebe (Enderassie)
17. Dej. Kebede Ali (Enderassie)

Category Two: Gross Abuse of Authority

18. Colonel Solomon Kedir (Chief of Security)
19. Afenigus Abeji Debalke (Judge)
20. At Yilma Aboye (Courtier)
21. Ato Tegegn Yetesha-Work (Vice Minister)
22. Ato Solomon Gebre Mariam (Vice Minister)
23. Ato Hailu Teklu
24. Lij Hailu Desta (an official of the Ethiopian Red Cross Society)
25. Beleta Admassu Retta (Courtier)
26. Fit. Demissie Alamerew (Awraja Governor)
27. Fit. Amede Aberra (Awraja Governor)
28. Fit. Taddesse Enqu Selassie (Awraja Governor)
29. Lieutenant-General Abiye Abebe (Minister)
30. Lieutenant-General Kebede Gebre (Minister)
31. Lieutenant-General Dressie Dubale (Commander, Ground Force)
32. Lieutenant-General Abebe Gemeda (Commander, Imperial Body Guard)
33. Lieutenant-General Yilma Shebeshi (Police Commissioner)
34. Lieutenant-General Haile Bykedagn (Commander, Ground Force)
35. Lieutenant-General Assefa Ayene (Minister)
36. Lieutenant-General Belete Abebe

37. Lieutenant-General Isayas Gebre Selassie (Senator)
38. Lieutenant-General Assefa Demissie (Aide-de-camp of the emperor)
39. Lieutenant-General Debebe Haile Mariam (Enderassie)
40. Major-General Seyoum Gedle Giorgis
41. Major-General Gashaw Kebede
42. Major-General Tafesse Lemma
43. Rear Admiral Iskinder Desta (Commander of the Navy and grandson of the emperor)
44. Major-General Mulugetta Wolde Yohannis
45. Brigadier-General Wondimu Abebe
46. Brigadier-General Girma Yohannis
47. Colonel Yalem-Zewde Tessema
48. Colonel Tassew Mojo
49. Colonel Yegezu Yimer
50. Major Berhanu Metcha
51. Captain Molla Wakene
52. Ato Nebiye-Luel Kifle (Security Chief)

Category Three: Plotting to Incite Civil War and Disrupting the Popular Movement

53. Captain Demissie Sheferaw
54. Captain Belaye Tsegaye
55. Captain Wolde Yohannis Zergaw
56. Lance Corporal Tekle Haile
57. Private Bekele Wolde Giorgis

Category Four: Breach of Military Oath and Attempt to Create Division Among the Different Units of The Armed Forces

58. Lieutenant-General Aman Michael Andom (Chairman of the Dergue and Council of Ministers, Defence Minister and Chief of Staff of the Armed Forces)
59. Lieutenant Tesfaye Tekele (Dergue Member)
60. Junior Aircraftman Yohannis Fitiwi (Dergue Member)

The news of the execution of fifty-eight government officials and two members of the Dergue was announced in the early radio programme on Sunday 24 November 1974. The official statement which was entitled 'A Major Political Decision', was read by the well-known news presenter, Assefa Yergu. Till this day there are individuals who shiver when they hear his voice. The tragic news of mass-execution caught the nation by surprise. No rational soul was prepared to condone such a flagrant viola-

143

tion of a basic human right. The public was too dumbfounded to react either for or against the execution. However, the astounding silence and depressed mood of the people was a sign of disapproval of the unwarranted waste of human lives. Many people demonstrated their disgust and deep sense of shock by mourning for the victims with the bereaved families. The summary execution of the sixty officials was the most damaging political blunder of the Dergue that discredited it both at home and abroad. In the domestic scene the enthusiasm to support the Dergue and its policies waned and even instigated pockets of armed resistance. The international community was equally shocked by the tragic news of the execution. The United Nations' Secretary-General expressed in writing the concern of his organisation for the safety of the remaining officials under detention, to the new chairman of the Dergue, General Teferri Bente. The Dergue's chairman responded by giving the Dergue's assurance that the remaining prisoners would be given a fair trial by a court of law. The execution also put the Dergue at loggerheads with the Carter Administration which resulted in serious deterioration of relations between the United States and Ethiopia. The United States Government ceased to be the major development partner of Ethiopia while participating in humanitarian assistance only. The other Western democracies followed in the footsteps of the United States. Thus the PMAC was domestically discredited and internationally isolated, except in the socialist bloc. The summary execution of the officials was a turning-point in the domestic and foreign policies of the country. All platitudes and promises for peaceful change 'without letting any blood let Ethiopia advance' was conveniently replaced by the slogan 'a revolution devours its children'.

NOTES

1 Education Sector Review Report, Ministry of Education, Addis Ababa, 1974, p. 51.
2 ibid., p. 25.
3 ibid., p. 26.
4 ibid., p. 6.
5 ibid., p. 13.
6 *The Ethiopian Herald*, vol. xxx, No. 967, Addis Ababa, 24 February 1974.
7 *The Ethiopian Herald*, vol. xxx, No. 968, Addis Ababa, 26 February 1974.
8 ibid.,
9 *The Ethiopian Herald*, vol. xxx, No. 1139, Addis Ababa, 22 September 1974.

10 ibid., No. 971, 1 March 1974.

11 ibid., No. 972, 2 March 1974.

12 ibid., No. 979, 15 March 1974. The list shows the cabinet ministers as of 15 March 1974. It should be noted that up to the resignation of Lij Endalkatchew in July of that year a number of cabinet changes had taken place. For instance Lij Michael Imru and Ato Mohammed Abdurhaman had swapped posts. Ato Bulcha Demekssa and Dr Minassie Haile had resigned. Lieutenant-General Assefa Ayene, after the Armed Forces charged him with corruption, was forced to resign from the cabinet and eventually was arrested by the Co-ordinating Committee of the Armed Forces, Police and the Territorial Army.

13 ibid., No. 976, 12 March 1974.

14 ibid., No. 1003, 12 April 1974.

15 ibid., No. 1003, 12 April 1974.

16 ibid., No. 1074, 26 April 1974.

17 ibid., No. 991, 29 March 1974.

18 ibid., No. 1078, 10 July 1974; No. 1080, 12 July 1974; No. 1083, 16 July 1974; No. 1104, 20 August 1974. The members 1–6 were chosen by the Chamber of Deputies; out of the six members Ato Zenbe Haile, Ethiopia's Ambassador to Senegal, declined to accept the membership to the Commission and was replaced by Ato Baro Tumsa an employee of the Ministry of Commerce and Industry. Baro Tumsa was also a leader of one of the leftist political organisations known under the Amharic acronym, ECHAT.

19 *The Ethiopian Herald*, vol. xxx, No. 1085, 18 July 1974.

20 ibid.

21 ibid.

22 ibid., No. 1086, 20 July, 1974.

23 ibid., No. 974, 6 March 1974.

24 ibid., No. 984, 21 March 1974.

25 ibid., No. 994, 2 April 1974.

26 ibid., No. 1045, 1 June 1974.

27 ibid., No. 1000, 9 April 1974.

28 ibid., No. 1073, 4 July 1974.

29 ibid., No. 1074, 5 July 1974.

30 ibid., No. 1059, 18 June 1974.

31 ibid., No. 1089, 23 July 1974.

32 ibid., No. 1009, 23 July 1974.

33 ibid., No. 1094, 31 July 1974.

34 ibid., No. 1099, 4 August 1974.

35 ibid., No. 1125, 5 September 1974.

36 The Provisional Military Government Establishment Proclamation no. 1/1974.

37 *The Ethiopian Herald*, vol. xxx, No. 1131, 13 September 1974.

38 ibid., No. 1132, 14 September, 1974.

39 ibid., No. 1133, 15 September 1974.

40 ibid., No. 1135, 18 September 1974.

41 ibid., No. 1133, 15 September 1974.
42 ibid., No. 1136, 19 September 1974.
43 Proclamation No. 2/1974.
44 *The Ethiopian Herald*, vol. xxx, No. 1127, 7 September 1974.
45 ibid.
46 ibid., No. 1192, 24 November 1974.
47 ibid., No. 1194, 27 November 1974.
48 Address to the People of Eritrea, Lieutenant-General Aman Michael Andom, Asmara, October 1974.
49 ibid.
50 Speech at the Graduation of Officers' Ceremony of the Harar Military Academy, Lieutenant-General Aman Michael Andom, Harar, October 1974.
51 Statement of Clarification, Provisional Military Administration Council, Addis Ababa, 27 November 1974.
52 *The Ethiopian Herald*, vol. xxx, No. 1193, 26 November 1974.

Chapter Four

Critical Stage of the Revolution

Every reform movement has a lunatic fringe.

Theodore Roosevelt

Appointment of a New Chairman for the Dergue

The execution of the Chairman, Lieutenant-General Aman Michael Andom, and two members of the Dergue temporarily had done away with dissension and opposition within the Dergue and the Armed Forces. However, the Dergue did not appoint a new chairman from its members. It rather chose a senior officer from the Armed Forces to avoid any further dissension and division within its ranks. By drawing a lesson from the appointment of the previous chairman, the Dergue, this time, was very careful not to appoint a popular and senior officer with an independent mind. The candidate who would qualify for the post had to be an ordinary officer who would be easily manipulated by the Dergue or rather one who would be suitable for a puppet chairman. According to the Dergue's assessment Brigadier-General Teferri Bente who had been appointed by the Dergue as Commander of the Second Army Division was the suitable candidate. He was, unlike the first chairman rather a humble and an unassuming character, a quality that had misled the Dergue to pick him as its puppet chairman. In announcing his election, the First Vice-Chairman, Major Mengistu Haile Mariam, said that the general was elected on his leadership qualities, integrity, patriotic feelings and humble origin.

In all meetings, including the Council of Ministers, he sat in the middle

147

flanked by the First and Second vice-presidents who, invariably, on all issues under the consideration of the Council held diametrically opposite views. A Council's meeting was an ordeal for him. He was very careful not to give the impression that he favoured the views of one over the other. In those days, when the competition between the two vice-presidents was evident, entertaining the views of one of them would have been interpreted as a preference for the one whose views had been entertained. It was difficult to escape from being labelled a supporter of one of the vice-chairmen. The position of the cabinet ministers was equally difficult. Free expression of views by ministers was invariably regarded as an exercise of choice of one vice-chairman over the other. The competitive disposition of the two vice-chairmen suppressed free and democratic debate on issues considered by the Council of Ministers. The meetings of Council were, as a result, dull and unstimulating. The chairman kept a reasonable balance in his dealings with the two vice-chairmen. However, he was swayed by Dergue members who loathed the ambition particularly of the first vice-chairman and his ideological allies in the Provisional Office for Mass Organisational Affairs (POMOA).

Yelewit Hawariat (*Apostles Of Change*)

Even though the struggle for power was settled, the Dergue did not feel secure unless potential sources of dissension and challenge to its survival were put under tight control. At the initial stage of the revolution the Co-ordinating Committee of the Armed Forces, Police and the Territorial Army had created Noos Dergues (sub-committees) mainly for maintaining liaison between the Co-ordinating Committee and the Armed Forces and the Police. To that end the contributions of the sub-committees were immense but on the other hand their close contacts with the different units of the men-in-uniform were a legitimate source of concern for the committee. Gradually, the sub-committees became conscious of their immense influence in the armed forces thereby posing a threat to the Co-ordinating Committee. This new development had made necessary the creation of a formula that would eliminate the threat and at the same time provide to the members of the sub-committees a significant role in the revolution. An outright disbanding of the sub-committees would have provoked a revolt in the armed forces. The Co-ordinating Committee requested each of the units of the armed forces to elect representatives who would be placed in the various ministries and other government institutions. The representatives would act as agents for the Dergue in popularising the philosophy of *Ethiopian Tidkem* and checking upon the

148

bureaucracy whether it executed its functions in line with the new philosophy. About 276 apostles of change were elected by the various units of the Armed Forces and the Police. They were placed in all government institutions including government owned industrial and commercial establishments in the capital city as well as in the fourteen administrative regions of the country. Responsibilities of *Yelewit Hawariat* were not properly defined in relation with powers and responsibilities of heads of government institutions. The ambiguity in the powers of the *Yelewit Hawariat* was a constant source of confusion and indecision. The net result was that the power for decision-making shifted from the institutional heads and executives to the *Yelewit Hawariat* while accountability still remained with the heads of institutions and executives of government-owned undertakings. Such an arrangement perpetuated inefficiency and indifference in the bureaucracy. As a result, distrust in the bureaucracy was aggravated. The confusion that was created by depriving heads and executives of institutions the power to act independently would be interpreted by *Yelewit Hawariat* as a deliberate act to obstruct the pace of the revolution. In some cases the indecisiveness of heads and executives of institutions would be interpreted as an outright sabotage and often would end in their being sacked. Eventually, the problem was resolved by absorbing *Yelewit Hawariat* into the bureaucracy. Having had the experience at the cost of bureaucrats, *Yelewit Hawariat* were appointed as permanent secretaries, department heads, managers and in a few cases ministers. *Yelewit Hawariat* served for the Co-ordinating Committee of the Armed Forces, Police and the Territorial Army as a recruitment reservoir of loyal cadres to man key positions. Moreover, the *Yelewit Hawariat* formula helped to abolish the Noos Dergues which were ideal sources for generating opposition and challenge to the power of the Dergue. It played a very crucial role in weeding out from the bureaucracy those elements who were not prepared to keep abreast with the pace of the revolution. To sum up *Yelewit Hawariat* were cadres upon whom the Dergue relied for the implementation of the political, economic and social changes that were in the making.

National Work Campaign for Development Through Co-operation (Zemecha)

The Dergue, having settled, at least temporarily its power struggle by placing *Yelewit Hawariat* in all government institutions, went out with full-scale agitation to involve the peasants who accounted for more than ninety per cent of a total population of 33.958 million.[1] The rural population was not participating in the changes that were ravaging the country.

Any change that failed actively to involve the rural population that was the primary victim of feudalism was bound to face difficulties. So it was in the Dergue's interest to give high priority to agitation among the peasantry. For this enormous task of synthesising and agitating the peasantry there was no better candidate than the exuberant youth of the country, particularly students whose slogan for change was 'land to the tiller'. The Dergue was cunning enough to exploit the exuberance of students. To this end, it announced that it would close senior secondary schools, universities and colleges and dispatch students and teachers to the *Zemecha* (campaign) as early as October 1974. The idea was rejected by the students who had felt that the campaign was a rather sinister design to drive them away from the hub of revolutionary turmoil. They were told that the poor peasants had financed their education and that the least they could do to repay their debts to the peasants would be to participate in a campaign whose major benefactors would be the peasants. Despite student protest the preparation for the *Zemecha* continued unabated. An elaborate organisation was created for the execution of the *Zemecha* in October 1975, a year after it was announced. A Dergue member, Major Kiros Alemayehu, was appointed as chairman of the *Zemecha*. Four programme co-ordinators for health, education, basic engineering and agriculture were appointed from universities.[2]

Some 60,000 students, teachers and a few men-in-uniform between the ages of 18–40 were mobilised for the campaign. Even though the initial announcement was made as early as October 1974, it was not launched until December 1975. The intervening period, between the announcement and the launching, was used for programme and logistic preparation. The campaign was launched with a colourful ceremony and parade in Addis Ababa. The chairman of the PMAC, Brigadier-General Teferri Bente, in his nationwide address on the occasion outlined the following ten principles[3] by which the campaign participants were to be guided:

1. To explain the philosophy of *Ethiopia Tikdem* and lay down a strong groundwork for it to flourish.
2. To open literary opportunities to the broad masses of the people.
3. To persuade the people that alcoholism, prostitution and luxury were hindrances to progress and suggest ways and means of eradicating these evils.
4. To explain to the people by deed the idea of self-reliance through co-operation.
5. To convince the people that everyone had to bear an equal share of

responsibility for the progress and development of the country and that nobody has the right to oppress another because of his wealth, birth, or authority.

6. To explain to the people that we should put the interest of the community above narrow selfish ends.
7. To bridge the wide gap between the educated and the uneducated through dialogue.
8. To carry out programmes aimed at fighting famine.
9. To impress the dignity of work in the minds of the people by fighting the elimination of certain caste practices which degraded the social status of labour.
10. To explain the aims and objectives of the land reform legislation when this was decreed. Students could also help in the registration and distribution of land. At the same time they could also initiate co-operative ventures and other agrarian reform.

Students, teachers and men-in-uniform were, with these general terms of reference, dispatched in batches to the rural areas for mass agitation and invoking political awareness. The country was, for the purpose of the campaign, divided into six regions, 56 provincial units and 505 districts: Each provincial unit had under it 8–12 district stations with 100–120 campaigners allotted to each station. Six thousand and twenty-four of the 60,000 campaign participants were assigned to work in government institutions, particularly with the Ministry of Education, and the Relief and Rehabilitation Commission.[4] The rest served in the rural areas until June 1976.

The contribution of the campaign participants was commended by the PMAC on several occasions. On the winding-up of the campaign, the chairman of the PMAC, in expressing the government's satisfaction with the results of the campaign, said:

> ' . . . we recall with admiration what you campaign leaders
> and campaigners were able to demonstrate in deeds,
> particularly things essential for the improvement of the daily
> lives of the masses, during the past 18 months, while
> politicising and organising them with no fear of the threats
> of reactionaries and undeterred by divisive and confusing
> propaganda and withstanding the adverse influence of the
> old order.'[5]

The students did a remarkable job in preparing the groundwork for the introduction of the most radical land reform since the October Revolution of 1917 in Russia. When the Proclamation to Provide for the Nationalisation of Rural Land No. 31 of 1975 was decreed, to the surprise of sceptics, it was gracefully accepted by the bulk of the population, particularly by the peasants. The students' contribution in the registration, distribution of lands and formation of peasants' associations was immense. However, their agitation of the peasants was not without danger. It was used to incite opposition to the Dergue's rule. The Dergue was worried about the extent of the infiltration, probably, of the Ethiopian People's Revolutionary Party (EPRP), a leftist organisation that refused to recognise the rule of the junta. The PMAC issued a warning to the campaigners as early as August 1975, instructing them to refrain from spreading malicious rumours about the revolution. As time went by, the campaigners became more susceptible to the influences of opposition forces and their presence in the rural areas was a cause for concern. Consequently the PMAC wound up the first round of the campaign by June 1976 and it was not followed by another round as originally planned. At any rate, the PMAC by dispersing the students to the rural areas had done away with most vocal and organised opposition to its rule. On the other hand, the students played a very constructive role to bring the peasantry within the ambit of the revolution. Furthermore, their contribution in the implementation of the Rural Land Nationalisation Proclamation was monumental. Just as they began to outlive their importance in the rural areas, the *Zemecha* was wound-up and the campaign participants were sent back to resume their vocations after an interval of eighteen months.

Hibretesebawinet (*Ethiopian Socialism*)

Up to the overthrow of the emperor, the men-in-uniform were satisfied with the slogan of *Ethiopia Tikdem* with its basic components of equality, justice, loyalty to the emperor and his government, and inviolability of the territorial integrity of the country. With the passage of time, the development of events compelled the military junta to assume state power and correspondingly the slogan was upgraded to a philosophy without any significant change to its contents. Similarly, the assumption of the power of the state made the adoption of some sort of political ideology imperative. The monarchy virtually ceased to function as a political institution and its replacement by either a capitalist or a socialist system was a foregone conclusion. The Dergue opted for the latter under the disguised designation of *Hibretesebawinet*. Delegations, before the declaration of Ethiopian Socialism, mainly composed of Dergue members made extended tours in Tanzania, the People's Republic of China and other socialist countries. Tanzania was forthcoming in its appreciation of the Ethiopian revolution. President Nyerere was the first leader from a progressive country who paid a state visit to Ethiopia after the deposition of the emperor. President Nyerere during his visit expressed his willingness to share with Ethiopia Tanzania's experience in socialism. The experience of Tanzania was cited by Dergue members as a success story whenever they embarked on their ritual exercise of expounding the philosophy of *Ethiopia Tikdem* on various forums. When the Dergue declared Ethiopian Socialism as its political ideology, the *Tanzania Daily News* commented: '*Capitalism has no room on this continent (Africa), no matter how long some regimes flirt with it . . . only socialism gives the people a say in the running of their affairs.*'[6]

The Dergue declared Ethiopian Socialism as the political philosophy of the nation on 20 December 1974. In its declaration, the new political philosophy of the country was defined as *Ethiopia Tikdem means Hibreteseba-winet and Hibretesebawinet means equality, self-reliance; the dignity of labour; the supremacy of the common good; and the inviolability of Ethiopian unity.*'[7] The ideas reflected in the definition were those concepts that were consistently expressed as the underlying principles of *Ethiopia Tikdem* at various stages of its evolution. However, the content of the declaration goes much deeper in articulating the political philosophy, economic, social and foreign policies of the country in line with scientific socialism.

The conditions that required the adoption of a political system were:

'1. First, having demolished the old order, it is necessary to demonstrate what political and social order takes its place. An act of demolition should be immediately followed by an act of creation. It is an unfinished job which starts with the former and shies away from the latter. We have said that the new Ethiopia will be created on the basis of our motto, *Ethiopia Tikdem*. But the full meaning of the motto ought to be spelled out. The political philosophy should provide the meaning of *Ethiopia Tikdem*.

2. Second, even an individual, let alone a country, ought to know the direction of his journey. It is not enough to say that Ethiopia will henceforth embark upon the avenue of progress. It is essential to pick one such avenue.

3. Third, there must be a political philosophy which springs

from the aspirations of the people and which is capable of
bringing them under one national goal. This will
strengthen our unity, ensure that the rights of the people
are respected, and restrain the Government from
embracing upon policies and actions outside the
philosophy.'[8]

The need to fill the void created by dismantling the monarchy; the
inherent necessity of a political philosophy that emerges from the cultural
values of the people for a sustained development; the Dergue's desperation to defeat the underground leftist organisations and other
progressive elements in the society were compelling reasons for adopting
socialism as the political philosophy of the country.

The philosophy that had to be adopted, according to the PMAC declaration, had to meet the following criterion:[9]

1. Originate from the cultures and soil of Ethiopia;
2. Emanate from the aspirations of the broad masses;
3. Be a philosophy which shares a certain level of commonalty with
   philosophies followed by her neighbours;
4. Provide solutions to the socio-economic problems of the country.

The Dergue in its declaration gave the verdict that the political philosophy that met the foregoing criterion was *Hibretesebawinet* which stemmed
from the traditions of the great religions of the country, Christianity and
Islam. The absurdity of the declaration was its characterisation of socialism
as the product of the great religions whose basic teachings are the antithesis of socialism. It was a dishonest and deceitful approach to justify the
introduction of socialism under the cover of the great religions. The
Dergue's false declaration gained currency and even acceptability by the
naïveté of some of the clerics of the Ethiopian Orthodox Church who
inadvertently in their sermons drew similarity between the teachings of
Christ and the fundamental principles of socialism.

The following were listed as the basic principles of *Hibretesebawinet*.[10]

1. All Ethiopians are equal and will be treated equally before the law.
2. The interest of the community will prevail over the individual interest.
3. The right to self-determination within a unified Ethiopia will be
   realised.
4. The respect for labour and the rejection of a parasitic and exploitative
   mode of life are the defining features of the new philosophy.

5. The unity of the country is the sacred faith of the people.

These were not new elements. They were elaborated on several occasions as the basic tenets of the motto and philosophy of *Ethiopia Tikdem*. The basic ideas were deliberately repeated in the declaration to show that the philosophy of *Ethiopia Tikdem* was identical both in content and form with Ethiopian Socialism.

According to the PMAC's declaration *Hibretesebawinet* or Ethiopian socialism comprised the following major policies:[11]

1. Government Structure: A decentralised government structure with a minimum interference from the centre to be introduced.
2. Political Organisations: There would be one political national party that would have as its members all progressive elements. No room for opposition parties.
3. Economic Policy: All resources of the nation and means of production would be owned by the state. The private sector would have a role in areas where it is beneficial for the development of the nation.
4. Social Policy: The Ethiopian family is an essential element of the society. It would be protected against negative forces that would undermine its cohesiveness and viability. All Ethiopians have a right to free basic education; and access to health services would be expanded.
5. Foreign Policy: The foreign policy would be essentially the same except a change of emphasis in the light of recent developments. Non-interference in the internal affairs of other nations, non-alignment, peaceful coexistence and the principles enshrined in the charters of the United Nations and the Organisation of African Unity would form the foreign policy component.

The PMAC's declaration was carefully designed to reflect the political direction of the new Ethiopia that was to be constructed upon the debris of the defunct monarchy. The declaration of Ethiopian socialism disclosed the policies of the regime on the structure of government, political organisations, economic, social and foreign policies. Their implications were subject to detailed policy guidelines that would be issued in the course of implementation of the political ideology. In some areas, particularly in the economic sector, nationalisation of the means of production preceded the issuance of an economic policy. Industries, banks, insurance companies and other financial intermediaries were nationalised before an economic policy was issued.

Seventy-two industries, thirteen insurance companies, eight banks and other financial intermediaries were nationalised after the declaration of Ethiopian Socialism in January 1975. From the eight banks only three of them, Addis Ababa Bank, Banco di Roma and Banco di Napoli were privately owned, the rest were under public ownership. Moreover other than the Addis Ababa Bank, the share in the financial market of the other two banks was insignificant. The major commercial bank, which had control of more than 80% of the financial market, with branches all over the country and even abroad in the Sudan and Djibouti, was fully owned by the government at the time of nationalisation. On the other hand, the thirteen insurance companies were under private ownership and the term nationalisation correctly applied to them.

The drive for nationalisation gathered momentum after the nationalisation of banks and insurance companies and hit its peak when seventy-two industries were nationalised. The state, as a result, became a major shareholder in twenty-nine enterprises on 4 February 1975. The nationalised industries comprised food, beverages, textiles, leather and shoe, chemical, non-ferrous, iron and steel, and miscellaneous enterprises. The industries over which the government had controlling shares were six food processing firms, four fuel distributing plants, three chemical plants, two textile factories, two iron and steel plants and one paper and pulp firm.

Nationalisation left no economic activity unscathed, except the transport sector where few firms were nationalised. Nationalisation of major economic activities was the first concrete measure the PMAC took in implementing Ethiopian Socialism which as its execution revealed was scientific socialism under disguise. The urge for nationalisation grew to a level where it became an obsession to grab any economic activity irrespective of its size and the significance of its service to the public. Without criterion for nationalisation and responsible government institution to direct the process of nationalisation individual members of the Dergue and sometimes *Yelewit Hawariat* took the initiative in instructing ministries to nationalise economic activities that they considered were essential to the public. The confusion that was created by the lack of a nationalisation policy and a responsible government institution to implement the policy was rectified when the Economic Policy of Socialist Ethiopia was issued on 11 February 1975.

The New Economic Policy

The economic policy clearly delineated the economic activities where the state alone operated, the state participated with the private sector in a joint venture and the activities left for the private sector. In other sectors such as education and health the role of the state and the private sector were defined too. The areas of competence of the state and the private sector were classified into the following categories.[12]

1. *Activities Which Were Exclusively Reserved for the State*

1.1. Exploration of Precious Metals (gold, silver, etc.).
1.2. Large-scale Salt Mining.
1.3. Petroleum Refining and Natural Gas.
1.4. Basic Industries, i.e. iron and steel, fertiliser, cement, etc.
1.5. Textile Industries.
1.6. Leather and Leather Products.
1.7. Large-scale Rubber Manufacturing and Fertiliser Industry.
1.8. Drug and Medicine.
1.9. Tobacco.
1.10. Glass and Bottle Manufacturing.
1.11. Large-scale Printing and Publishing.
1.12. Electricity, Gas and Water.
1.13. Railway, Air, and Sea Transport.
1.14. Radio, Television, Posts and Telecommunications.

2. *Areas Where the State and Foreign Capital Could Participate*

2.1. Exploration and Exploitation of Carbons and Hydrocarbons.
2.2. Mining of Ferrous and Non-ferrous Metals.
2.3. Mining Chemical and Fertiliser Materials (Potash, Phosphate and Sulphur).
2.4. Processing, Canning and Preserving of Meat.
2.5. Paper and Pulp Industries.
2.6. Manufacturing of Plastics and Other Synthetic Materials.
2.7. Large-scale Construction Works.
2.8. Tourism.

3. *Activities Which Were Left to the Private Sector*

3.1. Food Processing, Canning and Marketing.
3.2. Quarrying.
3.3. Dairy.
3.4. Small-scale Grain Milling and Pressing of Oil Seeds.
3.5. Bakery.
3.6. Small-scale Manufacture of Wood and Wood Products.

3.7. Fabricated Metal Products.
3.8. Small-scale Weaving, Knitting, Spinning, Sewing and Tailoring.
3.9. Cottage Industries and Handicrafts.
3.10. Repair and Maintenance of Vehicles and Appliances.
3.11. Small-scale Construction Works.
3.12. Export and Import Trade.
3.13. Wholesale and Retail Trade.
3.14. Surface Transport Other than Railway.
3.15. Small-scale Inland Water Transport.
3.16. Entertainment Services.
3.17. Other Services Including Hotels, Bars, Restaurants, Coffee Shops and Groceries.
3.18. Others not elsewhere classified.

The declaration of an economic policy cleared the confusion that was rampant for want of an unambiguous policy. The policy was pragmatic in recognising the role of the private sector and foreign capital in the economic development of the nation. Although the policy was for a mixed economy, the indiscriminate nationalisation of enterprises scared both local and foreign investors. Moreover, the government's reluctance to take measures that would have restored the confidence of investors largely contributed to the ceasing of capital inflows from overseas to the country. To make matters even worse the government issued an additional policy that put a ceiling on both foreign and domestic capitals for investment in the activities that were left in the economic policy to the private sector. Fixing a ceiling of 500,000; 300,000 and 200,000 Birr capital for industry, wholesale trade and retail trade, respectively and other restrictions such as limiting the number of licences an investor could hold to one, rendered the investment climate unattractive for domestic as well as foreign investors.[13] As if the policy restrictions were not enough, the government's media onslaught against the business community by blaming it for shortages of goods and services, was an additional obstacle for the recovery of business confidence.

Nationalisation of Rural Land

Nineteen seventy-five was the year of drastic change. The economic and social basis of feudalism was scrapped and replaced by a socialist socio-economic order. The nationalisation of rural and urban land was the most radical measure that the PMAC had taken since the revolution broke in 1974. The economic base of Ethiopia that sustained the livelihood of over 90% of the population was rural land, whose unequitable distribution was a matter of public knowledge. Even the defunct monarchy was aware of the shortcomings of the land tenure system but lacked the courage and political commitment to reform it. Any far-sighted regime could have foreseen the immense political dividend that would accrue from land reform. The Dergue was quick to appreciate the political advantage and to capitalise on it to win the support of the people. After it took power in September 1974, land reform was on the top of its priority list. To expedite the promulgation of a land reform proclamation, the leadership of the Ministry of Land Reform and Administration was put under the custody of progressive elements who had a very close relationship with influential members of the Dergue. The progressive elements rejected possibilities of introducing a land reform legislation that would improve the system of tenancy, more or less, an effort to regulate the landlord–tenant relationship without abolishing the system. Such a reform was not in line with socialism that the Dergue was intent on pursuing under the guise of 'Ethiopian Socialism'. Besides the political advantage that would have accrued from a radical land reform legislation would have been diluted, a proposition that was not appealing to the Dergue. The most advantageous option that would win the support of the rural people and at the same time give legitimacy to the Dergue's rule was the introduction of a radical land reform. The Dergue with its commitment to win the support of as many interest groups as possible, seized the land reform issue and then translated it into concrete terms by enacting the Proclamation to Provide for the Nationalisation of Rural Land No. 31 of 1975. The proclamation introduced the most radical land reform system since the October Revolution of 1917.

The reaction of the people to the proclamation was astounding. The citizens of Addis Ababa went out into the streets spontaneously to express their jubilation. The mammoth gathering and demonstration in the capital generated an attendance of over half a million people from all walks of life. Organised bodies such as CELU, teachers' and students' unions, and the men-in-uniform expressed their satisfaction with the reform. Even the underground leftist organisations such as EPRP and *MEISON* hailed the measure taken by the Dergue to dismantle the socio-economic base of feudalism. On the other hand, landlords who were not comfortable with the reform expressed their resentment by resorting to unsuccessful armed struggle. On balance, the supporters of the reform overwhelmingly outnumbered the handful of landlords. The land reform proclamation was a political victory for the Dergue. The proclamation helped it to regain the support of the people that had been lost

159

because of the summary execution of the former government officials. The land reform was the climax of the revolution. The Dergue had the apprehension that the reform would provoke a civil war but, to its pleasant surprise, it did not even provoke opposition that would have jeopardised its power.

In the northern provinces, Eritrea, Tigray, Begemidir, Gojjam, Wollo and Northern Shewa where the land tenure system was mainly communal (rist) the reform did not make significant change other than confirming possessory rights upon those who were using farm lands. In the rest of the country where individual ownership was prevalent and the majority of the peasants were tenants, the reform made a significant change in the land tenure system. The peasants were the major beneficiaries of the reform – a factor that induced the peasantry to give its full support to the rule of the Dergue.

The Dergue's chairman, in a speech on the eve of the first anniversary of the revolution said:

> 'That is why our revolution addressed itself almost
> instantaneously to the challenge of changing an old
> anachronistic land tenure system. Since a country where nine
> out of ten people derive their living from agriculture, land
> had been and continues to be an important factor of
> production. But the productivity of this land has for long
> been principally constrained by a land tenure system which
> had put most arable lands into the hands of a small group
> of owners, while the majority of the people worked for their
> subsistence as tenants and share-croppers. In order thus to
> raise agricultural productivity for the general well-being of
> our people, and with a view of introducing a measure
> of social justice by redistributing income, we have carried out
> a land reform programme under which those who were on
> the land have become direct beneficiaries of their labour.'[14]

Indeed the Rural Land Nationalisation Proclamation was a major instrument for redistribution of income and introduction of a system of agriculture based on socialist principles. Its main features were:[15]

1. It abolished private ownership of land;
2. Land became the collective property of the people held in trust by the state for their benefit;

3. No compensation was to be paid to a former landlord other than for improvements on land;
4. The maximum plot of land to be allotted to a farmer was not to exceed twenty hectares;
5. It prohibited the use of hired labour on farms except in cases where the beneficiary was infirm, sick, old or a child;
6. The transfer of land by inheritance or lease or sales or mortgages or any other means of transfer was prohibited provided that upon the death of the head of the family the use of the land was to be transferred to the spouse and/or minor children or in the absence of all, the offspring who had attained the age of majority may use the land;
7. It transferred the ownership of all large-scale private farms to the state and/or co-operative societies or peasants' associations;
8. It gave to nomads possessory right over the land they customarily used for pasture;
9. It annulled all customary payments to local chiefs;
10. It entrusted the implementation of the proclamation to peasants' associations.

Moreover, the proclamation served as an instrument to bring the peasantry within the ambits of the revolutionary process. It also provided for the formation of a three-tier peasants' association at the village, district and provincial levels. However, regional and national peasants' associations were not stipulated in the proclamation but they were created at a later stage of the revolution. Farmers within twenty Gashases or 800 hectares would form a peasants' association at a village level. Roughly, an association at a village level would have as members 80–100 heads of households who are tenants, farm labourers and landlords who possessed up to ten hectares of land before nationalisation. A village peasants' association was a vital instrument for the implementation of the proclamation. Its main functions were:[16]

1. To distribute land;
2. To administer and conserve any public property (soil, forest water, etc.) within its jurisdiction of 800 hectares;
3. To hear land disputes within its jurisdiction;
4. To establish marketing, credit and other forms of co-operative societies;
5. To build, in co-operation with the government schools, clinics and other similar services;

6. To cultivate lands of peasants who by age or health or in the case of a woman who is, by the death of her spouse, incapacitated.

A village level peasants' association was given judicial, administrative, developmental and welfare responsibilities within its jurisdiction. A village became the hub of the administrative structure of the government. The functions of a village level peasants' association were co-ordinated by a Wereda (district) peasants' association whose members were elected from the village peasants' associations.

The main functions[17] of a Wereda peasants' association, other than co-ordination of the activities of village peasants' associations in a district were:

1 To allot land to landless individuals;
2. To alter the area of operation of a village peasants' association;
3. To hear appeals against decisions of village peasants' associations;
4. To hear first instance disputes between village peasants' associations.

The activities of a Wereda peasants' association in turn were co-ordinated by an Awraja (provincial) peasants' association whose members were individuals elected by Wereda peasants' associations. An Awraja peasants' association was also responsible to hear appeals against decisions of Wereda peasants' associations.

Peasants' associations served as platforms for farmers to administer their own affairs. Litigation on land disputes that was, in the past, a major cause for communal and individual conflicts and waste of productive time disappeared with the right to private ownership of land. Peasants' associations acted as effective links between the government and the rural people. Government directives and policies percolated smoothly and effectively from the central government to the farmers in the villages. The organisational capability of peasants' associations tremendously increased with the maturity of the revolution. Initially, the participants of the National Work Campaign for Development Through Co-operation played significant roles in organising and politicising the peasants. The bulk of peasants' associations was formed during the campaign, 1975–76. Over 20,000 peasants' associations were established in the entire country when the People's Democratic Republic of Ethiopia was founded in 1987.[18]

Nationalisation of Urban Land and Extra Houses

The final radical measure taken by the PMAC to dismantle the remnants of the old socio-economic order was the issuing of the Proclamation Providing for Government Ownership of Urban Land and Extra Houses, No. 47 of 26 February 1975. The proclamation was as radical as the Rural Land Nationalisation Proclamation, No. 31 of 1975. It was intended to bring equitable redistribution of income, to regulate house rent and to allot urban land to landless urban dwellers. Underscoring the significance of the ideological component of the proclamation, the chairman of PMAC, General Teferri Bente, in his address to the nation on the eve of the first anniversary of the revolution commented: *'The urban land reform programme we have undertaken recently instituted aims at discouraging unproductive speculation in land transactions and enrichment at the impoverishment of others.'*[19]

The proclamation failed to provoke spontaneous mass support and demonstrations which the rural land nationalisation proclamation succeeded to do. In particular prohibiting the renting of houses by individuals and limiting citizens to possessing one dwelling-house was resented by the majority of the three million urban dwellers. However, these harsh provisions were sweetened when a monthly rent of less than 300 Birr was slashed down by 50%. Tenants, who were the majority of urban dwellers, gracefully accepted the reduction in house rents. The ceiling of 300 Birr was fixed to cover a substantial majority of salary and wage earners. The objective of the proclamation was to abolish private ownership of land and the evils supposedly associated with it. The main features[20] of the proclamation were:

1. To nationalise all urban lands without compensation to the owners;
2. To confer possessory rights on urban dwellers over 500 square metres of land;
3. To transfer houses in excess of one to the state without compensation to the owner provided that the former owner proves that he/she has no other source of income for his/her subsistence, the state might grant to the owner a monthly allowance not exceeding 250 Birr;
4. To abolish the tenant's obligation to a landlord, thereby conferring upon a tenant a possessory right over a piece of land a tenant had leased from a landlord;
5. To charge house owners a land rent that would be calculated on the rental value of a house;

The proclamation, following the pattern set by the Rural Land Nationalis-ation Proclamation, provided for the establishment of a three-tier urban dwellers' association, namely, a Kebele Urban Dwellers' Association (Neighbourhood Urban Dwellers' Associations), *Kefitegna* (Higher Urban Dwellers' Association) and Maekelawi (Central Urban Dwellers' Associations). A Kebele had direct contact with residents of a particular locality. It had 300–500 contiguous households. Membership to a Kebele was automatic. The fact of inhabiting in a Kebele made it mandatory, irrespective of one's wishes, on an individual to be a member of a Kebele. A Kebele was run by a 15-person executive committee elected by its adult residents. The functions[21] of a Kebele were, among other things, to register nationalised houses, collect house rents of up to 100 Birr, adjudi-cate land disputes and set up clinics, markets, consumer co-operative shops and safeguard its security. The executive committee members served on a part-time basis on two afternoons a week. A Kebele other than serving as a municipal ward also played an important role in regi-menting the people to comply with government directives. It was used by the government to conscript the youth for the national military service, to collect contributions for famine victims, to mobilise the people for the defence of the state, etc. Moreover, it was used as an effective instrument for the execution of Red Terror, rallying people behind government policies and organising demonstrations in support of such policies. A Kebele was placed in an unenviable position of being responsible to provide services to its members on one hand and on the other hand acting as a repressive arm of the government. In the scheme of things, the desire of the government was carried out to the letter with the unfortunate result of undermining the confidence of the people in the organisation supposedly run by the agents they democratically elected. A relationship of a Kebele and its members was built on fear rather than on a partnership to promote the interests of its residents.

A *Kefitegna* whose executive committee of 26 consisted of members elected from the members of executive committees of Kebeles. The func-tions of a *Kefitegna* included maintenance of nationalised houses, collection of rents, keeping public safety, co-ordinating and operating social service programmes, designating and supervising live-stock markets and running co-operative shops.[22] More than one *Kefitegna* could form a Central Urban Dwellers' Association which could have a status of char-tered or unchartered municipality depending on the level of its development. A chartered Central Urban Dwellers' Association was headed by a Kentiba (mayor), the unchartered by a Shume (chief). These officers were nominated by municipal congresses and appointed by the government. In the congress of a chartered municipality the government was represented with a voting power while in the unchartered municipality a government representative could participate in a debate without a right to vote. The chartered municipality had power to raise its revenue by levying taxes and imposing charges for the services it rendered whereas the unchartered municipality's revenue, plan and programme were approved by the government. Even in the case of a chartered Central Urban Dwellers' Association government control was exercised by the appointment of a mayor and by its voting power in the deliberations of a congress. A Central Urban Dwellers' Association, *Kefitegna* and Kebele due to the government's patronising approach failed to develop into democratic local governments.

New Labour Law

One of the most significant measures taken by the Dergue, following the nationalisation of economic activities, was the promulgation of a labour law that was in consonance with the new economic order. Moreover, the new labour law that was biased in favour of the workforce served as an effective instrument to win the support of workers whom the Dergue was wooing, ever since it came to power. Before the declaration of the political ideology of the country, the Dergue instructed, as a matter of urgency, the Ministry of Labour and Social Affairs to produce a draft of a new labour law that would replace the Industrial Relation Proclamation of 1964. Although the drafting of the legislation was left to the experts of the ministry, the Dergue had made it clear that the draft legislation should be based on socialist principles of industrial relations reflecting the cardinal principles of socialist organisation, democratic centralism. The drafters were hard put to produce a piece of legislation that provided adequate protection for workers; granted them extensive rights to organise themselves into trade unions of their choice; reflected certain socialist organisational principles; took into account the interest of the private sector; put the employment market under the full control of the government; and adhered to the International Labour Organisation's conventions and protocols which Ethiopia had ratified. The experts produced a draft legislation that, to a certain degree, struck a balance among the conflicting interests of the PMAC, the private sector and the International Labour Organisation. The legislation, above all, provided employment security to workers by curtailing employers' prerogative to hire and fire workers as they wished. Workers were given a role in the settlement of industrial disputes and through workers' councils to express

165

their views in such subjects as raising production and workers' productivity. Provisions for collective bargaining and agreement were liberalised in line with international standards. The principle of equal pay for equal work was recognised. Generous provisions on conditions of employment such as overtime payment, severance pay, hours of work, leaves, etc., were provided for in the law. The right to organise into trade unions was liberalised as well.

Workers of an undertaking with employees as few as five workers acquired the right to form trade unions by joining other workers in a similar undertaking. Furthermore, the law allowed the formation of only one national union running the risk of violating ILO's conventions on the right to organise to which Ethiopia was a party. Other than this and denying employers the right to organise into associations of their own choice, the law, largely, was not outrageous in disregarding the international instruments to which Ethiopia was a party. The government, as a result of nationalisation, became a major employer and consequently the right to organise was irrelevant to it as an employer. The employment market that was left to the forces of a free market economy was controlled and regulated by the state. Employers were required by the law to report all vacancies to government employment exchange offices and to make their recruitment through these offices. The compulsory notification of vacancies and recruitment of workers through employment exchange offices of the government worked satisfactorily in the socialised sector of the economy; but in the private sector due to lack of proper organisation and trained personnel for enforcement purposes, recruitment outside the employment exchange service was conveniently overlooked and tolerated.

In spite of certain shortcomings, the new labour law rectified most of the weaknesses of the old Labour Relations Proclamation of 1964, and provided workers with humane conditions of work and employment promoting industrial peace. Its promulgation was timely in responding to the pressing needs of the workers.[23]

Implications of the Gains of the Revolution

The declaration of Ethiopian Socialism made the political direction chosen for the nation clear. It was a response to the Dergue's desperate search for an ideology that would fill the ideological void created by removing the monarchy and at the same time would win the support of the underground Marxist organisations, particularly the EPRP and *MEISON*. Under the circumstances, Ethiopian Socialism was the nearest response to the Marxist organisations' cry for a classical Marxist–Leninist ideology; either of the Soviet or Chinese brand. The declaration of Ethiopian Socialism was followed by nationalisation of industries, rural land, urban land and extra houses, private schools including schools run by churches and missionaries. Moreover, the introduction of an education curriculum, based on socialist principles, contributed to narrowing the differences between the Dergue and the Marxist clandestine organisations, save the EPRP. The EPRP consistently demanded that the Dergue should hand over power to a broad-based 'provisional government' comprising the intelligentsia, workers, peasants, students and other progressive elements. Yielding to this demand was tantamount to the Dergue signing its own death warrant.

The measures that were taken by the Dergue were calculated steps to appease each segment of the society by accommodating its main concern. The nationalisation of rural land gave vested interest to the peasantry with an implied obligation to defend it vigilantly. As a result, the peasantry was swayed to contribute a fighting force of over 300,000 that helped the Dergue to keep its power under the guise of safeguarding the gains of the revolution, defending the unity and territorial integrity of the country. Similarly, the urban land and extra houses proclamation by slashing house rent by 50%, exerted a substantial impact on a family budget of a tenant who was paying a monthly rent of less than 300 Birr. The annulment of landlord–tenant relationship besides freeing a tenant of any obligation to a landlord vested in him/her possessory right to the piece of land he/she had leased. An urban dweller who had benefited from nationalisation had every justification to support the Dergue.

Workers, who were also beneficiaries of a new labour law, pension benefits and reduced house rent were not prepared to compromise on their demand for a civilian 'provisional government'. The Dergue's first cajoling and then arresting of the leaders of workers' organisations, who were deeply influenced by the EPRP, did not either succeed in restraining them from striking. The Dergue, true to its determination to subdue leaders of workers' organisations, took drastic action by temporarily closing down CELU under the pretext that rivalries for leadership in the trade union movement had endangered industrial peace. The Vice-President of CELU, Ato Alem Abdi, who had sensed earlier the determination of the Dergue appeared to be conciliatory and hailed the revolutionary measures that the Dergue had undertaken in his May Day speech. He said:

> 'CELU had on several occasions expressed its solidarity with
> and supported the steps taken by the Provisional Military

Government in proclaiming *Hibretesebawinet* nationalising rural lands, transferring the ownership of the means of production and distribution to public holding and in initiating all other policies that reflect the true aspiration of the masses.'[24]

However, this conciliatory gesture did not succeed in bridging the rift that was created as a result of CELU's adamant demand for replacing the Dergue by a civilian provisional government. Without any change of stance from CELU, the Dergue had to create a conducive condition that would favour a change of the leadership by individuals who would be amenable to its whims and ambition. To this end a meeting of some members of CELU was convened and elected a five-man executive committee with a mandate to make the necessary preparations and call a meeting of the congress of CELU. The ban on CELU was lifted enabling the executive committee to make arrangements for convening a congress. The congress was convened on 5 July 1975 and elected a 13-man executive committee chaired by Ato Markos Hagos to run CELU until a general election was held. Strikes and other forms of resistance to the rule of the Dergue, instead of subsiding, were intensified. Finally, it was discovered that the chairman and some members of the new executive committee were either supporters or sympathisers of the EPRP. The chairman, Ato Markos Hagos, who went into hiding after the exposure of his allegiance to the EPRP, was killed by a search team while resisting arrest at the end of March 1977.

The men-in-uniform, with a generous salary and allowance increase, improved pension benefits and a change of uniforms which was a sensitive issue in those days, were contented with their privileged position.

Students who were vocal critics of the Dergue had also their share of the spoil. The ban on their union and publication was lifted. Their slogan 'land to the tiller' for which they had made great sacrifices, saw the light of day when rural land was nationalised – a measure more radical than they had hoped for. As a recognition of the students' struggle for agrarian reform the slogan 'land to the tiller' was adopted as a title for Article Four of the Rural Land Nationalisation Proclamation of 1975. On the whole, the students were convinced that most of their demands were realised under the military junta even though their dream for a civilian government was outstanding. Moreover, they were scattered all over the country to participate in the National Work Campaign for Development Through Co-operation that effectively excluded them from being a nuisance to the Dergue.

In spite of hiccups here and there, the Dergue's one year performance was satisfactory. The chairman of the Dergue, General Teferri Bente, addressing the nation on the occasion of the first anniversary of the revolution said:

> 'I am happy to say today our revolution is on a correct and
> positive course. It is not directed against any external factor.
> Within the specific Ethiopian context it is dedicated to
> finding solutions to the crying needs of our people.'[25]

The Socialist states were, in spite of the radical reforms introduced by the PMAC, reluctant to welcome the regime to their bloc. However, closer diplomatic ties and exchange of goodwill delegations were frequented. Dergue members were sent for ideological training and study tours to the Soviet Union, China and other socialist countries. The Soviet Union was extremely careful not to tread freely into the sphere of influence of the other superpower. However, it did not remain a passive spectator but signalled interests in developments in Ethiopia by sending delegations of the Russian Orthodox Church prelates. The Dergue tried very hard to win the friendship and recognition of socialist countries, particularly that of the Soviet Union. The ecclesiastical delegation from the USSR was followed by a delegation from Cuba. The visit of the Cuban delegation was a signal that the regime was to be accepted in the socialist bloc. The Cuban delegation made several meetings with the PMAC and POMOA leadership followed by visits of development projects. The delegation was impressed by the achievements of the revolution and the enthusiasm and dedication of revolutionaries and offered to share Cuba's experience in socialism. The visit by a high-level Cuban delegation reassured the regime of acceptance in the socialist circle. The chairman of the Dergue in underlining the international significance of the Ethiopian revolution commented:

> 'We recognise that we would be making a mistake if we
> believed that the Ethiopian Revolution is a unique
> phenomenon. We assert today, that the Ethiopian Revolution
> is an integral part of a global process of economic and
> social change which has a historical continuity.'[26]

The Western democracies were watching developments with anxiety. The declaration of Ethiopian Socialism and the radical measures taken were sources for serious concern for the United States that had uncontested

169

influence in Ethiopia for over a quarter of a century. Surprisingly, even after the abolition of private ownership of land and the nationalisation of the means of production and distribution the USA signed an agreement with the regime for an assistance of 14.5 million dollars to finance a malaria control project.[27]

Some Arab countries showed their disapproval of the new political orientation of the country by stepping up their assistance to the Eritrean secessionists in the northern part of the country. The scale of their interference was worrisome to the regime. Moreover the Arab interference was exploited by the regime to rally the Ethiopian people behind it under the pretext that the territorial integrity of the country was threatened by the collusion of external forces with secessionists. The Eritrean problem had always been a cause for straining relations between Ethiopia and some Arab nations even under the monarchy. During that time the radical Arab states of Syria, Iraq and Libya and from the moderates Egypt and the Sudan were assisting and harbouring secessionist elements. But after the revolution the number of Arab states entertaining a secessionist cause grew and their financial, arms, diplomatic and material assistance and support were intensified even though the Dergue was making an effort to resolve the problem by peaceful means. The imperial regime, let alone attempting to solve the problem by peaceful means, did not recognise the Eritrean problem. The Dergue on the other hand recognised the problem and made it one of its major preoccupations when it assumed power in 1974. The following were some of the measures taken by the Dergue to resolve the problem in Eritrea by peaceful means:

1. A message of goodwill was conveyed to the rebels to join hands with the rest of the Ethiopian people in building a new Ethiopia;
2. The late chairman of the PMAC, Lieutenant-General Aman Michael Andom, who was an Eritrean, briefed the Eritrean people of the government's desire for a peaceful solution of the Eritrean problem;
3. The government instructed its security guards to stop tracking rebels and confined them to their camps as a sign of a goodwill gesture;
4. An Eritrean, Ato Amanuel Amde Michael, was appointed as chief administrator of the region;
5. A delegation of elders of the region was sent to convey the goodwill of the PMAC to the rebels;
6. Government delegations were dispatched to a number of Arab governments to explain to them the government's readiness for a peaceful resolution of the problem and to persuade them to support the peace effort of the government;

170

7. A deputation of elders from the capital led by a prelate of the Ethiopian Orthodox Church, Abune (His Grace) Philipos, was sent to the region to appeal to the Eritrean people and the rebels to stop the unnecessary loss of lives and destruction of properties.[28]

Although its efforts were not reciprocated by the rebels, the PMAC did not cease to press for a negotiated settlement. On the first anniversary of the revolution, the chairman of the PMAC made the following appeal to the rebels:

'We would like to appeal once more on this occasion to our Eritrean brothers not to be accomplices in designs of others who do not have their interests at heart and join the Ethiopian people in building one Ethiopia based on social justice and co-operative endeavours, an Ethiopia which embraces all her sons and daughters on the basis of equality, an Ethiopia which allows for the realisation of the full potential of every and all its national groups.'[29]

Again this appeal fell on deaf ears and the situation in the region deteriorated leaving no option to the PMAC other than reciprocating the guerrilla activities of the rebels in kind to uphold the cardinal principles of the revolution of safeguarding the unity and territorial integrity of the country.

Marxist-Leninist Organisations Join the Revolution

The radical measures that were taken by the PMAC to change the socio-economic system of the country was a political reality which the leftist underground organisations could not afford to ignore. The support of the masses to the regime's reforms was also a compelling factor for a change of mind of most leftist organisations to be partners of the PMAC in intensifying the revolution. They realised that the revolution had in spite of their opposition to the rule of the PMAC, gathered a momentum and failure to recognise this political fact was counter-productive. It was time for the leftists to change their strategy lest they would be excluded from the revolutionary process. They realised that instead of remaining disgruntled underground oppositions it would pay a handsome political dividend to collaborate with a military junta that was desperately looking for partners who would make good for its deficiency in ideology. The Marxist-Leninist organisations joined the revolution with the hope of

171

snatching the leadership from the PMAC whose ideological deficiency was misconstrued as political naivety. The PMAC regarded the partnership with leftist organisations as a calculated move to diffuse their opposition to its rule. Each having its own hidden agenda made tacit agreement to create a common revolutionary front to expedite the pace of the revolution in unison. The secret pact of the PMAC and leftist organisations culminated into the declaration of a National Democratic Revolution Programme of Ethiopia (NDRPE) and the establishment of a Provisional Office for Mass Organisational Affairs (POMOA) on 20 April 1976. On the same day, the first Vice-Chairman, in launching NDRPE, revealed to the public that progressive forces had urged to join the revolution. The NDRPE and POMOA were the concessions that leftist organisations won from the PMAC to join the revolution. Among the Marxist-Leninist underground organisations, the All Ethiopia Socialist Movement (known under its Amharic acronym, *MEISON*), *Waz* League, Ethiopian Marxist-Leninist Revolutionary Organisation (Amharic acronym, *MALRED*) and Ethiopian Oppressed People's Struggle (Amharic acronym, *ECHAT*) joined the revolution while the Ethiopian People's Revolutionary Party or EPRP (well known by its Amharic acronym, *EHAPA*) rejected any possibility of collaborating with the PMAC and its Marxist allies thereby being isolated and labelled as an enemy of the revolution and revolutionaries.

The NDRPE was the most important document in shaping the course of the revolution. It was drafted by the progressive forces who joined the revolution and endorsed by the PMAC which had already committed itself to Ethiopian socialism. The NDRPE was the final stage in the evolution of the slogan *Ethiopia Tikdem*. It was the nearest adaptation of classical Marxism-Leninism to the realities of Ethiopia. It endorsed scientific socialism as the basis of its political ideology and consequently stipulated a new socio-economic system identical to the one prevailing in the Soviet Union and Eastern European Socialist countries. Unlike its predecessor, Ethiopian Socialism, the NDRPE clearly articulated the political, economic and social policies of the government. Moreover, in its operative paragraphs the following goals were set:

'1. Complete elimination of feudalism, bureaucratic
   capitalism and imperialism from the country, to build a
   new People's Democratic Republic of Ethiopia on solid
   foundations through the concerted collaboration
   among anti-feudalist, and anti-imperialist forces and to
   pave the way for transition towards socialism.

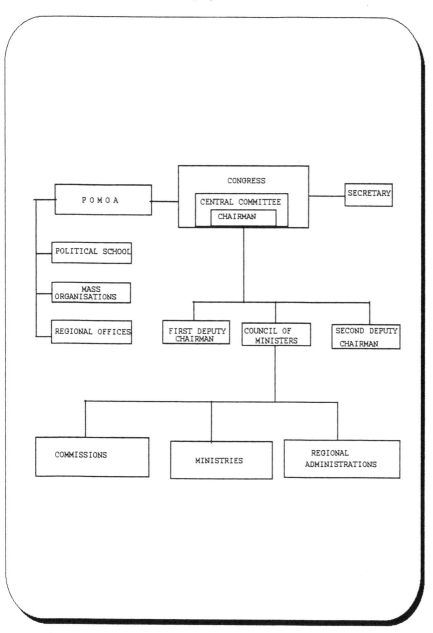

Chart 2
Organisation chart of PMAC, PMG and POMOA, 1976

2. To this end a Peoples' Democratic Republic of Ethiopia will be established in Ethiopia under the proletariat leadership in close collaboration with farmers and the support of *petit-bourgeois*, anti-feudalist, and anti-imperialist forces to guarantee to the Ethiopian people their rights to freedom, equality, unity, peace and prosperity as well as self-determination at various levels and unrestricted human and democratic rights.'[30]

The programme unequivocally made its pronouncement on the type of government and those who would be eligible to participate in it. It also identified the enemies of the revolution and the measures that would be taken to eliminate them. The course for class struggle was charted and the protagonists classified according to their class origin. The progressive forces – workers, peasants, *petit-bourgeoisie* and other – anti-feudalist, anti-bureaucratic and anti-imperialist individuals on one side were lined up against reactionaries – landed aristocrats, compradors and bureaucratic bourgeois classes, and imperialism. The programme stressed the need to win the unemployed proletariat lest it would be used by the reactionary camp to undermine the revolution. As a precondition for the execution of class struggle the need for politicising, organising and arming progressive forces was emphasised. The creation of a common front for all the progressive forces was recognised as a precondition for the class struggle and as a nucleus for the creation of a workers' party. Another preoccupation of the programme was to create a progressive structure that would be responsible for its implementation. The bureaucracy whose class allegiance by reason of its nature was with the reactionary camp could not be entrusted with the implementation of a basic revolutionary policy. The exclusion of the bureaucracy made the establishment of a new and a progressive organisation composed of Marxist-Leninists imperative. The creation of the new organisation, the POMOA, was made to coincide with the declaration of the NDRPE. It had its headquarters in Addis Ababa with branches corresponding to the government's administrative structure at the regional, provincial and district levels. The POMOA, to insulate itself against the undue influence of the bureaucracy which by definition was non-revolutionary, was made accountable to a Supreme Organising Committee composed of revolutionaries. The PMAC appointed members of the committee in consultation with the members of POMOA.

The main functions[31] of POMOA included:

1. To ensure the proper implementation of the NDRPE;
2. To create the necessary conditions for the People's Democratic Republic of Ethiopia;
3. To make recommendations for changing the existing bureaucracy;
4. To enforce a democratic rights' proclamation which was to be issued during the life of the office;
5. To train cadres either locally or by sending them abroad;
6. To disseminate socialism;
7. To run a political school.

Representatives of *MEISON, Waz, ECHAT* and *MALRED* constituted the 15-person commission of POMOA; until they were joined by *Abiyotawe Seded,* a Marxist organisation headed by Colonel Mengistu Haile Mariam, in the latter part of 1976. Seven of the members of the commission including its Chairman and Secretary-General were members of the *MEISON,*[32] thus giving it a decisive edge over the other organisations which were relegated to play a role of junior partners to *MEISON.* The office enjoyed the full support of the PMAC. A very generous budget of seven million Birr was allocated for it. The Commission members weilded enormous power and influence both as a group and individually as well. For a brief period they were privy to the PMAC and virtually vetted appointments of individuals to ministerial and other key positions in the Government. Their influence was also reflected in the distribution of portfolios in the cabinet. Education, Planning, Housing and Urban Development and the mayoralty of the capital city went to *MEISON.* Labour and Social Affairs and Health were given to *Waz* and Agriculture to *ECHAT.* Moreover, at department levels they had quite a sizeable number of key positions replacing career civil servants. Their ultimate aim was to control the government machinery, trade unions, peasants' and urban dwellers' associations and other mass organisations. The POMOA's sole responsibility of politicising and organising put them in an ideal position to have their members elected for leadership of mass organisations. The PMAC soon realised the threat that control of the bureaucracy and mass organisations by progressive forces posed to its power. To check the influence of the revolutionaries and at the same time to control the POMOA it organised its own brand of a Marxist organisation, *Abiyotawe Seded* or Revolutionary Flame, with the assistance of *Waz* League which refused to come to terms with *MEISON's* domination of POMOA.

Seded mainly relied for its membership on the armed forces. Although it was not made public, the Secretary-General of *Seded* was Colonel Mengistu Haile Mariam who ran it by his proxy Sergeant Legessie Assfaw. The formation of *Seded* and its eventual membership to POMOA and its commission served as a safety valve against revolutionaries who were bracing themselves to take over power from the PMAC.

POMOA, provided with a comfortable budgetary provision, opened up offices right from the centre down to district level on an unprecedented scale. The best government offices were given to it free of charge. The latest office equipment and transport facilities were made available. All government institutions were instructed to co-operate with it and to give it their unreserved support and co-operation should it happen to require them. Having its working conditions arranged with the necessary conveniences it started, as a matter of priority, to train cadres who would spread the gospel of Marxism-Leninism, politicise and organise the people. The local training of cadres was augmented by sending them to socialist countries in their hundreds. In tandem with production of cadres the awakening of the masses through discussion forums was strengthened. Topics for discussion were published in the national papers and in the fortnightly publication of POMOA, *Abiyot*. All government institutions were required to subscribe to *Abiyot*. The chairmanships of discussion forums that were established in every government institution and government-owned factories were controlled by individuals recruited by one of the members of POMOA. On the other hand election and re-election of leaders of workers' organisations, peasants' and urban dwellers' associations were, in spite of the competing interests of the five members of POMOA to control the leaderships in the mass organisations, intensified.

POMOA Controls Mass Organisations

The workers were the most organised segment of society. They had experience in union elections and trade union politics. The Confederation of Ethiopian Labour Unions' affiliation with international workers' organisations particularly with the International Confederation of Free Trade Unions (ICFTU) and its association with American Federation of Labour-Congress of Industrial Organisations (AFL-CIO) had broadened the workers' perception of the role of trade unions in matters affecting their interests. The anti-Communist influence of the ICFTU and AFL-CIO in the Ethiopian Labour movement had manifested itself ever since the Dergue adopted socialism as its political ideology.

The promulgation of a new labour law was one of the steps the government took in reorganising the trade union structure and reformulating its role in a socialist state. By 1975 workers formed new unions in conformity with Labour Law Proclamation No. 64 of 1975. When the Marxist organisations opted to join the revolution and work in close collaboration with the Dergue, the workers had already reorganised their unions into 1,200 factory and ten industrial unions. Elections of trade union leaders were held without government interference complying with the International Labour Organisation's norms of non-governmental interference in trade unions' elections. It was the national union that was yet to be formed when the coalition of Marxist organisations, POMOA, took over the politicisation and organising functions of all mass organisations including workers' organisations. POMOA, having arrived at the scene after the elections for the most part were over, had to create conditions that would warrant re-election by instigating leadership rivalries. Soon two competing forces in the trade union movement appeared: one favouring the PMAC and the other opposing its stay in power. The former was influenced by the Dergue and POMOA while the latter was under the grip of EPRP. The trade unions became a bone of contention between the PMAC and its Marxist allies on one side and EPRP on the other. The most obvious struggle was to control the All Ethiopia Trade Union (AETU) whose leadership had yet to be elected by a congress of all registered trade unions. Representatives of more than 1,200 trade unions with a membership of 273,982 assembled in the old parliament building to form the national union and elect its officers. The meeting took place in the presence of representatives of the PMAC, POMOA and the Ministry of Labour and Social Affairs. The representatives of the Ministry were there to ascertain whether the congress was conducted democratically and the election of officers was free and fair. Everything went smoothly until PMAC and POMOA felt that the outcome of the election would not be as they anticipated. The congress was suspended indefinitely under the pretext that anti-revolutionaries had infiltrated the congress. A number of the delegates along with three officers of the Ministry of Labour were arrested and imprisoned. Two of the three were released when the Minister of Labour and Social Affairs interceded on their behalf; but the third who was a senior department head was indicted for anti-revolutionary activity and sentenced to five years imprisonment by a Special Court Martial.

After a long interval 65 delegates of eight industrial unions were gathered for a ten-day political awareness course that was conducted by a senior member of POMOA at Ambo, a resort town about 120 kilometres west of the capital. The Minister of Labour, who was opposed to the government's meddling in the trade union election, attended only the opening of the workshop and returned to his office on the same day leaving behind a senior officer of his Ministry. At the end of ten days of

177

indoctrination and lobbying an eleven-person executive committee was, free of any sympathiser of EPRP, elected according to a pre-determined plan.[33] By 1977 the leadership, in the Ministry of Labour and Social Affairs, AETU and most of the trade unions, was in the hands of Marxist revolutionaries.

By September 1976, 22,000 peasant associations with 5.5 million members[34] were established. The major part of organising peasants was carried out by the participants of the National Work Campaign for Development Through Co-operation. The credit for organising and, to a limited extent, the politicisation of the peasantry goes to the campaigners. POMOA was in time for the formation of peasants' associations at district, provincial, regional and national levels. POMOA did not face any serious challenge in putting its supporters in the leadership of peasants' associations. A lack of political consciousness of the peasantry and an absence of any influence from other political organisations were favourable conditions for POMOA to mould the peasants' associations into a structure that would fit its designs.

The organising of urban dwellers succeeded the formation of workers' and peasants' organisations. PMAC and POMOA had, when the formation of urban dwellers' associations started in earnest, already gained sufficient experience to influence the outcome of any leadership election to their satisfaction. Necessary preconditions such as replacing the minister and department heads of the Ministry of Urban Development and Housing by revolutionaries were satisfied, before they began organising urban dwellers' associations.

The ministerial portfolio was given to a senior member of *MEISON*, Ato Daniel Tadesse, who placed in key positions in the ministry including the Department of Organisational Affairs members of *MEISON*. After taking such decisive measures followed by agitation and propaganda works the formation of urban dwellers' associations was conducted systematically throughout the country. Election dates were declared public holidays to encourage massive turn-outs at polling stations. By September 1976, 1,500 urban dwellers' associations, including 291 in Addis Ababa, were formed. The outcome of the first election was not as the PMAC and POMOA hoped for because the infiltration and influence of the EPRP in urban centres was considerable. To weed out EPRP members and sympathisers, re-elections and by-elections were called under various pretexts. The results of the elections revealed the magnitude and the complexity of the problems that were created by the influence of non-revolutionary forces in urban centres.

POMOA, having sensed oppositions that were facing revolutionaries, constantly demanded the arming of revolutionaries and disarming all others. The Dergue did not entertain the demand until Colonel Mengistu Haile Mariam came into power in February 1977. Soon after his take-over of the leadership of PMAC, the government issued a public notice that required members of the public to surrender any fire-arms in their possession to a search team. The team was composed of representatives from urban dwellers' associations, the Police, the Armed Forces and peasants' associations. The search team conducted a house-to-house search for fire-arms and anti-revolutionaries from 24–29 March 1977. In the capital a search day was declared and all citizens were instructed to stay at home, a dawn to dusk curfew was imposed and vehicles were prohibited from circulation. The search was conducted in a very tense atmosphere. Fire-arms were collected and alleged anti-revolutionaries, including the leader of EPRP, Tesfaye Debesaye, were summarily executed by a search team. The search for arms and anti-revolutionary hunt was a prelude to the Red Terror.

Relapse into Power Struggle and Purges

The members of the PMAC, after the execution of the first chairman of the PMAC, Lieutenant-General Aman Michael Andom, two members of the PMAC and fifty-eight former government officials, formed a bond of solidarity and comradeship based on a blood-bath. The bond of solidarity was undermined when the Marxist-Leninists who were greedy for power joined the revolution and began to work with the PMAC. The short-lived solidarity gave way to a fresh bout of power struggle. The Marxist-Leninists who controlled the POMOA developed a close relation-ship with the First Vice-Chairman of the PMAC, Major Mengistu Haile Mariam who was covetous of the chairmanship of the PMAC. He con-sidered Major Sisaye Habte, the chairman of the Political and Foreign-Affairs Committee of the PMAC, as an obstacle to the realisation of his ambition. Major Sisaye excelled Mengistu in many respects. He had a university education which outshone Mengistu's junior secondary school education. Even though both were charismatic and eloquent Sisaye had depth in his views and was at ease with himself. Moreover, in the early years of the revolution he became a prominent figure when he acted as the spokesman of the Dergue. He had an opportunity to address the people as well as the military on the aims of the revolution. This was a golden opportunity for Major Sisaye to create a good impression on the people and to emerge as a leader, should a vacancy occur in the most coveted position of the PMAC. The author had, in his capacities as High

179

Commissioner of Labour and Permanent Secretary of the Ministry of Labour and Social Affairs an opportunity to meet him on several occasions. He had a remarkable quality for persuading others and putting his views across. In a short time, he proved his leadership qualities. No wonder that Major Mengistu and his Marxist-Leninist cabals considered him a dangerous candidate. They accused him of being pro-West and of anti-revolutionary disposition. Gradually, he was side-lined and his responsibilities of political and foreign affairs were taken over by Major Berhanu Bayih, a rather docile character. The last public appearance of Major Sisaye was in Asmara, Eritrea; when he and the chairman of POMOA, Ato Haile Fida, explained the NDRPE to over 2,000 representatives[35] of workers, farmers, government employees, elders and men-in-uniform in the last week of April 1976.

In July the PMAC issued a statement which revealed the alleged involvement of Major Sisaye Habte, two other PMAC members and Brigadier-General Getachew Nadew, the Commander of the Second Division of the Army in Eritrea, were found guilty by a Special Court Martial of conspiracy to disrupt the revolution. The statement also disclosed that the verdict of the court was upheld by the PMAC; and that Major Sisaye and General Getachew were executed while the other two officers were in hiding.

According to the PMAC's statement Major Sisaye was found guilty of the following charges:

'The officer was among the representatives of the Air Force in the PMAC. Since the establishment of the PMAC and until the overthrow of the king, he claimed to be a revolutionary, pretended to collaborate with the progressive change. Since then he gradually showed symptoms of his true colours. He played intrigues against the revolution and through subtle means misled the PMAC into mistakes.

In addition:

a) Although he had been entrusted by the PMAC with the important political post of the Chairmanship of the Political and Foreign Affairs Committee of the PMAC, he has used his office as a cover to make contacts with agents of imperialism by going to countries where he had not been sent after changing his flight schedules whenever he was sent abroad on political missions.

b) He had organised a personal anti-revolutionary group

180

known as 'Mafia' to divide the Air Force – a unit which
has in unison played a vital role in the ongoing revolution
and is committed to strengthen the struggle of the
oppressed broad masses. He has deliberately misled the
government by providing false information in an
attempt to divide the PMAC and the Air Force to pit and
divide the oppressed Ethiopian armed forces against one
another.

c) He had used for anti-revolutionary activities government
   funds allocated in connection with finding a practical
   solution to the problem in the Eritrean Administrative
   Region in accordance with the programme of the
   Ethiopian National Democratic Revolution.

d) He refused to undertake his revolutionary duty of leading
   a high-level delegation on an urgent national mission to
   the Soviet Union – exemplary founder of the socialist
   ideology – by giving unconvincing excuses in order to
   be able to conduct the anti-revolutionary activities
   hatched by him.

e) Finally he has been executed for having been found guilty
   with evidence of leading an anti-revolutionary conspiracy
   along with right-wing anti-revolutionaries and his
   accomplices in violation of the oath he had taken on
   behalf of the oppressed Ethiopian masses whose
   revolutionary struggle will never be retarded. This man's
   anti-revolutionary tendencies have been unmasked after
   his waivering reactionary stands when decisions on such
   crucial issues as the proclamation of rural land, urban
   land and extra houses, the programme of the Ethiopian
   National Democratic Revolution, and the People's
   Organising Provisional Office were taken.'[36]

The accomplice of Major Sisaye, Brigadier-General Getachew, was accused
and found guilty of the following charges:

'He was among the favoured few of the former feudal order
and was listed among those trusted strong-arms of the
feudal regime. Because of the then prevailing urgent
conditions and seemingly revolutionary stand, he was

retained and given a high post. Because of this and his
reactionary background:

a) Ever since the proclamation nationalising all rural lands
deprived him and his feudal accomplices of the large
farm he had owned in Meki, (Shewa Region) he had
amassed a vast fortune directly and indirectly from the
mess hall of the Airborne Unit in Debre Zeit with which
he built villas that were nationalised by the revolution
thus depriving him of his income as a military bourgeois
and cattle breeder. Overcome by the privilege of his
class stand, vain glory of his rank and self-admiration, he
had neglected under various pretexts the high trust put on
him by the government and the revolutionary masses.

b) During his service in the Eritrean region, disregarding
the highest duty entrusted to him, he took advantage
of the prevailing problem in the northern administrative
region to indulge in his habit of misappropriating funds
by deliberately creating outlets for such purposes. He had
collaborated with known anti-revolutionary groups for
sinister personal gains as well as self-serving power-hungry
plotters against the Ethiopian revolution. He was killed
while resisting arrest by security men at 3 p.m. on July
10, 1976, at his residence in Addis Ababa after he
refused to accept the summons for questioning in
connection with his anti-revolutionary activities and
opened fire and wounded a soldier who was sent to serve
him with notice.'[37]

The other alleged accomplices of Major Sisaye, Lieutenant Bewketu Kassa,
PMAC member and Assistant to the Major, and Lieutenant Seleshi Beyene
a member of PMAC were at large until they were tracked down and
killed by security guards in Gojjam. The other accomplice, Major Kiros
Alemayehu, member of PMAC and chief of the Zemacha, died in mys-
terious circumstances while he was under detention. Thus the second
round of the struggle for power ended with the liquidation of three
Dergue members and one general paving a way for a brighter future for
Colonel Mengistu and his Marxist-Leninist collaborators.

The Purge of the Patriarch of the Ethiopian Orthodox Church

Along with the liquidation of anti-revolutionaries, the Ethiopian Orthodox Church, the traditional partner of the monarchy, was targeted and undermined by the remote machination of the PMAC and the Marxist-Leninists. The Church was infiltrated by agents of the state who incited the clerics against the Patriarch of the Ethiopian Orthodox Church, Bitsue Wokidus Abune (His Holiness) Tewophlos. A demonstration was staged by some members of the clergy demanding his removal. The opposition to the Patriarch was given wide and biased coverage by the state-owned media. After continued denigration of the Patriarch by the media he was arrested and imprisoned as a common criminal. In circumstances that were not clear to the public, the spiritual father was dethroned against the law of the Church. The government statement that was released after his detention accused him of corruption, collaborating with the imperial regime and causing the death of certain members of the clergy.[38] The whereabouts of the Patriarch was, at least to the faithful, a mystery. His execution was revealed when the regime was overthrown in May 1991. According to the law of the Ethiopian Orthodox Church a new Patriarch could be appointed only upon the death of the incumbent. In flagrant disregard of this provision a council of the Church under the grip of the regime was convened and elected a new Patriarch. From five candidates an unknown monk, Aba Melaku, from Wollita province in the Sidamo administrative region was elected by winning 317 votes[39] out of 809.

The new Patriarch, Abune Teklehaymanot, was a holy man in the true sense of the word – a man who was detached from worldly trivialities, innocent and saintly.[40] His election was manipulated by the PMAC. The election of a Patriarch, who was detached from and lived in a spiritual world of his own, was a disservice to the Church and a great victory for the Dergue which was bent on having a puppet Patriarch.

The administrative aspect of the Church was normally handled by a Chief Administrator. Under the imperial regime an incumbent had the rank of a minister and was appointed by the emperor upon the recommendation of the Patriarch. The position was prestigious and wielded very strong power and influence in the Church. The power and influence of the Chief Administrator, even after the separation of Church and State, were not diminished. A person with a liturgical background, who had served as a member of the Dergue's Public Relations and Information Section and later as Deputy Chief Administrator of Begemidir, was chosen for the position of the Chief Administrator of the Church. The election of a puppet Patriarch and the subsequent appointment of an individual who had earned the trust of the Dergue brought the Church under the complete control of the PMAC. The Church's silence at the time of the Red Terror is a further proof of the extent of the PMAC's full control over its conscience.

Revolutionaries Compete for Power

With the relapse of the power struggle within the Dergue, a new front of struggle became visible. The self-alienated EPRP and its ideological foes, the PMAC and the four Marxist-Leninist Organisations – *MEISON, Waz, EMALRED* and *ECHAT* – reached a stage where their differences had to be settled by recourse to violence, EPRP, that was branded by its protagonists anti-revolutionary and an agent of imperialism took the initiative in perpetuating urban terror by assassinating revolutionaries and their sympathisers. Its primary targets were members of the PMAC and the Marxist-Leninist Organisations who were collaborating with the PMAC, trade union and urban dwellers' associations and other individuals whose active co-operation with the PMAC was in evidence. The EPRP unleashed 'White Terror' by assassinating one of the fifteen-person commission of POMOA, Comrade Fikre Merid. He was one of the few sober and rational members of the commission. On the day of his assassination he was attending a meeting of a committee that was reviewing the possibilities of launching the second round of the National Work Campaign for Development Through Co-operation. He took leave of the committee before the adjournment of the meeting to collect his wife from her office at the centre of the city. An assassin's bullet tragically ended his life while he was waiting for his wife. The assassination of Comrade Fikre Merid was a great shock for the revolutionaries. His assassination was used as a pretext to intensify their demand for arming revolutionaries that had a cool reception from the PMAC. The EPRP, however, broadened its targets of terror by blowing up industries, buildings and other establishments whose destruction would attract public attention.

Despite the havoc that was created by EPRP, the chairman of the PMAC, Brigadier-General Teferri Bente, on the occasion of the second anniversary of the revolution, not only failed to castigate and condemn it, but went out of his way to invite anti-revolutionaries for national reconciliation. It was a sensible call to avoid unnecessary bloodshed and damage to property. The gamble cost his life and the lives of the moderate members of the PMAC. The group which was led by Mengistu Haile Mariam and his close associates of POMOA had hoped to use the occasion for exposing EPRP, EDU and the Eritrean secessionist elements as the enemy of the people and the country. To their bewilderment the chairman appealing to all political forces said: '*We would like to reiterate that all the progressive forces bear a responsibility to create a united front on the basis of the Programme the Ethiopian National Democratic Revolution to enable the revolution of the broad masses to attain its objective.*'[41]

The appeal of the chairman was interpreted by Colonel Mengistu and his cabals as a proposition to negotiate with their enemies and an outright support for the reactionary camp. Nothing illustrates more vividly his anger than the statement he made soon after his take-over. He commented:

'These supporters not only turned a deaf ear to our pleas and demands, to add insult to injury, they invited us to co-operate with and re-embrace EPRP – the group which opposes both in theory and practice the progressive proclamations, namely, the fruits of our Revolution; a group which stands against the Programme of the National Democratic Revolution; co-operates with reactionaries in opposition to the unity of the oppressed masses; strives to hold power by killing activists and creating anarchy; engineers machinations so that the masses may turn against their known revolution; works with EDU and ELF and in general had been widely rejected and well known for its anti-people and anti-revolutionary activities. This was the group which was first of all invited to embrace and then to undertake a campaign against our external enemies. When we were asked to do this, we clearly realised that a counter-revolutionary activity was in progress.'[42]

The EPRP, which was not in a compromising mood, intensified its acts of terrorism by targeting members of the Dergue, leaders of mass-organisations and economic infrastructures. An attempt on the life of the First Vice-Chairman of the Dergue, Colonel Mengistu, was made on 23 September 1976. According to his version of the attempt he was ambushed by gunmen while driving from his office, in the old palace, to his residence in the headquarters of the Fourth Army Division. He and his drivers escaped the assassination attempt with minor injuries. The attempt on his life was fanned out of all proportion by the media accusing EPRP of being the culprit.

The incident was exploited on one hand to ostracise the EPRP and on

the other to popularise the First Vice-Chairman. The day after the incident urban dwellers' associations in the capital demonstrated against
EPRP, EDU, EPLF, feudalism, bureaucratic capitalism and imperialism.
The rally was addressed by the victim of the attempted assassination who
declared that he was targeted by reactionaries because of his dedication
to the cause of the revolution. Messages of good wishes and support for
his escape from the assassination poured in from the army, the bureaucracy, urban dwellers' and peasants' associations including the Ethiopian
Students' Association in Europe (ESAE), which was led by members of
the *MEISON*. The message of ESAE was a representative sample of the
messages that were sent by various sectors of the society. The ESAE
declaring its support to the First Vice-Chairman stated:

> 'The assassination attempt on the life of Major Mengistu
> cannot be isolated from the overall posture of a reactionary
> plot to disrupt the ongoing Ethiopian People's Revolution.
> The assassination attempt is part of a plot drawn up long
> ago by members of the anarchist group (EPRP) in close
> collaboration with the notorious CIA counter-revolutionary
> group. Therefore the crime was not committed on the spur
> of the moment.'[43]

The Socialist countries were not spared from joining the chorus of
sending congratulatory messages. The propaganda campaign against the
assassination attempt was a systematic approach in preparing the groundwork for taking stern measures against anti-revolutionaries. The alleged
attempt on the life of the First Vice-Chairman could have been a ploy
that was concocted by him and the leaders of POMOA for the purpose
of winning the sympathy and support of the people.

Restructuring of the Dergue

The excessive ambition of the First Vice-Chairman and his allies from
POMOA backfired. Most of the members of the Dergue were concerned
about the greed for power that was shown by the Vice-Chairman and the
members of the POMOA, particularly the *MEISON* leaders. To curtail this
unhealthy development the Dergue took a step in restructuring the PMAC
and properly defining its duties and responsibilities as well as the division
of labour among the chairman, the two vice-chairmen and the Secretary-
General. The relation of the POMOA was another area where clear

definition of accountability was required. Moreover, the pace of political development required reviewing the structure of the PMAC and POMOA.

In 1974 the military as the only organised power in the country took the historic responsibility to express to the authorities the popular demands of the people. To this end a co-ordinating committee consisting of representatives of the Armed Forces, the Police and Territorial Army was created. Since the major function of the committee was to make representation to the emperor and to round up former officials accused of maladministration, corruption and other improprieties in office an elaborate structure was not required. However, with the entrenchment of the military in politics its structure underwent a drastic change. The declaration of NDRPE, the creation of POMOA and developments there-after required revision of the functions and structure of the PMAC as stipulated in the Provisional Military Government Establishment Procla-mation No. 1/1974.

This proclamation was the first legislation that gave legal status to the Co-ordinating Committee of the Armed Forces, the Police and Territorial Army and a new designation, Provisional Military Government (PMG). The PMG assumed government power collectively. Its structure and the duties of the principal officers were not defined in the proclamation. The organisational inadequacies were compensated for by establishing different committees that were responsible for administration, legal, defence, economic, social, political and foreign affairs and public relations and information.

The committees were composed of members elected from a 125-man council. They issued policy guidelines to government departments as well as supervising and controlling their activities. The committee members would go out in teams of two or more to inspect the various government departments and sometimes give orders or directives on the spot without properly considering their implications. Attempts to explain the long-term implications of impulsive instructions would be considered as old bureaucrats' resistance to change. At best it would result in the loss of job and at worst imprisonment. The committee members were very powerful; a telephone call by them to the police would result in an immediate detention of the official who in earnest attempted to implore for reconsideration of the order or directive. The committee members were anxious and zealous to run the institutions under their supervision without any accountability for the consequences of their actions. They made major decisions but for the consequences of their decisions minis-ters and department heads were held responsible. Ministers and institutional heads would be accused of intentionally misleading committee members. The style of administration of the committees created an atmosphere of fear and anxiety that drastically affected the decision-making mechanism of ministries and other institutions. The lack of proper demarcation of the duties of committees and government institutions was a major problem that the Dergue was not prepared to entertain. The Dergue suffered from a paranoia of sabotage and even innocent mistakes were taken as deliberate acts to reverse the course of the revolution. This does not imply a denial of the existence of sensible committee members who appreciated suggestions. Of course, there were some who came to the rescue of ministers and institutional heads when they were in real trouble; but the prevailing mood was not to err on the side of the officials of the defunct regime.

Definitions of Powers of the Provisional Military Administration Council and its Chairman, Proclamation No. 2, 1974 did not go far enough to define the function of the Dergue in relation with various organs of the government. Its main objective was to fill the void that was created by the deposition of the emperor. The Dergue was enabled to assume the functions of the head of state until such time as the king-designate returned to the country. This additional responsibility of the Dergue made it imperative to define its role as head of state and government. The Dergue as head of state was empowered to ratify international treaties, to declare war, to ensure the defence and integrity of the nation, to enact laws other than regulations that were normally enacted by the appropriate ministries after they were approved by the Council of Ministers, to establish an advisory body of professionals that would give council to the government on political, economic and social affairs. Its function as a government essentially was a continuation of the powers and functions of the Council of Ministers of the monarchy.

Proclamation No. 2, on the other hand, was a marked improvement over Proclamation No. 1. Besides defining the powers of the head of state, it gave legal status to the positions of the chairman and vice-chairman of the Dergue, even though the functions were not adequately described. The functions of the Dergue, such as receiving dignitaries, granting audiences and bidding farewells to foreign emissaries, following-up implementations of decisions of the Dergue, chairing meetings of the Council of Ministers and submitting to the Dergue policies initiated by the Council of Ministers, were delegated to the chairman.

The Proclamation provided for one deputy whose duty was to act in the absence of the chairman, but in practice two deputies and a Secretary-General were appointed without specific duties. The *ad hoc* committees of the Dergue continued to operate as usual without any legal basis.

188

The deficiencies in the two proclamations were corrected by Proclamation No. 110, 1977 that restructured the Dergue in line with socialist organisational patterns of a congress, a central committee and a standing committee. The congress consisted of all the members of the Dergue, whose membership had, as a result of executions and other causes, dwindled from 125 to less than 100 by 1987. The proclamation did not refer to the size of the congress and the procedure of its appointment and dismissal. The Central Committee and the Standing Committee had 40 and 17 members respectively. The posts of two vice-chairmen and a Secretary-General were given legal status. The proclamation had properly defined the functions of the three organs and the officers of the Dergue as well as the Council of Ministers.

The distribution of powers and responsibilities, particularly among the officers of the Dergue, was a factor that led to a third round of major purges in the Dergue. The duties and responsibilities of the three organs and five of its principal officers are summarised hereunder:

The Congress was, among other things, responsible for

1. Determining the country's internal and external policies;
2. Approving the development plan and budget of the country;
3. Determining the defence strength of the nation;
4. Ratifying international treaties and agreements;
5. Declaring martial law and national disasters when the need arises;
6. Confirming or commuting death sentences and remitting punishments;
7. Issuing directives on the formation of political parties and other public organisations;
8. Reorganising existing or creating new government institutions:
9. Approving the report of the Auditor-General;
10. Considering recommendations from the Central Committee;
11. Electing and dismissing members of the Central and Standing Committees, chairman, vice-chairmen and the Secretary-General of the Dergue.

The Central Committee was responsible for

1. Exercising the collective leadership of the country;
2. Ascertaining the implementation of the economic, social and political policies of the country;
3. Supervising the security and defence activities of the country;
4. Deciding on matters relating to foreign aid and loan;

189

5. Determining the foreign policy components of the nation;
6. Approving the governments proposal on revenue and forms of taxation;
7. Approving the promotion of senior officials.

The Standing Committee was accountable to the Central Committee for

1. Leading the nation on behalf of the central Committee and the Congress;
2. Safeguarding the unity of the country;
3. Issuing directives for politicising, organising and arming the broad masses for the implementation of the NDRPE;
4. Heading and supervising the Provisional Office for Mass Organisational Affairs;
5. Deciding on statements to be announced by the mass media;
6. Directing the country's defence and intelligence and controlling the movement of forces within the country;
7. Approving policy decisions referred to it by the Council of Ministers;
8. Approving the establishment and/or severance of diplomatic relations including cultural, and economic ties with other countries.

The organisational reform and the distribution of functions in those organs of the Dergue were not controversial because of the collective nature of their decision-making processes. The most sensitive decision was the allocation of functions among the four officers of the Dergue.

The Chairman of the Dergue was responsible for

1. Acting as head of state for the Dergue;
2. Receiving foreign guests, ambassadors and other diplomatic envoys and emissaries;
3. Presiding over the meetings of the Congress, the Central Committee and the Standing Committee;
4. Presiding over the meetings of the Defence and Security Council;
5. Supervising the implementation of the decisions of the Dergue and the Council of Ministers;
6. Acting as the Commander-in-Chief of the Armed Forces:
7. Approving decisions of the Council of Ministers;
8. Ensuring peace and order in the country;
9. Appointing high officers of the Armed Forces and the Police.

The chairmanship that was occupied by an officer who was not a Dergue member became a very powerful position. It conferred upon the incumbent, power and prestige similar to an executive president of a country. The liberal allocation of powers to the chairman and making the vice-chairmen, who were Dergue members and nominal office bearers, were causes for dissatisfaction as will be discerned from the functions allocated to each one of them.

The First Vice-Chairman was responsible for chairing the meetings of the Dergue in the absence of the chairman and to preside over the meetings of the Council of Ministers.

The Second Vice-Chairman was responsible for

- politicising and organising militia;
- supervising auxiliary sections of the Dergue including its Security Guards; and
- acting in place of the First Vice-Chairman in the event of his incapacity.

The Secretary-General was responsible for

- Serving as the Secretary-General for the Congress, Central and standing committees;
- Heading and running the secretariat of the Dergue;
- Presenting businesses addressed to the Dergue to its appropriate organs;
- Co-ordinating the activities of the three organs of the Dergue;
- Preparing agendas for the Dergue and recording the proceedings of its meetings.
- Transmitting the decisions of the Dergue and following up their implementations.

The allocations of functions and powers were biased in favour of the chairman, the Second Vice-Chairman and the Secretary-General. The First Vice Chairman, the most ambitious of the lot, was given the responsibility to chair and co-ordinate the activities of the Council of Ministers, an organ without power. The PMAC revamped it quite often with cabinet reshuffles, but was reluctant to delegate to it powers that could have made it an institution that could have played a vital role in shaping the policies of the government. The members of the Council were largely civilian technocrats who were chosen to run the bureaucracy in compliance with the directives of the Dergue. The First Vice-Chairman was made responsible to chair the regular meetings of the Council whose agenda was restricted in considering budgets and programmes of govern-

191

ment institutions. Naturally he was quite unhappy with running an institution that was not influential.

The Second Vice-Chairman was responsible for politicising, organising and arming militia all over the country. The position conferred upon its occupant a high profile of public life and influence over the peasantry, a class that was considered vital in the development of the revolution. In a polity where the gun plays a crucial role in changing the locus of political power, the post of the Second Vice-Chairman was a position to be coveted by ambitious Dergue members. Besides his responsibility for the militia, a force that was developing in parallel with the regular army, the Second Chairman was in charge of the Security Guard of the PMAC. The guard was a rapid deployment force for crushing opposition. This post was given to Colonel Atnafu Abate, who was the founder of the Co-ordinating Committee at the beginning of the revolution in 1974.

Another important officer was the Secretary-General who ran the day-to-day activities of the Dergue and co-ordinated the functions of its three organs. The Secretary-General also acted as a link between the Dergue and other government institutions directly accountable to it. One of these institutions, POMOA, was, under the restructuring of the Dergue, put under the supervision of the Standing Committee – an arrangement that ended the First Vice-Chairman's role of liaising between the Dergue and POMOA. Ever since the Marxist-Leninists opted to join the revolution they had developed a close tie with the First Vice-Chairman. The relationship of the First Vice-Chairman and the Marxist-Leninists of the POMOA was of mutual political benefit. The new restructuring of the Dergue and POMOA broke any official link between the First Vice-Chairman and POMOA. What made matters unbearable to them was not only the measure taken to break their discreet relationship but the appointment of the chairman of the Administration Committee of the PMAC, Captain Alemayehu Haile, who was suspected of being a sympathiser of the EPRP, as the Secretary-General of the PMAC. The First Vice-Chairman and his cabals of the POMOA had taken the appointment of Captain Alemayehu Haile as a great blow to their political aims. The First Vice-Chairman could not come to terms with the restructuring of the Dergue that reduced him to a political nonentity. He felt so dejected and depressed – a feeling that he was not able to conceal at the first meeting of the Council of Ministers following the reorganisation and redistribution of functions. His presence in the meeting was in body; he was elsewhere in mind and spirit, perhaps brooding over the sophisticated measures that had been taken to strip him of political power under the guise of organisational reform.

The Marxist-Leninists of the POMOA who had, from their student days, been at loggerheads with the leaders of EPRP, were unhappy and not certain of their future under a reform that gave a key position to a sympathiser of EPRP. Sharing a common experience of injustice with the First Vice-Chairman created an ideal condition for conspiracy against the leadership of the Dergue.

The initiators of the restructuring of the PMAC, Colonel Asrat Desta, Captain Alemayehu, Captain Mogesse Wolde Michael and their associates, failed to anticipate the capability of those seriously affected to retaliate. The forces behind the restructuring of the Dergue made a major mistake by retaining the head of the Security Guards of the PMAC, Colonel Daniel Assfaw, a close friend of Colonel Mengistu Haile Mariam. Colonel Daniel caught the reformers unaware and executed them summarily.

Internal and External Threats

The PMAC, having made the necessary changes in structure and functions, directed its attention towards making the people aware of the dangers that were hovering over the unity and territorial integrity of the country. The collusion of the Sudan and Somalia with internal reactionary forces was given prominence in the government's propaganda offensives.

The President of the Sudan, Neimerie, declared that he would assist secessionist elements in Eritrea and the newly-formed Ethiopian Democratic Union. The EDU was led by General Iyassu, an Eritrean, who was an ambassador of the imperial regime in the United Kingdom. The grandson-in-law of Emperor Haile Selassie and great grandson of Emperor Yohannis IV, Leuel Ras Mengesha Seyoum, and another grandson-in-law of the Emperor Haile Selassie, Major-General Nega Tegegn, governors of Tigray and Begemidir, respectively were among the prominent leaders of the EDU.

Somalia had also stepped up its barrage of propaganda against Ethiopia to promote its irredentist interest in the Ogaden region of Ethiopia. Moreover, other Arab countries were also apprehensive of the revolutionary movement in Ethiopia. They intensified their moral support, material and financial assistance to the Eritrean secessionists and other organisations opposed to the rule of the PMAC. The Western democracies were not indifferent to developments in Ethiopia since the regime was striking closer ties with the socialist countries.

The internal situation had become more volatile than ever. The EDU and EPRP had conceded to the ELF's demand for an independent

Eritrea, thereby forging an alliance to fight against their common enemy, the PMAC. The PMAC, who had believed that the unity and territorial integrity of the country were under serious threat, took it upon itself to bring the dangerous situation to the notice of the people. It made a national call to the people to rally behind it in the defence of the revolution and the 'revolutionary motherland'. On 29 January 1977 the chairman of the PMAC, Brigadier-General Teferri Bente, in his address to the nation called upon progressive forces and patriots to form a common front to defend the motherland. The chairman, in his speech enumerated the achievements of the revolution, the sacrifices made in the furtherance of the objectives of the revolution, the collusion of the EDU and secessionist elements in the northern part of the country: the threat of invasion by the Sudan and Somalia, imperialist plots and the steps that the revolutionary camp was expected to take. The speech was a detailed appraisal of the magnitude of the problem that the nation was facing because of the revolution. Although his speech covered a wide variety of issues, its central theme was the immediate creation of a common front by the alliance of all progressive forces. Nothing illustrates this better than the following passage from his speech:

> 'Progressive anti-feudal, anti-imperialist and anti-bureaucratic
> capitalist and all other democratic forces bear historic
> responsibility of closing ranks and forming a common front
> by sinking their minor differences in the spirit of the
> Programme of National Democratic Revolution in full
> awareness of the menace hovering over the country. There
> is no greater clarion call that the motherland can make on
> them. We have no reason to believe that there is any
> progressive group or individual who will not respond to this
> call. Nor can there be. It is imperative that all progressive
> forces concerned with the welfare and interests of the masses
> should at this critical point when enemies are poised on
> numerous fronts, close ranks, co-ordinate their efforts and
> set an example in spearheading any undertaking
> demanding sacrifices. It must be recognised that the
> responsibility for defending the unity and territorial
> integrity of the motherland and placing the country on a
> firm foundation by no means rests on the men-in-uniform
> alone. There is no alternative to this decisive struggle in so
> far as Ethiopians, jealous of their country's honour and
> freedom, are concerned.'[44]

194

The chairman's speech was an invitation to all progressive forces other than the EDU that was labelled as reactionary, and condemned. The EPRP and ELF, on the other hand, were not condemned nor excluded from the invitation. The chairman's approach to these two organisations was conciliatory. He made it clear in his speech, given the colossal problem the country was facing, that the progressive forces should over-look their minor differences and act in unison to safeguard the unity and territorial integrity of the country. The chairman and his associates in the PMAC believed that the minor differences among progressive forces, including secessionist elements, could be resolved by dialogue. Colonel Mengistu and his Marxist-Leninist cabals of the POMOA, on the other hand, held the view that their differences with the EPRP, EDU, ELF and other opposition forces were irreconcilable and it had to be resolved by crushing them.

The day after the chairman's speech to the nation, a mammoth rally was held at the Revolution Square to support his national call to defend the country against internal and external enemies. Addressing the rally the chairman repeated his call for the formation of a national front of all progressive forces and even went to the extent of pronouncing that the difference among them was nothing other than the struggle for power. He said: *'In time of revolutionary ferment differences are bound to be more pronounced for reasons that have to do with power struggle. We have seen and heard that this is a universal phenomenon. I said a while ago such differences should in no way be allowed to provide an opportunity for either external enemies or the exposed reactionaries who had been uprooted.'*[45]

He down-played the differences among progressive forces as struggle for power rather than ideology. Imploring them to put aside their differences he said: *'The appeal I made to all progressive Ethiopians at this particular moment from this square is that you unite, establish a party and form a common front. As long as this is not done, our revolution will continue to be on the verge of disaster.'*[46]

The other speakers at the rally, the representatives of the POMOA, AETU, Central Urban Dwellers' Associations of Addis Ababa and peasants' association of its environs made speeches whose content and mode of delivery were contrary to the chairman's conciliatory speech. All of them condemned the EPRP, EDU and ELF as enemies of the revolution and demanded that stern action should be taken immediately against them. They emphatically echoed the Marxist-Leninist demands for arming with weapons the revolutionary camp, the creation of defence committees to safeguard the revolution and a host of other issues. The POMOA and mass organisations excluded peaceful dialogue with other groups and

195

advocated their total elimination. The only point of agreement between the chairman and the POMOA and its surrogates was the condemnation of the EDU. The speeches of the chairman of the PMAC on 29 and 30 January 1977 and the speeches of the representatives of the POMOA and its surrogate mass organisations made clear the two opposing views in dealing with anti-revolutionary forces. The chairman of the Dergue and the majority of its members favoured dialogue with anti-revolutionaries while a few PMAC members, including Colonel Mengistu and the Marxist-Leninists of the POMOA, opted for a violent class struggle.

The difference of views in the PMAC and POMOA on measures to be taken in dealing with the EPRP, EDU and ELF culminated in the palace coup of 3 February 1977. On that fatal day the chairman of PMAC was conducting a meeting of the Central Committee when Colonel Daniel, accompanied by security guards, burst into the meeting and arrested the chairman, General Teferri Bente, along with Lieutenant-Colonel Asrat Desta, chairman of the Information and Public Relation Committee of PMAC, Lieutenant-Colonel Hiruy Haile Selassie, member of the PMAC, Captain Alemayehu Haile, Secretary-General of PMAC, Captain Mogesse W/Michael, chairman of the Economic Committee of PMAC, Captain Teferra Deneke and Corporal Hailu Belai, both members of the PMAC. They were taken away immediately and ruthlessly executed by a firing squad. This unfortunate episode silenced the voice of moderation and reason in the PMAC. It was a victory for Colonel Mengistu and his cabals of the POMOA.

A statement issued by the PMAC after the execution alleged that a coup attempt by some members of the PMAC in collusion with the EPRP, EDU and ELF was foiled. The statement declared that revolutionary measures had been taken against the plotters, the chairman and six members of the Dergue. The statement in underscoring the dangerous nature of the alleged plot said:

> 'Today's coup, which was foiled through the committed
> action of the Provisional Military Government and
> dedicated men-in-uniform was a sophisticated and deep-
> rooted plot. It was masterminded by hired recruits within
> the PMAC used by imperialists, EDU and EPRP and was
> carried out with an aim to rid the country from various
> directions and thereby demoralise the men-in-uniform, but
> also to take advantage of the unfavourable situation so that
> the hired members of the Council could bring about a
> fascistic *coup d'état* in the capital identical to what had taken

place in Chile and restore the oppressive rule of Assfaw-Wassen Haile-Selassie, Mengesha Seyoum and their like cohorts. Revolutionary forces, including progressive educators, youth workers, soldiers – in general the vanguards of the struggle against EPRP, EDU, ELF and imperialism were to be subjected to the fate which once fell upon progressive Chileans.'[47]

This official statement was aimed at agitating the masses to rally behind the regime's actions and as such could not be taken as credible explanation of the circumstances that led to the execution of the alleged plotters of the coup. It was a statement that was issued to justify the execution.

The alleged plotters were accused of the following crimes:[48]

– Supplying anti-revolutionaries with arms and provisions belonging to the state;
– Openly siding with the EDU and EPRP in the fight from behind against the men-in-uniform, the broad masses and the Ethiopian Revolution;
– Seeking to replace genuine revolutionaries with EPRP recruits and by infiltrating mass organisations;
– Lobbying in the PMAC ranks for bringing the EPRP to the revolutionary camp;
– Sanctioning unfavourably mentioning the EPRP on the media;
– Plotting to reverse the revolution and to abduct members of the POMOA.

Moreover, Brigadier-General Teferri Bente was accused of failing to denounce the EPRP in public as the enemy of the revolution in his speeches to the nation on the 29 and 30 January 1977.

The statement further alleged that the commander of the PMAC's Security Guards, Colonel Daniel Assfaw, three security guards and the Vice-Chairman of the POMOA, Dr Senay Likie, were killed during the exchange of fire with the plotters. This statement was far from the truth, for the alleged plotters of the coup were arrested while they were in a meeting unarmed. According to the insiders' version, the Vice-Chairman of the POMOA was shot by the deputy commander of the Security Guards while he was heading toward the commander's office immediately after the execution of the seven officers of the PMAC. The commander was killed when he peeped through a window of his office in response to the sound of sudden shots. The three security guards were killed in an exchange of shots with Captain Yohannis, Deputy to Colonel Daniel. Captain Yohannis also lost his life in the exchange of fire with the security guards.[49] Following the PMAC's statement, in keeping with its standard practice, a rally was held at Revolution Square in the capital. Representatives of mass organisations and the POMOA gave speeches that condemned the alleged plot of a coup as a treacherous act. The ring leaders of the alleged coup were castigated for collaborating with enemies of the revolution – the EPRP, EDU and ELF, who were accused of plotting with reactionary neighbouring countries and assisted by imperialist forces to dismember the country. The speeches were carefully orchestrated to create the impression that the internal enemies (EDU, EPRP and ELF) were colluding with external enemies (neighbouring and certain imperialist countries) to reverse the revolution and subvert the territorial integrity of the country. In the face of a threat to the nation and the revolution the speakers demanded arms and for the taking of decisive measures against reactionaries and anarchists.

Colonel Mengistu also addressed the rally revealing the direction of the revolution and announcing with a great sense of satisfaction the PMAC's decision to meet the demands of revolutionaries for arms and taking stern measures against reactionaries. In explaining these actions he declared:

> 'Terror and anarchy will vanish from the camp of the broad masses and reign in that of the reactionaries.
>
> We will duly reciprocate the campaign of terror being spread by reactionaries by launching a barrage into their very camp.
>
> To this end, we will arm the allies and comrades of the broad masses without giving respite to reactionaries and to avenge the blood of our comrades double and triple.'[50]

He went ahead and sanctioned the immediate establishment of revolutionary committees at the national, regional, provincial, local levels and at workplaces to safeguard the victories of the revolution against anti-revolutionaries. His declaration was the official launching of the Red Terror that was responsible for the unnecessary loss of many innocent lives. Liquidation of enemies rather than their political accommodation became the norm for settling differences – a view advanced with conviction by the members of the POMOA particularly by the members of the

MEISON.[51] As will be seen in the following section, the *MEISON* eventually was a victim of its own convictions.

Mengistu's take-over of power by eliminating the moderates from the PMAC paved the way for meeting the demands of Marxist-Leninist organisations of the POMOA for arms and taking stern measures against so-called reactionaries and anarchists. The terms reactionaries and anarchists were liberally interpreted to include anyone who opposed the policies of the regime and the modes of their implementation.

The tempo of distribution of arms to executive committees and revolutionary squads of urban dwellers' associations and trade unions with assault guns increased substantially. The arming of the peasant militia that had the full support of the PMAC since it assumed power was pursued with vigour. Disarming ordinary citizens, on the other hand, by launching house-to-house searches and night raids of selected residential areas was rigorously carried out. During the searches and night raids, individuals who were suspected of membership in the EPRP, EDU and ELF, were arrested and/or shot on the spot on the pretext of resisting arrest. The house searches and night raids were planned and executed by revolutionary development committees in collaboration with the government's security guards. The committees were established parallel to the state structure with members from mass organisations, the POMOA and certain government departments.

The night raids, more often than not, resulted in the execution of individuals suspected of being members, sympathisers of agents of reactionary or anarchist organisations. The swift action of the search teams did not spare those who distributed or who were innocently in possession of clandestine leaflets. Simultaneously with the searches and nocturnal raids the propaganda offensives against the EPRP, EDU and ELF were systematically conducted. Reactionaries and anarchists particularly the EPRP, in retaliation to the regime's measures against its members, stepped up assassinations of revolutionaries. Assassinations were carried out under the cover of darkness as well as in broad daylight. So much so, that the government-owned media's preoccupation became the disclosing of atrocities of the anti-revolutionary forces quite often singling out the EPRP. The successes of the search teams were also given prominence. The display of caches of weapons allegedly captured from the anti-revolutionaries was routine.

The assassinations and executions combined created a sense of insecurity and uncertainty. It seemed both the government and anti-revolutionaries welcomed the effect that was created by their acts. The government's propaganda onslaught also aggravated the effects of

199

executions and assassinations. People were not sure whether those alleged assassinations were committed by anti-revolutionaries or the government. The regime was capable of committing such acts to discredit anti-revolutionaries. The way some of the assassinations were used for propaganda purposes compels a detached observer to conclude that the PMAC and POMOA had staged the scenario to create public antipathy against reactionaries and anarchists. A case in point was the assassination of the chairman of the AETU, Ato Tewodros Bekele. He was assassinated by armed men in military uniform. The assassins, in broad daylight, walked into the headquarters of the AETU, shot down the chairman in the presence of his colleagues and drove away. The manner in which the assassination was committed was quite different from the pattern established by oppositions particularly the EPRP. An assassin of the EPRP invariably attacked a victim in an isolated place, mostly under the cover of darkness; avoided public places where he/she could be easily apprehended. The assassination of the chairman of the AETU did not fit into this pattern. Besides, the assassination of the chairman created an ideal condition for the labour unions to demand more aggressively for the execution of the EPRP members and sympathisers.

The day after the assassination a mass rally was held at Revolution Square where his remains were laid in state before they were taken for burial. At the rally representatives of the PMAC, POMOA, AETU, Central Urban Dwellers' Association of Addis Ababa and Peasants' Association of the Menagesha Province made speeches. The theme was the condemnation of the assassins as paid agents of the EPRP, EDU, ELF and CIA. The need to create a common front of the progressive forces against enemies of the revolution was underscored.

A representative of the PMAC, Major Endale Tessema, articulating the steps that ought to be taken against anti-revolutionaries, said:

> 'The Ethiopian revolution which has now taken an offensive course by getting rid of reactionary infiltrators in high positions, is determined to defeat the White Terror of its enemies with Red Terror through sacrifices of genuine revolutionaries in the forefront of the struggle, like Comrade Tewodros.'[52]

The rally was stage-managed by the PMAC and POMOA to incite the people, particularly the workers, against the enemies of the revolution. From the way the death of the unfortunate union leader was manipulated for political ends one cannot help suspect that the revolutionary camp was responsible for the union leader's assassination. On the other hand, the state burial ceremony that was televised created the impression that the PMAC honoured those whose lives were sacrificed in the name of the revolution. In a society that attaches great importance to burial ceremonies, the state burial given to the chairman of the AETU, was a calculated step to win the support of the people, particularly the workers. The occasion was also used to convey a message to counter-revolutionaries that White Terror would be reciprocated with Red Terror.

Although the execution of suspected assassins was intensified after Mengistu's take-over of power, Red Terror was not announced until the assassination of the chairman of AETU. Searches and night raids were intensified along with meetings at workplaces to expose anti-revolution-aries. The meetings were usually chaired by cadres of POMOA or its agents. A chairperson would make a lengthy speech which usually would start with enumerating the achievements of the revolution and the sinister designs of the enemies of the revolution to reverse it and end by stressing the need to expose individuals who were either members or sympathisers of the enemies of the revolution. Following a chairperson's speech the ordeal of exposing suspects would begin. Those present at the meeting would be given the opportunity to expose themselves by making a confession in front of their colleagues. Failure to make voluntary confession would provoke the chairperson to invite others in the meeting to expose anarchists and reactionaries. Those who would take the initiative to expose others were individuals planted by the POMOA. Exposing suspects continued until the names on a black list of the POMOA were exhausted. The wretched individuals who were exposed either voluntarily or by others would be paraded on a stage and finally taken to Keble detention centres. In Addis Ababa alone the 291 Kebeles and 26 *Kefitegnas* each had a prison that was used for the detention of anti-revolutionaries. Urban dwellers' associations were given *carte blanche* power to execute prisoners. Every night Kebeles, one after the other, would execute some of the detainees and display their bodies in public squares where passers by were forced to look at bodies drenched with blood. The mass killing of citizens without due process of law continued unabated. The executions, in most cases, were used for settling old scores and other reasons unrelated to the revolution. Young, old, pensioners and even children as young as 10–12 years were not spared the wanton killings of individuals. A competition among urban dwellers' associations in scoring the highest number of executions senselessly increased the toll. Besides urban dweller's associations, there were other killing squads, probably organised by the PMAC and POMOA to eliminate those who had escaped the notice of Kebeles. By the end of the summer of 1977 the first round of the Red Terror broke the backbone of the major enemy of the PMAC and POMOA, the EPRP, and by the end of 1978 the second round of the Red Terror effectively uprooted it from all cities and towns. The surviving members of the EPRP retreated to the mountains of Asimba in the Tigray administrative region. Even though it is difficult to give the exact number of victims of the Red Terror, one could claim that several thousands of lives were lost. The cruelty and the indiscriminate nature with which it was executed are an affront to humanity.

Colonel Mengistu, once more, turned his attention towards the unfinished business of cleansing the PMAC of members who challenged his leadership. The only member who questioned the decision of Mengistu was his deputy, Colonel Atnafu Abate. He was in many respects the antithesis of Colonel Mengistu. He was a sincere nationalist but hopelessly naive in politics. However, he advocated gradual change and hand over of power to a civilian elected government and did not subscribe to the introduction of scientific socialism as practised in the USSR and other socialist countries. Besides, he resented the execution of the Second Chairman and six members of the PMAC. He was very naive to make his views about the execution of his colleagues public. Mengistu, who believed that he could not have peace of mind unless he got rid of the only person who challenged him openly, convened the third ordinary session of the congress of the PMAC.

At the meeting of the congress some members who had connived with Mengistu provoked Colonel Atnafu into an argument. As a result of heated arguments Atnafu innocently questioned the wisdom of the execution of the chairman and members of the PMAC, the launching of Red Terror and the adoption of socialism as an official ideology of the state. He also appealed to the congress to proceed with caution and moderation. He even suggested to the congress to defer the consideration of some of the issues that required the consent of the people until such time an elected government took over. Atnafu, without realising the trap set for him, expressed his sincere views that were vital to the revolution. His comments were taken by the congress as a confession of his reactionary stands, particularly his resentment of the execution of the chairman and members of the PMAC as endorsing counter-revolutionary activities. The congress, as would be expected of a rubber stamp body, condemned him to share the fate of counter-revolutionaries. A statement of the PMAC, that was issued after his execution, summarised the verdict of the congress as:

'It is scientific truth that as the revolution advances, gaining strength and depth, the PMAC too has come cleansing itself of and eliminating from time to time those members of the PMAC engaged in shifting class alliances thus reaching the present stage. Similarly, during the third regular session of the PMAC congress, Lieutenant-Colonel Atnafu Abate whose reactionary stand has been precipitating in the history of the struggle of the PMAC, has more than ever before brought out into the open his long-hidden stand. The PMAC Congress heard Lieutenant-Colonel Atnafu personally exposing himself and after giving the matter serious consideration, it found him to be very dangerous for the revolution. A revolutionary measure (execution) was taken against him on Saturday on the basis of the decision of the PMAC Congress.'[53]

The only voice of moderation in the PMAC was lynched by a congress that had reduced itself to a tool of an aspiring despot.

The following is a summary of the charges[54] against Colonel Atnafu Abate from the statement of the PMAC:

1. He had not given his support to the NDRPE and failed to participate actively in discussions on the programme.
2. Opposed all progressive proclamations that had been issued and held views that were against the wishes of the people.
3. In the discussion of vital issues in the Dergue he had invariably placed himself in opposition.
4. Manifested feudal arrogance and neglected the allies of the revolution.
5. Displayed an anti-cadre position.
6. Provided solace and support to anti-revolutionaries.
7. Conspired with Brigadier-General Teferri Bente and associates who were executed for having conspired with EDU, EPRP and ELF to reverse the course of the revolution and made secret contacts with the enemies of the revolution.
8. Confessed to the congress that he did not believe in scientific socialism.
9. Advocated a military dictatorship.
10. Opposed the measures taken against reactionaries and secured the release of assassins who had slain revolutionaries from detention.

11. Opposed the politicising, organising and arming of the masses and on the other hand, supplied arms to anti-revolutionaries.
12. Opposed the setting up of the Provisional Office for Mass Organisational Affairs.
13. Abused his power to further his personal interest and those of his associates.
14. Opposed the search operations that were carried out in two rounds to weed out anti-people, anti-revolutionary and anti-unity individuals and groups from the broad masses.
15. Argued that the interest of Ethiopia should have precedence over the ideology.
16. He said: *'We have deprived the country of friends in the name of socialism. I do not believe that Ethiopia alone can build socialism in Africa. We have to be friendly to the East and the West and this is mixed economy.'*[55]
17. He argued: *'In the name of socialism and class, the entire people are today deprived of justice, peace and democracy. How many are those who had fled the country? A way must be found for releasing those in jails and reconciling with others.'*[56]

The charges against vindicate him as the only sensible person with an independent mind in the Dergue. His prophecy that socialism would not work in Ethiopia was proven right by the collapse of the socialist system.

The news of the execution of Colonel Atnafu was not a surprise to the people. It was public knowledge that, after the assassination of the Second Chairman and six members of the Dergue, he would be the next victim. Clandestine leaflets were being circulated warning him that he would be another target. His complacency made him easy prey to the predatory instincts of Mengistu. His execution deprived the PMAC a sense of moderation and an opportunity to introduce a reform that recognised and respected the intrinsic nature of man.

Socialist Countries Express Solidarity and Support

Socialist countries who were pleased with developments in Ethiopia poured their congratulations and support on Mengistu. They were convinced that the revolution under the radical leadership of the PMAC was serious enough to merit welcome to the socialist bloc. Soon after the execution of the ring leaders of the alleged coup, the German Democratic Republic (GDR) sent a high-level delegation led by Comrade Lambez, a politburo member and Secretary-General of the Central Committee of the Socialist Unity Party. That the delegation was led by a senior member

204

of a politburo was recognition of the Ethiopian revolution which in the past the communist bloc withheld, in spite of the PMAC's desire to seek closer links with it. Comrade Lambez's visit was an overt demonstration of a change of outlook in the communist bloc. At the end of the visit of the delegation Comrade Lambez commented:

> 'Members of my delegation and myself are very pleased to be able to hold meetings with the genuine revolutionary leaders of Ethiopia and Comrade Mengistu Haile Mariam, since our arrival here. As a result we have been convinced that the Ethiopian popular revolution is in the hands of genuine revolutionaries. Furthermore, we have been convinced that the revolutionary leaders stand for the interest of the broad masses and determined to lead the revolutionary struggle to the ultimate objectives. We have been able to confirm the progressive Ethiopian leaders and genuine revolutionaries are struggling for the interests of the broad masses. Because of this, the people of GDR will stand on their side and the broad masses of Ethiopia.'[57]

The verdict of Comrade Lambez opened the door for other socialist countries who began to send delegation, after delegation. President Castro of Cuba endorsed the GDR's appraisal of the Ethiopian revolution by paying a state visit to Ethiopia. He was the first head of a socialist country to have visited Ethiopia since the 1974 revolution. His satisfaction with the Ethiopian revolution was reflected in the joint communique released at the end of the visit. The communique stated:

> 'Referring to the solidarity of the Cuban people with the people of Ethiopia, the Cuban side expressed admiration and support for the anti-feudal, anti-imperialist and socialist stand of the Ethiopian people. Condemning the interference in Ethiopia's internal affairs by imperialists and reactionary states, the Cuban side also reaffirms total support for the Ethiopian revolution.'[58]

The communique in endorsing Ethiopia's legitimate concern over the Red Sea further stated:

> 'They discussed the counter-revolutionary activities of imperialism and its puppets in the Red Sea region and

205

expressed the need for the progressive forces in the area to
co-ordinate their struggle against machinations of their
common enemy, imperialism. Further the two sides
emphasised that the peace of the region requires that the
Indian Ocean remains a zone of peace.'[59]

The positive evaluation of the Ethiopian revolution by the two most important proxies of the USSR encouraged other socialist countries to exchange delegations with Ethiopia and to sign all sorts of economic, cultural, technical assistance and military co-operation agreements. Ethiopia's position in the socialist bloc was assured when Colonel Mengistu, upon the invitation of the USSR, paid a state visit from 4–8 May 1977. A communique issued at the end of the visit characterised it a success. The communique expressed the common stands of the two countries on world problems, including the situation in the Horn of Africa. Furthermore, the Ethiopian delegation expressed its loyalty to the USSR by pledging that, '... *Ethiopia firmly intends to follow the anti-imperialist and anti-colonialist course of its foreign policy and wishes to develop and strengthen friendship and co-operation with all countries and peoples.*'[60] The Soviet side being satisfied with the vow of allegiance of the Ethiopian side to the ideals of socialism reciprocated by saying that it '*welcomed the progressive transformations that are being carried out in Ethiopia, and wished the Ethiopian people every success in building a new life. It also voiced solidarity with the efforts of the people and leadership of Ethiopia in defending the revolution.*'[61]

The visit was of immense political benefit for both countries. For Ethiopia it was an end to political isolation imposed by the West, particularly the US under the Carter Administration that stopped military as well as development assistance to it. Moreover, the Carter Administration's intention to review its policies on the problem in Eritrea and its readiness to supply weapons to the Republic of Somalia that was prepared to declare war on Ethiopia had strained the Ethio-US relations beyond any repair. In the Ethio-Somalia conflict, Somalia was the aggressor and Ethiopia the victim of aggression. Imposing an arms embargo on the victim of aggression gave good cause to the leaders of Ethiopia to interpret the action of the Carter Administration as an act of endorsing Somalia's irredentism. The new friendship struck with the USSR was an assurance that Ethiopia could rely on the USSR's friendship.

The USSR's adoption of Ethiopia as a new satellite state in the Horn of Africa was timely. For Ethiopia was diplomatically isolated by the West, the Eritrean secessionists and EDU with the assistance of the Sudanese Government and other Arab countries had intensified their armed struggle in the northern part of the country and Somalia had already opened two fronts in the East and the South under the guise of the Western Somalia Liberation Front. The sense of diplomatic isolation that was felt when Mengistu took over power compelled him to look for a superpower ally. Expressing the sense of isolation he said: *'Except for the People's Democratic Republic of Yemen, mother Ethiopia does not have a single revolutionary friend in the region! The broad masses of Ethiopian people must take this potent fact to heart!'*[62] The new friendship with the socialist bloc lifted the fear of isolation. The friendship with the USSR and other Socialist countries gave to the Ethiopian leadership a sense of security and confidence to intensify the revolution.

Control of the People's Office for Mass Organisational Affairs

Colonel Mengistu, after his take-over of power, had restructured the PMAC and filled all key positions both in the PMAC and in his government with loyalists. The POMOA grew very powerful, partly due to his support. Its members' greed for power inflated unabated and Mengistu had to take steps to check this development. Steps were taken to amend the proclamation that provided for the establishment of the POMOA. A restructuring of the POMOA curtailed its freedom of action. The political school, which was under its supervision in the new proclamation, became directly accountable to the PMAC. This change transferred responsibility of selecting and training of cadres from the POMOA to the PMAC. The selection and appointment of regional officers of the POMOA was also transferred to the PMAC with the consequence of bringing it under the virtual control of the PMAC. The impact of the consequence of restructuring frustrated the ambition for power of the dominant member of the POMOA, the *MEISON*. With its control and influence curtailed, the *MEISON* had no cause to continue to work with the PMAC. Moreover, the *MEISON* members were better placed than anybody else to asses the PMAC's fortune to remain in power. For this was a time when intensive war was being waged against the EDU forces and Eritrean secessionists in the northern and northwestern part of the country. The forces of both organisations had the upper hand in the battles and succeeded in excluding vast regions from reach of the government. The EDU forces captured Setit Humera, a province bordering the Sudan. Eritrean secessionists also succeeded in chasing out the government from most of Eritrea, including part of the port of Massawa. The city of Asmara and the port of Assab were the only places under government control. In the east Somali forces penetrated 700 kilometres into Ethiopian territory and a full-scale war was being waged between the forces of the two countries. The Ethiopian forces were defending the city of Dire Dawa, which was the site of the second Air Force base of the country and a major terminal of the railway line that links the capital, Addis Ababa, with the port of Djibouti, against the invading Somali forces. This was indeed a time when the disintegration of Ethiopia and the demise of the military junta was considered by political pundits to be a foregone conclusion. The leaders of the *MEISON* seemed to have reached the same conclusion and to have chosen this moment to disassociate themselves from a beleaguered regime and to go underground. The *MEISON*'s decision to abandon the revolution when the people were rallying behind the government in response to the call for the defence of the country was an error of judgement that cost the lives of its leaders and its own existence as a credible political organisation.

The *MEISON*, with the other members of the POMOA, had prepared the nation for an inevitable war against the internal and external enemies of the country, in defence of the revolutionary motherland. In spite of the atrocities perpetrated by the PMAC in collusion with the members of the POMOA particularly the *MEISON*, the Ethiopian people, setting aside their legitimate right of retribution for the injustices done to them, rallied behind the junta in defence of the country. The response of the people ranged from voluntarily joining the front to financial and material contributions. A militia force of 300,000 strong was mobilised and trained in a short time, mainly with public support. Such was the scale of the people's concern for the territorial integrity of the country. The Ethiopian people again were proving that they were still true to their tradition of rallying behind their leaders regardless of their shortcomings. The Marxist-Leninist leaders of the *MEISON* seemed to have overlooked the history of their country. Running away from the revolutionary camp when the entire nation was determined to defend the country was unwise and an act offensive to Ethiopian social values. The defection of the *MEISON* was also considered by the ordinary people as an act of betrayal. On the other hand, the defection of the *MEISON* was an unexpected bonus for Colonel Mengistu Haile Mariam who was eagerly awaiting for an opportune time to deal with it. The opportunity to act swiftly in eliminating the *MEISON* leadership was made possible by their foolish decision. The PMAC handled the defection of the *MEISON* with a sober mind. It broke the news of the defection to the nation and at the same time appealed to the functionaries of the *MEISON* to continue with their normal duties in spite of the defection of their leaders.

The leaders and members of the *MEISON* withdrew from the POMOA and government institutions at the national and regional levels in August 1977. They drove out from the capital in three directions.[63] The PMAC which was aware of their plan let them drive out from the capital under the watchful eye of its spies. Running, as fugitives in the countryside where their presence could easily arouse suspicion, was another unmitigated disaster. Upon information received from local peasants' associations the fugitives were pursued by security guards. Those who failed to give themselves up were liquidated on the spot and others who co-operated were arrested and imprisoned. Those who gave themselves up shared the fate of those individuals whom they had branded as reactionaries and anarchists. The *MEISON* leaders or 'right roaders', as they were referred to by the government media, including the highly regarded ideologist of the *MEISON* and the chairman of the POMOA, Comrade Haile Fida, languished in prison and died a slow death in unknown circumstances. The entire leadership of the *MEISON* was liquidated. It died a premature death because of its leaders' excessive ambition for power and their decision to abandon the revolution to which it gave a sense of direction in its formative years, at the wrong time.

The leaders of the remaining four Marxist-Leninist organisations either defected to *Seded* or pledged the allegiance of their organisations to Mengistu by joining the Union of Ethiopian Marxist-Leninist Organisations – which was supposed to serve as a nucleus of a workers' party. The *ECHAT* and *MALRED* who resisted disappeared from the political map of Ethiopia by the liquidation and/or the detention of their leaders.

Confrontation with the Sudan and Somalia

By the end of the summer of 1977, Mengistu had emerged as an undisputed leader and a strongman. Among the Marxist-Leninist organisations the most dominant one, the *MEISON*, was obliterated by its own folly of premature defection from the revolutionary camp. From the so-called reactionary camp the EPRP was ousted by the Red Terror. The EDU which, with the support of the Sudanese Government and other countries, had captured a few regions in the northwestern part of the country was defeated by the Dergue forces. Although these victories on the home front were sources of encouragement for the PMAC, the situation in Eritrea was disheartening. The Eritrean secessionists with the assistance of the Sudan, Egypt and other Arab countries had captured the towns of Teseneye, Keren, Karora and Naqfa in the provinces bordering the Sudan.

On the eastern front, the Somali forces had occupied the towns of Gode, Qebridehar and Warder in the Ogaden region. The Ethiopian regular army and militia were engaged in fierce battles with Somali forces nearby Jigiga and Dire Dawa. Somalia had also opened other fronts in the south and south-east.

Along with the invasion from three fronts, the governments of the Sudan and Somalia launched a synchronised propaganda offensive against the Ethiopian Government. The propaganda offensive exceeded the bounds of acceptable behaviour and civility. Particularly President Nimerie personalised the propaganda and began to call the chairman of the PMAC as 'Mengistu the pirate'.[64] On the other hand, Colonel Mengistu *'With all his excesses, tried to avoid personalising the conflict.'*[65] Besides the personal insults, President Nimerie declared that he would assist the Eritrean secessionists and if need be mobilise the thousands of Ethiopian refugees in the Sudan to fight against the Ethiopian Government. Although Nimerie's threat was a bluff, it strengthened Ethiopia's case against Sudanese interference in its internal affairs. The tension created between the two neighbouring countries became even worse when the Sudan signed a joint defence pact with Egypt. Egypt never restrained herself from meddling in Ethiopia's internal affairs since the time of the Egyptian leader, Khedive Ismail. Egypt and other Arab countries expressed their commitment to support the Sudan if Ethiopia and the Sudan clashed. Similar gestures of solidarity were expressed in support of Somalia which was invading Ethiopia. The military manoeuvre of Egypt, the Sudan and the US, Operation Bright Star, in the Red Sea, increased the tension in the Horn. The Ethiopian Government condemned the military exercise as an unwarranted demonstration of force and its new friends, the socialist countries, expressed their solidarity with Ethiopia by castigating the military manoeuvre.

Ethiopia, while defending itself against invasion on three fronts, stepped up its diplomatic offensive by submitting its case to the regular meeting of the Heads of State and Government of the OAU at Libreville, Gabon 1977.

Chairman Mengistu passionately addressed the summit of OAU accusing the Sudan of interfering in the internal affairs of Ethiopia by assisting and harbouring secessionists from Eritrea in violation of the charter of the OAU. The Sudanese President made counter accusations. The angry exchange of words between the two heads of state revealed the seriousness of the deterioration of relations. The Ethiopian Chairman in articulating his charges against the government of the Sudan said:

'The Sudanese Government opened more than ever before,
the ports, towns and frontiers of the Sudan for the

subversive activities of the secessionist groups against
Ethiopia. Arms and all other supplies sent to the groups by
imperialist and reactionary Arab regimes were shipped to
Port Sudan and from there transported by land with a
Sudanese military escort to the Ethio-Sudanese border.
Several training and operation bases were set up all along
the Sudanese side of our common border . . . The Sudan
became the rear base and its military forces the rearguard
for the secessionist groups. In addition the Sudanese
Government has been providing full assistance to a
collection of runaway monarchists, feudal barons and other
reactionaries with a view to subverting the Ethiopian
revolution. To this group the Sudanese Government did not
only render material and moral support but also has put at
its disposal propaganda facilities, especially radio Omdurman
– Sudan's national radio station.'[66]

Although the Sudanese interference was endemic and of public knowledge, it denied the charges and made counter charges by accusing
Ethiopia of harbouring secessionists from southern Sudan. However, the
summit, having listened to the recriminations, charges and counter
charges of interference in the internal affairs of one another, appointed
a Good Offices Committee to resolve the conflict. The conference
appealed to the two sides to restrain themselves from any activity that
would undermine the easing of tensions between the two countries. In
spite of the dislike of the two heads of state for each other, the politicians
and diplomats of the two countries worked hard to reduce tension and
restore normal relations. In less than a year from the Libreville summit
the heads of states of the two countries met at Freetown, Sierra Leone,
to resolve their differences. In the case of Ethio-Sudanese conflict the
Good Offices Committee's effort bore fruit when the two sides accepted
its recommendations for the normalisation of their relations.

   The problem with the Ethio-Somali conflict was of quite a different
nature from the Ethio-Sudanese dispute. Somalia in violation of the
charters of the UN and OAU desired to annex one fifth of Ethiopia
inhabited by Somali-speaking Ethiopians. Somalia's irredentism since its
independence in 1960 had resulted in two wars between the two countries
with humiliating defeats to Somalia. After having built up its forces for
seventeen years with generous military assistance from the USSR, Somalia
began to infiltrate into the Ethiopian territory under the guise of the
Western Somalia Liberation Front, a phoney organisation created by

the Somali Government. Taking advantage of the upheaval that was antecedent to the Ethiopian revolution, it intensified its aggression and by the end of the summer of 1977 its forces penetrated about 700 kilometres into the Ethiopian territory. The Ethiopian forces were outnumbered both in men and weapons and retreated abandoning the entire Ogaden region to the Somali invading forces. It was at this time of disadvantage that the Ethiopian authorities protested to the OAU against the aggression of Somalia with full confidence to win the support of the OAU. The Ethio-Somali dispute was well known to both the UN and OAU. It was raised on several occasions and it was the view of the international bodies that Somalia's claim was in violation of international treaties. The head of the Ethiopian delegation to the Summit of the Heads of State and Government of OAU held in Libreville, Gabon, 1977, made the following statement:

> 'We cannot re-draw the map of the world to satisfy the whims
> of the Somali Government. Africa has already come out with
> a solution to this fundamental question. Res. AGH/16/I of
> July 1964 of the OAU Assembly of Heads of State and
> Government solemnly declared that all member states pledge
> themselves to respect the borders existing on their
> achievement of national independence. Moreover the
> Second Conference of the Heads of State and Government
> of the Non-aligned countries in its Cairo Summit of October
> 1964 declared that the countries participating in the
> conference pledge themselves to respect frontiers as they
> existed when the states gained independence.'[67]

Somalia's claim on Ethiopian territory was in violation of these international declarations. On the other hand, Ethiopia argued its case in compliance with these declarations. On the basis of these international declarations she sought the intervention of the OAU for condemning Somalia's aggression against it and to require the withdrawal of Somali forces from Ethiopian territories.

The Assembly of Heads of State and Government at its meeting in Libreville, Gabon, established a Good Offices Committee consisting of eleven members to submit to it recommendations on the resolution of the Ethio-Somali dispute. The committee heard the arguments of both sides but the Somali delegation walked out from the meeting anticipating that the outcome of the deliberation of the committee would favour Ethiopia.

The committee considered the case, in spite of Somalia's withdrawal from the meeting and made the following recommendations:

1. Reaffirms resolution AGH/Res./16(I) and the resolution AHG/27(II) which bind member states in accordance with the charter of the OAU to respect the borders existing at independence as well as adherence to the cardinal principle of holding inviolable sovereignty and territorial integrity of member states,

2. Appeals to the parties to the conflict, Ethiopia and Somalia, in conformity with the aims and purposes of the charter and the relevant resolution of the OAU, to cease all acts of hostility,

3. Reaffirms the opposition of the OAU to the interference of all foreign powers, and in particular that of extra-African powers, in the internal affairs of OAU member states and to repudiate such unwarranted interference in accordance with the decision of the 14th Assembly of Heads of State and Government,

4. Appeals to all states to refrain from any action that could be detrimental to the achievement of understanding between the parties to the conflict or exacerbate the tension and conflict threatening peace and security and the territorial integrity of the neighbouring states,

5. Recommends, in view of the gravity of the situation, that the current chairman of the OAU Good Offices Committee undertakes contacts with the heads of states of Ethiopia and Somalia with a view to effecting a cessation of the hostilities and creating the atmosphere conducive to the peaceful solution of the problem.'[68]

The recommendations were a diplomatic slap in the face for Somalia. They upheld the correctness of Ethiopia's position, even though they were short of condemning Somalia's aggression. Given the weakness of the OAU as an ineffective regional organisation a more precise formulation of recommendations could not have been feasible. However, even the reaffirmation of OAU's resolutions was a diplomatic victory for Ethiopia because Somalia had rejected the resolutions. Somalia ignored the recommendations and intensified its military offensive. It captured the

213

entire region of the Ogaden and established a government of Western Somalia with the town of Jigiga as its administrative capital. Somali forces advanced to capture other parts of the administrative region of Harargie and some other regions in southern Ethiopia. The Ethiopian forces, short of weapons and troops, were defending the cities of Harar and Dire Dawa.

The Carter Administration had already ceased supplying weapons to Ethiopia. On the other hand the USSR, although it had promised to support Ethiopia, was still supplying weapons to Somalia during its invasion of Ethiopia. Mengistu, who felt betrayed by his socialist friend, lamented:

> 'Even though we had not suspected that they would wage an attack against the Ethiopian revolution with the arms which the socialist countries had given them for their defence, we did not expect that one of the main towns of Ethiopia, our industrial town Dire Dawa and the revolutionary workers in it, would be bombed by tanks and artillery produced by socialist workers.
>
> We did not imagine that defenceless children and old women would be mercilessly and ruthlessly butchered.
>
> We have found the situation extremely controversial, difficult to believe and one which perplexes genuine revolutionaries.'[69]

The fact was that the USSR wanted to have both Ethiopia and Somalia as its client states, until the latter unilaterally abrogated its Agreement of Friendship and Co-operation with the USSR. Somalia was enjoying the political support of the US, UK, France, Germany and Italy on one hand and on the other, arms and financial support of Iran, Egypt and the Gulf countries. Somalia, buoyed by the promises of arms and huge financial assistance of Arab countries and the political support of the West, unceremoniously expelled Russia and gave the Russian naval base at Berbera to the US. Russia, which had been humiliated by Somalia, had every reason to give its full support to Ethiopia. Russia delivered massive military hardware to Ethiopia with unprecedented efficiency that caught the West by surprise. Russian military advisers and trainers soon filled the void created by the expulsion of the American Military Advisory Group (AMAG). Along with their military hardware the Russians brought valuable information that they had collected over their long period of association with Somalia. The shift in alliance of Russia from Somalia to

Ethiopia had rallied the entire socialist bloc to the support of Ethiopia. The socialist countries provided political, diplomatic, morale, arms, material support and assistance; in particular Cuba and the People's Democratic Republic of Yemen contributed troops.

On the domestic front, the response of the Ethiopian people to the general mobilisation was beyond the expectation of the PMAC. The spontaneous and overwhelming reaction of the people to the unprovoked aggression of Somalia was harnessed and properly put in use by the creation of a National Revolutionary Operation Command (NROC) at the level of the central government with branches reaching the smallest administrative units. The NROC's branches at the various levels played significant and effective roles in co-ordinating the material, financial and human resources of the nation to be deployed in the defence of the country. In a very short time a militia force of 300,000 strong was drawn from workers and peasants. It was trained and was ready to be deployed at the front. Another force of 500,000 was being prepared to serve as rearguard with the final target of a force of 6,000,000 — more than the entire population of Somalia.

The militia and the regular army, equipped with Russian weapons, supported by the Cuban and Yemenese troops, changed the balance of power in favour of Ethiopia.

Ethiopia took the initiative in a counter-offensive which soon began in earnest. Somalia, that consistently denied the invasion of Ethiopia, raised a hue and cry that Ethiopian forces assisted by foreign troops were advancing to invade her. The United States, its allies and certain Arab countries rallied behind Somalia and warned that should Ethiopian forces cross the international border, they would not be passive spectators. Egypt and Iran threatened that they would field their troops on the side of Somalia. The socialist countries, on the other hand, put their diplomatic support behind Ethiopia and demanded the unconditional and total withdrawal of all Somali forces from Ethiopian territories. They further required that Somalia should renounce its claim over Ethiopian terri- tories. The Ethio-Somali dispute became a subject of exchange of demands between Ethiopia and the socialist countries on one side and the West, most of the Arab countries and Somalia on the other. A leader of a Russian delegation, who was on a visit in the United States in January 1978, addressing the House of Representatives, pointed out to them that the unconditional withdrawal of Somali forces from Ethiopian territory was a precondition for any peaceful negotiations. He also reassured the House that Ethiopia and its allies had no intention of invading Somalia.

He added that the allegation of Somalia was unfounded and was made with a motive to secure more weapons.[70]

At the same time the Ethiopian leader, in his nationwide address on the status of the war against Somalia, declared:

> 'What we Ethiopians would like to remind the world is that apart from opposing and defending ourselves against colonialists and expansionists, racists and fascists at no time in our long history did we cross as invaders the borders of our neighbours and desecrate the rights of others. Even today, we have no territorial question with anyone, no expansionist aims nor designs to carve out the territory of our neighbours.
>
> What we are struggling to do is to uphold our territorial integrity and national independence.'[71]

In spite of the assurances given by Ethiopia and its allies, Somalia and its allies failed to restrain themselves from harping on about an impending invasion by Ethiopia. The Ethiopian forces, nonetheless, continued to make advances to their borders chasing the fleeing Somali forces. The Somali force that had penetrated about 700 kilometres into the Ethiopian territory failed to sustain its supply line and retreated in haste in the face of an Ethiopian counter-offensive. The Ethiopian infantry, enjoying the air cover of one of the best air forces in Africa south of the Sahara, drove out Somali forces from Ethiopian territories by the end of March 1978. Although the Ethiopian forces could have exercised their right in hot pursuit of the enemy, they restrained themselves from crossing the international border.

In April of that year, immediately after the defeat of Somalia, Colonel Mengistu Haile Mariam paid an extended visit to Nigeria, Tanzania, USSR, GDR, Czechoslovakia, Romania, Bulgaria and Cuba. The purpose of the visits was to express the gratitude of the Ethiopian people for their support and assistance in the defence of the country to all those countries which had supported the cause of Ethiopia. Other objectives of the visit was to assess the extent of the financial and material support that would be obtained for launching a campaign for a reconstruction of the economy and taking offensive measures to subdue secessionists in Eritrea. In a statement issued upon his return Colonel Mengistu expressed his satisfaction with the success of the visit. He reiterated that the socialist countries had promised him their support and assistance in the efforts of his government in consolidating the gains of the revolution and maintaining the territorial integrity of the country.

The Campaign in Eritrea

Colonel Mengistu, encouraged by the promises of the socialist allies decided to take counter-offensive measures against the secessionists in Eritrea. In a nationwide address he recounted the efforts of the PMAC to settle the problem peacefully, and the intransigence of the secessionists to any peace initiative. The loss of life and destruction and damage to property were presented with astounding figures and facts. The public was told that a total of 13,000 men-in-uniform and 33,000 civilians including children, were slaughtered by the secessionists and 200,000 people were forced to emigrate to a neighbouring country. The properties that were destroyed by the secessionists were worth over two and half billion Birr.[72] The destruction caused to bridges, hospitals, schools, factories and other public properties, were listed in a manner that would persuade the people of the need of some government action. The secessionists' rejection of any peaceful negotiation was also stressed. The involvement of foreign countries in the Eritrean problem was underscored in these words: *'Imperialist and reactionary Arab governments who want to see a weak Ethiopia, but not an Ethiopia strengthened by the revolution of oppressed people, seek to undermine our country and subvert our revolution by interfering in our internal affairs.'*[73]

The statement emphasised the point that the secessionists were collaborating with foreign countries in undermining the territorial integrity and unity of the country. Again these points were stressed to justify the need of a general mobilisation. In articulating the measures needed he said:

> 'Just as you have earlier scored a major victory in the east
> and in the south by co-ordinating your efforts and strength
> and risen with determination under the call of everything to
> the war front, so also you must stand firm to repeat that
> victory by winning the war which had been intensified against
> you in the north – a war which is being waged against you
> since a long time with a view to disrupting your unity and
> reversing your revolution.'[74]

On the day after the nationwide address of the chairman, a demonstration was, as usual, staged to express support for a military campaign in Eritrea.

The state propaganda machinery was unleashed in denigrating and demanding annihilation of the secessionists. A ten-day workshop for 800 representatives of mass organisations, military, government institutions and other revolutionaries was organised in the capital to make a Marxist-Leninist analysis of the Eritrean problem and to suggest a solution. The whole exercise was a propaganda stunt directed to whipping up the wrath of the people against the secessionists and to rally the support of the people behind the government.

The National Revolutionary Operation Command and its branches at various levels were activated to mobilise the human and material resources of the nation for the campaign. The campaign was launched in June 1978. In a very short time, the secessionists were ousted from the major towns of Eritrea and the road leading from Addis Ababa to Asmara, which was inaccessible for over a year, was opened. Part of the port of Massawa that was in the hands of the secessionists was recaptured facilitating transport to Asmara. The siege of Asmara was successfully broken. By the time of the Fourth Anniversary of the Revolution, 12 September 1978, the Second Liberation Army had recaptured all of the towns of Eritrea; save Keren that was recaptured in November 1978. The loss of lives on both sides was heavy. The secessionists having sustained heavy losses in the conventional battles fled to their safe haven, the Sudan, and reverted to their guerrilla warfare. The campaign in the north, even though of a limited duration, brought a semblance of government presence in most of the provinces of Eritrea. The defeat of the secessionists, although short of annihilation as planned, was a source of encouragement and gave the regime a breathing space to launch a campaign for the rehabilitation of the war-torn economy of the country.

Reconstruction and Rehabilitation of the National Economy

The power struggle in the PMAC and the Marxist-Leninists of the POMOA being resolved in its favour; having come out victorious over the EPRP and EDU; having crushed the Somali invading forces; and having defeated and chased away secessionists in the North; the PMAC braced itself for a campaign to reconstruct and rehabilitate the economy that was shattered by war and misguided economic policies since 1974. The PMAC's approach to tackling national problems was an emergency and campaign approach – a legacy of its military orientation. For the reconstruction of the economy, a National Revolutionary Development Campaign and Central Planning Supreme Council Establishment Proclamation was issued. The general objectives of the campaign were to rehabilitate the economy and to lay a firm foundation for a command economy. An elaborate organisation, a National Revolutionary Development Campaign and Central Planning Supreme Council, with a power to mobilise the human, financial, and material resources of the nation, was created. The major objectives of the Central Planning Supreme Council (CPSC) were to:

1. 'Prepare and ensure the implementation of a plan centred on the revolutionary and immediate solutions of the major and most pressing economic and social problems of the country;

2. Bring about the mobilisation of the broad masses and government participation in the campaign;

3. Issue directives to ensure the increase of production in various sections of the economy, ensure the implementation of these directives through a revolutionary means and provide and co-ordinate all the necessary facilities;

4. Identify and follow-up, in a revolutionary way, closely, activities in the major areas of development activity and work out solutions to outstanding problems on the basis of the priority of their emergency;

5. Explore all ways and means to acquire from internal and external sources, all that is necessary for ensuring the success of the campaign;

6. Prepare short, medium and long-term economic plans by assessing campaign activities focusing on the major and most pressing national problems taking into account the ultimate goals of the revolution and, having regard for the objective reality of the country, ensure that the plan is implemented;

7. Ensure that the economic campaign is inseparable from the struggle on the political front and lay the groundwork for the establishment of a workers' party and ultimately of a people's democratic republic of Ethiopia;

8. Issue regulations, orders and directives necessary for the attainment of the goals of the campaign, devise ways and means for full participation in the campaign and

undertake agitational activities to enhance the full and
correct understanding of the objectives of the campaign.'[75]

The extensive powers for introducing a new socio-economic order were
bestowed upon the CPSC. Its powers and responsibilities were carved out
from the powers of the PMAC and the Council of Ministers. The creation
of this body undermined the Council of Ministers. In matters pertaining
to the formulation of social and economic policy the Council of Ministers
became irrelevant. The Supreme Council had the power to allocate
budgets and determine economic priorities. The Council of Ministers
was, as a justification for its existence, given the responsibility to approve
the recurrent budget of the government and to sanction transfer of
budgetary allocations from one item to the other. Even personnel allocations to government institutions were controlled by the Supreme
Council. The creation of institutions that duplicated the functions of
existing organs of government was a standard practice of the PMAC style
of management of the affairs of state, without taking into account the
wastage of skilled manpower and financial resources.

The CPSC's elaborate structure[76] at the national level consisted of a
congress, an executive committee and a secretariat. At the regional level
a provincial development campaign and a planning office, at Awraja
and district levels development and planning congresses, and executive
committees were established. The structure was designed to serve as
a forum for public participation in the initiation and formulation of
development plans.

At the national level the congress and the executive committee of the
CPSC were chaired by the chairman of the PMAC. The membership of
the congress reflected a cross-section of society. It consisted of the
members of the Standing Committee of the PMAC, the Secretary-General
and department heads of the CPSC, members of the Council of Ministers,
commissioners, chief regional administrators, the Chief of Staff and
Sector Commanders of the Armed Forces, the Police Commissioner, the
Mayor of Addis Ababa and representatives of mass organisations. A similar
pattern of representations in the regional, provincial and district level
was followed. The power and responsibilities of the various organs of the
CPSC were clearly defined and the best brains from public institutions
were selected and deployed to the gigantic structure. By the end of 1981
the workforce of the CPSC was over a thousand. Budgetary provisions,
office facilities, equipment, vehicles and other requirements were generously provided by the government. With the entire nation being alerted
to wage war against economic deprivation and underdevelopment, the

campaign was launched with big fanfares and publicity at the end of October 1978.

During the campaign period, 1979–84, five annual plans were designed and executed. In the first two plans, 1979/80 and 1980/81, the GDP grew by an annual rate of 5.2 and 5.5%[77] respectively. The annual growth rates when compared to the less of than 1% in 1978 were remarkable and a cause for jubilation for the regime. However, the growth rate of the GDP for the period 1980/81, 1981/82 and 1982/83 plummeted to 2.9% per annum. The hope for a surge in the annual growth rate was lost when in 1984 a famine affecting 5.2 million people broke out.

The campaign, more than anything else, had contributed to developing expertise in formulating, implementing and evaluating plans. The annual workshops of CPSC, where evaluation reports on sectorial plan implementation were discussed, encouraged the development of a system of critical self-analysis. The campaign had brought to the fore the paucity of reliable data for planning. To meet this deficiency institutions were encouraged to create a system for recording and processing data. The shortage of reliable demographic data was overcome when the CPSC took a general census for the first time in the history of Ethiopia. By the time of the creation of the Workers' Party of Ethiopia in 1985 the CPSC had made the necessary preparation and its continuation with the same powers and responsibilities was superfluous and in conflict with the leadership role of the vanguard party. To this end, the CPSC was restructured with a new designation, National Committee for Central Planning, responsible for formulating broad national economic and social policies in conformity with the programme of the party.

National Literacy Campaign

The level of illiteracy under the imperial regime had reached 93%. It was not recognised as a serious problem until the earlier part of 1960. The awareness to the problem of illiteracy came to the forefront when an educator and independent thinker, Dr Tickher Hailu, suggested to the Ministry of Education that illiteracy could be tackled by expanding the formal education system and by launching a literacy campaign. According to his suggestion access to formal education would be increased by the efficiently use of teachers, classrooms and other teaching facilities without incurring a major financial burden on the government. The rational use of resources would be achieved by introducing a shift system. It was the adaptation of a method that was used in industries to maximise the optimum use of manpower, machinery and equipment. For instance an industry that operates one eight-hour shift could triple its manpower requirement by changing to three shifts in twenty-four hours. Dr Tickher adapted the shift system to schools. Enrolment in schools could be doubled or tripled by introducing a shift system. The Ministry of Education of the imperial regime adopted the system – it was called the 'Tickher's Method' and was authorised to be used in elementary schools throughout the country.

Similarly the other suggestion on literacy campaign (which Dr Tickher named *Yefidele Serawit*) was also entertained but the government was not prepared to take full responsibility to launch it. Instead it delegated the literacy campaign to a non-governmental and charitable institution. In 1962, *Yefidele Serawit* (a National Literacy Campaign) under the chairmanship of the Minister of Education was formed. To give it a veneer of prestige the emperor was made its patron, the Crown prince, honorary president and other prominent personalities, the Prime Minister and the Patriarch of the Ethiopian Orthodox Church were also members. The organisation depended on voluntary contributions and volunteers for the execution of its campaign. It lacked the resources and the organisational capability to face the problem of illiteracy squarely. By 1974, when the revolution broke out, the campaign boasted making some 27,000 people literate.[78]

At the early stages of the revolution, illiteracy was not on a priority list of the military junta even though the participants of the National Development Through Co-operation Campaign had made some useful contributions towards literacy in the rural areas. The literacy programme was discontinued when the development campaign was wound-up in 1976. Due to the lack of a definite policy on literacy and proper follow-up the effort of the development campaign did not leave a lasting impact on the rural population. From 1974 to 1978 the priorities of the Dergue were seizure and consolidation of power and defending the territorial integrity of the country against internal insurrection and external invasion. However, by 1979 it was well established and confident enough to launch a national development campaign whose success depended on the eradication of illiteracy. Besides illiteracy was an obstacle to disseminating socialism among workers and peasants who were groomed for the dictatorship of the proletariat. Eradication of illiteracy was, therefore, considered a precondition for the spread of socialism. In 1979 the regime took the full responsibility of eradicating illiteracy by issuing a proclamation that provided for the establishment of a National Literacy Campaign Co-ordinating Committee (NLCCC) under the Ministry of Education and relevant ministries and mass organisations as members.

The national level organisational structure was replicated at regional, Awraja, district and Kebele (sub-district) levels and committees at these levels planned and implemented literacy programmes. Moreover the committees were actively involved in fund-raising by soliciting assistance from external as well as internal sources. The government-owned media was effectively deployed to promote the campaign.

The campaign was launched in July 1979 with great pomp and publicity. PMAC members, including Chairman Mengistu Haile Mariam and other senior government officials and leaders of mass organisations, conducted classes on their respective Kebeles. The response of the public was impressive too. Teachers, students, factory workers and civil servants volunteered to give lessons in the several thousands of centres scattered through the length and breadth of the country. The literacy campaign was the only one of the many campaigns of the Dergue that succeeded to muster the voluntary support of the entire nation. The support and active public participation guaranteed its success. Funds and other resources for the campaign were largely met by voluntary contributions of the people. International organisations in particular UNESCO and friendly countries, gave valuable donations both in cash and kind.

The campaign was executed in two phases. The first phase was making illiterate people literate. The second phase was a follow-up to the first phase to prevent relapse to illiteracy. The campaign was initially conducted in five main languages, including Amharic, Oromigna, Tirigna, Wolayitigna and Somaligna. Later on the number of media of instruction was increased to fifteen dialects. The selected fifteen languages were spoken by nearly 95% of the total population of the country. The strategy of the campaign was, in the first instance, to rid urban areas of illiteracy. The overall plan was to eradicate illiteracy in seven years – by 1987. On implementation it was discovered that the target was too ambitious and the period was extended to 1991.

Illiterate persons between the ages of 8 and 50 were required to attend illiteracy classes. Although there was an element of compulsion, generally the classes were attended with enthusiasm and interest. Lessons were arranged without clashing with the normal activities of participants. In urban areas classes were normally held in evenings. In rural areas, classes were held during the daytime taking into consideration daily routines of farm families. Schools, community halls, offices, temporary shelters and even shades of trees were used for literacy classes. Teaching aids were improvised from locally available materials. Trees, walls, fences were used for displaying posters. Employers were required to release their domestic workers for at least 2–3 hours a day to enable them to attend classes.

223

The literacy campaign was conducted in two consecutive rounds of four months each in a period of twelve months. In the first round all illiterates in a community were registered and taught the basic skills of reading and writing for 240 hours. The second round, remedial or mop-up round targeted those who were omitted from the first round and failed to attain a satisfactory level of literacy. For the remedial task 210 hours were allotted[79]. Every round was preceded by a carefully planned publicity offensive soliciting from the public donation of funds and teaching materials such as paper, pencils, chalk, blackboards, etc. The intensity of publicity, the organisational capability of mass organisations and professional associations, in particular the National Teachers' Association, the overwhelming support of the public for the campaign and the commitment and resolve of the government facilitated efficient execution.

In the first two rounds 5.4 million people were freed from the bondage of illiteracy. Of the total of 5.4 million, 2 million and 3.5 million were from urban and rural areas respectively. This remarkable performance was acknowledged by international organisations, in particular UNESCO. It gave its full backing by appealing to the international community to render its assistance to the campaign. The Director-General of UNESCO, Mr Amadu Maktar M'Bow, in his appeal to the international community for assistance to the campaign said:

> 'By supporting the action, the international community will
> be doing more than answering a call of solidarity; it will be
> participating in an endeavour whereby the continent, in its
> entirety, will recover its historic momentum, build once
> more its forces whose strength has long been sapped and
> finally set about assuming the responsibilities incumbent
> upon it in a world of freedom, justice and shared progress.'[80]

UNESCO further demonstrated its support to the literacy campaign by conferring on it the 1980 UNESCO Literacy Award.

In 20 rounds (1979–89) 21 million people participated and out of which 18.7 million were successfully made literate reducing illiteracy from 93% in 1974 to 25% in 1989. The credit for such an impressive performance primarily goes to the 1,788,000 instructors[81] and the Ethiopian people for carrying the financial and organisational burdens of the campaign.

NOTES

1 Central Statistical Office, PDRE Facts and Figures, Addis Ababa, 1987, p. 22.
2 *The Ethiopian Herald*, vol. xxxiv, No. 1161, 19 October 1975.
3 ibid., No. 1216, 22 December 1975.
4 ibid.
5 Address to the Nation on the Occasion of the Winding-up Ceremony of the *Zemecha*, Brigadier-General Teferri Bente, Chairman of PMAC. Addis Ababa, 16 July 1976.
6 *The Ethiopian Herald*, vol. xxx, No. 1227, 4 January 1975.
7 ibid., No. 1424, 23 December 1975.
8 Objectives of Ethiopian, Socialism, *The Ethiopian Herald*, vol. xxx, No. 1230, 9 January 1976.
9 ibid.
10 ibid.
11 ibid.
12 The Economic Policy of Socialist Ethiopia, PMAC, Addis Ababa, 11 February 1975.
13 Proclamation of Commercial Activity in the Private Sector, No. 76 of 1975.
14 Address on the Occasion of the First Anniversary of the Revolution, Brigadier-General Teferri Bente, Chairman of the PMAC and the Council of Ministers, Addis Ababa, 13 September 1975.
15 Rural Land Nationalisation Proclamation, no. 31, Addis Ababa, 1975.
16 ibid.
17 ibid.
18 Peoples' Democratic Republic of Ethiopia, Facts and Figures, Central Statistical Office, 1987, p. 35.
19 Address on the Occasion of the First Anniversary of the Revolution, Brigadier-General Teferri Bente, Chairman of the PMAC and the Council of Ministers, Addis Ababa, 13 September 1975.
20 Proclamation Providing for Government Ownership of Urban Land and Extra Houses, no. 47, 1975.
21 ibid.
22 ibid.
23 The author was the Permanent Secretary of the Ministry of Labour and Social Affairs at the time of the drafting of the labour proclamation.
24 May Day Speech of the Vice-President of CELU, Ato Alem Abdi, Addis Ababa, 1 May 1975.
25 Address on the Occasion of the First Anniversary of the Revolution, Brigadier-General Teferri Bente, Chairman of the PMAC and the Council of Ministers, Addis Ababa, 13 September 1975.
26 ibid.
27 *The Ethiopian Herald*, vol. xxx, No. 1353, 27 September 1975.

28 ibid., No. 1331, 3 September 1975.

29 Address on the Occasion of the First Anniversary of the Revolution, Brigadier-General Teferri Bente, Chairman of the PMAC and the Council of Ministers, Addis Ababa, 13 September 1975.

30 National Democratic Revolutionary Programme of Ethiopia, PMAC, Addis Ababa, 20 April 1976.

31 People's Organising Provisional Office Establishment Proclamation of 1976.

32 Yedrese Lebaletariku, Tesfaye Mekonnen, Artistic Printing Press, Addis Ababa, 1985 (EC), pp. 195–8. Ato Tesfaye was the Secretary-General of MALRED and a member of POMOA. He had served for a short period as the Secretary of POMOA after *MEISON* defected from the revolution in August 1977.

33 The author was Minister of Labour and Social Affairs at the time of the election of the Executive Committee of AETU.

34 Address on the Occasion of the Second Anniversary of the Revolution, Brigadier-General Teferri Bente, Chairman of the PMAC and the Council of Ministers, Addis Ababa, 12 September 1976.

35 *The Ethiopian Herald*, vol. xxxiv, No. 97, 29 April 1976.

36 PMAC Confirms Verdict, *The Ethiopian Herald*, vol. xxxiv, No. 162, 14 July 1976.

37 ibid.

38 ibid.

39 ibid. No. 157, 8 July 1976.

40 The author in his capacity as Vice-Minister of Administrative Affairs in the Office of the Chairman of the Council of Ministers was responsible for matters dealing with religious affairs.

41 Speech by Brigadier-General Teferri Bente, Chairman of the PMAC and the Council of Ministers, On the Occasion of the Second Anniversary of the Revolution, Addis Ababa, *The Ethiopian Herald*, vol. xxxiv, No. 214, 13 September 1976.

42 Address to a Rally Held at the Revolution Square, Major Mengistu Haile Mariam, *The Ethiopian Herald* vol. xxiv, No. 334, 6 February 1977.

43 Statement of the Ethiopian Students' Association in Europe, *The Ethiopian Herald*, vol. xxxiv, No. 228, 1 October 1976.

44 Nationwide Address, Brigadier-General Teferri Bente, Chairman of PMAC and the Council of Ministers, *The Ethiopian Herald*, vol. xxxiv, No. 328, 30 January 1977.

45 ibid.

46 Speech Addressing a Mammoth Rally at the Revolution Square, Brigadier-General Teferri Bente, Chairman of the PMAC and The Council of Ministers, *The Ethiopian Herald*, vol. xxxiv, No. 329, 1 February 1977.

47 PMAC Statement on the Foiling of a Counter-revolutionary Coup, *The Ethiopian Herald*, vol. xxxiv, No. 333, 5 February 1977.

48 ibid.

49 Yedrese Lebaletariku, Tesfaye Mekonnen, Artistic Printing Press, Addis Ababa, 1985, pp. 225–6.
50 Addressed to a Rally Held at Revolution Square, Major Mengistu Haile Mariam, First Vice-Chairman of the PMAC, *The Ethiopian Herald*, vol. xxxiv, No. 334, 6 February 1977.
51 Tesfaye Mekonnen, op. cit., p. 219.
52 PMAC Message to the Workers of the Country, *The Ethiopian Herald*, vol. xxxiv, No. 352, Addis Ababa, 27 February 1977.
53 As the Class Struggle Intensifies Reactionaries will be Ejected at Every Stage, PMAC's Statement, *The Ethiopian Herald*, vol. xxxiv, No. 672, Addis Ababa, 15 November 1977.
54 ibid.
55 ibid.
56 ibid.
57 *The Ethiopian Herald*, vol. xxxiv, No. 339, 12 February 1977.
58 Ethio-Cuban Joint Communique of 18 March 1977, Ministry of Foreign Affairs, Addis Ababa.
59 ibid.
60 The Ethio-Soviet Joint Communique, May 1977, *The Ethiopian Herald*, vol. xxxiv, No. 411, 19 May 1977.
61 ibid.
62 Speech Addressing a Rally at the Revolution Square. Major Mengistu Haile Mariam, First Vice-Chairman of the PMAC, *The Ethiopian Herald*, vol. xxxiv, No. 333, 5 February 1977.
63 Tesfaye Mekonnen, op. cit. pp. 249–60. Tesfaye was appointed Secretary for POMOA after the defection of *MEISON* and enjoyed the favour of Colonel Mengistu for a short period until he was imprisoned in July 1978.
64 Nimerie and the Revolution in Dismay, Mansour Khalid, London 1985, p. 326. Mr Mansour Khalid had served under President Nimerie's government in various ministerial capacities including that of the Foreign Minister of the Republic of the Sudan.
65 ibid., p. 326.
66 The Speech of the Leader of the Ethiopian Delegation to the Assembly of Heads of State and Government of the Organisation of African Unity, Libreville, Gabon, Ministry of Foreign Affairs of the PMAC, Addis Ababa, July 1977.
67 ibid.
68 As reproduced in *The Ethiopian Herald*, vol. xxxiv, No. 490, Addis Ababa, 10 August 1977.
69 Address to the Nation on General Mobilisation, Colonel Mengistu Haile Mariam, Chairman of the PMAC and Commander-in-Chief of the Armed Forces, *The Ethiopian Herald*, vol. xxxiv, No. 500, Addis Ababa, 21 August 1977.
70 *The Ethiopian Herald*, vol. xxxiv, No. 734, 28 January 1978.
71 Nationwide Address on the Somalia Aggression, Colonel Mengistu Haile

Mariam, Chairman of the PMAC and the Commander-in-Chief of the Armed Forces, *The Ethiopian Herald*, vol. xxxiv, No. 736, 31 January 1978.

72 Nationwide Address on the Eritrean Problem and the Efforts of the Government to Find a Peaceful Solution, Colonel Mengistu Haile Mariam, Chairman of the PMAC and Commander-in-Chief of the Armed Forces, *The Ethiopian Herald*, vol. xxxiv, No. 843, 8 June 1978.

73 ibid.

74 ibid.

75 The Statement of PMAC on the Establishment of a National Revolutionary Development Campaign and Central Planning Supreme Council, *The Ethiopian Herald*, vol. xxxv, No. 40, 29 October 1978.

76 National Revolutionary Development Campaign and Central Planning Supreme Council Establishment Proclamation of 1978.

77 The Ethiopian Famine, Kurt Jackson, Michael Harris and Angela Penrose, London, Zed Books Ltd. 1978, p. 114.

78 A Blindfold Removed: Ethiopia's Struggle for Literacy, Chris Searle, London, Karia Press, 1991, p. 52.

79 *The Ethiopian Herald*, vol. xxxiv, No. 305, 9 September 1980.

80 *The Ethiopian Herald*, vol. xxxiv, No. 245, 28 June 1981.

81 Searle, op. cit. p. 105; *The Ethiopian Herald*, vol. xlv, No. 168 and 243, 1989.

Chapter Five

Major Political Developments of the Revolution

Many forms of government have been tried, and will be tried in this world of sin and woe. No one pretends that democracy is perfect or all-wise. Indeed, it has been said that democracy is the worst form of government except all those other forms that have been tried from time to time.

Sir Winston Churchill

A Prelude to the Formation of a Vanguard Party

The Ethiopian revolution in many respects differed from the classic revolutions of other socialist countries. The main differences were that it took place without the benefit of guidance of a vanguard communist party and without a political ideology. Despite these preconditions it broke out spontaneously and introduced radical reforms thus defying the *raison d'être* for the need of a Marxist-Leninist vanguard party. Nevertheless, the PMAC and its Marxist-Leninist cohorts lamented the absence of a vanguard party. They referred to the situation as the main weakness of the Ethiopian revolution. Emphasising this Chairman Mengistu Haile Mariam said: "*It has been reiterated that a shortcoming of the Ethiopian Revolution is that it has no political organisation which, either in secret or openly, has been tested in struggle and which equipped with the working-class ideology, would give it direction.*"[1] The formation of party, notwithstanding the awareness of the need for a vanguard party and the USSR's insistence on its formation, was delayed until the leftist contenders for power became subservient to the PMAC. The formation of the vanguard party was a

229

slow and an evolutionary process; it was formed after passing through three stages. In the first stage the PMAC and four Marxist-Leninist underground organisations agreed to work for a common cause. The agreement resulted in the establishment of the POMOA.

The POMOA was a forum created to involve Marxist-Leninist organisations in a revolutionary process. The creation of the POMOA and the adoption of a National Democratic Revolutionary Programme went a long way in giving a sense of direction to a revolution that broke out spontaneously. However, the amorphous nature of the POMOA was revealed by the extreme feeling of parochialism of its members. Each one of the members instead of working as a team in the political process made relentless efforts in using the POMOA for controlling the government machinery and mass organisations. The domination of the POMOA by civilian Marxist-Leninist individuals and their greed for power were a cause of concern for the PMAC. To counter this trend the PMAC created a Marxist-Leninist organisation under the name *Abiyotawi Seded* (Revolutionary Flame). *Seded* was chaired by Mengistu and most of its members were men-in-uniform. Soon it was co-opted as a member to the POMOA.

The second stage in the development of party formation was to work for the merger of Marxist-Leninist organisations to create a conducive condition that would gradually lead to a single party. The five members of the POMOA, including *Seded*, formed a union of Marxist-Leninist Organisations (known under its Amharic acronym, *EMALEDH*) in February 1979. *EMALEDH* served as a platform whereby revolutionaries capitalised on the things they had in common by forging an alliance. The members of *EMALEDH* took a common stand on controversial political issues of the time such as class content and the revolutionary nature of the PMAC; question of the formation of a vanguard party; strategies to be adopted by the revolution in solving the question of nationalities and the place of the Ethiopian revolution in the international communist movement. These broad agreements on issues vital to the revolution on one side and on the other the members desire to down-play the issues that divided them contributed to rallying the members of *EMALEDH* behind the NDRPE. However, after seven months of political infatuation a leading member of the POMOA and *EMALEDH*, *MEISON*, broke away from the revolutionary camp and went underground.

MEISON's defection was followed by the expulsion of *ECHAT*, an organisation closely identified with *MEISON*, from the POMOA and *EMALEDH* for promoting ethnicity. These developments convinced the PMAC that

230

a vanguard party could not be formed by a merger of Marxist-Leninist organisations. For the PMAC, *EMALEDH* was a failure and other ways had to be devised for the creation of a vanguard party. In describing the failure of *EMALEDH* and the need for seeking an alternative route for forming a vanguard party Chairman Mengistu stated:

> 'Although Marxist-Leninist organisations and individual communists who stand genuinely for the revolution have struggled for ideological and organisational unity, many were those who found their attention on the form rather than on the lasting union of progressives. Struggle made it evident, therefore, that the working-class party cannot come into being through the merger of organisations.
>
> Today at this stage of the progress of our revolution the working-class party can be formed only with the genuine communists who stand for the ideological and organisational unity of progressives and who are tested in struggle.'[2]

It is evident from the quotation that the fate of Marxist-Leninist organisations was sealed. A new pivot was needed for co-ordinating the efforts of revolutionaries. To this end, a seminar was organised by Mengistu's henchman, Sergeant Legessie Asfaw, head of the Military Political Affairs Section of the PMAC, for military commissars, leaders of discussion groups and mass organisations in the latter part of August 1979. The seminar passed a resolution requesting Chairman Mengistu to take the lead for the formation of a vanguard party. Mengistu obliged by accepting the request. Resolutions of meetings of such importance were normally drafted by the organisers with the advance blessing of PMAC and then submitted to participants for endorsement. We have no reason, in this particular case, to assume a deviation from this standard procedure of the PMAC in influencing the outcome of the seminar. Taking the resolution of the seminar as the democratic expression of the will of the participants, Mengistu took the responsibility of uniting revolutionaries for the formation of a party. This was a calculated step taken by the PMAC to undermine Marxist-Leninist organisations which were weakened by detaining and executing their leaders.

Mengistu, no sooner than he obliged to lead the pivot for the formation of a vanguard party, constituted a committee chaired by him including as members the Deputy Senior Minister, the Minister of Information and National Guidance, an ideologist from the POMOA and the head of the Institute of Management and Training who served as member-secretary.

At the first meeting of the committee the chairman made it clear to the other members of the committee that due to the realities obtaining in the country to imagine the formation of a vanguard party was unrealistic. He said that he wanted the creation of an organisation that was a hybrid of the powers and duties of a governmental institution and a vanguard party. It was an organisation that would be accountable to the PMAC for creating the necessary conditions for the formation of a vanguard party and at the same time would function as a party. With these unambiguous terms of reference the committee decided to consider the function, organisational structure and legal basis of the establishment of a commission. After accepting 'commission' as a designation for the new institution, the committee discussed the objectives, its powers, duties, structure and other relevant issues, such as criterion for membership and recruitment of members. Mengistu did most of the talking. He read to the other members of the committee his views on each of the foregoing issues. His notes and explanations constituted the terms of reference of the committee. The first meeting was wound-up with a clarification on terms of reference. He instructed the committee to produce its report in two weeks, working full-time under the chairmanship of the Deputy Senior Minister. To facilitate ease of consultation the committee was given an office nearby Chairman Mengistu's office and secretarial facilities were made available from there. Besides the oral term of reference a poorly researched document on the functions and organisational structure of parties of socialist countries and a recommendation on the nature and structure of a vanguard party for Ethiopia was made available to the committee for its reference.[3]

The secretary of the committee prepared a working document on the basis of the terms of reference given by the chairman. It was comprehensive enough to include objectives, an organisation chart and a detailed job description of a commission and its organs. The committee then considered the draft thoroughly and the final version was submitted for Chairman Mengistu's approval. He went through the document with the committee article by article and made sure that the commission was accountable through him to the PMAC. On the basis of the approved structure and job description, a proclamation on the establishment of a commission for organising the Workers' Party of Ethiopia was drafted by the Deputy Senior Minister and vice-chairman of the committee who was an accomplished lawyer. Furthermore the committee by co-opting experts constructed a salary scale for the commission. A draft speech for the chairman that he would make on the launching of the commission was drafted by the Minister of Information and National Guidance and an

ideologist from the POMOA. A manual of the commission, a draft proclamation which provided for its establishment, a salary scale and a draft
speech were submitted to Chairman Mengistu and through him to the
Standing Committee of the PMAC which endorsed the package.

The establishment of the Commission for Organising the Workers'
Party of Ethiopia (COWPE) was declared on the 17 of December 1979.
Chairman Mengistu made a nationwide address labouring at length in
explaining the objectives of COWPE. As a sequel to his address a proclamation was issued the next day providing for the establishment of COPWE
with the following broad objectives:

> '1. To cause the dissemination and propagation of the
>   philosophy of Marxism-Leninism among government,
>   mass organisations, co-operative societies and the broad
>   masses;
> 2. To organise a sole and strong party of the working people
>   based on the teachings of Marxism-Leninism whose
>   historical mission shall be to liquidate from the land of
>   Ethiopia feudalism, imperialism, bureaucratic
>   capitalism, and to establish the new People's Democratic
>   Republic of Ethiopia and to guide the people to
>   socialism and consequently communism.'[4]

At the time of drafting of the objectives of COPWE neither Chairman
Mengistu nor the other members of the drafting committee were certain
of its life span. The fact that the creation of the People's Democratic
Republic was included in the goals of the organisation was an indication
that the committee was not sure which one would be realised first, the
party or the republic. As events later on proved the party came first and
the republic was created four years later.

From its start COPWE was provided full government support, including
a huge budget, luxurious offices and facilities to enhance its prestige. For
all intents and purposes it was given a role and a status of a vanguard
party. Although COPWE was a government institution in name, it was
a party in form and content. A glance at Article Six of the proclamation
would suffice to prove this point, Article Six reads:

> 'COPWE shall have the following powers and duties:
> a. organise the working people to be firmly and purely
>   based on the principle of Marxism-Leninism;
> b. disseminate among the broad masses the Marxist-Leninist

ideology free from revisionism through study circles, discussion forums, government and mass organisations and the mass media;

c. agitate, politicise and organise the various sections of the population by disseminating Marxism-Leninism;

d. establish political schools, prepare curricula, train and assign qualified teachers and organise other necessary facilities thereof;

e. prescribe criteria according to which students be admitted to political schools; ensure that students follow-up properly their courses and, upon completion of their education, assign them to places where they can best serve the revolution and the people;

f. issue directives in accordance with the curricula of regular and vocational education which shall be based on the philosophy of Marxism-Leninism and ensure that its directives are carried out;

g. strengthen existing Marxism-Leninism study circles and discussion forums in government and mass organisations, establish new ones, issue directives to them, co-ordinate their activities and extend to them material assistance;

h. in co-operation with the appropriate government and mass organisations establish, politicise, assist and consolidate professional associations and mass organisations to be effective executors of the directives of the party of the working people;

i. produce, translate, import and distribute books, periodicals, newspapers, films necessary for the building of a socialist society and other written materials useful for education, political consciousness, and research;

j. prohibit and control, through the appropriate offices and organisations, written materials, films, tapes, records and the like that come into the country by direct or indirect channels from imperialist countries for purposes of cultural adulterations or for counter-revolutionary activities, provided that such prohibition and control shall not apply to materials dealing with science, technology or subjects contributing to the building of a socialist society;

k. find ways to develop and enrich the useful traditional

cultures, customs and practices of the society in a
manner conducive to the building of a socialist society;
and, in co-operation with offices and organisations,
liberate the people from backward cultures, customs and
practices;

l. prepare the criteria in accordance with which prospective
members of COPWE may be admitted and co-opted;

m. establish, direct and supervise such committees and
divisions of operations as are necessary for its work;
employ the necessary staff and issue special regulations
with which they will be administered;

n. co-operate with the appropriate offices and organisations
in making the necessary efforts and agitations with a
view to enforcing laws, regulations, government directives,
orders, decisions and the implementations of economic,
and cultural campaign plans, their class and ideological
content being strictly adhered to;

o. establish fraternal relationships with Marxist-Leninist
parties, liberation movements and other democratic
organisations with a view to enabling the Party of the
working people that will be established to discharge its
international call Workers of the World, Unite.'[5]

These powers and duties of the commission and its structure were identical to the functions and structures of vanguard parties in other socialist
countries. If this was so why was not a vanguard party declared instead
of a commission for organising a party? Mengistu replying to this question
said:

'This is a legitimate question. In particular, since a party plays
a decisive role in the victory of a revolution, it would have
been desirable if it had manifested its existence in the pre-
February 1974 period. The heavy sacrifices that we had
been incurring would have been minimal if, instead of
counting a few isolated victories in the course of the
revolution, the party of the working people of Ethiopia had
from the very beginning been a vanguard force leading the
struggle to victories.
This is a general view and wish. But because objective
conditions are not governed by mere wish, the Ethiopian

Workers' Party did not achieve its existence easily either
before or in the course of the revolution.

Even now the very fact we have braced ourselves up to realise
not the party but the commission to organise the party is a
clear reflection of the objective conditions in which we find
ourselves.

Even the revolutionaries, organised piecemeal by force of
circumstance, were working together for a specified period
of time, because their unity had no profundity and
permanence, it was only recently that they shared a united
stand for the creation of a centre embracing them all by
doing away with internal friction and conflict.

Unless this is merely for namesake during such a time it
would not be easy to establish a party which in its contents
embraces the whole country and in practice does some justice
to its name.

Right from the beginning when we declared that socialism is
our guiding principle, we would have announced the
establishment of a "Socialist Party" if our fundamental aim
was the pursuit of mere name and form.

That is why the establishment of an organising commission
possessing the confidence of the broad masses which create
the desirable conditions for the party to be created on a
sound foundation is, in itself, something that should not
only be given high consideration but is also a measure that
marks a historic step forward for the long journey ahead of
us.'[6]

Mengistu was not prepared to allow the repetition of the struggle for
power that bedevilled Marxist-Leninist organisations when they were
operating under the umbrella of POMOA and *EMALEDH*. Besides the
creation of COPWE as a government organisation was an effective strategy
for excluding revolutionaries from organising themselves into organisations of their choice. Politicising the people and organising them into
a political party by law became a government monopoly. The rationale
for creating COPWE was political expediency rather than as alleged by
Chairman Mengistu the dictate of the realities obtaining in the country.
COPWE was nothing other than an organisation bestowed upon it rights

and privileges of a government body and a vanguard party to ensure the PMAC'S monopoly of power and control over the political rights of the people. An in-depth examination of the structure of COPWE would throw some light on the foregoing assertions.

The organisation of COPWE consisted of:

1. A Chairman (Secretary-General);
2. A General Assembly;
3. A Central Committee;
4. An Executive Committee;
5. Regional committees;
6. Awraja committees;
7. Wereda committees and
8. Basic organisations (at the Kebele, village, association and workplace).

The chairman's post was the most powerful position in the structure of COPWE. The chairman was empowered to select, assign, transfer, suspend or dismiss the General Assembly, the Central Committee (CC), the Executive Committee and other organs and members of COPWE. All positions in the secretariat of COPWE were held by appointments. Power was concentrated in the hands of the chairman who was in control of the PMAC, the Council of Ministers and the Armed Forces.

The membership of the General Assembly comprised members selected by the chairman from the members of the PMAC, government officials, officers from the Armed Forces and mass organisations. There was no ceiling to the size of membership. The chairman determined the size of the General Assembly as he deemed fit. The frequency of meetings were also determined by him. The assembly would consider broad domestic issues and foreign policies when the chairman would invite it to do so. It had no power to initiate proposals on its own accord. For all intents and purposes it was an advisory body consisting of a cross-section of society.

The Central Committee of COPWE consisted of full and candidate (alternate) members selected from the members of the General Assembly by the chairman. Membership in the Central Committee was prestigious. It had served to fill the void that was created by abolishing the various titles and honours of the imperial regime. The candidate members would participate in the debates and deliberation of the committee without the right to vote. The size of the membership of the committee was not determined. However, at the first COPWE congress the names of 90 full and 30 candidate members were announced. More than 60% of the

members were from the Armed Forces and the Police. Civilian government officials accounted for the remaining 40%. Mass organisations,
including trade unions and peasant associations, were not given seats in
the Central Committee. Their omission from the Central Committee
revealed the emptiness of the PMAC's declaration of creating necessary
conditions for the dictatorship of the proletariat.

The Central Committee was responsible for considering all policy issues
affecting the government and COPWE. It had the power to make its
rules and formulate programmes. It was also in charge of safeguarding
ideological purity. Besides between meetings of the General Assembly the
Central Committee assumed the powers and responsibilities of the
General Assembly. This principle of a lower organ assuming the powers
of a superior body were replicated in the powers and duties of the
Executive Committee. In the intervening period between the meetings
of the Central Committee the Executive Committee assumed its powers.
This formula made frequent meetings of the Central Committee and the
General Assembly unnecessary with the effect that the decision-making
process was concentrated in the Executive Committee whose members
were drawn from the Standing Committee of the PMAC. The size of
membership of the Executive Committee was also left to the discretion
of the chairman of COPWE. However at the first congress of COPWE
the names of the following seven members were announced:

1. Colonel Mengistu Haile Mariam, chairman of COPWE (including the
   General Assembly, the Central Committee and the Executive
   Committee),
2. Captain Fikre Selassie Wogderese,
3. Colonel Fiseha Desta,
4. Colonel Tesfaye Gebrekidan,
5. Colonel Hadis Tedla,
6. Colonel Berhanu Bayih and
7. Sergeant Legessie Assfaw.

All of them were members of the sixteen-man Standing Committee of
the PMAC. The most important decision-making body of COPWE was
dominated and controlled by the military to the total exclusion of civilian
revolutionaries. Marxist-Leninists who dissolved their political organisations in the hope that they might be rewarded with important positions
in COPWE were left out. The size and composition of the Executive
Committee remained unchanged until the formation of the Workers'
Party of Ethiopia in 1984.

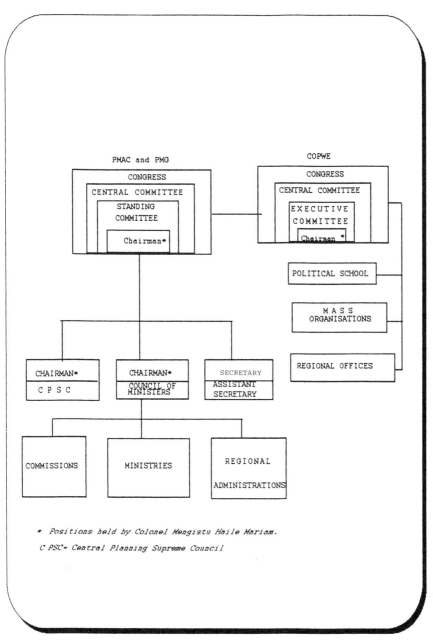

Chart 3
Organisation chart of PMAC, PMG and COPWE, 1979

239

At regional levels a similar pattern of appointment of representatives of COPWE was adhered to. Thirteen of the fifteen regional representatives of COPWE were from the Central Committee of PMAC and the remaining two from the Armed Forces. Civilians were further excluded from sharing power in the regional bodies of COPWE. Even in the secretariat of COPWE all departments were headed by members of the PMAC and military officers, save the Co-operatives' Development Department which was allotted to a civilian. Most of the important positions in COPWE and the government were held by the PMAC members and officers of the Armed Forces by 1980. The appointment to high positions, both in COPWE and the government, followed this order of priority: the PMAC members, members of the Armed Forces and the Police, Marxist-Leninists, persons whose vices would make them vulnerable to blackmail, and, lastly, technocrats with long years of experience.

The basic organisation of COPWE was its most important link with the people at the grass-roots level. It was established in all government offices, educational institutions, industries, factories, state farms, co-operative societies, mass organisations, professional associations, the Armed Forces and the Police and in other places of work where three COPWE members were working. It was responsible for disseminating Marxism-Leninism, recruiting members for COPWE and facilitating implementation of decisions of COPWE.

All workers irrespective of their views and beliefs were required to belong to study circles or discussion forums that were conducted by basic organisations. Discussions were held during working hours once a week lasting for two hours. It was from these forums that secretaries of basic organisations identified prospective members and eventually recruited them for membership in COPWE. Secretaries of basic organisations were leading cadres who were selected on the merits of their commitments to Marxism-Leninism and democratic centralism which was and still is a cardinal principle of communist parties. Democratic centralism boils down to implementing the decisions and directives of superior organs correctly and without delay by lower organs of a party. Formation of basic organisations at grass-roots level provided COPWE favourable conditions — for formulating a work plan which will be examined in the following section.

COPWE's Plan of Work

COPWE executed its plan of work in three phases. The first phase covered the period from the formation of COPWE in December 1979 to the convening of its first congress in June 1980. This phase was used for establishing the organs of COPWE at various levels, acquiring offices, recruiting staff, preparing internal rules and regulations, making preparation for its first congress and mobilising resources for the second phase of its plan of work.

The second phase was the period when COPWE began full-scale operational activity. Politicising and organising the people were actively pursued. Existing mass organisations, AETU and AEPA, were restructured and strengthened; their officers were re-elected ensuring that leadership of mass organisations was in the safe hands of individuals who were loyal to the regime. An unorganised segment of the society was organised. In particular the youth of the country between the ages of 14–30 and women were organised into youth and women's associations. At national level a Revolutionary Ethiopian Youth Association (REYA) and a Revolutionary Ethiopian Women's Association (REWA) were established. With the formation of these associations the task of organising society into mass associations was successfully accomplished, creating conducive conditions for indoctrinating the people with Marxism-Leninism. In 1983, when the second congress of COPWE was convened, 1,300,000 persons[7] had held elective posts in AETU, AEPA, REYA and REWA.

Professional organisations, Ethiopian Teachers' Association, University Students' Union and Health Workers' Associations were also restructured and re-elections of officers were held. Other professional organisations of musicians, artists, journalists were formed at national level. During the second phase of COPWE's plan of work the formation of organisations reached its peak. There was no citizen who did not belong to a mass organisation or a professional association or both. Underscoring COPWE's impressive achievement in organising the people the chairman of COPWE reported:

> 'Today one can hardly find a citizen who in one way or
> another does not participate in a mass organisation either
> at residential area or place of work. All citizens are thus
> being judged for their active participation, an ideal situation
> has thus been created to determine how an individual views
> the political and organisational leadership of the working
> people and his loyalty to the objectives of COPWE.'[8]

This statement is evidence of the extent of regimentation that citizens were subjected to. The PMAC's slogan, 'the revolution will knock at the door of everyone' became a reality. At the workplace an individual's life was governed by a basic organisation and at his place of residence by one or more mass organisations and in some cases a professional association.

The third and last phase of COPWE was a period of consolidation of its power, refining its ideological leadership and preparing to transform itself from a commission to a fully-fledged vanguard party. The period from the first (1980) to the second congress (1983) was devoted to refining the organisational capability of COPWE and gaining valuable experience in running a vanguard party. It had also helped in developing a system of self-evaluation and taking corrective measures in areas where weakness was discovered. One glaring area where flaws were observed was in the recruitment of members for COPWE. From 1979 to the third plenary meeting of the Central Committee of COPWE, 1981, the recruitment of members did not reflect a balanced composition of various segments of society. The class composition of the membership was skewed in favour of the intelligentsia. The working class accounted for 2.9%, peasants 1.2% and the intelligentsia (teachers, civil servants, men-in-uniform and others) 95.9% of the total members of COPWE.[9] However the third plenary meeting of the Central Committee of COPWE gave a directive for correcting this trend of preparing the intelligentsia rather than the working class for the dictatorship of the proletariat. By 1982 the share in membership of the workers, peasants and the intelligentsia was 21.7%, 3.3% and 75% respectively. Although these were improvements over the 1982 figures, the dominance of the intelligentsia over COPWE did not show any drastic change when its conversion from a commission to the Workers' Party of Ethiopia (WPE) took place in 1984.

By 1980 COPWE's leadership in ideological, political, social and economic matters was firmly established. The decision-making mechanism shifted from the PMAC to COPWE, although there was no difference in the leadership of both bodies, COPWE was given prominence and its directives constituted state policies. It approved appointments to key positions in the civil service, government-owned enterprises and the military. Both at home and abroad COPWE was treated as a vanguard party. Even the Russians, who were insisting on the formation of a civilian vanguard party, accepted COPWE as a substitute for a party. COPWE signed agreements of friendship and co-operation with communist parties, exchanged visits with them and even attended their congresses as an observer.

COPWE's foreign policy proved its success when the strained relations of Ethiopia and the Sudan began to improve. Mengistu took the initiative in inviting the First Vice-President of the Sudan, General Abdul Majid Hammid, for an official visit which took place in March 1980. At the end of the visit the two sides agreed to respect the territorial integrity of each others' country, not to interfere in the internal affairs of one another, to strengthen economic and cultural relations between the two countries and to reactivate the Ethio-Sudanese Border Commission. In May of the same year Chairman Mengistu reciprocated by making a four-day state visit to the Sudan upon the invitation of President Gaffar Mohammed Nimerie. At the end of the visit a joint communique reiterating the principles of the charters of the UN and the OAU such as respect for sovereignty and territorial integrity of a state, non-interference in the internal affairs of a state, good-neighbourliness, was issued. The restoration of friendship and close relations between the two countries reached its climax when President Nimerie paid a state visit to Ethiopia in October 1980. The restoration of normal relations between the two states was demonstrated in practical terms. The Sudanese Government discontinued to support and assist the Eritrean rebels openly. President Nimerie even went to the extent of promising the Ethiopian Government to close the rebels' office in his country and to discontinue harbouring in the Sudan any force that was anti-Ethiopia, promises which he failed to fulfil. At any rate, normal relations were restored as a result of exchange of visits and lasted until November 1983 when President Nimerie in one of his hysterical outbursts accused the Ethiopian Government of harbouring rebels of the Southern Sudan in breach of the agreement between the two countries. The Ethiopian Government categorically dismissed the charge as false accusation with a sinister motive. Since Mengistu was planning to launch a Red Star campaign he could not have dreamt of any action that might antagonise and provoke the Sudanese Government to retaliate. However, during the political honeymoon of Nimerie and Mengistu two important political developments had taken place. President Gaddafi of Libya whom Nimerie called 'a mad dog' made a state visit to Ethiopia and at the same time a tripartite treaty of friendship, co-operation and joint defence was signed among Ethiopia, Libya and the People's Democratic Republic of Yemen. Nimerie's alleged charge against Ethiopia for harbouring Sudanese rebels was a demonstration of his resentment at the Ethio-Libyan friendship and the tri-partite agreement. It was a political blunder on the part of Mengistu to associate himself and Ethiopia with a leader who, was condemned not only by the Sudan, but by the international community as a leader who pursued state terrorism and supported terrorist organisations.

The Ethio-Libyan friendship was short-lived. It might have brought some financial benefit to Ethiopia and partnership in investment which fell apart before it began. On the other hand the political damage it did by tarnishing the prestige of Ethiopia was immense. It was a major factor in causing the deterioration of relations between the Sudan and Ethiopia. The friendship with Libya was a major flaw in the political leadership of COPWE. It served as an excuse for the Sudan to revert to its policy of openly supporting and assisting Eritrean rebels.

COPWE and the PMAC, having made a political blunder which antagonised the most important country that was committed to the cause of Eritrean rebels, made a naive decision to launch a multi-faceted campaign in Eritrea. Chairman Mengistu genuinely believed that the problems of Ethiopia would be solved by mobilising the resources of the country and launching a series of campaigns. Some past campaigns, such as distributing nationalised land to landless farmers, defending the country against the Somali invasion of 1977 and the National Literacy Campaign, were successful. The leadership of COPWE decided to solve the Eritrean problem by mobilising the entire nation for a campaign named Red Star. Before launching the Red Star Campaign, an elaborate organisation with detailed job descriptions of the various organs of the campaign excluding its military aspect was made.

The multi-faceted Red Star Campaign was in many respects an extension of the National Development Campaign that was launched in the other parts of the country in 1979. However, its military dimension made it different from the National Development Campaign. It aimed at reconstructing the infrastructure that had been demolished by the rebels and routing them from their last stronghold in the rugged mountains of the province of Sahale. The difficult terrain of the province had made it a safe haven for the rebels. Normal life was, except in the Sahale, reasonably restored to other provinces under government control. The organisational structure of the Red Star provided for a congress consisting of the First Secretary of COPWE for Eritrea, the Chief Administrator of Eritrea, the Commander of the Second Revolutionary Army, other representatives of government departments and mass organisations of Eritrea. The secretariat of the campaign was headed by a secretary who was the chief executive of the development aspect of the campaign. Despite the interest of certain members of the Executive Committee of COPWE in the post, the Deputy Senior Minister, Ato Amanuel Amde Michael, an Eritrean, was appointed to this prestigious position.

The Red Star Campaign was launched in January 1982 with fanfare and pomp. The participants of the campaign were senior officials of the central government, members of the Central Committee of the PMAC, senior officers of the Armed Forces and the Police Force, religious leaders, elders from Eritrea, representatives of national and regional mass

244

organisations and the Ethiopian Patriotic Association. The meetings of the campaign were held in Asmera and Massawa. The festival for launching the campaign lasted for a week. Between meetings the participants attended important events, such as laying cornerstones of monuments for two national heroes, Ras Alula Ingda and Zerai Dresse, in Dogali and Asmera respectively.[10]

At the conclusion of the congress of the Red Star the participants issued the Asmera Manifesto. It covered issues such as the history of Ethiopia with particular emphasis on its northern part, the history of colonialism in Eritrea, the emergence of secessionists and the crimes they had perpetrated against the Eritrean people, the measures taken by the government to end the problem in Eritrea by peaceful means and secessionists refusal to enter into any peaceful dialogue with the government. The following were the operative paragraphs of the manifesto:

'1. We have issued today the Asmera Manifesto containing our assessment of and decisions on the national, regional and international issues deliberated at the meeting and later reviewed in a revolutionary and patriotic feeling.

We unanimously endorse the historic statement made by our determined and wise leader, Comrade Chairman Mengistu Haile Mariam, chairman of the PMAC and of COPWE and Commander-in-Chief of the Revolutionary Army, to the entire Ethiopian people when addressing the Red Star multi-faceted revolutionary development campaign meeting in Asmera on January 17, 1982 regarding the objective reality of Ethiopia in the context of the world situation and in particular the problem in theEritrea Region.

We pledge our readiness to implement the directives given by Comrade Chairman Mengistu to rebuild the economic infrastructure destroyed by the secessionist bandits in the region and to bring genuine freedom to the people and to make every sacrifice, including that of life, demanded of us to spearhead the execution of work strategies which the revolutionary government will conceive in future.

2. The anti-freedom, anti-unity and anti-peace bandit gangs who have been rejected by the society and who represent

245

no one except the forces of imperialism and reaction should no longer be allowed to continue creating destruction and must be therefore, reduced to smithereens by the united might of the broad masses.

We moreover pledge to crush those who provided support to the bandits, including fifth columnists, because they are enemies of the people. We thus affirm in unison that we not only support any measure which the Revolutionary Army takes in its defensive posture but we are also behind it and ready to give rearguard support.

3. The meeting unanimously calls on both compatriots who joined the ranks of the bandits either out of innocence or forced to do so and Ethiopian refugees living abroad to abandon those who trade in the blood of people, to take advantage of the amnesty granted by the revolutionary government and to return home without delay and join the broad masses.

4. It is well recognised that organisation is the guarantee for the success of socialist economic construction now underway in Revolutionary Ethiopia and particularly in view of the acute problems prevailing in the region and efforts towards the resurgence of such problems. We, therefore, call on the peasantry to organise itself immediately into peasant producers' co-operatives in line with programmes and directives given by our revolutionary leader, Comrade Chairman Mengistu. We at the same time express our readiness to make the necessary support.

5. We strongly condemn all foreign forces and intelligence agencies which support hired assassins who trade with the lives of the oppressed in pursuit of their anti-freedom, anti-unity and anti-peace mission. We also warn that they cease channelling such support forthwith.

6. Recognising the colonialist disposition of Ethiopia's honour and millennial history and the gravity of corrosive imperialist influence and alien culture forced on the Ethiopian people, the Revolutionary Government, after thorough assessment of Ethiopia's saga of freedom

and struggle, has revived the history which was muffled by the discredited feudo-bourgeois order, and decided that monuments be erected in honour of those who died for the cause of the freedom and unity of the country as well as for other Ethiopian heroes.

Sincerely appreciating the initiative Comrade Chairman Mengistu Haile Mariam, Chairman of the PMAC and of COPWE and Commander-in-Chief of the Revolutionary Army, to lay the cornerstones for monuments in honour of the famed Ras Alula at Dogali, Zerai Dresse in Asmera, as well as for those who struggled and died for the cause of unity under the banner of "Ethiopia or Death" and members of the Revolutionary Army who have fallen defending the cause of unity and revolution carrying aloft the banner "Revolutionary Ethiopia or Death".

We request the Revolutionary Government to study the history of the region and take measures to put history in its proper context by erasing place names given and cultural influence bequeathed by colonialists.

7. Viewing the present class struggle in light of the confrontation between imperialism and socialism on the global scale it will be seen that the imperialist plot hatched against the Ethiopian Revolution aims at changing the balance of forces in the region in favour of imperialism. We realise, in solemn recognition of our internationalist responsibility, that the victory of the Ethiopian revolution means the victory of the anti-imperialist force and that the failure of Ethiopia's revolution means the defeat of these forces and that therefore, our struggle influences developments in the region and in the ultimate sense of the world. Recognising this and that our bitter struggle against imperialism is part and parcel of the worldwide anti-imperialist struggle, we call on all anti-imperialist forces to step up the support which they had been providing in the past.'[11]

COPWE and PMAC with the support of mass organisations of the entire country and the Armed Forces executed the Red Star Campaign. The reconstruction aspect and the military component of the campaign were implemented simultaneously. The reconstruction of infrastructures in the six districts where the rebels were routed by the 1979 military campaign was successful. Schools and health facilities began to give their services to the people. Factories and other enterprises were rehabilitated and provided employment opportunities for thousands who were deprived of the right to work due to circumstances beyond their control. Factories of Eritrea, which had accounted for one-third of the industries of Ethiopia, began to produce at full capacity goods that were in shortage in Eritrea and other parts of Ethiopia. Moreover the opening up of land transport from Eritrea to the other parts of Ethiopia facilitated an unhampered flow of goods and services.

The military component of the campaign was directed by the Commander-in-Chief of the Revolutionary Army, Comrade Chairman Mengistu. He monitored and directed the military operation from the State House of Asmera. The objective of the military operation was 'the elimination once and for all of such anti-society elements.'[12] The army, the largest and best-armed force in Africa south of the Sahara, was mobilised for this purpose. The attacks on the rebels were directed from three directions in an attempt to close routes of escape to the Sudan. Many decisive battles were fought. Although both sides suffered casualties, the rebels sustained heavy losses and were besieged. It was the natural terrain of Sahale Awraja that rescued them from total annihilation. The government forces advanced despite the resistance of the rebels and routed them from most parts of the province. The rebels concentrated their forces in the provincial town of Naqfa. It is a town on the top of a mountain range. The topography of the region provided a natural fortress against air as well as ground attack by government forces and they sustained heavy losses in their attempt to dislodge the rebels from Naqfa. At one moment when the government forces were advancing to capture the town, they were instructed to stop advancing until the Lion Regiment (the regiment where Mengistu had served as an officer before the revolution) took the lead in capturing the town and taking prisoners of the surrendering rebel forces. Overriding military gains for personal vanity was a blessing in disguise for the rebels who were crying in desperation for the intervention of the international community. The Lion Regiment lost its direction somewhere in the desert. In the meantime the rebels received a breathing space to regroup and dig themselves into the mountains of Naqfa. The only two entrances to the town were easy to defend from the attacks of government forces. The mountain range surrounding the town made air strikes difficult.

248

Mengistu was certain of victory. So much so, while the advance of the government forces was interrupted the Institute of Management and Training as a matter of urgency was instructed to dispatch to Asmera management experts. Upon their arrival at the Asmera airport the experts were rushed to Chairman Mengistu's office. He instructed the management experts to prepare a new administrative structure for Eritrea with a degree of operational autonomy – more or less an arrangement that prefigured the old federal system.

The management team produced a discussion paper in a couple of days for the consideration of a committee presided over by Chairman Mengistu and comprised as members the Secretary-General of the Red Star Campaign, Cde. Amanuel Amde Michael, the First Secretary of COPWE for Eritrea, Cde. Dawit Wolde Giorgis, the Chief Administrator of Eritrea, Colonel Fikru Woldetensaye, the Minister of Justice, Cde. Getachew Kibret, the Minister of Labour and Social Affairs, Cde. Kassa Kebede and the Minister of Agriculture, Cde. Dr Geremew Debella. The draft was sent back to the team for further refinement with the comments of the committee. While the team was working on its final version of recommendations Chairman Mengistu unceremoniously flew back to Addis Ababa. The management team soon learned that the military operation had failed due to a decision motivated by vanity. However, the development component of the Red Star Campaign was continued and gradually phased out. Its failure is a black spot in the history of COPWE.

Another significant development in the third phase of COPWE's plan of action was the prevalence of corruption in public offices and mass organisations. To curtail such unhealthy development COPWE decided to create a Peoples' National Control Committee (PNCC) whose objectives included stamping out of corruption, individualism, greed and abuse of office from society. It was organised at national, regional, provincial, district, Kebele and village levels. It was accountable to the PMAC and it had eleven members elected by mass organisations. Although the PNCC and its branches at the various levels contributed to checking wastefulness, abuse of office and misappropriation of funds, they had on the other hand created much confusion at workplaces by labelling senior government officials and executives of public-owned enterprises as remnants of the old order who encouraged the spread of unacceptable practices and modes of behaviour. People were judged by their social background rather than by their deeds, which was a totally wrong approach to the problem. Corruption was worse than it was under the imperial regime. Although corruption and other forms of impropriety in public offices exist in any system, the Ethiopian experience of almost two decades indicates that corrupt practices flourish under a system where religion is regarded as the 'opium of the people'.

The introduction of a national military service was another radical institutional innovation of COPWE. The service was introduced to protect the victories of the revolution and the unity of the country against anti-revolutionary forces including imperialism. To this end a National Military Service Proclamation No. 236/1983 was issued. The proclamation made an obligation on everyone in the age limit of 18–50 to be inducted for military service. After six months of training (Article 9) recruits were placed in the Armed Forces and Police and served for 24 months. Those who had fulfilled their obligations of service were placed on a reserve list until the age of fifty (Article 18/1). The proclamation as usual was greeted with demonstrations and speeches of support from leaders of mass organ-isations who welcomed the timeliness of the proclamation and expressed their support for its implementation. The demonstrations and the speeches of functionaries of COPWE created a semblance of national support for the military service whereas the true feelings of parents were outright rejection. Parents did not entertain the idea of sacrificing the precious lives of their children for the cause of the revolution. Anyhow, citizens' feelings do not count in a totalitarian system. The PMAC/COPWE went ahead and created a military commissariat for the implementation of the proclamation, including organising the peasantry into a people's militia (The Territorial People's Army Proclamation No. 239 of 1983).

Commissariats were established at national and regional administrative levels. They inducted the youth of the nation and prepared them for the fratricidal war that was ravaging the country. Upon the completion of their training many were rushed to fronts to replenish regiments of the Revolutionary Army. The purpose of the national military service and the manner with which it was implemented forced the young men of the nation to flee the country in great numbers. Even those who were rushed to fronts swayed by the propaganda of insurgent movements defected in large numbers. Despite the youths' defections from the front and their exodus to neighbouring countries to escape induction, the service was pursued with greater intensity. The national military service was one of the major blunders of the third phase of COPWE's plan of work. It was wound up by convening the second and last congress of COPWE. Comrade Chairman Mengistu made a lengthy report to the congress underscoring the achievements of COPWE in ideological, economic, social and cultural spheres. The report also chalked out actions that ought to be taken in the intervening period between the congress and the formation of the party. The phasing out of COPWE was suggested as well. The congress endorsed the report and commended the achievements of COPWE as historic.

The recommendations of the congress were:

1. Phase out COPWE.
2. Convene the founding congress of the Workers' Party of Ethiopia.
3. Recruit more members from workers and peasants in the run-up to the formation of the party.
4. Prepare party rules, programmes and a ten-year perspective development plan;
5. Reorganise the government structure in line with requirements of a vanguard party.
6. Prefigure the working relationships of COPWE and government institutions with practices of other socialist countries.
7. Establish an institute of nationalities which would study varied nationalities of the country for making recommendations on safeguarding and protecting their rights.
8. Establish a social science school for training cadres and facilitating the dissemination of socialism.
9. Strengthen the relationships of COPWE and mass organisations with their opposite numbers in other socialist countries.
10. Strengthen the defence of the nation.

The leadership of COPWE implemented the recommendations with vigour and interest. Upgrading the political school of COPWE to an institute of social sciences was one of the significant developments of the last phase of COPWE's activities. The political school was established in haste at the initial stage of the revolution to meet a shortage of cadres properly equipped with socialist ideology. It conducted short-term courses lasting from three to six months. It had trained several government officials and cadres of COPWE as well as leaders of mass organisations. On the eve of the formation of the vanguard party, all cadres of COPWE, persons in key government positions and leaders of mass organisations participated in one of the courses offered by the school.

Along with the establishment of an institute of social sciences other institutes, in some cases, duplicating the efforts of existing higher institutions were opened up. Some of these were the Ethiopian Institute of Management and Training, Co-operative Training and Development Institute, Institute of Water Technology, Agarfa Farmers' Training Centre,

251

Power and Light Development Institute and Institute for the Study of Nationalities.

Among these institutions, the Institute for the Study of Nationalities was unique. We shall consider its area of competence briefly. The problem of nationalities was not recognised by the imperial regime. As a result of this, arrangement was not made for the development of the languages and cultures of over 80 ethnic communities of the country. COPWE and PMAC demonstrated their awareness of the problems and the need for finding amicable solutions by issuing a proclamation providing for the establishment of the Institute for the Study of Nationalities, No. 236 of 1983. According to this proclamation the objectives of the institute were:

1. Studying the political, social, economic and cultural conditions of Ethiopian nationalities.
2. Conducting studies concerning constitution, state structure and administrative set-up on the basis of which a people's democratic republic could be established.

The head of the institute was a political appointee and its experts were professionals selected from the University of Addis Ababa and other government institutions by the chairman of PMAC and COPWE. To their credit the professionals of the institute made valuable studies on social, economic and cultural conditions and settlement patterns, geographic locations and distributions of over eighty ethnic communities. The findings of their studies were useful contributions to understanding and resolving the problems of nationalities. Whether policy makers used the findings or not for solving the problems associated with nationality and ethnicity, is a totally different issue. The efforts of the experts were commendable. They laid down a basis for formulating a sound solution to the problem of nationality and ethnicity. The institute had also produced a draft constitution within the constraints of its term of reference. Since the term of reference was to draft a socialist constitution based on the experiences of other socialist countries, the experts had operated within these constraints. Each draft was submitted to the scrutiny of the Executive Committee of COPWE which vetted it for ideological conformity with socialism. In particular the distribution of power among the different organs, including the share of the president of the republic, was of utmost interest to the leadership. So much so that the experts had liberally drawn on the experiences of Romania. The institute's draft served as a working document for a constitution drafting commission. Upon the completion of drafting a constitution, the institute served as a secretariat for constitution drafting and referendum commissions. Consequently its activity was scaled down. After the creation of a republic most of its experts were appointed to cabinet and other senior posts in the new structure.

Formation of a Vanguard Party

COPWE, at its second congress in July 1983, declared that it had made the necessary ideological and organisational preparation that would justify the formation of a vanguard party. The intervening period between the second congress and the founding congress of a vanguard party was used for recruiting members, preparation of party rules and programmes and requiring of members of COPWE to adhere strictly to party practices and discipline. At the time of the formation of the party in 1984 all the necessary preparations were accomplished satisfactorily with active participation of basic organisations. Draft rules of the party were sent to all basic organisations for discussion. Their comments were used for improving the draft. Discussion on rules provided opportunities for members of basic organisations to acquaint themselves with party rules. Besides, the discussions facilitated the transformation of the organs of COPWE into corresponding bodies of a vanguard party. The conversion of COPWE into a vanguard party was begun at the basic organisation and worked upward. Party formation meetings were conducted throughout the nation with a high pitch of publicity. Basic organisations, district and provincial COPWE branches elected their officers in conformity with the draft party rules that were yet to be adopted by the founding congress of the vanguard party. Preparations for the founding congress were carefully and efficiently executed by committees established from the national to the basic organisation levels. Along with the preparation for the formation of the vanguard party COPWE was being phased out. Some heads of departments and other senior officers of the secretariat of COPWE were transferred to high positions in the government. For instance COPWE's head of Ideology Department and secretary of the PMAC, Captain Fikre Selassie Wogderese was appointed Deputy-Chairman of the Council of Ministers. The head of COPWE's Foreign Affairs Department, Colonel Berhanu Bayih and the First Secretary of COPWE for Eritrea, Major Dawit Wolde Giorgis, became Minister of Labour and Social Affairs and Commissioner for Relief and Rehabilitation, respectively. As a result of these changes the cabinet was also reshuffled and in the process the posts of senior and deputy senior ministers were abolished. The reshuffles both in COPWE and the cabinet were additional measures to facilitate placements of revolutionaries in the party structure. After having created conducive conditions for the formation of a party, the leadership of COPWE and PMAC diverted their attentions to making arrangements for the celebration of the tenth anniversary of the revolution and the Founding Congress of the Workers' Party of Ethiopia (WPE). The whole nation was put into a celebration mood when the 1983/84 famine was taking its toll on many regions, including those regions that were affected by the 1974 famine. The Relief and Rehabilitation Commission disclosed to donors the news that five million people were affected in the drought-prone regions of Tigray and Wollo. The severity of the famine did not escape the attention of the PMAC and COPWE, but they chose to behave as if things were normal. The preparation for the celebration of the tenth anniversary of the revolution and the founding congress continued. The news on the famine was kept at a low profile so as not to disrupt the celebration. Probably the transfer of Commissioner Shimelis Adugna, who had earned the respect and confidence of the international donor community, to the Children's Commission was a deliberate step to suppress the news on the famine that was claiming thousands of lives. Kurt Jansson who was head of the United Nations Relief Operation in Ethiopia observed: *'Ato Shimelis Adugna, the first commissioner of RRC, was universally respected ... Commissioner Dawit's main fault (until he defected to the USA) appears to have been his manner which clearly thought inappropriate in one asking for aid.'*[13] Besides Major Dawit was an extremely ambitious person who had loyally served the PMAC and COPWE in senior positions including as first secretary of COPWE for Eritrea. He had played a prominent role in the Red Star Campaign. He was one of those revolutionaries who had made major contributions to the revolution and was rightly expecting a position in the Politburo of the WPE.

As if everything was normal, the prelude to the celebration began in the first week of September 1984. Industries and factories were commissioned and cornerstones were laid for others. Statues were unveiled including the bust of Karl Marx opposite to the main gate of the Addis Ababa University. At the same time delegations to the founding congress of the party were arriving from provinces in the capital. They were received with pomp and publicity. Invited guests from socialist countries and communist parties, including the Communist Party of America, were also arriving in the capital. The founding congress of WPE was convened on the 17 September 1984 in a hall built for the occasion. The nation was rejoicing the celebration of the formation of the party while the victims of famine from Wollo and Tigray were trekking to urban centres, in particular to the town of Korem (Wollo administrative region) where over 60,000 emaciated people of all ages had over-flooded RRC's feeding shelters. The agonies of those unfortunate souls were not allowed to spoil the festive mood of the nation and the lavish celebration. The celebration lasted for a week. It was observed with pomp, and graced with sumptuous receptions and dinner parties.

The long-awaited party was formed fulfilling the aspirations of revolutionaries for a vanguard party. The founding congress was convened by an address from the chairman of COPWE and PMAC, Cde. Mengistu. His extensive report to the congress covered the history of Ethiopia, causes of the revolution, problems of the revolution at its various stages of development, efforts made in guaranteeing equality of nationalities, direction of economic and social development, ideological work, process of introducing a socialist education system, efforts in building a new culture, building a strong national defence and a host of other things that had been accomplished in the last tens years. The report was comprehensive in content. By transcending its domestic frontiers it reviewed the development of communism in other socialist countries and concluded that the Ethiopian revolution was an integral part of the international communist movement. The report also succinctly pointed out that the creation of the vanguard party was not an end in itself, but a means for the creation of a people's democratic republic that would eventually facilitate the dictatorship of the proletariat. In expounding this point the report observed:

> 'Above all, we are confident that the realisation of the
> Workers' Party of Ethiopia, which has emerged through
> immense sacrifice, will enable us to enhance further our
> endeavours to build socialism and attain successful results. In
> this process, the primary task of our party in the
> establishment of the new state will not be to bring about
> the dictatorship of the proletariat directly, but rather to
> establish a people's democratic state which will lead us to the
> dictatorship of proletariat.'[14]

The report broadly defined the new state with reference to Marxist-Leninist principles of democratic centralism, socialist legality, proletarian internationalism and conscious participation of citizens in affairs of the state. The state, which was to be built on these lofty principles, was defined in the report as: *'The People's Democratic Republic that we shall establish is a state where no citizen will be discriminated against on the basis of sex, religion, race or nationality, or in which a society of justice, of equality and progressive human relations shall come to exist. The principles of its organisational structure and functioning, as well as the basic rights of citizens, shall be guaranteed constitutionally and through appropriate legislations.'*[15] In elaborating further the state structure the report stated: *'State power ranging from the lowest administrative unit to the national level, will rest in the hands, and be expressed by, popularly elected bodies. With respect to structuring and functions of the republic, the Workers' Party of Ethiopia will give special attention to ensuring that the working class gains supremacy, and the participation of the nationalities is guaranteed at all levels and in all the organs of the state power.'*[16] Despite these pious declarations the organs of the new state were controlled by the military and the intelligentsia.

Another major issue which was dealt with at length in the report was the question of nationalities. With respect to this question the role of WPE was spelled out:

> 'The aspirations of all peoples is for development, equality
> and a meaningful life, and their ultimate aim is not disunity
> but close ties and unity on the basis of identity of aims. On
> this basis the aims of the Workers' Party of Ethiopia
> concerning nationalities is that the democratic rights of each
> shall be recognised, and that they shall build their common
> prosperity together by co-ordinating their resources and
> abilities in the spirit of brotherhood and equality. This
> natural concern which is in line with the principles of
> proletarian internationalism is not limited to Ethiopian
> nationalities, but will also be realised amongst all people
> through the human race, ultimately leading to the
> establishment of the communist world, where everyone will
> lead a communist life completely free of insecurity and
> want.'[17]

The report also notified that COPWE and the National Democratic Programme of 1976 were replaced by WPE and the programme of WPE, respectively. The report was adopted by acclamation and the congress continued with other items of its agenda, including adoption of rules and programme of WPE and election of members of the Central Committee (CC). Members of the CC were elected by a secret ballot among the members of the congress. Members of the congress cast three votes each. The election was conducted in conformity with standard election procedures to create a semblance of a free and democratic election. In actual fact the congress, under the guise of election, endorsed a list of names of all prospective full and alternate members that was prepared by the chairman of COPWE. After the drama of an election of members of CC of WPE, the result of the election was submitted to the chairman who announced the names of the persons who were elected for the CC of WPE. A congress of over 1,000 delegates drawn from the various parts of the country and meeting for the first time elected full and alternate members for the CC. The result of the election caught many revolutionaries by surprise. Those who were certain of securing seats in the CC were left out and others who were not even members of COPWE obtained them. The results of the election although biased towards men-in-uniform included persons from all walks of life. The names of 136 full and 64 alternate members of CC of WPE were disclosed. Alternate members were those who had full right to participate in the deliberations of the CC without the right to vote.

The dominance of the members of the armed forces was a defining aspect of the CC. They accounted for 64% of the full and 39% of the alternate members of the CC. Since alternate members did not have the right to vote, power of decision-making was in the hands of the military just as it was in COPWE.

The next ritual of the founding congress was the election of a Secretary-General and members for the Politburo of WPE. Members of the CC, including alternate members, elected Cde. Mengistu as Secretary-General, and the following persons as members of the Politburo

1. Cde. Captain Fikre Selassie Wogderesse,
2. Cde. Colonel Fiseha Desta,
3. Cde. Major-General Tesfaye Gebre Kidan,
4. Cde. Colonel Haddis Tedla,
5. Cde. Colonel Berhanu Bayih,
6. Cde. Sergeant Legessie Assfaw,
7. Cde. Hailu Yimenu,
8. Cde. Amanuel Amde Michael,
9. Cde. Dr Alemu Abebe,
10. Cde. Shimelis Mazengia,
11. Cde. Colonel Tesfaye Wolde Selassie, alternate member,
12. Cde. Colonel Teka Tulu, alternate member,
13. Cde. Tesfaye Dinka, alternate member,
14. Cde. Fasika Sidelil, alternate member,
15. Cde. Shewandagn Belete, alternate member and
16. Cde. Kassa Gebre, alternate member.

The pattern of domination of the military in the Central Committee was also repeated in the Politburo. Seven out of eleven full members were from the military. This ensured the dominance of the military and revealed its unwillingness to share power with civilians. Although the civilians faired much better in securing seats in the Politburo than they did in the Executive Committee of COPWE, their representation did not alter the dominance of the military. Despite the semblance of involving civilians in the highest organs of WPE power still remained in the hands of the members of the PMAC.

The election of Cde. Mengistu as the Secretary-General of WPE was a centre for attraction when the stage-managed election results were reported to the congress. One of the politburo members in breaking the news of the election to the congress said:

> 'Believing that the CC will implement the slogan "Forward with Comrade Mengistu Haile Mariam" echoed from one corner to the other by WPE Founding Congress at every level, it is with a great feeling of joy and revolutionary honour that I announce the election of Comrade Mengistu Haile Mariam as Secretary-General of the Central Committee of WPE for his untiring and unrelenting effort, for his tested, unparalleled, incomparable and distinguished leadership ability, for his ardent and popular stand, his unflinching loyalty to Marxism-Leninism and to the working people.'[18]

Cde. Mengistu in his acceptance speech said:

> 'On the other hand comrades our aim is not to adhere to and sanctify the party, but as Lenin once said: "Give us an organisation of revolutionaries, and we will overturn Russia." We must not merely and soothingly touch Ethiopia's scars but overturn Ethiopia and transform it radically under the leadership and through the instrumentality of the party.'[19]

The congress proceeded to consider the party programme after the election fanfare was over. It was the most important document of the party that set its aims, objectives and plan of action. It was the result of ten years of experience in a revolutionary process that had radically changed a traditional polity. It was divided into seven chapters that comprised detailed policies for economic, social cultural and political transformation of the nation.

The programme included such issues as laying down the foundation for socialism, setting up a new political system, policy on nationalities, economic, education, science, technology, culture, foreign affairs, defence and enhancing the leadership role of the party. It also defined the relationship among the party, state and mass organisations. It delineated their spheres of competence and interdependence in building socialism and eventually communism. The party's leading role was, in building a communist polity, unequivocally defined as: *'The Workers' Party of Ethiopia is a vanguard organisation of the working class and of its ally, the peasantry, and of all the working people. It holds Marxism-Leninism as its guideline and struggle for socialism and communism.'*[20]

The celebration for the formation of WPE and the tenth anniversary of the revolution was over at the end of September 1984. Then the entire party and state machinery diverted their attentions to combating famine as if it were a new phenomenon that happened after the celebration and festivities.

Turning a Blind Eye to Famine

The PMAC, in spite of RRC's notification of the famine situation to donors in March 1984, turned a blind eye to it until the celebration for the formation of WPE and the tenth anniversary of the revolution was over. In October 1984, two weeks after the end of the celebration, the PMAC declared a state of emergency acknowledging the severity of the famine. The Politburo of WPE took charge in combating the effects of the famine. It established several committees chaired by its members and representatives of government institutions and mass organisations serving as members. The committees were assigned activities such as transport, relief assistance, fund and assistance raising, settlement and so on. The PMAC and WPE in tandem with the creation of high-level committees took such austerity measures as restricting the import of luxury goods, rationing of fuel, earmarking 80 million Birr for combating famine and imposing a levy on income.

The state-run media unleashed its campaign for soliciting assistance targeting the domestic public as well as the international community. The international press was invited to visit the scenes of emaciated victims of famine in the RRC's feeding centres in particular in Korem in the administrative region of Wollo. Korem, a small town with a population of less than five thousand, was inundated with 60,000 victims of famine

259

posing a serious health hazard to the community. Most of the towns in Wollo, Tigray and northern Shewa regions were also flooded with famine victims who had abandoned their homes in search of food. The exodus of peasants to outskirts of towns would have been prevented had the government put its priorities right and the international donor community reacted in time to RRC's appeal for assistance. An Independent Commission on International Humanitarian Issues regarding the indifference of the PMAC and the international donor community to RRC's plea for assistance commented:

> 'The Ethiopian Government had certainly been sounding the alarm internationally for over a year before a television team suddenly brought the crisis alive and galvanised international action in October 1984. But the Government had not come clean with its own people about the famine. It had not undertaken the belt-tightening measures, such as cutting back on arms' purchases or foregoing the expensive celebration of the revolution, which a government with real accountability to those in the countryside might have been obliged to do. Only a much more unequivocal clearing of the desks on its part to fight famine at the expense of other government priorities might have persuaded sceptical food donors to act sooner.'[21]

The international donor community, in particular governments who were reluctant to give assistance, succumbed to public opinion and pressure that were generated by the Western media, in particular the British films on the horrors of famine produced unprecedented public sympathy that any sensible government could not afford to ignore. The international donor community gave generous assistance. Even the United Nations, an organisation, more often than not, that dances to the political tunes of a superpower, appointed an assistant-under-secretary for co-ordinating the flow and distribution of international relief assistance to Ethiopia. The concerted action of the Ethiopian people and the international donor community was able to contain gradually the worst tragedy since the famine of 1888–92.

Settlement Scheme

Mengistu, having successfully mobilised the resources of the nation for combating the effects of famine and being encouraged by the positive response of the international donor community, flew to Cuba to visit his role model, President Fidel Castro. He sent a cable to Cde. Amanuel Amde Michael, Politburo member of WPE, Minister of Justice and chairman of the Emergency Relief Assistance Committee of the Politburo, while he was in flight. The short message from Mengistu instructed him to prepare logistic requirements for a massive settlement scheme to be undertaken upon Mengistu's return from Cuba. The message was so brief that it could not be used as a term of reference for a preliminary study in resettlement. Cde. Amanuel consulted the members of the relief committee who advised him to constitute an *ad hoc* committee which was composed of the Minister of Industry, the head of the Economic Department of the CC of WPE, a vice-minister from the Office of the Chairman of the Council of Ministers and a representative of RRC. The committee under the chairmanship of the Minister of Justice and Law discussed such issues as target groups for a settlement scheme, the number of people to be relocated, sites, financial implications and its logistic requirements. It also prepared a cost estimate and logistic requirements for three schemes consisting of 5,000, 10,000, and 50,0000 persons each.

Although Chairman Mengistu had in a press conference before he left for Cuba stressed the significance of resettlement in relieving the population pressure from over-populated regions, no one with any sanity, could have imagined projects that would have involved millions of people. Moreover, the resources of the country then were overstretched by the government's attempt to combat the effects of famine. The committee, therefore, of the three options it had considered, recommended a scheme for relocating 5,000 heads of families to be undertaken as a pilot project. The recommendation of the committee was submitted to Chairman Mengistu upon his return from Cuba, but he put it aside and mobilised the nation for resettling peasants from drought-stricken regions to other parts of the country. Senior officials of the party and government, including Chairman Mengistu, were on tour by helicopter over certain parts of western and south-western regions of the country for locating settlement sites. Several sites in the administrative regions of Wellega, Keffa, Gonder and Gojjam and Illubabor were identified from the air without making any investigation of climate, soil and other factors. Heavy tractors and bulldozers were soon dispatched to open up access roads to some of the sites. From the haste with which the relocation took place it was clear that the recommendation of the *ad hoc* committee failed to impress Mengistu. He again resorted to his standard approach of attacking massive problems by launching campaigns. The resources of the country, including trucks and other vehicles of the private sector, were commandeered for resettlement. Sergeant Legessie Assfaw, politburo member and first secretary of the CC of WPE for organisational affairs, took charge of transporting settlers to sites. Mass organisations were mobilised for making necessary arrangements, including providing hospitality to settlers *en route* to the sites. Advance parties from relevant government organisations were sent to open up access to the sites and make other necessary arrangements for the settlers. Then university students and their instructors were sent to settlement sites to construct huts for the settlers. Also wherever communities existed near sites, they were mobilised to participate in land clearance, building huts and providing provisions for settlers.

Recruitment of settlers began in earnest. Settlement was executed in two stages. The first stage was integrating new settlers in existing settlements where 32,000 heads of families with 106,000 dependants[22] from drought-prone regions had been settled. However, under this scheme the scope for absorbing large numbers of settlers was limited. The settlement scheme relied heavily on new sites as a result.

The existing settlement schemes were of two types. In one of them settlers were given plots of land and owned the means of production. Farmers ploughed their own plots of land without being induced or persuaded to join producers' co-operative societies where means of production were owned collectively. This scheme proved realistic and successful. Members were, in a relatively short period, able to support themselves. In the second type of settlement, farmers were organised into producers' co-operative societies and the means of production were owned by the society. The farms were mechanised and largely depended on government subvention. Producers' co-operative farms in most cases were not cost efficient. Despite the use of modern agricultural machinery and government subsidy they did not attain levels of production that could have justified the heavy subsidy from the Government. Yet it was the producers' co-operative societies that were replicated for settling half a million victims of famine, mainly from the regions of Tigray, Wollo and Northern Shewa.

The number of victims of drought in Tigray, Wollo and Northern Shewa surged to 1.4 million, 2.59 million and 850,000 respectively.[23] The size of the affected population in these three regions was 53%, 65% and 10% respectively. The drought victims in these regions accounted for more than 50% of the victims of famine in the whole country.

Peasants were recruited from Tigray, Wollo and Northern Shewa where lands had become unproductive due to years of over use, mismanagement and environmental degradation. Some of the districts in these regions had reached such irreversible environmental degradation that they were unable to produce crops even when nature kept its normal climatic rhythm. The World Bank study on these regions in 1971 had recommended resettlement as a solution for restoring ecological balance. Resettlement was not an innovation of the 1974 revolution. It had been going on in an unplanned fashion under the imperial regime. For instance, from 1950–70 farmers from the highlands of Tigray, Wollo, Gonder, Gojjam and Eritrea had spontaneously settled in the Shire lowlands of Tigray, Metema and Agew Midir provinces of Gojjam and Settite Humera of Gonder. These spontaneous resettlements of farmers had prompted the imperial regime to undertake benchmark surveys in resettlement. In the early 1970s the Upper Dedessa Settlement Project was studied by Tippets–Abbot–McCarthy–Straton for USAID financing and settlement schemes were undertaken by missionaries in the Bako district of Shewa, Gode and Kelafo and in the Harargie administrative region.[24]

After the 1977–78 Ethio-Somali conflict 400,000 displaced people were settled in the Bale administrative region. In the province of Ogaden 30,000 drought victims were settled on 150,000 hectares of irrigated land along the Wabi Shebeli river. According to government sources both these settlements were financed by USAID and World Vision.[25] Furthermore, in the latter part of 1970, the Food and Agricultural Organisation (FAO) and the PMAC had made investigations in the highlands of Tigray, Wollo, Shewa and other drought-prone regions. The findings of their studies had confirmed the conclusions of earlier surveys of the World Bank that the effects of drought in these regions could be managed by relocating the people to other parts of the country where climatic conditions were favourable for agriculture and settlement. According to the studies relocation of farmers from drought-prone regions to other parts of the country would reduce population pressure and consequently create opportunity for rehabilitating degraded regions.

The PMAC and WPE, however, added another dimension to resettlement by using it as a means for the formation of producers' co-operative societies that were accorded a high priority in the transformation of the rural areas. The WPE programme articulating the role of producers' co-operative societies stated:

'The expansion of peasant co-operative societies, beyond yielding economic benefits, lays down the necessary material base for alliance of the working class and peasantry. As this alliance is one of the vital preconditions for ensuring the dictatorship of the proletariat, special significance should be

given to the expansion and consolidation of such co-
operatives.'[26]

Drought victims, who had lost all their possessions, left their birthplaces,
robbed of their self-esteem, lost their loved ones and depended for their
survival on handouts, were soft targets for trying out the party's programme. The party cadres organised them into producers' co-operative
societies without going through the three stages of the formation of co-
operative societies laid down by the Government.

The PMAC had adopted three stages in the development of producers'
co-operative societies and followed them rigorously since 1975. In the
first stage farmers would retain the ownership of oxen and other means
of production and cultivated their plots. For services such as marketing of
their products, acquiring agricultural inputs and consumer goods they
would join service co-operative societies. In the second stage they were
required to pool their means of production and products in common.
Products were shared among members in proportion to their contribution. The last stage was the creation of producers' co-operative
societies. The means of production were owned by co-operative societies
and a member was given a share of the collective produce according to
norms fixed by a society. Distribution of product was, at this stage, governed by the Marxian axiom, '*from each according to his abilities to each
according to his needs*'.

The 1984/85 drought affected over seven million people in more than
half of the fourteen administrative regions of the country. The national
Relief and Rehabilitation Committee set a target for settling 1.5 million
in two phases of 50,000 and 250,000 heads of family or 250,000 and
1,250,000 family members. The movement of these people started in
haste. The socialist countries, in particular Russia which was thrilled by
the prospects of the emergence of collectivisation, provided several air-
craft and 300 hundred trucks with 700 drivers for transporting settlers to
new sites. Settlers were recruited by committees consisting of representatives of peasants' associations, RRC and local administrations. Initially
recruitment was carried out in the feeding camps and shelters in Wollo,
Tigray and Northern Shewa. Markets, and other places of public gather-
ings were used as recruitment venues when shelters were unable to
provide settlers. Finally quotas were imposed on peasants' associations for
supplying settlers. Although willingness, youth, full health and physical
fitness were criteria for recruitment, there were instances where these
criteria were overlooked to meet quotas.

For the first round, 600,000 peasants[27] were recruited for relocation in the administrative regions of Illubabor, Keffa, Wollega, Gojjam, Shewa and Gonder. These settlers were recruited from Tigray, Wollo and Northern Shewa. Of the total recruits 63% were from Wollo, 18% from Shewa and 15% from Tigray.[28] They were transported by air to the nearest place where land transport was available and then transferred to buses and trucks. *En route* and at resettlement sites some died but this did not compare the daily death rate of over 100 persons in the feeding camps of Korem, although unnecessary loss of lives could have been avoided by taking precautionary measures. Despite the hazard involved in moving huge numbers of peasants, in one year more than half a million people were moved to Assosa (Wollega), Gambella (Illubabor), Metekele (Gojjam) and Keffa.

The settlement scheme outraged certain Western democracies and their human rights organisations. It was condemned as gross violation of human rights. The Western media unleashed a concerted campaign against settlement demanding its suspension. The PMAC was portrayed as the worst form of dictatorship since the Third Reich. Some resourceful reporters likened the settlement scheme with the atrocities of Pol Pot in Cambodia. The government of the United States of America was an outspoken critic of the scheme. Although the use of force in recruiting settlers was vehemently criticised and a plethora of violation of human rights was used as a pretext for castigating the scheme, the ulterior motive of the critics was to object to the ideological transformation of Ethiopia. An outright criticism against the political system of the country would have been undue interference in the internal affairs of a sovereign state which the critics were careful to avoid. We are not arguing here to extricate the PMAC and WPE from violations of certain basic human rights of settlers but to underscore the use of alleged violations of human rights for political motives rather than for concern of the plight of settlers. Persuasion and compulsion had always been basic components of the PMAC's strategy for executing its policies since the revolution of 1974. The procedures it followed in relocating peasants were not deviations from its standard practice.

The USA and its allies refused to give relief assistance for settlers and even prohibited the transfer of some of their aides to the settlement sites. Their decision to deny any form of assistance to the settlement scheme was in accord with their aid policy that they were following since the PMAC declared socialism as its political system. The USA, the major partner of Ethiopia, under the imperial regime, had discontinued its development as well as military assistance since 1977. Settlement being a long-term development programme geared towards advancing socialism

265

the PMAC and WPE did not expect assistance from the Western democracies. While the Western countries were preoccupied with unconstructive criticism of the settlement programme, the socialist countries, in particular the USSR, supported the programme by providing medical services, agricultural machinery, vehicles, hand tools and so forth. The USSR, in one of the major sites in Assosa, provided a fully-equipped and mobile hospital with doctors and other medical staff. The socialist countries, even though suffering from the lack of disposable surplus, expressed their full support of the programme by providing food aid, medicine, medical personnel, agricultural machinery, water pumps, etc.

Lack of assistance from the West did not restrain the government and the party from carrying out resettlement. By the end of 1985 over half a million people had been relocated in clusters of villages each consisting of 500 heads of family. The financial, manpower and social services requirements for sustaining life in villages was horrendous. The government had to provide food aid until settlers were able to support themselves which would have taken three to five years. Also it had to meet housing and domestic needs of settlers which ranged from cooking utensils to clothing. Moreover the means of production such as hand tools, oxen, tractors, had to be provided and schools, health facilities, water supplies, feeder roads and other facilities constructed. By April 1986, 200,000 dwelling units, 46 primary schools, 946 clinics, 10 health centres, three hospitals, 1,500 kilometres of feeder roads, 54 airstrips, 1,446 deep-water wells were giving their services to settlers. Of the overall target of 300,000 hectares of land 231,733 hectares were cleared and cultivated. Deployment of manpower to settlement sites was impressive as well. Over 2,259 WPE cadres, 545 agricultural experts, 270 surveyors as well as necessary staff for running social services and local administration were made available. Also 1,800 tractors, 180 bulldozers, 1.2 million hand tools and 18,773 plough oxen were supplied.[29]

The commitment of the PMAC and WPE, and the financial and material support of the people, were major factors in settling 510,287 peasants in less than a year.[30]

However the scale of financial, material and manpower requirements forced the PMAC and WPE to reconsider their plan of relocating additional settlers. It was decided to suspend new resettlements and to concentrate on consolidating the existing schemes. Although the programme suffered from a number of constraints such as lack of social, hydrological and soil studies, shortage of resources, settlers were provided with decent shelters, medical service, education, potable water, community centres, etc., which were not available to ordinary farmers in most parts of the country. Leaving aside the ideological dimension of resettlement a tour to the feeding shelters in Tigray and Wollo followed by visits to resettlement sites would have invariably convinced a sceptic that life in the new sites was not as dreadful as the critics of resettlement painted it.

The government on several occasions admitted flaws in the execution of resettlement, but it was determined to prove the advantages of resettlement to the international community. As a result settlement sites were open to foreign visitors and media. As more and more foreigners visited the sites a gradual change of attitude was visible. Most countries of the West, except USA, allowed relief assistance to be used in settlement sites. Canada and Italy broke ranks with the West and gave development aids to settlement schemes. Italy in particular undertook a multi-purpose agricultural development project near one of the settlement sites at a cost of over 200 million dollars. Some non-governmental organisations followed suit by involving themselves in small agricultural and health projects. By 1986, the vehement criticism of settlement subsided. Some congress men of the USA who visited the sites generated public opinion that tended to neutralise the views of their government. The critics of settlement conceded that there was nothing inherently wrong with it, but they objected to the modality of its implementation. Resettlement is not a new phenomenon in Ethiopia. For centuries there were out-migrations, in particular from the northern regions to other parts of the country due to natural and man-made disasters. Ever since 1945 some peasants were migrating to cash-crop regions in the south and west where labour was scarce during harvest. Migrant labourers usually returned to their homes in time for cultivating their plots. This type of migration had benefited farmers in supplementing their meagre incomes from over-used farms. Another type of out-migration was where peasants left their farms and homes for good to go to other parts of the country and in some cases crossed borders to neighbouring countries. Spontaneous settlement had served as a natural means for regulating over-population and as an escape from the adverse effects of recurrent drought. Any rural development strategy has to rationalise spontaneous resettlement from over-populated and environmentally degraded parts of the country to under-populated regions where conditions are suitable for settlement and agriculture.

Villagisation

Villagisation and resettlement were two sides of a coin. Whereas the resettlement programme had as its target victims of drought, villagisation on the other hand aimed at changing the rural settlement pattern of the entire country by regrouping villages. It affected over 90% of the population. The PMAC had the desire of changing the ruler settlement pattern of the country since 1979 when the restructuring of the Ministry of Agriculture was considered by the Council of Ministers. Chairman Mengistu strongly argued for making explicit provision on villagisation in the revised attribution of the Ministry. A sizeable number of cabinet ministers argued that villagisation ought to be a result of rural development rather than an object to be pursued for its own sake. Moreover, other considerations such as political and economic implications dictated deferring any attempt to cluster the countryside into villages. The 1984/85 famine was used as a pretext to revive it. The settlement programme was villagisation on a smaller scale. The 510,287 peasants from the northern parts of the country were settled in 994 villages each consisting of 500 families.

The obvious advantage of villagisation as its proponents presented it was that it facilitated the delivery of services such as education, health, water, electricity, telephone, transport, markets, etc. The fallacy of this line of argument was that it assumed these services could not be delivered due to the sparse settlement pattern of the rural area. It was far-fetched and did not correspond to the realities in the country. Let alone the countryside, in urban centres where settlement patterns were favourable, services were not delivered due to shortage of resources. How could a government which lacked the necessary resources to deliver services for an urban population of less than 5 million have contemplated providing services for over 90% of the population of the country? The government did not possess the resources to meet the requirements of such magnitude. The ulterior motives of the government and the party were to create favourable conditions for the development and growth of socialism.[31]

Natural and man-made disasters, in particular the Ethio-Somali conflict of 1977/78, displaced people from their homes in several thousands. After the war the government took a major step in rehabilitating displaced people in the administrative region of Bale. In this region alone 789,891 of a total population of 929,284 or 85% was reorganised into 562 villages. The experience acquired from the Bale villagisation programme was used to undertake similar ventures in the Arsi administrative region where farmers displaced by state farms were resettled along the Wabi Shebli river.[32] The Wabi Shebli project was supported by generous government assistance and often was cited as a success story.

The first secretary of the administrative region of Harargie who was inspired by the experiences of Bale and Arsi embarked upon a villagisation programme without guidance from the central government. A regional villagisation committee for planning and execution was formed. This was a first attempt of the region to institutionalise villagisation. The committee prepared standards for housing and other facilities including criteria for selection of sites. Sub-committees at various administrative levels were entrusted with responsibilities for preparing logistic require-ments. After preliminary preparation the construction work for the first round of the villagisation of Harargie began in February and was com-pleted in March 1977. In one month 2,365 villages with 182,000 houses were built and 815,277 people were moved to new villages.[33]

Villagisation in the Harargie administrative region was started at the same time with the huge settlement programme of the central govern-ment. This was a period where regional first secretaries of WPE were racing ahead without central direction to solve problems related to drought. Their initiatives were appreciated and encouraged by Chairman Mengistu who was making regular inspection tours to administrative regions. The first administrative region which was graced by his inspection tour was Harargie. He was impressed by the work that was in progress. Upon completion of his tour he wrote a letter of commendation to the first secretary of the region, Cde. Kassaye Aragaw. Kassaye, who was elated by the letter of appreciation of the Chairman, sent copies of the letter to his colleagues, and first secretaries of thirteen administrative regions. Whether this move had been instigated by Chairman Mengistu to spite and motivate other regional first secretaries to follow suit or was initiated on his accord is a matter for speculation. The way the letter was publicised suggested that the first secretary of Harargie circulated copies of the letter in connivance with the Chairman. As would have been expected the distribution of copies of the letter created a spirit of competition among the regional first secretaries of WPE in embarking upon villagis-ation. The race for villagisation began in earnest in the entire country. By March 1986 in the administrative regions of Shewa, Arsi and Harargie 2,839,293 people were moved into 6,523 new villages.[34]

After the Fourth Plenum of CC of WPE, April 1986, villagisation gath-ered momentum. The PMAC and WPE, established a national villagisation committee for issuing uniform policies and monitoring their execution. The committee was created when villagisation reached its peak. It was chaired by Cde. Fikre Selassie Wogdrese, secretary of PMAC and Politburo member of WPE, and ministers and commissioners whose departments were relevant to villagisation served as members. The Ministry of Agri-culture rendered secretarial services to the committee. The committee met as often as required to issue directives and evaluate the progress of villagisation. The creation of a national committee was a delayed response though it served to regulate the execution of villagisation which in some regions, in particular in Gojjam and Illubabor, provoked armed resistance. However, involvement of peasants' associations in the execution of villagisation kept peasant opposition in check.

Other than villages selected for show-pieces the bulk of them did not get social services which the government promised to deliver at the new sites. The peasants were disillusioned when they discovered that facilities were not provided as promised. They had lost their vegetable gardens and trees surrounding their old dwellings and the houses were constructed from the ruins of their former dwellings which in the process of demolishing and movement to new locations were damaged hindering the provision of better accommodation. As a result, in some villages the quality of housing was inferior to those the farmers owned prior to moving to the new sites.

One positive contribution of the national committee was its national villagisation policy. The policy classified rural settlement into three categories, cereals, cash crops and pastoral areas. The directive was to implement villagisation in cereal producing regions and to exclude the cash crop and pastoral areas until proper studies were made. At any rate 33% of the rural population, or 2.6 million families or 12.2 million people, were moved to 12,013 villages consisting of 1,138,265 houses[35] by June 1988.

The absence of a vanguard party was lamented by revolutionaries including Chairman Mengistu as a major weakness of the Ethiopian revolution; but the radical measures it took since its creation including villagisation proved otherwise. The measures it took generated dissatisfaction and negative sentiments toward the PMAC and WPE. Perhaps villagisation was a major factor that contributed to the downfall of the government and WPE.

NOTES

1 Chairman Mengistu's Address to the Nation in Announcing the establishment of the Commission for the Organising of the Workers' Party of Ethiopia, *The Ethiopian Herald*, vol. xxxiv, No. 82, 18 December 1979.

2 ibid.

3 The author was head of the Institute of Management and Training from 1976–82.

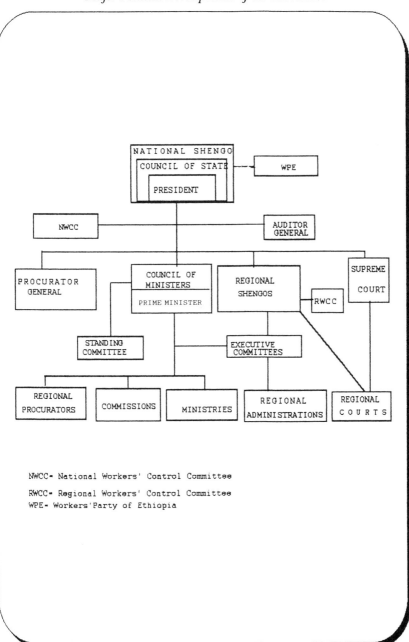

NWCC - National Workers' Control Committee

RWCC - Regional Workers' Control Committee

WPE - Workers' Party of Ethiopia

Chart 4
Organisation Chart of PDRE, 1987–91
271

4 A Proclamation Providing for the Establishment of a Commission for Organising the Workers' Party of Ethiopia of 1979, Article 5.

5 ibid., Article 6/1.

6 Chairman Mengistu's Address to the Nation Announcing the Establishment of COPWE, *The Ethiopian Herald*, vol. xxxiv, No. 82, 18 December 1979.

7 The Documents and Resolutions (The Amharic Version) of the Second Congress of COPWE, Addis Ababa, December 1984, p. 23.

8 Central Report to the Second COPWE Congress by Chairman Mengistu Haile Mariam, *The Ethiopian Herald*, vol. xxxix, No. 97, 4 January 1983, p. 6.

9 The Documents and Resolutions of the Second Congress of COPWE, p. 10.

10 Ras Alula Ingda was one of the most trusted generals of Emperor Yohannis IV. He was governor of Tigray, a province which included most of Eritrea with the exception of the ports of Massawa and Aseb. Both ports were occupied by Italy. Alula's army defeated and annihilated an Italian contingent of 500 men which was advancing to invade the hinterland in 1887 at Dogali.

   Zerai Dresse was an Eritrean patriot who was in Rome at the time of the Italian invasion in 1935. He is considered a hero on account of his opposition to the Italian occupation of Ethiopia.

11 The Asmera Manifesto, *The Ethiopian Herald*, vol. xxxvii, No. 120, 2 February 1982.

12 See the preamble of the Asmera Manifesto.

13 The Ethiopian Famine, Michael Harris, Kurt Jansson and Angela Penrose, London: Zed Books Ltd., 1990, p. 142.

14 Central Report to the Founding Congress of the Workers' Party of Ethiopia, Cde. Chairman Mengistu Haile Mariam, Addis Ababa, September 1984, p. 26.

15 ibid., p. 30.

16 ibid., p. 31.

17 ibid., p. 47.

18 *The Ethiopian Herald*, vol. xl, No. 1, 11 September 1984.

19 ibid., Acceptance Speech of Cde. Mengistu Haile Mariam.

20 The Programme of the Worker's Party of Ethiopia, Addis Ababa, September 1984, p. 32.

21 Famine: a Man-Made Disaster? A Report of the Independent Commission on International Humanitarian Issues, London and Sydney, 1985, pp. 43–44.

22 Ethiopia: Laying the Foundation for a Sustained Socio-economic Development, Ministry of Information, Addis Ababa, 1988, p. 30.

23 Harris, Jansson and Penrose, op. cit. p. xii.

24 Ethiopia: Laying the Foundation for a Sustained Socio-Economic Development, Ministry of Information, Addis Ababa, 1988, p. 29.

25 ibid., p. 30.

26 The Programme of the Workers' Party of Ethiopia, Addis Ababa, 1984, p. 22.

27 Ethiopia: Laying the Foundation for a Sustained Socio-Economic Development, Ministry of Information, 1988, p. 31.

28 Harris, Jansson and Penrose, op. cit. pp. 171–176.

29 The figures in this section are quoted from Chairman Mengistu's reports to the Third and Fourth Plenum of the Central Committee of the Workers' Party of Ethiopia.

30 Report to the Third Plenum of the Central Committee of the Workers' Party of Ethiopia, Chairman Mengistu Haile Mariam, Meskerem 1978.

31 Report to the Fourth Plenum of the Central Committee of the Workers' Party of Ethiopia (Amharic text), Chairman Mengistu, Addis Ababa, Miazia 1978, p. 14.

32 *Meskerem*, vol. 6, No. 26, Addis Ababa, Sene 1978, p. 57.

33 ibid., p. 78.

34 Report to the Fourth Plenum of the Central Committee of the Workers' Party of Ethiopia, Chairman Mengistu Haile Mariam, p. 16.

35 Report to the Ninth Plenum of the Central Committee of the Workers' Party of Ethiopia, Chairman Mengistu, Addis Ababa, *Tikmit* 1981, p. 50.

Chapter Six

The People's Democratic Republic of Ethiopia

You can fool all the people some of the time, and some of the people all the time, but you cannot fool all the people all the time.

Abraham Lincoln

Constitutional Development

The culmination of the Ethiopian revolution was the creation of the People's Democratic Republic of Ethiopia. Much hard work had gone into it before its declaration in September 1987. Initially an Institute for the Study of Nationalities, under the guidance and supervision of the Department of Nationality Affairs of the Workers' Party of Ethiopia, whose primary function was to draft a constitution, was established. The Institute made a socio-cultural survey of the entire country, as well as acquainting itself with constitutional developments in socialist and some developing countries. Then it drafted a constitution which was tailored to meet the requirements of a socialist state. The Institute's draft was an instrument designed to make the status quo lawful and formalise the establishment of a unitary state with certain of its powers devolved to its administrative subdivisions. A federal republic was not considered as an alternative form of government at the drafting stage. The draft that served as a working document for the Constitution Drafting Commission was for the creation of a unitary state. A constitution drafting commission was established by Proclamation No. 291, 1986 with the power to draft a constitution, to conduct a public discussion on it, to promote public awareness and

274

to invite suggestions from the public that would enrich the final draft. The commission comprised 347 members, who were drawn from the WPE, appropriate state organs, mass organisations, professional associations, the heads of the major religions and individuals renowned for their professional and/or patriotic services to the nation.

The members were hand-picked by the WPE leadership to which the commission was accountable. The public was not invited in either nominating or electing members of the commission. Representatives of the major religions and renowned individuals were included in the membership of the commission to give credence to it. The irony was the participation of the heads of the Ethiopian Orthodox Church, the Catholic Church, the Evangelical Church and Islam in drafting a constitution whose long-term goal was the creation of a communist society. The presence of the heads of the major religions and their active participation in the debate misled the public into believing that the constitution had the blessings of the holy fathers, an impression which the authorities desired to create.

The commission, at its first session, elected Chairman Mengistu as its chairperson by acclamation. He was nominated by a politburo member of the party, an initiative which was intended to discourage the possibility of other nominations. The chairperson of the commission, in turn, presented a list of names for membership of an executive, drafting, and discussion recording committees. The commission again endorsed the nomination from the chair without even pausing to seek other nominations. The WPE leadership controlled the composition of the committees of the commission by failing to invite open nomination from the floor. An examination of the membership of the composition of the committees shows the extent of the WPE leadership's determination to control the deliberations of the commission.

The Members of the Executive Committee of the Commission were:

1. Chairman Mengistu Halie Mariam, Secretary-General of the WPE, Chairman of the Council of Ministers and the Commander-in-Chief of the Armed Forces – chairperson;
2. Cde. Fikre Selassie Wogderese, Deputy Chairman of the Council of Ministers and politburo member of the WPE, member;
3. Cde. Fiseha Desta, politburo member of the WPE, member;
4. Cde. Legessie Assfaw, politburo member of the WPE, member;
5. Cde. Amanuel Amde Michael, politburo member of the WPE and Minister of Justice and Law, member;

6. Cde. Alemu Abebe, politburo member of the WPE, member;
7. Cde. Shimelis Mazengia, politburo member of the WPE, member;
8. Cde. Shewadagne Belete, alternate member of the politburo of the WPE, member-secretary;
9. Cde. Tesfaye Dinka, alternate member of the politburo of the WPE and Minister of Finance, member;
10. Cde. Taddesse Tamrat, member of CC of the WPE and Chairman of ETU, member;
11. Cde. Abdella Sonessa, member of CC of the WPE and Chairman of EPA, member;
12. Cde. Getachew Robelie, alternate member of CC of the WPE and Chairman of REYA, member;
13. Cde. Asegedech Bizuneh, alternate member of CC of the WPE and chairperson of REWA, member;
14. Cde. Yayehyirad Kitaw, alternate member of CC of the WPE and Head of the Institute for the Study of Nationalities, member;
15. Cde. Dr Haile Gebrel Dagne, alternate member of CC the WPE and Chairman of the Teachers' Association, member.

The Executive Committee was only composed of the Politburo and Central Committee members of the WPE. The other important committees for drafting, discussion and comments recording, and propaganda, comprised persons who were in key leadership positions in the party, government, mass organisations, professional associations, religious institutions as well as a few renowned private individuals. Incidentally all the committees were chaired by a politburo member of the WPE. The procedures by which members were nominated and chairpersons appointed protected the draft constitution from any substantive changes.

The commission, in three sessions, concluded its assignment of drafting a constitution. In the first session a general debate on the draft was conducted and it was then referred to a drafting committee. At the second session of the commission the draft of the Committee, which comprised 17 chapters and 121 articles and 181 sub-articles, was adopted without any substantive amendment and submitted for the approval of the WPE. Between the second and the third sessions of the commission the draft was made available for public debate. To facilitate the participation of the public in the debate the draft was prepared in fifteen local and three foreign languages, including English, French and Arabic. Free public discussion on the draft was conducted in 25,388 discussion fora including Ethiopian missions abroad.[1] Individuals raised pertinent points questioning the appropriateness of socialism for Ethiopia. All comments, questions and amendments were duly recorded and transmitted to the commission's secretariat. At the end of the discussion which lasted three Sundays 500,000 questions, comments and amendments were recorded.[2]

The articles which attracted the highest number of comments, questions and amendments were those articles dealing with nationality, individual rights, freedom and citizens' obligations followed by political and socio-economic systems, in particular the types of ownership of property and the leadership role of the working class. The third group of subjects which provoked public interest was the state and its organs. Those amendments which did not challenge the tenets of the political system were incorporated in the constitutions while the others were dubbed revisionist tendencies and discarded. At any rate the discussion contributed immensely to awakening the political consciousness of the people.

The final draft, which was allegedly enriched by public debate, was adopted by the congress of the commission in the first week of July 1986 and was then submitted for approval by the Fifth Plenum of the Central Committee of the WPE which approved the draft and decided its submission for a referendum. Pursuant to the decision of the central committee a Referendum Commission was created by Proclamation No. 365/1986. The task of the commission was to submit the draft constitution to a referendum and to report the result to the CC of the WPE. The members of the commission were again hand-picked from the WPE, mass organisations, professional associations and government organisations, and a few individuals of repute were once more included. The commission elected a 15-man executive committee with branches at the local and regional levels. The Executive Committee's role was to conduct a referendum. The commission was chaired by Chairman Mengistu Haile Mariam, politburo members of the WPE and the chairpersons of ETU, EPA, REYA and REWA served as members.

The structure of the state, the party and mass organisations from the central to the local level served as venues for registration and polling. Registration for the referendum lasted from 11 to 18 January 1987. The registration books were kept open for public inspection from 19–21 January. Any person 18 years of age and above was eligible for registration. The referendum took place in the entire country on 1 February 1987 between 6 a.m. and 6 p.m.

277

Out of 14,035,718 registered for the referendum 96% cast their votes; of this 81% voted YES, 18% NO and 1% of the votes cast were invalidated.[3] The result of the referendum was hailed by the state-run media as a victory of the Ethiopian people and a concrete testimony to a high level of political consciousness of the people that was achieved by arduous efforts of revolutionaries. The drafting and the referendum exercise led to a final drama, the creation of an Electoral Commission by Proclamation No. 314 of 1987. The Electoral Commission was chaired by Cde. Amanuel Amde Michael, politburo member of the CC of the WPE and Minister of Justice and Law.

The proclamation among other things defined those who had the right to nominate candidates (Article 28) for the National Shengo (Parliament). Candidates were nominated by a joint forum of the WPE, mass organisations and units of the military. Registration for electing representatives for 835 constituents began on 3 May 1987. At the end of May a list of the nominations of candidates was submitted to the Electoral Commission. The commission approved the list of nominees drawn up by a joint forum. Those members of the Electoral Commission who were nominated, including the chairperson of the commission, were replaced by other persons who were not nominated as candidates. Following the decision of the commission, that meetings should be organised to introduce the candidates to constituencies, meetings were held throughout the country. The candidates were duly introduced to the members of their constituencies. Chairman Mengistu was present at the meeting of Kebele 1, Kefitegna 14 in Addis Ababa. Other officials and party functionaries were dispatched to various meetings held throughout the country. Some candidates were introduced to constituencies where they were total strangers to the people. When the names of three nominees were disclosed to each of the constituencies one or in some cases two of the candidates withdrew their candidacy in favour of one candidate whom they regarded that he/she had contributed to the revolution more than they had. As a result of this comradely gesture 12%, 7% and 81% of the constituencies had respectively one, two or three candidates standing for election. Practically all the important members of the WPE including Chairman Mengistu were sole candidates in their respective constituencies.

The election was held on 13 June 1987 from 6 a.m. to 6 p.m. According to the report of the Electoral Commission 20 million people cast their votes to elect 835 representatives. The composition of the representatives elected to the National Shengo was as follows:

Social Composition	%
Workers	12.1
State functionaries	36.5
Party functionaries	23.6
Members of the Armed Forces	12.9
Artisans	1.5
Others	4.9
Age	
21–30	18.2
31–59	79.6
60 and above	2.2
Education	
Literate	4.7
Elementary and secondary	67.1
Higher education	28.2*
(RA 8.1%, MA 4.4%, PHD 3.1% and others 12.6%)	

Source: People's Democratic Republic of Ethiopia, Facts and Figures, Central Statistical Office 1987 p. 9.

This classification gives the wrong impression that only 23.6% were party members. The fact is that those classified as workers, state functionaries and members of the Armed Forces were members of the party as well. This means that 93.6% of the members of the Shengo were party members.

The Founding Congress of the PDRE was convened with pomp in the presence of distinguished guests from socialist and neighbouring African countries on 11 September 1987. At its first session the Shengo endorsed the constitution, issued a proclamation that formally established the PDRE, elected the President of the Republic, the various state organs including the Vice-President of the Republic, members of a 24-man Council of State, three Vice-Presidents of the Council of State, the Prime Minister and five Deputy Prime Ministers, members of the Council of Ministers, the President, Vice-Presidents and judges of the Supreme Court, the Procurator-General, the Auditor-General and members of the National Working People's Control Committee. The results of the election for these state organs were as follows:

1. Cde. Colonel Mengistu Haile Mariam, President of PDRE;
2. Cde. Colonel Fiseha Desta, Vice-President of PDRE;
3. Cde. Captain Fikre Selassie Wegderese, Prime Minister;

279

4. Cde. Colonel Addis Tedla, Chairman of the Central Planning Committee;
5. Cde. Hailu Yemenu, Deputy Prime Minister;
6. Cde. Dr Alemu Abebe, Deputy Prime Minister;
7. Cde. Tesfaye Dinka, Deputy Prime Minister;
8. Cde. Dr Teferra Wonde, Deputy Prime Minister;
9. Cde. Amanuel Amde Michael, Vice-President of the Council of State;
10. Cde. Colonel Debela Dinsa, Vice-President of the Council of State;
11. Cde. Yusuf Ahmed, Vice-President of the Council of State;
12. Cde. Assefa Liben, President of the Supreme Court;
13. Cde. Bililign Mandefro, Procurator-General;
14. Cde. Lemma Aragaw, Auditor-General, and
15. Cde. Tilahun Haile-Selassie, Chairman of the National Working People's Control Committee.

The Council of State, the most important organ of the PDRE, included the officials listed in numbers 1–11 above as well as the following persons:

1. Cde. General Tesfaye Gebre Kidan
2. Cde. Colonel Berhanu Bayih
3. Cde. Fasika Sidelil
4. Cde. Shoandagn Belete
5. Cde. Colonel Endale Tessema
6. Cde. Dr Ashagre Yegletu
7. Cde. Captain Kassaye Aragaw
8. Cde. Colonel Embibel Ayele
9. Cde. Taddesse Tamrat
10. Cde. Abdella Sonessa
11. Cde. Dr Haile Gebrel Dagne
12. Cde. Asegedech Bizuneh
13. Cde. Getachew Robelie

Of the 24-man Council of State 12 members were Politburo and the remaining 12 were Central Committee members of the WPE. The important positions of PDRE, the Presidency, the Vice-Presidency and the Premiership were occupied by the members of the Dergue. An innovative aspect of the membership of the Council of State was the inclusion in its membership the chairpersons of mass organisations ETU, APE, REWA, REYA and ETA.

The other organs of the PDRE, the Council of Ministers, the Office of the Auditor-General, the Procuracy and the Presidency of the Supreme

Court, were filled by personalities hand-picked by the President and endorsed by the congress of the Shengo. The top-heavy state structure comprised a president, a vice-president, a 24-man Council of State with three vice-presidents, a prime minister and a 26-man Council of Ministers with four deputy prime ministers. The elections of the officials of the PDRE was applauded by the state-run media as democratic. Invited guests also joined the chorus by extending their congratulations to the elected officials, particularly to Chairman Mengistu upon his unanimous election as president of the PDRE. The first speaker among the prominent guests was President Kenneth Kaunda of Zambia, current chairman of the Organisation of African Unity, who in his address to the National Shengo, said that the member states of the OAU fully supported the changes that were taking place in Ethiopia. He concluded his speech with a touch of emotion that was typical of him. At the end of his speech he asked the members of the congress of the National Shengo to repeat after him the slogan. '*There is one nation and that nation is Ethiopia; there is one leader and that leader is Comrade Mengistu Haile Mariam.*'[4]

The National Shengo at its first session, besides the election of officials for the various organs of PDRE, adopted laws and directives that would facilitate the implementation of the constitution. It also made a call to all insurgent movements to join the PDRE. This was the first public indication of the government's desire to enter into peaceful dialogue with insurgent organisations. However, none of them responded positively.

The National Shengo gave its priority to the creation of regional Shengos at various administrative levels. The state structure that was enforced since 1941 was reorganised on the basis of the constitution. Criteria developed by the Institute for the Study of Nationalities for restructuring the state were adopted. Although the criteria for the reorganisation of the state were not debated in public, it could be assumed that the Institute took into consideration language, culture, economic resources and political factors into reorganising the state structure. The state was divided into 25 administrative and autonomous regions[5] replacing the former 14 administrative regions, 101 Awrajas and 500 Weredas. The new structure was a two-tier system consisting of autonomous and administrative regions and Awrajas both smaller in their areas and population than the former regions and Awrajas. The Wereda or district, the smallest administrative unit under imperial rule, was absorbed in the Awraja under the new state structure.

The PDRE constitution did not make distinction between administrative and autonomous regions. Articles 97 and 98 conferred similar powers and duties on both types of administrative units. Both were meant to serve as

281

instruments for implementing the decisions of the central government. Their programmes and budgets were approved by the National Shengo. On the other hand, they were empowered to supervise and co-ordinate the activities of their administrative subdivisions, elect judges and regional councils and appoint chairmen of regional control committees. The constitution fell short of giving them the power to legislate on local matters, but by subsequent directives and seminars held on to the implementation of the constitution, distinction was made between administrative and autonomous regions. The autonomous regions were allowed to enact legislation as long as this did not clash with directives of the central government. In the delegation of legislative power, distinction was made among the five autonomous regions. The Eritrean Autonomous Region was empowered to issue legislation without seeking the prior approval of the National Shengo in so far the legislation did not conflict with the constitution and other laws of the state. The other four autonomous regions, Tigray, Dire Dawa, Aseb and the Ogaden, were given the power to issue legislation subject to the approval of the National Shengo before it was enforced. The Eritrean region was given more latitude for freedom of action in economic, education, health and other fields. It could establish educational institutions up to and including junior colleges, provide health services, and set up industries without obtaining the approval of the National Shengo. The other four autonomous regions could give secondary education, and provide health services in clinics and health centres, and set up small-scale and medium-scale industries. In the case of Eritrea there was an attempt to restore the powers and responsibilities of the Eritrean Legislative Assembly under the federal arrangement.

The administrative divisions of the PDRE were the result of political expediency. The five regions accorded autonomous status had one thing in common; in all of them there was some form of armed resistance to the central government. The government hoped that the new political map of the state would appeal to insurgents, but none of the insurgency movements were tempted to accept the new arrangement. They intensified the armed struggle after the creation of PDRE.

The government nevertheless went ahead in implementing the constitution. The strategy adopted to reorganise the state on the basis of the new administrative structure was in stages. Three autonomous and 11 administrative regions were first selected for introducing the new system of administration. These three autonomous regions were Dire Dawa, Aseb and the Ogaden. Eritrea and Tigray autonomous regions were not included due to the deterioration of the security situation there. The

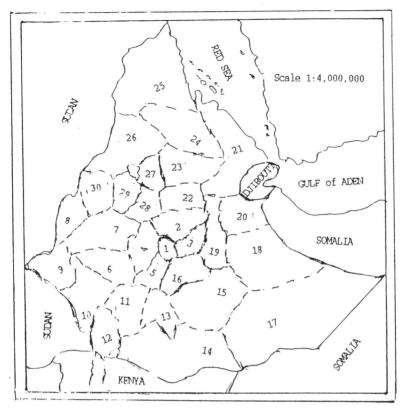

LEGEND

1 Addis Ababa	11 Northern Omo	21 Aseb
2 Northern Shewa	12 Southern Omo	22 Northern Wollo
3 Eastern Shewa	13 Sidamo	23 Southern Wollo
4 Southern Shewa	14 Borena	24 Tigray
5 Western Shewa	15 Bale	25 Eritrea
6 Illubaor	16 Arsi	26 Northern Gonder
7 Wellega	17 Ogaden	27 Southern Gonder
8 Assosa	18 Eastern Hararge	28 Eastern Gojjam
9 Gambella	19 Western Hararge	29 Western Gojjam
10 Keffa	20 Dire Dawa	30 Metekele

— — International Boundary

——— Regional Boundary

Map 6 Autonomous and administrative regions of the PDRE, 1987–91. Adapted
from the Institute for the Study of Nationalities

selected eleven administrative regions were Northern Wollo, Southern Wollo, Metekel, Assosa, Bale, Gambella, Western Harargie, Eastern Harargie, Southern Omo, Northern Omo and Wellega. The criteria for the selection of these regions were not disclosed, but a close examination indicates that most of them were frontier regions and relatively backward in development. They met the government's policy that development ought to be carried from the periphery towards the centre.

Election for the regional Shengos for three autonomous and eleven administrative regions were carried out as a matter of priority. They were carefully planned to facilitate manipulation of the elections as was the case with the election for the National Shengo. To ensure that the chairmanship of the regional Shengos were in the hands of party officials, one first secretary of the WPE for each of the thirty administrative and autonomous regions was appointed. After the assignment of party secretaries the elections for the regional Shengos were carried out under their direction and supervision. When the results of the elections were disclosed all first secretaries of the WPE were elected as members of their respective regions and subsquently as chairmen of the Shengos. The regional Shengos were controlled by the party. Besides chairmen, the Shengos elected executive committees, which according to Article 98 of the constitution, had responsibility to implement laws, directives and decisions of higher bodies, supervise and co-ordinate the activities of their respective regions. Members were elected from the Shengo members. The first election of regional executive committee membership was dominated by party members.

War and Peace

Since the formation of PDRE two contradictory developments were unfolding. The government took a series of peace initiatives while the insurgent fronts, the EPLF and TPLF, particularly the latter intensified its offensive on many fronts. Tigray was put under marshal law administration. Cde. Sergeant Legessie Assfaw, politburo member, was appointed Chief Administrator of Tigray and Supreme Commander of the Third Revolutionary Army. This army initially had some successes but was later defeated and disintegrated. It was an unprecedented reverse and a turning point in the military operation of the government. The massive weapons, armoured vehicles, tanks, ammunition etc., which were captured at the headquarters of the army in Enda Selassie, Shire, completely changed the balance of power in favour of TPLF. The disintegration of the Third Army was due to lack of able leadership.[6] The TPLF, fortified with the captured weapons, was able to extend its military operation to Southern Gonder, Wollo and by the summer of 1989 when the Rome Peace Talks were in progress, their forces had penetrated deep into Northern Shewa, some 200 kilometres away from the capital city.

The withdrawal from Tigray undermined the government's position both at home and abroad. Domestically, particularly in the countryside, the government lost the support of the peasants while the TPLF gained their co-operation and assistance. The flight of government officials, including the Chief Martial Law Administrator of Tigray, created a bad precedent. Administrators and party officials from regions adjacent to areas where TPLF was operating fled to the nearest towns when they heard rumours on the advance of TPLF forces. The number of party and government officials who abandoned their posts became so serious that some members of the National Shengo raised the problem at its First Extraordinary Congress where the President promised to take corrective measures. Abandoning posts was not limited to civilians, army units were equally guilty; but their flight was covered by military jargon, strategic retreat or withdrawal. Even the withdrawal of the entire government machinery from Tigray was explained as tactical retreat.

The government's military performance at the battle of Shire was a disgrace. A division well-armed with modern weaponry and supported by air cover was shamefully annihilated by a rag-tag guerrilla force. More than the loss of the Army the government's decision to withdraw from Tigray was a blunder of incalculable political repercussion. The decision for withdrawal was made by the President in consultation with the top military officials in the Army and Ministry of Defence. It was decided that the administration should pull out of Mekele, the capital of Tigray, gradually in six days, but the high command made its withdrawal in two days to a new provisional site, Dessie.[7] Internationally the TPLF gained recognition as a force that could be relied upon to overthrow one of the most hated regimes by the West in Africa. It was after the fall of Tigray that the United States began closely to associate itself with the TPLF.

In Eritrea, as in Tigray, the government brought about its own downfall. The Second Revolutionary Army in Eritrea was a formidable force and the elite of the Ethiopian Armed Forces. Many of its operations against insurgents were successful. However, its officers' corp was frustrated by the Commanders-in-Chief's instituting a system which deprived them of exercising full command and control over their men. The commanders at the front were placed in a very difficult position of making strategic decisions independently. They had to consult military commissars, who were picked from the non-commissioned and junior officers, and inspectors of the Army. The triumvirate command, comprising a commander, a commissar, who was a political cadre, and an inspector, replaced the single command which is typical of any modern army. The system was effective in checking dissension in the Army, but killed the initiative of the officers and encouraged insubordination and indiscipline. In this connection Major-General Gizaw Belayneh, who was the Chief of Staff of the Armed Forces for a brief period, after the execution of Lieutenant-General Aman Michael Andom observed that he had witnessed the deterioration of discipline which was actively encouraged by the state-controlled media.[8] The restoration of the single command in the Army had been raised on several occasions at the meeting of the Central Committee of the party by concerned senior officers, but it was conveniently shelved by the President.

President Mengistu regularly flew to Eritrea to review the military situation and to resolve problems that surfaced from time to time. He was displeased to hear at one of his meetings after an inspection tour, the commanding officers of the Second Revolutionary Army informed him of the weakness in the force. Particularly the commander of the Afabet Front, General Tariku Ayne, who frankly disclosed the weakness of his force and in the process a heated exchange of words took place between him and the President and the Commander-in-Chief of the Armed Forces. At the end of the meeting the General was arrested and summarily executed. Major-General Regassa Jima, the Commander of the Second Revolutionary Army was pensioned, and a number of other senior officers were demoted in rank. Brigadier-General Kebede Gashu, a sector commander, was stripped of his rank and dismissed from the force.

The arbitrary action by the Commander-in-Chief of the Armed Forces destroyed the combat spirit of the Armed Forces, particularly that of the Nadew Division at the Afabet Front. A few days from the execution of the General, the demoralised division was overrun and the largest military depot and strategic post in Eritrea was captured by the EPLF in 1987. The weapons, ammunition and armoured vehicles, including over hundred tanks, changed the balance of power in favour of the EPLF. The fall of Afabet was a turning point in the Eritrean war. The Minister of Industry and ex-commander of the Ethiopian Air Force, Major-General Fanta Belay, who was in London when Afabet was lost to the EPLF, observed: '*The fall of Afabet was the secession of Eritrea*' Such was the gravity of the consequence of the loss of Afabet as a result of the execution of the commander at the front. Subsequently the fall of Afabet led to another major disaster, the capture of the Port of Massawa, on the Red Sea Coast, in 1990.

It was when the balance of power was tilted towards the insurgents that the government intensified its peace initiative. The Founding Congress of the PDRE appealed to the insurgents to settle their differences with the government by peaceful dialogue. Both the EPLF and TPLF rejected the call. Gradually, the government's concerted effort convinced the international community of the sincerity of its proposal and the insurgents succumbed to public pressure. Ex-President Carter seized the opportunity to act as a mediator and held a number of meetings with the President of PDRE who was desperate for a negotiated settlement. Mr Carter, having obtained the assurance of the government, contacted the EPLF leadership, who because of their military successes, were not keen to participate in peaceful dialogue. The government, however, intensified its peace efforts and was determined to expose the intransigence of the rebels. To this end an extraordinary congress of the National Shengo was convened to assess the situation in Eritrea and other parts of the country, and to endorse the peace initiative of the government. President Mengistu opening the Extraordinary Session said:

'The main objective of the congress is to deliberate and formulate a strategy on ways of ending with a stepped up peace effort the problem that has persisted as the main obstacle to our progress and the fulfilment of the wishes of the entire working people and in particular wrought unparalleled destructions in the northern part of our country. As our National Shengo collectively and each deputy individually and fully realises our aim is to build the nation and raise the standard of living of the people. That is why we have given priority to peace. In this we have not limited ourselves to a mere declaration of intent to give priority to the peaceful solution of our problems, but have actually taken practical measures to that end.

Although the anticipated full result to ceaseless effort made in this regard has yet to be attained, we have found it necessary to devise a new peace initiative taking into consideration the wishes of our people and the prevailing overall international situation. This Extraordinary Congress of the National Shengo is convened by the President in accordance with Article 67 of our constitution, in order to facilitate conducive situations for a reinforced peace initiative. Now the various efforts have been made for the practical implementation of the peace call made by the

National Shengo at the First Congress and reiterated by
the Second Congress.'[9]

Peace talks had been tried on several occasions before the creation of
the PDRE. Secret contacts had been made, in particular with the EPLF.
The talks stalled due to the uncompromising attitude of both the government and the insurgents. The insurgents demanded independence and
the government wanted to find a solution within the unity of Ethiopia.
The government claimed that it had made several attempts for a negotiated settlement since the Ethiopian Revolution of 1974. The initiatives
of the government were both on the domestic and international fronts.

On the domestic level a committee composed of 38 Eritrean elders was
established in 1974 to make contacts with the insurgents and to express
to them the Dergue's readiness for a negotiated settlement, but the effort
failed on account of the insurgents' intransigence. Despite this obstinacy
the First Chairman of the Dergue, Lieutenant-General Aman Michael
Andom, who was an Eritrean, made two trips to convey the military
government's willingness for a negotiated settlement to the Eritrean
people, and through them, to the insurgents, but the reply was an intensi-
fication of the conflict. By 1975 the insurgents were too close to capture
the city of Asmera to favour negotiation.

When the Dergue declared its National Democratic Revolutionary Programme in 1976, it made an effort to address the problem of nationalities,
including in Eritrea. The Dergue was under the naive impression of
assuming that the programme would be a panacea to the problem
of Eritrea. The provision of the NDRPE on nationalities reads:

'The right to self-determination of all nationalities will be
recognised and fully respected. No nationality will dominate
another one, since history, culture, language and religion of
each nationality will have equal recognition in accordance with
the spirit of socialism. The unity of Ethiopian nationalities
will be based on the common struggle against feudalism,
imperialism and bureaucratic capitalism and all reactionary
forces. The united struggle is based on the desire to construct
a new life and society based on equality, brotherhood and
respect.'[10]

Based on this principle of socialism which the PMAC and EPLF had in
common, the government issued a Nine-Point Peace Policy on 20 April
1976. It aimed at the peaceful resolution of the problem in Eritrea within

the principle of self-determination of nationalities leading to a regional autonomy. The following were the nine points:

1. The anomalies which had existed before will be done away with and the people of the Eritrean Administrative Region will, in a new spirit and in co-operation and collaboration with the rest of the Ethiopian people, have full participation in the political, economic and social life of the country. They will in particular plan their full role in the struggle to establish the people's democratic republic in accordance with the programme of the Ethiopian Democratic Revolution.

2. The Programme of the Ethiopian National Democratic Revolution has affirmed the right of self-determination of nationalities can be guaranteed through regional autonomy which takes due account of the objective realities prevailing in Ethiopia, her surroundings and in the world at large. To translate this into deeds, the government will study each of the regions of the country, the history and interactions of the nationalities inhabiting them, their geographic position, economic life and their suitability for development and administration. After taking this into consideration the government will at an appropriate time present to the people the structure of the region that can exist in the future. The entire Ethiopian people will then democratically discuss the issue at various levels and decide upon it themselves.

3. Having realised the difficulties existing in the Administrative Region of Eritrea and the urgency of overcoming them, in order to apply in practice the right of self-determination of nationalities on a priority basis, the Provisional Military government is prepared to discuss and exchange views with the progressive groups and organisations in Eritrea which are not in collusion with feudalists, reactionary forces in the neighbourhood, and imperialists.

4. The government will give full support to progressives in the Eritrean Administrative Region who will, in collaboration with the progressives in the rest of Ethiopia

289

and on the basis of the Programme of the Ethiopian National Democratic Revolution, endeavour to arouse, organise and lead the working mass of the region in the struggle against the three enemies of the Ethiopian people, feudalism, bureaucratic capitalism and imperialism, and thereby promote the unity of the oppressed class of Ethiopia.

5. The government will give the necessary assistance to those Ethiopians who, because of the absence of peace in the Eritrean Administrative Regions for a long time, have been in exile in neighbouring countries and in far-off alien lands so that they may, as of today, return to their country.

6. The government will make a special effort in rehabilitating those Ethiopians who might have lost their property because of the adverse conditions that had existed. All those who have been dislocated from jobs and education as a result of the existing problem will be enabled to avail themselves of the employment and educational opportunities which Ethiopia can offer in any part of the country.

7. People who have been imprisoned as a result of the existing problem will be released. The case of those who have been sentenced to life imprisonment or death will be carefully examined and reviewed as soon as peaceful conditions are restored and, on the basis of their offence, they will either receive reduced prison terms or be altogether released.

8. The state of emergency will be lifted as soon as major decisions begin to be implemented and peace is guaranteed in the Eritrean Administrative Region.

9. A special commission entrusted with the task of ensuring the implementations of decisions 5 and 7 above will be established by proclamation.'[11]

The commission was established for implementing the peace plan but was closed down after a year due to lack of co-operation from the insurgents.

After the failure of successive domestic attempts to resolve the Eritrean problem, the PMAC took the initiative to involve governments, who had contacts with the insurgents, Cuba, Libya and the People's Democratic Republic of Yemen, to mediate. The result of this fresh attempt with the use of third parties was not different from the unilateral and direct attempts of the Dergue. Ultimately the German Democratic Republic succeeded in bringing the EPLF to the negotiating table. A delegation of the PMAC and the EPLF met for the first time in East Berlin in February, March and June 1978. The PMAC and EPLF delegations were led by Colonel Berhanu Bayih, in charge of PMAC's Foreign Affairs Committee, and Isayas Afeworki, Secretary-General of the EPLF, respectively. The two sides, at these meetings, tabled their positions formally. The PMAC expressed its readiness to discuss the problem within the framework of its Nine-Point Peace Policy and the National Democratic Programme of Ethiopia which upheld the principle of self-determination of all nationalities within a united Ethiopia. The EPLF presented the following pre-conditions[12] for any peace dialogue with the government:

1. The PMAC should recognise Eritrea's right to independence.
2. The government's forces should be withdrawn from Eritrea.
3. Socialist countries should guarantee the independence of Eritrea.

After three unproductive rounds of discussions the peace effort was abandoned. Although the meetings failed to bring the parties to an agreement they created an opportunity for direct and secret contacts between the PMAC and EPLF.

The stalled peace initiative once more was reactivated by the government when the PDRE at its first and second congresses issued calls for a negotiated settlement. Although the invitation of the National Shengo was well received by the international community, it needed more articulation. The peace initiative which was rejected by both the EPLF and TPLF gathered momentum when all those concerned countries and international organisations welcomed it; then the insurgents bowed to international pressure to enter into a peaceful dialogue with the government. Moreover, the latter was also required to be more explicit in its peace initiative. To this end the First Extraordinary Congress of the National Shengo issued the following peace plan:[13]

– to meet and engage in peace talks with anyone;
– to begin the talks without any preconditions;
– to conduct the talks in the presence of an observer to be selected by mutual agreement;
– to conduct the discussions publicly at a mutually chosen venue; and

– to take any other additional measures that would help the progress of talks.

The major insurgent organisations, the EPLF and TPLF, which at this time had successfully co-ordinated their armed and propaganda offensives against the PDRE, did not accept the government's peace initiative on the grounds that they did not trust it. In particular the TPLF argued that the peace initiative was not addressed to it. President Mengistu in a press conference in giving clarification to TPLF's concern reiterated:

> 'The peace initiative and indeed all the various invitations to
> peace that have been made over the years, are addressed
> to all parties that have for different reasons remained outside
> of the revolutionary democratic process and who have the
> good will for peace and co-operation.'[14]

The government's peace initiative generated immense domestic as well as international support and appreciation which the insurgents could not have afforded to ignore by giving flimsy excuses for rejecting it.

The government aggressively promoted its peace initiative at home and abroad. Internally the WPE cadres held public discussions on the peace plan throughout the country by mobilising the people in support of the peace talks. Moreover, the government dispatched delegations abroad to explain the content of its plan, determination and sincerity for a nego- tiated settlement. The superpowers and a number of European countries expressed their support for the government's peace initiative. The African head of states and governments, who were in Addis Ababa for the 25th Regular Session of the OAU, also gave their full support to the peace initiative. The systematic government diplomatic offensive in promoting its peace initiative generated a tremendous international support which compelled the EPLF and TPLF to review their stance for a negotiated settlement. The EPLF expressed its readiness to enter into a peace dia- logue with the government through ex-President Carter who by this time had established a reasonable rapport with both the government and the EPLF.

The TPLF disclosed its readiness to begin peace talks with the govern- ment through its clandestine radio station. Its radio message was later put in writing and delivered to the Ethiopian Embassy in London which forwarded it to the government in Addis Ababa. The government's letter of acknowledgment was sent to the TPLF through the same Embassy which by this time had become the official channel of communication between the PDRE and TPLF. After a preliminary exchange of letters the London Embassy was authorised to meet and discuss with the representatives of the TPLF the venue, date, observers and mediator of the peace talks in August 1989. The London Ambassador and a Politburo member of the TPLF met and discussed those issues for four weeks. Though tempers were lost at times and heated exchanges of words were made, the meetings were conducted with cordiality and dignity. However, the major obstacle for the discussion was the lack of trust of each other coupled with the delay that was created in getting directives from the TPLF's office in Khartoum. The lack of an adequate mandate to make decisions on the spot was a common problem shared by both delegations. After four exacting weeks of discussions in various hotels in London, an agreement was reached to hold the first meeting in Rome under the chairmanship of the Italian Government. The parties to the Rome Peace Talks as identified in the agreement were on one side the PDRE and on the other side, the TPLF. Regarding observers it was agreed in principle to select them by mutual consent but their identity and number was left to be determined at the Rome Peace Talks. The Preliminary London Agreement between the representatives of the PDRE and TPLF constituted the basis for the subsequent meetings between the PDRE delegation led by Dr Ashagre Yigletu, Deputy Prime Minister, and the TPLF delegation by Ato Melese Zenawe, Secretary-General of the TPLF, in November 1989 and March 1990.

The Italian Government, although accepting the trust that was placed in it by the two sides, was not enthusiastic to serve as a mediator and without any modesty the officials did not hesitate to indicate to the government delegation that they were more interested to participate in the peace talks that the government had begun with the EPLF under the chairmanship of ex-President Carter. At any rate, they accepted the mediation role and provided all necessary facilities, including conference hall, secretarial services and transport vehicles to both delegations. An Italian ex-ambassador to Ethiopia was appointed as mediator. The ambassador to his credit led the discussion with extraordinary skill, sense of humour and patience. In the first round of talks which took two weeks, agreement was reached on some procedural issues, including working language, recording the minutes of the proceedings of the meetings, press, the numbers of observers, etc. The outstanding issues including the nomination of observers and drawing up the agenda for the substantive talks were delayed until the next meeting which was held in March 1990.

The parties met for the second time in Rome. In the intervening time between the first and second talks the situation at the front had favoured the TPLF. It had extended its offensives from its home base, Tigray, to Gonder, Wollo and Northern Shewa, only two hundred kilometres from the capital. Besides the Rome Talks had helped it to broaden its contacts with several countries, including the United States which began to show active interest in the TPLF. Buoyed by its advances in the field and its diplomatic contacts the attitude of the TPLF delegation was not helpful for the continuation of peace talks. It demanded that it should be allowed to negotiate on behalf of its close ally, the Ethiopian People's Democratic Movement (EPDM), which was not a party to the London Agreement signed between the PDRE and TPLF. The government delegation, by invoking the London Preliminary Agreement, rejected the TPLF's new demand and further argued that the EPDM could in its own right contact the PDRE either to join the on-going discussion or to enter into other peace talks with the PDRE. These differences of positions of the parties to the peace talks led to the breaking up of discussion without even agreeing to meet again.

The peace talks with the Eritrean fronts began at two venues simultaneously. In one venue the PDRE started discussion with five factions of the ELF in Khartoum who were the first among the Eritrean fronts to respond positively to the peace call of the PDRE. At another venue, Atlanta, Georgia, the PDRE entered into peace talks with the EPLF under the chairmanship of ex-President Carter in September 1989. The PDRE and EPLF delegations were led by Dr Ashagre Yigletu, Deputy Prime Minister, and Isayas Afeworki, Secretary-General of the EPLF, respectively. At this meeting general matters were discussed and agreements were reached on such issues as venue, working language, co-chairman, observers, minutes and agenda for substantive peace talks. The second meeting took place in Nairobi, in November 1989 and discussed outstanding procedural items from the Atlanta meeting and selected jointly ex-President Neyrere of Tanzania as co-Chairman. However, on the third round of talks held in Nairobi, April 1990, the EPLF insisted including OAU and the UN as observers. Accordingly the Chairman Mr Carter requested the UN and OAU in writing but both of them declined to accept the invitation in comformity with their charters, particularly the UN made it clear that it would not participate in the peace talks unless it was invited by a member state, the PDRE. The EPLF took the positions of the two international organisations as an excuse to walk out from the peace talks.

The stalled peace talks between the PDRE and EPLF were reactivated by the US on 21 February 1991. The two delegations met in Washington

DC under the chairmanship of Mr Herman Cohen, Assistant Secretary for Africa.

In a two-day meeting the parties did not achieve anything worth mentioning other than agreeing to meet at some future date for further discussion. The timing was unfortunate for the PDRE to participate in any serious discussion because both the EPLF and TPLF had the upper hand on the battlefields. The loss of Afabet, the military fortress and depot in the North, the port of Massawa, the government's withdrawal from Tigray and the TPLF's extension of its military operation to Gonder, Gojjam, Wollo and Northern Shewa had effectively weakened the government's bargaining position with either the EPLF or TPLF. Besides the execution of the most experienced officers of the Armed Forces due to their involvement in the Generals' abortive coup was a significant factor in reversing events in favour of the insurgents. The PDRE was a beleaguered government whose days in power were numbered. It was from this position of hopelessness that the government and EPLF's delegation met in Washington. In the meantime the US Government suggested joint talks, which will shortly be discussed, involving the EPLF, TPLF and OLF to which the government promptly replied that it favoured peace talks which would involve all insurgent groups. London was chosen as the venue, perhaps for the obvious fact that the EPLF, TPLF and OLF had offices there. This issue would be discussed in greater detail in the London Peace Talks.

The Coup d'état *of the Generals*

Ever since the execution of General Tariku, Commander of the Nadew Division, and the disciplinary measures taken against some officers of the Second Revolutionary Army, including its commander, the officers and men were disillusioned, and felt that their fate might not be different from their colleagues. The Asmera execution was an incident that triggered the suppressed dissatisfaction of the officers of the Armed and the Police forces that led to a conspiracy to overthrow the Commander-in-Chief of the Armed Forces. The conspiracy was kept a secret among a few senior officers for the obvious reason that most of the junior officers, those in the commissariat of the forces who had more power and prestige than their commanding officers, were loyal cadres of the leadership and their exclusion from the plot was for security reasons. The plotters were waiting for an opportune time. According to statements obtained from the interrogation of some of the plotters the idea to overthrow the President was hatched as early as 1985, but delayed for want of an opportune time.[15] The advantageous moment arrived when President Mengistu flew to the German Democratic Republic for a state visit on 16 May 1989. As soon as the presidential plane was airborne most of the plotters who were at the Bole Air Port, Addis Ababa, to see him off drove to the Ministry of Defence to meet in the office of the Chief of Staff of the Armed Forces, Major-General Mered Negussie. Others were also invited to the Chief of Staff's office for an urgent meeting. Someone must have reported to the President's aide-de-camp, Captain Mengistu Gemechu, the unusual meeting of senior officers from the Armed Forces and the Police. An emergency meeting of the Council of State under the chairmanship of Cde. Feseha Desta was convened while the meeting of the plotters was in progress unaware of the their vulnerability. The Council of State decided that they should be advised to break up the unauthorised meeting. The Defence Minister was sent to the meeting to inform them of the Council of State's decision while the aide-de-camp of the President, with the assistance of the Chief of Security, Colonel Tesfaye Wolde Selassie, moblised the elite presidential guards and besieged the Ministry of Defence where the plotters were meeting. When they realised that they were surrounded by armed guards and the Defence Minister was there to request them to surrender, one of them, General Abera, shot to death the Minister, General Haile Giorgis Habte Marim, on the spot. The Chief of Staff, Major-General Mered Negussie and the Commander of the Ethiopian Air Force, Major-General Amha Desta, committed suicide. General Abera and General Fanta Belay, Minister of Industry and ex-commander of the Air Force, escaped. The remaining generals gave themselves up to the elite force without a shot. The commander of the Second Revolutionary Army, Major-General Demissie Bulto, who was also involved in the plot, without knowing that the coup was aborted, sent two contingents by air from Asmera to the capital. One of the contingents was intercepted by the presidential guards and disarmed and the other arrived after the conspirators had been arrested. It tried to force its way to the Ministry of Defence, but failed to break the defence of the elite guards. After a short exchange of shots it was defeated and its commander, General Kumlachew Dejene, escaped and finally ended up in the United States. The coup was crushed in only a few hours. But one of the ring leaders, Major-General Demissie Bulto and his colleagues were active in Asmera. The Council of State imposed a dusk to dawn curfew in the capital and ordered all citizens to stay at home until further announcement to the contrary was made. Having averted the danger in the capital the Council of State contacted the President in GDR to apprise him of the situation in the country. The news of the attempted coup was broken to him by the Ambassador to the GDR, Commander Lemma Gutema. The President interrupted his visit and flew back to Addis Ababa on 18 May 1989. On the same day the Asemra plotters were killed by junior officers loyal to the President, a dividend of the triumvirate system of leadership in the army. Twenty-seven officers, including the Commander of the Second Revolutionary Army and ten generals, were slaughtered.[16]

The official version of the coup as disclosed by the President was:

> 'As soon as it was realised that a number of generals were meeting in the Ministry of Defence with the tragic and hopeless purpose of launching a *coup d'état*, a message was sent from the party Central Committee and the Council of State ordering them to cease their conspiracy forthwith.
>
> When the Minister of Defence arrived there to give his order, he was shot dead in cold blood by one of the conspirators. At this point, troops were mobilised and surrounded the area where the conspiracy was being held and the officers were asked to surrender.
>
> Two of these, the Armed Forces Chief of Staff and the Commander of the Air Force, fully aware of the nature of their crime committed suicide on the spot. Otherwise everyone of the rest surrendered without a fight and peacefully.
>
> In Asmera, the coup was led by the commander of the forces in the region with a number of other generals. There, too, as soon as it was realised within the armed forces that these generals were engaged in committing treason, loyal troops took the initiative to set up their own leadership and demanded the surrender of the treacherous generals. A shootout ensued and a total of twenty-seven officers, including eleven generals, were killed. The rest surrendered and were put under arrest.
>
> The total number of officers under arrest in Addis Ababa is forty-three, of whom seventeen are generals. Two generals who escaped in the confusion at the Ministry of Defence are still at large and the search for them is continuing. In Asmera, a total of one hundred and thirty officers, seven generals among them, are under arrest.'[17]

One hundred and sixty senior officers of the Army and the Police, including 39 generals, were involved in the attempted *coup d'etat*. The arrest and execution of most of the generals deprived the forces of their seasoned leadership. President Mengistu, who was scared by the nightmare of the attempted *coup d'état*, appointed to commandant positions loyal ex-officers, who had served at various levels in the government and party structure since the revolution. The only exception to this was Brigadier-General Alemayehu Agonafer who was appointed commander of the Air Force. The following is a list of the new appointments to senior positions in the Army and the Police:

Name, Rank and Position	New Rank and Position
1. Col. Addis Tedla, Member of the Politburo of the WPE and the Council of State, and Head of Central Planning Committee	Lt.-General, Chief of Staff of the Armed Forces, Member of the Politburo and the Council of State
2. Maj.-General Seyoum Mekonnen, Commissar of the Militia and National Military Service and CC Member of the WPE	Maj.-General, Deputy Chief of Staff of the Armed Forces and CC member of the WPE
3. Col. Embible Ayele CC Member of the WPE and Secretary of the Council of State	Maj.-General, Commander of the Ground Forces and Member of CC of the WPE
4. Commander Yehoalaesht Girma, First Party Secretary for Addis Ababa and CC Member of the WPE	Rear Admiral, Commander of the Navy and CC Member of the WPE
5. Maj. Girma Newaye Regional First Secretary and CC Member of the WPE	Maj.-General, Commander of the Police Force
6. Brig.-General Alemayehu Agonafer, Head of Logistics in the Ministry of Defence and Member of the WPE	Maj.-General, Commander of the Air Force and Member of the WPE
7. Maj. Berhanu Jembere, Commissioner of the Relief and Rehabilitation Commission	Maj.-General, Commander of the First Revolutionary Army
8. Maj. Webeshet Dessie, Head of Administration and Finance of the WPE and CC Member	Maj.-General, Commander of the Second Revolutionary Army

These officers were generously rewarded with military titles and reinstated in the forces without consideration of the aspirations of career officers. The appointment of these officers was a reflection of desperation and the sense of insecurity of the Commander-in-Chief of the Armed

Forces. The appointment damaged the morale of the forces beyond any glimmer of hope for its restoration.

The time of the *putsch* was suitable, but its execution lacked proper planning and foresight. Given the experiences of the generals, it was absurd to have had held their meeting in the most conspicuous place and in broad daylight. The plotters' over-confidence was responsible for underestimating the capacity of the presidential elite force to strike. The need for a *putsch* was overdue, but its execution was reckless.

The President, addressing a rally after the coup had been foiled, made this remark:

> 'The generals who wished to quench their power thirst with
> the blood of the sons of the people have tried to present me
> as the enemy of the majority of my compatriots. But one
> would sincerely ask whether their hatred was against me or
> against the popular order which had made it impossible for
> them to realise their selfish pursuit. Let the people give
> their verdict.'[18]

The President used the occasion to dismiss the *putsch* as a struggle for power rather than a movement against his style of leadership and the policy of his government. He seized the opportunity to apportion blame to the generals for the military set-backs and defeats of the government forces. In a calculated attempt to exonerate himself from the poor performance of the army he interjected in his address:

> 'In fact the people have begun to wonder of late why our
> combat forces, for all their determination to fight, had to
> face unexpected and at times serious set-backs despite the
> people's full co-operation with the government in giving
> their sons as well as the necessary logistic support for the
> defence of the Motherland. The recent event has, I think
> made the answer clear.
>
> Following the concrete condition of the country the task
> of leading the army at different levels was entrusted to these
> same generals whose treachery has just been unmasked. If
> those individuals had a degree of patriotism and
> demonstrated some concern for the forces under their
> command rather than peruse their material and power
> ambition, we could not, as we have been exposed to repeated
> reverses. There were often cases when our forces were

whistled back when they appeared to be on the brink of
victory over the enemy. It was such inexplicable orders that
led many to ask angrily at times whether the real purpose
was to win the war or that there is any seriousness in
continuing the effort.'[19]

The charges levelled against the generals was the President's desperate
attempt to regain the sympathy and support of the people, but the mood
of the nation was disappointment with the failure of the coup rather
than feeling sympathy for the President. The generals would have won
the support of the people had the coup succeeded, but had to face the
ordeals of being tried for treason. The President, who was known for his
vindictiveness, established a special military court to try the generals.
After a year of gruesome trials the court found the accused guilty and
imposed penalties ranging from life imprisonment to death. Fourteen
faced the death penalty for criminal conspiracy, attempt to overthrow the
government and violating military discipline. The most amazing part of
the trial was the speed with which it was carried out. The convicted were
executed on the same day without giving them an opportunity to appeal
for clemency pursuant to Articles 82/1e and 86/3d of the PDRE constitution. The executions were unexpected, and shocked the conscience of
the nation. It was a blunder that generated intense hatred to the beleaguered government. Had the President shown magnanimity, either by
pardoning the convicted or changing the death verdict to imprisonment,
he might have won the respect and support of the people. He normally
acted on vengeance rather than exploiting situations to further his own
political ends. This was an ideal situation for making a political point,
but it was wasted and perhaps expedited his shameful flight from the
country.

Too Little Too Late

The year, 1989, was a period when events were dictating changes in
Ethiopia. Particularly the poor performance of the military and the collapse of the socialist system and its replacement by a market economy in
many countries including the USSR, had their impact on the situation
in Ethiopia. President Reagan's and Prime Minister Thatcher's administrations exerted pressure on socialist countries, particularly on Russia, to
stop its military assistance to the Ethiopian Government. By 1990 the flow
of weapons and ammunition from the socialist camp ceased, thereby
creating a shortage. This shortage of supplies was aggravated by low

morale in the Armed Forces which was mainly induced by the liquidation and imprisonment of senior officers. On one hand, to check the mounting internal and international pressures exerted on the government to change its political orientation and economic system, and on the other, to improve its chances of remaining in power, the regime declared a new economic policy and a change in the political system, Mengistu's style of *perestroika*.

Although the Ethiopian revolutionaries frowned upon the changes which were sweeping Russia and other socialist countries, the escalation of domestic problems, the mounting pressure from the Western Democracies and Russia's unwaivering commitment to abandon communism, forced them to follow suit in changing the economic as well as the political system of the country with the expectation that the change would pacify Western countries and dilute the internal problems. The President in his report to the Eleventh Plenum of the CC of the WPE recommended a change in the political and socio-economic system of the country, including a suggestion for changing the name and programme of the WPE. In his address he said: *'By taking the objective condition of our country on the one hand and giving due attention to the changing international situation on the other, it is all too clear that there is a need for charting a new development plan that will be to the advantage of and benefit to our country and people.'*[20] The report further declared that the country's economic system would be a mixed economy where the state, co-operative societies and the private sector would flourish in close co-operation in the development of the national economy. With this marked departure from the party programme which aimed at gradually phasing out the private sector and replacing it either by the state or co-operative societies. In underscoring the importance of the private sector in the new economic reform, the report stated:

> 'The other participant in the mixed economy is the private
> entrepreneur. One of the major factors of this economic policy
> being to assist and promote small-scale producers attain
> higher stages of production along with the path they
> choose, the private sector will from now on be encouraged
> and strengthened in all ways. According to our new
> economic policy, Ethiopian nationals will thus be able to
> participate without any capital limit, in any field privately,
> in partnership or through share companies. The private
> entrepreneur will therefore work side by side with the state

301

enterprises and co-operatives in industrial, agricultural, mining, transport, trade and other fields.'[21]

This policy declaration was a significant change from a command to a market economy. The private sector was recognised as a useful partner in national economic development. Besides the government committed itself to encourage the private sector to strive, a measure which was regarded as revisionist, in the past. Unfortunately without assessing the depth of the new economic policy the Western press dismissed it as a change which was 'too little and too late'.

The economic declaration was not an empty reform aimed at pacifying Western critics. Given the government's socialist economic policy, it was a radical change. The seriousness of the government in changing its economic direction was manifested when it introduced a number of legislative measures, including a liberal investment proclamation to facilitate the implementation of the policy. The agricultural policy restored to peasants the right of use and transfer to legal heirs plots of land which were allotted to them. The prohibition of employment of farm labour was lifted and entrepreneurs were allowed to take lands on concession from the government for commercial agriculture. These measures were profound amendments to the Public Ownership of Rural Lands Proclamation No. 31 of 1975. Trade, particularly external, which was dominated by the public sector, was liberalised by allowing the private sector to participate. This change repudiated the party's programme on external trade which stated: *'Since import-export trade has a great effect in determining the direction of the country's trade and increasing the State's accumulation capability and since it has a significant influence on the national economy in general, it will be placed entirely under state control.'*[22]

The housing policy was also drastically revised allowing individuals without any restriction to capital to build, rent, lease and sell buildings, including residential houses. The changes on the housing policy were drastic revisions of the *raison d'être* of the Urban Land and Extra Houses Proclamation No. 45 of 1975.

Along with economic changes, the Eleventh Plenum of the party emphasised the need of reforming the country's political system, and revising its international and foreign relations in the light of new political changes that were sweeping the socialist countries. The report of the Secretary-General of the Party drawing the attention of the Central Committee to the urgency of institutional reforms stated:

'International relations have shown pronounced change as

well, since it is impossible to continue under the former
conditions, it is necessary to chart the nation's foreign
relations attuned to the changing situation. In considering the
realities obtaining in the international scene the Central
Committee was requested to adopt a foreign policy which
was neutral to associating the country with any particular
bloc. The policy, therefore, was based on collaboration with
other nations for mutual benefit, peace, upholding the
principles enshrined in the charters of the United Nations
and Organisation of African Unity, and in general co-
operating with all democratic nations committed to peace
and development. This was a revision of the foreign policy
of the WPE which was "based on the objective of
contributing towards strengthening proletarian
internationalism, the development of socialism, the success
of world revolutionary movement and the attainment of
world peace.'[23]

The revision of the party's foreign policy to meet the conditions created
by the sudden collapse of the socialist bloc was under the circumstances
a timely and prudent course of action. The change in foreign policy was
not, however, appreciated by the international community which was not
prepared to accommodate any declaration short of handing the government over to a democratically elected party. The regime was in
desperation as a result of the external and internal pressures exerted on
it to institute a change in the system of government. The President was
indiscreet in revealing the fact that the various economic and political
changes that were proposed to the Central Committee of the party were
the result of changes in the international situation, the poor performance
of the military in the conflict with the insurgents and a demand for a
change of the system from various quarters. In conceding the need
for change the President retorted:

'As pointed out in the earlier report, we find ourselves at a
unique period, when the internal situation and the
international development are appraised, they indicate
different characteristics that require a different approach.
  It is believed that internally this new approach should
embrace and involve the various sectors and classes of
society in an indivisible spirit of being all Ethiopians. At the
international level too, it has been accepted that it will help

303

ensure that relationships are anchored on mutual benefits
and the interests of peace.'[24]

The admission that the changes were proposed because the changing of
circumstances rather than the regimes conviction and desire to introduce
change cast doubt on its commitment to implement its policy declarations.

The regime at the height of its desperation to retain its power
announced its intention to change the objectives of the Workers' Party
of Ethiopia. In explaining his vision of changing the political system to
the Central Committee the President stated:

'In the context of the newly developed economic system and
the theory of international relations, the WPE should change
its nature and even name. The move of this change will be
towards representing all the different classes and sections
of the society on the basis, in particular, of the Ethiopian
people's democratic unity. This means that the party which
will embrace all nationals irrespective of their class, and
religion, tenets, groups or a follower of this or that faith,
who are genuinely committed to Ethiopia's unity and
progress, will be represented with a common objective. In
regard to goals and tasks the party will have a framework
which will co-ordinate a doctrine, programme, and similar
other attributes while it may not be necessary that members
follow an identical ideology.

The party will have a broad popular base and will be
organised on the basis of the nature and content mentioned
earlier to serve, above all and in the spirit of representing
the whole society, the interest of our country's unity and
progress, the exercise of democratic rights by all nationals
and development of their personality.

Moreover, opportunities are open to opposition groups
which bring themselves through their organisations under
the umbrella of the democratic unity of the Ethiopian
people, after conditions of peaceful dialogue have been
discussed by the Ethiopian people and subject to their will
and decision in order that the group could participate in
the country's politics.'[25]

The proposal did not go as far as to allow a multi-party system of government. The regime was adamant to control the political life of the people by changing the name of the party and its ideology. The proposed change was a significant departure from a vanguard party to a single party which would have as members all those who believed in the unity and territorial integrity of Ethiopia. The new party, which was not following any political persuasion, was to be named the 'Ethiopian Democratic Party' (EDP). Insurgents too were invited to join the EDP, provided that they abandoned their armed struggle and subscribed to the unity and territorial integrity of the country. As the regime had done in the past, when it changed its name from Dergue to COPWE and then from COPWE to the WPE, it now sought to change its name from the WPE to EDP. This old trick with which the Ethiopians were familiar in their seventeen years of association with Dergue, its capability of changing names of institutions without changing the leadership, failed to strike a cord with either the people or the insurgents. The popular demand for a multi-party system was not met by a proposal of a single party system.

Both the economic and political reforms of the regime were not considered a breakthrough at the international level. Internally the economic reform was well received, but the political reform was not appreciated by the people.

Measures Taken in Desperation

When the government's economic and political reforms fell short in meeting the popular demand for a change in the system of government, the regime resorted to sacking the party's Politburo and Central Committee members (all of them were veteran members of the Executive Committee and Central Committee of the Dergue). They were pensioned on the grounds of poor health. The first casualties were Colonel Debella Dinsa, Central Committee member of WPE and Vice-President of the Council of State, and Colonel Teka Tulu, alternate member of the Politburo and head of the Party Control Commission. Both of them were retired on grounds of poor health. The official explanation given for the sacking of these veteran members of the Dergue was true in the case of Colonel Teka who was suffering from a debilitating disease which had left a visible impairment on his body. But in the case of Colonel Debella the official reason for his retirement was not consistent with the robust state of health that the victim was enjoying. He was the sober conscience of the Dergue during the Red Terror. As the representative of the Dergue in the most populous regional administration, Shewa, during the Red Terror campaign, he had won the respect and adoration of the people for his fairness and sense of justice. Particularly the restraints he had imposed on the cadres under his supervision during the Red Terror had made him popular. Besides his charismatic personality and his ability of conveying his thoughts to others with humour and friendly disposition were additional factors for his growing popularity. Ever since the Red Terror his popularity was steady, which might have worried President Mengistu. Had a vacancy occurred in the presidency Colonel Debella would have been a favourite candidate. His premature retirement on the grounds of poor health was a cover for a political motive. Anyway the retirement of these two ex-police officers did not make any difference to the popular demand in the change of leadership.

The next casualty from the inner circle of the ruling clique was Captain Fikre Selassie Wogderese, Politburo member, Prime Minister, member of the Council of State and ex-secretary of the Dergue. He was a person who was quite content with his post as second to the President. His name was associated with a scandal of gold smuggling from the Gulf states allegedly in complicity with an old friend from the Air Force who was the head of Air Security in the Ethiopian Airlines. The chief of security was suspended pending an investigation of the alleged scandal. The Prime Minister's name was linked with this serious crime when the witch-hunt for political scapegoats was in full swing. The rumours on the Prime Minister's complicity in the scandal soared to a height where his position was rendered a liability to the government. With the hope this unfortunate predicament of the Prime Minster would have improved the beleaguered government's position, he was also retired on the ground of poor health. The retirement of the Prime Minister pending the outcome of the investigation was tantamount as confirming the rumour and a revelation of impropriety of those in leadership positions.

The momentum that was created by sacking the inner circle of the ruling clique continued unabated and Sergeant Legessie Assfaw, Politburo member, Chief Marshal Law Administrator of Tigray, ex-member of the Executive Committee of the Dergue, who was in the capital having fled from Tigray in the wake of TPLF's offensive, was fired. He was the President's henchman and his dismissal without any reason was a delayed disciplinary measure taken against him for his incompetence in leading the Third Revolutionary Army in Tigray. His leadership was an unmitigated disaster to the regime.

The purge of the inner circle of the military junta reached its climax when Colonel Fiseha Desta, member of the Politburo, Vice-President of the PDRE and ex-Assistant Secretary of the Dergue, was pensioned. His position was an unenviable one, being from Tigray, some of his close associates questioned where his loyalty lay. Anyhow the third man in the ruling class was made a sacrificial lamb for political expediency.

The dismissal of senior members of the government and party was followed by a reshuffle of the administration. The most significant aspect of the shake-up was that for the first time since the revolution the Premiership was given ` to a civilian who was asked to form a cabinet. The appointments[26] to the highest positions in the state were:

1. Lieutenant-General Tesfaye Gebre Kidan, Vice-President of PDRE;
2. Cde. Hailu Yemenu, Vice-President of the Council of State;
3. Cde. Tesfaye Dinka, Prime Minister;
4. Commander Lemma Gutema, Vice-President of the Council of State;

The new Prime Minister was a veteran who had served as Minister of Industry, Finance, Deputy Prime Minister and Foreign Minister since the revolution. As a Foreign Minister (1989–91) he had done much to improve the country's relations with the Western democracies and the image of the country internationally. He was the best Foreign Minister that the country had ever had since the revolution. In the Gulf crisis of 1990 his contribution, representing Ethiopia in the Security Council, to the UN debate on Iraq was appreciated by the United States and its allies. Mr Cohen had expressed the USA's appreciation to President Mengistu for Ethiopia's active role in the Security Council and voting with the USA on an economic embargo against Iraq, when he was in audience with the President, after the Gulf War, in September 1990. All these positive developments in relations with the West perhaps had contributed more than other factors in the Prime Minister's appointment. Following his appointment the Prime Minister reorganised the government structure. The number of Deputy Prime Ministers was reduced from four to two; the ministries of Agriculture, State Farm, Coffee and Tea Development were merged; Internal and External Trade were combined, Finance and External Economic Relations were integrated, and a new Ministry of Environmental Affairs was created. On the basis of these reorganisations the following appointments[27] were made:

1. Cde. Yusuf Ahmed, Deputy Prime Minister for Economic Affairs,
2. Cde. Shimelis Adugna, Deputy Prime Minister for Social and Administrative Affairs.
3. Cde. Colonel Tesfaye Wolde Selassie, Minister of Internal Affairs.
4. Cde. Abdulhafez Yusuf, Minister of Information,
5. Cde. Tesfaye Tadesse, Minister of Foreign Affairs,

307

6. Cde. Merse Ijigu, Minister of Agriculture,
7. Cde. Tekze-Shewa Aytenfisu, Minister of Energy,
8. Col. Wondayen Mihiretu, Minister of Justice and Law,
9. Cde. Dr Yayeherad Kitaw, Minister of Education,
10. Cde. Afework Berhane, Minister of Health,
11. Cde. Colonel Mersha Wodajo, Minister of Transport and Communications.
12. Cde. Aklilu Afework, Minister of Planning,
13. Cde. Tadesse Kidan Mariam, Minister of Urban Development and Housing,
14. Cde. Tadiwos Hagrework, Minister of Industry,
15. Cde. Hambissa Wakoya, Minister of Internal and External Trade,
16. Cde. Bekele Tamirat, Minister of Finance and External Economic Relations,
17. Cde. Zegaye Assfaw, Minister of Labour and Social Affairs,
18. Cde. Aragaw Tiruneh, Minister of Construction,
19. Cde. Tewlde-Berhan Gebre Egziabher, Minister of Culture and Sports,
20. Cde. Tsegaw Ayale, Minister of Environmental Affairs.

Of the 20 ministers six had never had ministerial positions and the remaining 14 were ministers, including Cde. Zegaye Assfaw who had important ministerial portfolios as Land Reform, Agriculture, Justice and Law, until he fell out of favour in 1979 and was imprisoned. He was incarcerated without trial and released along with 907 inmates of which 84 were political prisoners, in 1989. His inclusion in the cabinet was an indication that the government was prepared for reconciliation with its political foes.

The dismissal of five senior members of the ruling clique and the cabinet reshuffle still failed to satisfy the public demand for a change of leadership. Now, the arrow of discontent began to focus more sharply on the President himself.

Pressure groups continued to make appeals to the government to do whatever it could in the interest of promoting peace in the country. The Eleventh Conference on Ethiopian Studies, held in Addis Ababa between 1–6 April 1991, supported the public demand by including peace in its agenda. It passed a resolution endorsing a peace plan put forward by a veteran academic, Professor Mesfin Wolde Mariam, and appointed an eleven-man Committee for Peace and Reconciliation in Ethiopia. The committee members were:

1. Professor Mesfin Wode Mariam
2. Dr Fiseha Haile Meskele

 3. Dr Seyoum Gebre Selassie
 4. Dr Azeb Desta
 5. Dr Mekonnen Bishaw
 6. Dr Assefa Desta
 7. Dr Aminu Hussen
 8. Dr Sebehat Mersiehazen
 9. Dr Solomon Teferra
10. Dr Taye Woldesemaite
11. Ato Isaac Kifle

The Committee after several meetings endorsed the professor's peace plan and issued an open letter addressed to 'all friends of Ethiopia' to support the peace initiative and requesting the President to implement it. The peace initiative which was endorsed by the committee of Eleven, contained the following points:

'1. A council of elders will be elected by the people from every region and they will be authorised to appoint a trusteeship government under their control.

2. The first duty of the trusteeship government under the control of the council of elders will be to sign an agreement with the present government on matters relating to the safety and security of party members, functionaries and party officials. This is a practical necessity not only for the sake of those involved, but also for the country and the nation which cannot afford another occasion for losing its trained manpower in one way or another.

3. The other duty of the trusteeship government will be to ensure that the sovereignty of the Ethiopian people and not the possession of guns will be the source of power. Therefore, all groups who have different and opposing ideas, no matter how unfashionable they may be, will debate freely and publicly with a view to winning the support of the Ethiopian people.

4. After ratifying the constitution that will be fully and freely debated by the whole population, and after legislating the functions, operations and the standards for contests between parties, both the council of elders and the

trusteeship government will hand over authority to the
winning parties and leave. Their roles will be terminal,
that is, neither the members of the council of elders nor
the members of the trusteeship government will seek any
position in the succeeding administration.'[28]

The letter was a courageous act of its signatories. It, for the first time,
challenged a regime that was notorious for its ruthlessness in dealing with
those who questioned its legitimacy. The regime conveniently dubbed the
letter as a dream of misguided scholars. Although it pretended to dismiss
it as a phantasy of scholars, the damage it had caused by undermining
the beleaguered government was immense. It motivated and encouraged the people to discuss openly the need for a change of leadership.
Optimism gave rise to the suspicion that the government would resign
of its own accord. At the height of speculation on the resignation of the
regime, it was announced that the President would address the nation.
The publicity given to the address further raised the expectation of the
people for a radical change in the leadership. On the day the speech was
made all government offices and institutions were closed to enable the
citizens to listen to it. The nationwide address was made on 19 February
1991. But to the surprise of everyone the speech was a report on the
achievement of the government and victories of the revolution that
the people were accustomed to hearing in the last seventeen years. In
particular, the President spoke at length on the procedures that were
adopted in drafting and ratifying of the constitution and concluded that
his responsibility was to the National Shengo and he would not succumb
to any external pressure. The speech conveyed the message that he was
determined to cling to power, and there would have been no question
of him resigning. He concluded by stating that unless every citizen recognised the threat to the unity of the country and was prepared to make
the necessary sacrifices, it would break into pieces. The statement that
was expected to be an announcement of a change of government was
nothing other than a call for general mobilisation. By this time the
military position had deteriorated and the rebels were taking the initiative
and fierce fighting was going on between the government and the insurgent forces within a radius of 125 to 130 kilometres from the capital.
The only sea port, Aseb, in government control was on the verge of
falling to the joint forces of EPLF and TPLF. The forces of the insurgent
fronts were advancing in all directions pursuing the fleeing government
forces. It was under such a desperate situation that the government
accepted the American proposal for a new peace dialogue with the EPLF,

TPLF and OLF instead of a separate negotiation with each of them. Although the President promptly accepted the American proposal, the peace dialogue was twice postponed at the request of the insurgents. The mediator, the United States Government, the avowed enemy of President Mengistu and his regime, was not keen to press the insurgents to start the peace talks. The government's position was getting precarious as a result of the delay in the peace talks while the insurgents were benefiting from the delay by advancing and controlling more regions. Deferring the peace talks improved the bargaining position of the insurgents. In the meantime, the President frantically campaigned to mobilise the people particularly university students and industrial workers who were rushed to training centres to prepare them for the final showdown with the insurgents pending the Peace Talks.

The Flight of the President

The President in one of his regular inspection tours to training centres for conscripts was due to fly on 8 May 1991 to the southern part of the country where university students were under training. Instead he landed in Nairobi, Kenya. No sooner had the President's landing in Nairobi become known than the Council of State met in an emergency meeting and issued a statement announcing the flight of the President and the appointment of the Vice-President, Tesfaye Gebrekidan, as an Acting President. The circumstances of the flight of the President were not made clear to the public. There were two versions. One was that the pilot was instructed by the aide-de-camp of the President in consultation with the Chief of the Security and a few members of the Council of State to fly the President to Nairobi and return immediately leaving him behind. No reliable evidence was available as to whether the Kenyan authorities were apprised of the President's trip to their capital. According to the briefing the Kenyan High Commissioner to the United Kingdom gave to the Ethiopian Ambassador in London, the Kenyan Government was not informed of the President's trip to Nairobi. As soon as the news of the President's arrival was relayed to the Kenyan authorities by the Nairobi Air Port management, an officer was immediately sent to meet him and to find out the circumstance of his unexpected arrival. Even the Ethiopian mission was not aware of his trip to Nairobi. The President explained that he was deported by some members of his Government, and sought the assistance of the Kenyan Government to make an arrangement for him to fly to Zimbabwe. The Kenyan Government provided him with some cash in US dollars and obliged by facilitating his trip to Harare.

On the other hand, the President's confession from Zimbabwe stated that he flew to Nairobi for an important errand related to the acquisition of weapons. But how could a head of state fly to another country without informing the host and his diplomatic mission? The official version of the Kenyan Government as conveyed to the Ethiopian Ambassador in London, was at variance with the President's story. This version was that the CIA had played a role in co-ordinating the efforts of certain officials of the Ethiopian Government and the Kenyan authorities to make the necessary arrangement in changing the course of his flight to Nairobi. But certain steps that the President had taken prior to his defection indicate that he was preparing contingency plans for future eventualities. A year prior to his flight he transferred his uncle, Ambassador Asrat Wolde, from Moscow to Harare and on the morning he fled, his wife and children accompanied by the ambassador flew by the Ethiopian Airline to Harare. These events indicate that the President was preparing himself for a rainy day.

His defection was a turning point in the fighting between the government and the insurgent forces. The flight of the Commander-in-Chief of the Armed Forces not only killed the fighting spirit of the army, but set a bad example which field commanders emulated. Many commanding officers of the Armed Forces abandoned their troops, including the Commander of the Second Revolutionary Army, General Hussen. Accompanied by his senior officers, he flew to neighbouring countries, leaving his army of over 100,000 to its devices. The impact of the defection of the President was a shattering blow to the Armed Forces. Within two weeks from the date of his flight the entire army collapsed, thereby facilitating the advance of the insurgents unopposed. The leader who in his public utterances said: 'We will fight until the last man and a single bullet is left' was the first to break his vow.

The London Peace Talks

The London Peace Talks between the government and three insurgent organisations, EPLF, TPLF and OLF were to be convened in London under the chairmanship of Mr Herman Cohen, Assistant Secretary of State for African Affairs, in London in the Old Admiralty Building on 28 May 1991. The major parties to the talks were the EPLF and EPRDF/ TPLF which had the upper hand in the fight against the government forces and were certain that they would dictate the course of the peace talks to their advantage, which they did. The insurgents, with the support of the mediator, determined the participants to the talks despite the governments insistence to involve all organised opposition forces, including the EPRP. Representations were made to the Western allies by the Ethiopian embassies, including the London mission which explained the need to include all opposition groups in the talks, in the interest of a lasting and durable peace. The view of the UK Foreign and Commonwealth Office was to start the Peace Talks with the EPLF, EPRDF/TPLF and OLF, and to co-opt others as the talks progressed. According to their views the other organisations did not count in the armed struggle against the government. Had military strength been the only criterion for determining participants the EPRP would have had precedence over the OLF which was a junior partner to the talks. The diplomatic representations did not bring any change on the position of the mediator. Since the government was joining the Peace Talks from a position of weakness, it had no alternative other than to be guided by the wisdom of the mediator. For a detached observer the three participants identified by the mediator and those excluded from the talks had conflicting stances on the territorial integrity and unity of Ethiopia.

Notwithstanding the choice of the parties to the Peace Talks, a government delegation led by Prime Minister Tesfaye Dinka arrived in London on 25 May 1991. On the 26th the Ethiopian delegation met at the London Tara Hotel where the delegation was staying, to get briefings from the London mission on the general situation and in particular the views of the UK Government on the Peace Talks, and the attitude of the press and other pieces of information that might have been inputs to the Conference. The meeting decided to contact the mediator, Mr Cohen, who was in London, to assess his views and to have an idea of how he intended to conduct the Peace Talks. On the basis of this decision the Prime Minister contacted Mr Cohen and they met at the latter's hotel on 26th. At this meeting the Prime Minister was accompanied by Dr Ashagre Yigletu and the Ethiopian ambassador to the United Kingdom. The Prime Minister in outlining the position of his government raised with Mr Cohen the following issues:

The composition of a provisional government, which would include the present government, the EPLF, EPRDF/TPLF, OLF, other opposition forces, academics and ethnic groups, and its terms of reference in administering the country:

– The resolution of the Eritrean question on the basis of a constitution to be drafted by the provisional government and approved by the Ethiopian people;
– The withdrawal of the government and the opposition forces from

Addis Ababa and its environs; and entrusting the security of the city to the Police Force and the Urban Dwellers' Associations;
- The unhampered delivery of assistance to drought-stricken regions;
- Guaranteeing no vindictive measures against members of the PDRE government and WPE;
- Granting amnesty to party and government functionaries as well as to insurgents.

Mr Cohen declared that the points raised by the Prime Minister were not different from his line of thinking. He, however, advised the Prime Minister that at the meeting the question of proportion of representation in a future transitional government should not be emphasised and a special package for Eritrea must be considered. He reassured the Prime Minister that any unilateral action by the EPLF to change the status of Eritrea prior to the adoption of a new constitution would be resisted by the US Government and this had been made clear to the EPLF leadership. Should they declare independence unilaterally, the United States Government would use its influence to deprive them of any recognition by its friends and allies. On the security of Addis Ababa he concurred with the views expressed by the Prime Minister. He also informed the Prime Minister that he had a plan to meet the parties separately on 27 May, starting with the government delegation. The exploratory meeting of the Prime Minister with Mr Cohen was informative.

The Prime Minister on his return from the meeting briefed his delegation of the constructive discussion he had with the mediator. The delegation was relieved to hear that the briefing of the London Embassy, that the mediator would require it to sign a draft agreement favouring the other parties to the Peace Talks, was different from the discussion the Prime Minister had with Mr. Cohen. The delegation, then began preparing itself in earnest for the Peace Talks by forming a subcommittee to give a final touch to the speech of the delegation that would have been made at the opening of the Talks. On the morning of the 27th the Prime Minister convened a further meeting of the delegation, and informed it that he had been requested by Mr Cohen to meet him in his hotel and that he had suggested to him not to be accompanied by more than two of his assistants. Under such circumstances the Prime Minister informed the delegation that he would have to take with him Dr Ashagre Yegletu and Major-General Mesfin Gebrekal, Deputy Chief of Staff of the Ethiopian Armed Forces. The rest of the delegation was instructed to stand by. After an hour the Prime Minister and his two colleagues were back from the meeting with a draft agreement. He said that they were asked to go through it since it would have to be signed after the opening ceremony. The Prime Minister in presenting the draft to his delegation stated that his colleagues had suggested to him that the government delegation should withdraw from the Peace Talks rather than become a party to an agreement which was biased against the government.

Having weighed the advantages and disadvantages of participating and withdrawing from the Talks the delegation decided to participate, and to consider the mediator's draft as a working document and submit a counter proposal of the government. The following were the texts of the mediator's draft agreement and the government's counter-proposal:

A. *The Proposed Agreement of the US Government*

London Accord

1. A Provisional Government should be established in Addis Ababa as early as June 1 which will assume all legal and political responsibility for the governance of the country. This government should be broadly representative of all parts of the society and should utilise the current administrative structure in carrying out its responsibilities.
2. In co-operation with the Ethiopian Ministry of Defence, elements of the EPRDF armed forces will enter Addis Ababa beginning 12 noon local time, Thursday, May 30, and take up garrison positions. It is envisaged that at some point the city will be generally demilitarised during the transitional period. All military operations should cease as of 12 noon Thursday 30 May.
3. Responding to the proposal of the EPLF, it is agreed that:

    - An Eritrean administration will be set up immediately in Asmera.
    - This administration will co-operate with the Provisional Government in Addis Ababa and members of it will sit on the Provisional Government,
    - On June 1, 1993, a referendum will be held in Eritrea under appropriate international supervision to determine the political future of Eritrea.

4. The primary responsibility of the Provisional Government will be to prepare the country for free, democratic, internationally monitored elections in six months, to produce a Constituent Assembly to prepare

a constitution for the country. An independent electoral commission will be established for this purpose.

5. All parties to this agreement pledge to conduct their activities in the spirit of reconciliation and justice and the rule of law for all Ethiopians.

6. All parties to this agreement pledge continued co-operation with ongoing international relief efforts in Ethiopia.[29]

B. *The Counter Proposal of the Delegation of the Ethiopian Government*

London Accord

1. A Transitional Government will be established in Addis Ababa as early as June 15 and will assume full responsibility for the governance of the country by utilising the current administrative structure in carrying out its responsibilities.

2. The Transitional Government shall be composed of government, all opposition forces and representatives of all segments of the population in the following proportion:

   a. The Ethiopian Government, Internal and External, Independent and representatives of all segments of the population 55–60%. Independents shall include movements such as the ELF, COEDF and professional associations, religious and other organisations, local intellectuals and renowned individuals.

   b. EPLF, EPRDF, OLF 40–45%.

3. The primary responsibility of the Transitional Government will be to prepare the country for free, democratic, internationally monitored elections in nine months. It shall also establish a constituent assembly whose task shall be to draft a constitution for the country. An independent electoral commission will be constituted for that purpose. The Transitional Government shall ensure the human and political rights of the people during the transition.

4. As of 12 noon local time, May 30, Addis Ababa shall be declared a demilitarised zone. All government forces shall be withdrawn from Addis Ababa to a point to be fixed by the Ministry of Defence and the EPRDF military leadership. The government police force shall maintain law and order in the capital city.

5. The EPRDF military forces shall be withdrawn from around Addis Ababa to a point to be fixed by the Ministry of Defence and the EPRDF military leadership.

6. All military operations shall cease as of 12 noon Thursday, May 30, 1991.
7. The EPLF shall participate in the Transitional Government in Addis Ababa in the proportion specified in 2(b) above.
8. A referendum shall be held, under appropriate international super-vision, within a period of 3–5 years after the establishment of an elected government in Ethiopia, on the basis of a negotiated solution of the Eritrean issue.
9. A general amnesty shall come into force on the day of the cessation of hostilities. Such amnesty shall be extended to government and party officials, as well as to members of all opposition forces. The amnesty shall be irrevocable and internationally guaranteed.
10. All parties to this agreement pledge to conduct themselves in a spirit of reconciliation and undertake to uphold justice and the rule of law. In particular, they shall refrain from all acts of reprisal.
11. All parties to this agreement pledge continued co-operation with ongoing relief efforts in Ethiopia'.[30]

The two texts were at variance on three major issues, the composition of the transitional government, the Eritrean question and the demilitaris-ation of Addis Ababa and were inconsistent with the discussion the Prime Minister and the mediator had on 26 May. Despite these facts the govern-ment delegation was prepared to use the mediator's draft as a working document for the peace negotiation that was to be convened on 28 May.

In the afternoon of 27 May the Prime Minister accompanied by the two members of the delegation who were with him at the morning meeting, met the mediator to discuss with him the counter-proposal of the Ethiopian delegation. While the Prime Minister was explaining the counter-proposal the mediator interrupted, and announced that he had received information from the American Chargé d'affaires in Ethiopia that the Acting President, Lieutenant-General Tesfaye Gebre Kidan, had asked the US Government to invite the EPRDF forces to enter the capital and that he would make a press statement to that effect. Since the Prime Minister was not advised of such developments by his government he requested the mediator to withhold his statement until he had checked the information. The Prime Minister then immediately returned to the Ethiopian Embassy and contacted on the telephone the Acting President who denied the alleged invitation to the EPRDF to enter the capital. On the other hand he said that because of the deterioration of the security condition in the city he had declared a unilateral cease-fire. This infor-mation was relaid to the mediator, but he had already given his press

statement inviting the EPRDF to enter Addis Ababa without the courtesy
of waiting to hear what the Prime Minister would have to say after his
conversation with the Acting President.

The following is that text of the mediator's press statement issued on
27 May:

> 'As I speak, a cease-fire is being announced in Addis Ababa
> by the interim government. In order to reduce uncertainties
> and eliminate tension in the city, and after consulting with
> all parties, the US Government is recommending that the
> forces of the EPRDF enter the city as soon as possible to
> help stabilise the situation.
>
> The EPRDF leadership here in London has assured us that
> they continue to plan for a broadly-based provisional
> government leading to a democratic constitution for
> Ethiopia.
>
> We are asking all parties in Addis to co-operate in
> maintaining law and order.'[31]

The assertion that the press release was made after consulting all the
parties was not consistent with the fact that the government delegation
was not consulted nor was the mediator prepared to hear its views. The
press release had made two of the most important issues for negotiation,
the formation and composition of transitional government and the
demilitarisation of Addis Ababa, a *fait accompli*. Under the circumstances
the Ethiopian delegation was left with no choice other than making a
statement in response to the press release of the mediator. The following
is the text of the Ethiopian delegation's statement issued on the eve of
the London Peace Talks:

> 'The Ethiopian Government delegation to what had been
> billed round table Peace Talks, regrets to announce that its
> participation in the projected negotiation has been rendered
> impossible after the first day, even before formal meetings
> had taken place among the parties to the round-table.
>
> The hope that the Ethiopian people and the international
> community had placed in these talks has been shattered as
> a result of a dubious reading of developments in the country
> as well as backdoor deals. Ethiopia's yearning for peace and
> democracy has thus been crushed and its people are now in
> mortal danger. The positive steps taken in the last few weeks

by the Ethiopian Government as well as various Ethiopian groups and individuals had created a good opportunity to take Ethiopia out of the civil violence and instability and, in their place, bring about peace, democracy and prosperity.

The government had expressed great misgivings when the United States Government limited the talks to a few participants despite our call to involve all opposition groups who had wanted to engage in peaceful dialogue. We had feared and sensed that preference was already being given to a few groups. But we had placed reasonable expectations that this bias would be rectified early.

This intention was apparent in the fact that the invitation to the negotiations was extended only to those organisations that have either explicitly negative or, at best, a dubious attitude to the paramount question of the integrity of the Ethiopian state. The forces of unity were pointedly excluded from the early phase of the negotiations. The government came to the talks with the hope and belief that other interested groups will be invited to join the talks at an early stage, and in particular, that all political groupings will participate in the Transitional Government.

Thus while the vital issue of the composition of the Transitional Government should have been the subject of honest negotiations among all the political forces in the country, the mediating party, the government of the USA, has regrettably entrusted the entire task to the EPRDF alone.

Furthermore, this was done without even the pretence of the proper negotiations being entered in-to. It is during the very preliminary phase of separate contacts with each delegation that the mediating party saw fit to invite the military forces of the EPRDF to enter Addis Ababa in the form of a 'recommendation' with the pretext that these forces will ensure the maintenance of law and order in the city. Not only will this heighten the possibility of a terrible and bloody conflict in a densely populated urban centre, but it also makes virtually certain that the civil strife that has torn the fabric of the Ethiopian society over the past decades will continue on a new and even deeper dimension.

This all-to-easy temptation to be impressed by and favour the party that appears to have temporary military advantage,

319

sacrifices the prospect of finding an enduring political solution to the conflicts in Ethiopia.

The government delegation is convinced that a unique golden opportunity to address the root causes of political stability in Ethiopia is being missed. By encouraging a narrowly-based group to take power, the long-term interest of peace and stability in the region are being severely and dangerously compromised.

The government delegation strongly believes that for durable peace to be attained the following steps need to be taken:

1. All interested political groupings within and outside the country should be represented in the Peace Talks.
2. The talks should lead to a Transitional Government composed of all political and social groupings.
3. All military forces shall be immediately withdrawn from Addis Ababa in order to bring about a peaceful environment for a setting up of an all inclusive Transitional Government.
4. An internationally supervised election should be held that will lead to the emergence of a democratic government that enjoys the broad support of the entire nation.

The government delegations, therefore, deeply regrets the outcome of the London Peace Talks and expresses its bitter resentment at the readiness which some parties have shown to reach hasty conclusions before actual negotiations had commenced between the parties concerned.

The delegation condemns in the strongest possible terms the step taken to hand power to a narrowly-based group and totally dissociates itself from the London Talks.'[32]

On 28 May the EPLF, EPRDF and OLF delegations met under the chairmanship of the mediator, Mr Cohen, to co-ordinate their press statements. In his second press release the mediator made the following statement:

'I would like to summarise for you our consultation in London with representatives of the outgoing government,

the EPRDF, the OLF, and the EPLF. The subjects covered were:

- the establishment of a Transitional Government;
- the situation in Addis Ababa; and
- the facilitation of international relief efforts.

At this point the United States Government makes the following recommendations and observations:

Transitional Government

A Transitional Government should be established in Addis Ababa as soon as possible. The Transitional Government should assume all legal and political responsibility for the governance of Ethiopia.

The Transitional Government should be broadly representative of all Ethiopian society, including diverse political groupings, and should, where appropriate, utilise the existing civil administrative structures in carrying out its responsibilities.

The primary responsibility of the Transitional Government should be to prepare the country for free, democratic, internationally monitored elections in nine to twelve months to produce a Constituent Assembly to prepare a new constitution for Ethiopia.

The new constitution should guarantee fundamental individual rights and should respect the identity and interests of all the different peoples of Ethiopia.

The Transitional Government should consider an appropriate amnesty or indemnity for past acts not consisting violations of the laws of war or international human rights. Any person accused of such offences should be afforded due process of law in accordance with international norms, and all procedures should be open to observers from internationally recognised organisations.

Discussion should continue in London regarding the composition of the Transitional Government.

Addis Ababa

Elements of the EPRDF armed forces have entered Addis Ababa and taken up garrison positions. The city should be demilitarised as soon as possible. Hostilities throughout Ethiopia should cease as soon as possible.

International Relief

All parties should continue to co-operate with ongoing international relief efforts. The United States Government calls on the international donor community to make all possible efforts to help maintain essential services and continue providing relief assistance.

The United States calls on the parties to conduct their activities in the spirit of reconciliation and justice and to create the conditions necessary for the establishment of democracy. The United States stands ready to assist them to achieve this goal.'[33]

Subsequently the EPLF, EPRDF and OLF made the following joint statement:

> 'The EPRDF, EPLF, and OLF have agreed to hold a follow-up conference not later than July 1 to discuss the details of the transitional period in general and the formation of a broad-based provisional government in particular. The precise time and venue will be announced later.
>
> They have agreed that such a conference is important in order that a wider range of parties and interests be included. The EPRDF, EPLF, and OLF will welcome the presence of the US and other international observers. In the meantime, the EPRDF will assume state responsibility in Addis Ababa pending the formation of a broad-based provisional government at the proposed conference. The three parties conclude by appealing for peace and tranquillity.'[34]

The joint statement empowered the EPRDF to head an interim government pending the convening of a conference on 1 July 1991. As the head of the interim government, the EPRDF leader, Ato Melese Zenawe, made the following statement in a press conference:

> 'As you know the London peace conference has come to a successful conclusion. The participants of the conference have agreed to hold a follow-up conference within a month. This was agreed upon in order to include other parties and interests in the discussion on the transition period in general and the formation of a broad-based provisional government in particular.

In the meantime, the EPRDF is assuming state power in Addis Ababa pending formation of broad-based provisional government.

I am pleased to inform you that peace and order has now been re-established in Addis Ababa. We feel confident that foreign embassies and international organisations in Addis Ababa will resume their normal duties over the next few days.

The priority of the interim EPRDF administration will be to ensure law and order, facilitate the distribution of relief aid and mainly essential services.

The EPRDF looks forward to participating in the proposed conference in a constructive manner. At the conference the EPRDF will work for an agreement on the formation of a broad-based provisional government, the peaceful and democratic resolution of the problem in our country, and the holding of an internationally supervised election to form an elected government. In other words the EPRDF still stands by its transitional programme.

Now that we are well on the way to resolving all our political problems and defining a democratic future for our country, we hope those who have been providing relief and other assistance to the people of Ethiopia will not only continue to do so but also augment their assistance.'[35]

On 29 May Isayas Afeworki, the Secretary-General of the EPLF, who was silent in the previous few days, issued a statement which was regarded by political observers as his interpretation and understanding of the joint declaration. He made the following statement:

'History is often punctuated by momentous episodes that radically shape the course of the future events. I believe you would agree with me that the turbulent developments that occurred in Eritrea and Ethiopia in the past ten days with such intensity and rapidity fall within the historical category. To appraise current realities and ponder on future prospects at this important and sensitive chapter in the history of Eritrean and Ethiopian peoples is thus timely and appropriate. The EPLF had refrained from expressing its views, both prior to and during the conference held in London, on the modalities of a transitional process as well

323

as the disparate interpretations maintained by various parties. It is with this general context and in order to clarify our standpoints and views on all relevant questions on the matter that we have called this press conference today. Allow me briefly to state, on this occasion, the broad outline of EPLF position on this issues:

- I. The EPLF announces that it will form a provisional government in Eritrea in order to facilitate and until such time as a UN supervised referendum is conducted and a durable and just solution to the Eritrean case realised.

- II. Paramount functions of the provisional government shall include:
- 1. To guarantee the national security of Eritrea and safeguard the hard-won achievements of the Eritrean people;
- 2. To ensure the rule of law and order;
- 3. To shoulder the requisite administrative duties of a functional society;
- 4. To assume authority and accountability for all other matters that concern Eritrea in the interim period;

- III. Until such time as a referendum is implemented and power duly transferred to the legitimate authority (in accordance with the results of the referendum), and in order to promote democracy, stability and peace in Ethiopia by averting turmoil and bloodshed, the provisional Eritrean Government shall maintain wide-ranging co-operation in economic, and other sectors of mutual interest with the provisional government in Ethiopia. The EPLF's commitment to participate in the follow-up conference scheduled before the beginning of July is guided by this spirit and will naturally be restricted to the agenda dealing with co-operation in the transitional period. It does not otherwise imply nor should it be misconstrued to mean Eritrea's active participation in the provisional government in Ethiopia, as the EPLF does not indeed have the mandate to do so from the Eritrean people.

324

- IV. The provisional Eritrean Government will exert maximum efforts to facilitate relief work as a first priority. It will also encourage economic reconstruction and the repatriation of dispersed citizens. All these undertakings evidently involve hard work and resources. But they remain urgent tasks that require immediate action.
- In this context, the EPLF appeals to the United Nations to shoulder its moral responsibilities without further delay. The EPLF also calls on all governments, NGO's and concerned bodies to grant assistance required to heal the wounds of war and destruction that have devoured our country for three decades.'[36]

The press statement was a declaration of independence for Eritrea pending the formalities of a UN supervised referendum without the consent of the entire Ethiopian people.

The Ethiopian Government delegation was not alone in condemning the lack of fairness and objectivity in the circumstances leading to the Peace Talks. An independent group of Ethiopians, who came from the US, Ethiopia, Switzerland and Kenya to follow-up the Peace Talks, in a press release expressed its dissatisfaction with the US Government's handling of the talks in the following terms:

'I. We are a group of Independent Ethiopians who came to London from Ethiopia, Africa, Europe, and the United States. The members of the independent committee are:

Mr Adbul Mohammed (Kenya)
Dr Andreas Eshete (Philadelphia, USA)
Dr Henock Kifle (Geneva, Switzerland)
Dr Hizkias Assefa (Kenya)
Mr Issac Kifle (Ethiopia)
Mr Jalal Abdel-Latif (Los Angeles, USA)
Professor Mesfin Wolde Mariam (Ethiopia)
The independent committee came to London with two aims:

1. First to present our views on a peaceful transition to democracy to all parties and the public;
2. Second to observe the talks in London.
   The committee intends to pursue these aims throughout the transitional period.
   The Committee has met in London with each party. We are grateful

to all for affording us the opportunity to hold free and extensive exchanges.

II. Obscurity surrounds the proceedings in London and the fateful decisions that issued from them. This in turn has led to dissatisfaction among citizens in the country and in exile as well as among certain parties to the talks. Reasons and merits to one side, it is noteworthy that the negotiations between the Ethopian Government, EPRDF, OLF and EPLF announced by the US Government never took place.

There were no talks among principal parties. Instead, there were US consultations, conducted separately, with representatives of the Ethiopian Government, EPRDF, OLF and EPLF. In addition, the US entered separate accords with EPLF and EPRDF.

Representatives of the Ethiopian Government abandoned the talks at an early stage because they felt that the crucial decision to let EPRDF take the military and political control in Addis Ababa has been decided unilaterally by the US without the consultation and consent of the Ethiopian Government.

The OLF has also expressed misgivings over the fact that there were no negotiations, and that an EPRDF government was formed without OLF's participation and consent.

In sum, two far-reaching actions, the formation of a provisional government in Ethiopia and a provisional government in Eritrea, were undertaken by the US in accords separately entered into with EPRDF and EPLF. It is therefore difficult to escape the public impression that two acts that will set the stage for the post-Mengistu era were, in large measure, made by US Government fiat.

Regrettably, the fact that the US reached its accord solely with EPRDF and EPLF, who are now the sole bearers of governmental power, also feeds an impression for long cultivated by the powerful propaganda machinery of the deposed government that there is an EPLF and EPRDF conspiracy to partition and control the country.

In the committee's considered view the serious problem with the procedure that governed the decisions made in London is that it failed to provide fair representation of fundamental interests in Ethiopian society. In consequence, the legitimacy of the decision and the resultant authorities remain dubious.

This is unfortunate and sad. It is unfortunate because the present conditions are not conducive to peace and stability, which are indispensable for an orderly transition to democracy. It is sad because it robs citizens of the full benefit of the victory won against a deeply-hated tyranny, an achievement to which the political groups now in power made the greatest contribution. The absence of any public celebration of the fall of the tyranny attests to the prevalent atmosphere of fear, uncertainty and profound civic mistrust.'[37]

The independent committee's assessment of the situation of the Peace Talks was also supported by the European Parliament which passed a resolution expressing its displeasure with the US Government's handling of the Conference and its concern about developments in Ethiopia after the EPRDF's take-over. The operative paragraphs of its resolution dealing with the Peace Talks read:

'The European Parliament:
Deplores the fact that, at the first negotiation held in London on 27 and 28 May 1991 under the auspices of the United States, only three opposition groups were invited; – regrets, as its Committee on Development and Co-operation has indicated to the current Presidency of the Development Council, that the European Community has failed completely to take the political initiative with far-reaching consequences, thereby leaving the field open to the United States;
Believes that a peaceful and democratic solution to the problem tearing the country apart must be found first and foremost by the Ethiopians themselves, without outside interference and in the presence of all the organisations and movements representing the Ethiopian civilian population.'[38]

The London Peace Talks were faulty from their very inception for they fell short of providing essential conditions for national reconciliation. The mediator's high-handed decision, in restricting the number of participants to the peace talks to the government and three from a dozen of opposition forces, wasted a favourable opportunity for national reconciliation. The mediator, the United States Government, could, if it had wanted to, have used its good offices for bringing about genuine peace and tranquillity to Ethiopia and its people.

Although the military performance of the government was in decline when the US Government initiated the London Peace Talks, it had still a formidable force to stifle the initiative of the opposition forces. In the past, all sides had met reverses and successes at battlefields which convinced them that the fratricidal wars they were waging could not have been resolved by force. It was the realisation of this fact and the changes in international political situation that compelled both the government and the opposition forces to accept the peace initiative of the United States Government which was emerging as the only superpower. However, before the peace process began to gather momentum the Ethiopian Government began to crumble. The President and the Commander-in-Chief of the Armed Forces fled the country setting a precedent for his field commanders to follow suit. The commander of the Second Revolutionary Army in Eritrea was the first to emulate the example of his commander. He with most of his senior officers abandoned an army of over 100,000 and sought refuge in a neighbouring country. Other government forces on other fronts disintegrated with meteoric speed. The government was only in control of Addis Ababa which was besieged by the joint forces of EPLF and TPLF. The government delegation to the peace talks arrived in London under such unenviable circumstances. To make matters even worse than they were, while the government delegation was discussing the peace accord proposal with the mediating party, the Acting President of the PDRE, Lieutenant-General Tesfaye Gebre Kidan, without the courtesy of informing the Prime Minister, declared a unilateral cease-fire, a news that was broken to him by the mediator who was apprised of the Acting President's latest move in advance. The cease-fire was an invitation to the besieging forces to occupy the capital, the last hold of the government, which the delegation in London was arguing to prevent its occupation. Declaring a cease-fire on the eve of the opening of the peace talks made the government delegation's participation irrelevant. The unwarranted collapse of the government as a result of the cease-fire created a power vacuum in the country, thereby tempting the mediator to take the initiative in inviting the EPLF and TPLF forces to occupy the capital and to assume state power under the pretext of preventing a breakdown of law and order.

To sum up, the London Peace Talks became irrelevant on account of the disintegration of the government's armed forces caused by the flight of the Commander-in-Chief of the Armed Forces, the appalling ineptitude of the government in Addis Ababa to provide a leadership that was required in a crisis, the absence of neutral international observers and impartial mediators.

NOTES

1 Report to the Fifth Plenum of the Central Committee of the WPE, Chairman Mengistu Haile Mariam, Addis Ababa, Pagume 1978(EC), Ref. No. 77–02–04/78. p. 2.
2 ibid., pp. 5–9.
3 Report to the Sixth Plenum of the Central Committee of the WPE, Chairman Mengistu Haile Mariam, Addis Ababa, Megabit 1979 (EC), Ref. No. 77–02–04/79, p. 8.
4 *The Ethiopian Herald*, vol. xlii, No. 302.
5 Ye Ethiopia Hizb Ena Ye Mengist Tarik, Dr Lapiso Dilebo, Addis Ababa, 1982 (EC), p. 18.
6 Ex-President Mengistu's Confession to the Ethiopian People, released on tapes, from Harare disclosed the fact that the Third Army disintegrated on account of the incompetence of its leaders.
7 Mengistu's Confession from Harare, *Aimro*, vol. I, No. 11, Addis Ababa, Tahsas, 1986 (EC), p. 3.
8 Rasoon Yebetene Serawitu (The Army Disbanded Itself), *Tobya*, vol. 2. No. 5, Addis Ababa, Nehasse 1985 (EC), pp. 26–29.
9 President Mengistu's Report to the First Extraordinary Congress of the National Shengo, Addis Ababa, 5 June 1989.
10 National Democratic Revolutionary Programme of Ethiopia, Addis Ababa, April 1976, Article 5.
11 Class Struggle and the Problem in Eritrea, Ethiopian Revolutionary Information Centre, pp. 64–66.
12 ibid., p. 48.
13 Press Conference on the New Peace Initiative, the Attempted *Coup d'état* and Other Issues, President Mengistu, Ministry of Information, Addis Ababa, 6 June 1989, p. 18.
14 ibid., p. 13.
15 Press Conference on The New Peace Initiative. The Attempted Coup and Other Issues, President Mengistu Haile Mariam, p. 28.
16 ibid., p. 27.
17 ibid., pp. 26–27.
18 President Mengistu's Speech to a Rally, *The Ethiopian Herald*, vol. xlv, No. 208.
19 ibid.
20 Central Report to the Eleventh Plenum of the Central Committee of the Workers' Party of Ethiopia, President Mengistu Haile Mariam, Addis Ababa, Yekatit 1982 (EC), p. 50.
21 ibid. p. 56.
22 Programme of the Workers' Party of Ethiopia, p. 69.
23 ibid., p. 114.
24 Central Report to the Eleventh Plenum, President Mengistu Haile Mariam.

25 ibid.
26 *The Ethiopian Herald*, vol. xlvii, No. 194, 27 April 1991.
27 ibid.
28 Speech Delivered to XI International Conference on Ethiopian Studies, Professor Mesfin Wolde Mariam, Addis Ababa, 1–6 April 1991; Letters to the President and Friends of Ethiopia, Peace and Reconciliation Committee, Addis Ababa, Miazya 1 ken 1983 (EC) and 5 April 1991.
29 The London Accord, The Proposal of the US Government, London, 27 May 1991.
30 The London Accord, the Counter-Proposal of the PDRE Delegation, London, 27 May 1991.
31 Statement by Mr Herman Cohen, Assistant-Secretary of State for African Affairs, London, 27 May 1991.
32 Statement by the Ethiopian Delegation to the London Peace Talks, London, 27 May 1991.
33 Statement by Mr Cohen, 28 May 1991.
34 Joint Statement by the EPRDF, OLF and EPLF, London, 28 May 1991.
35 Press Conference by Mr Melese Zenawi of the EPRDF, London, 28 May 1991.
36 Press Conference by EPLF Secretary-General, Isayas Afeworki, London, 29 May 1991.
37 Statement by the Independent Committee for a Peaceful Transition to Democracy in Ethiopia, London, 6 June 1991.
38 Resolution on the Situation in Ethiopia, European Parliament, Strasburg, 13 June 1991.

Bibliography

I. Books and Articles

Abir, M., The Era of the Princes, London: Longmans, 1968.

Addis Hiwet, From Autocracy to Revolution, London 1975.

Andargachew Tiruneh, The Ethiopian Revolution 1974–1987, Cambridge: Cambridge University Press, 1992.

Assefa Endeshaw, The February 1974 Ethiopian Revolution, Ethiopian Studies: Social Science Monograph Series, London 1994.

Bahru Zewde, A History of Modern Ethiopia: 1855–1974, London, Athens and Addis Ababa, 1991.

Bailey, Glen, An Analysis of the Ethiopian Revolution, Athens, Ohio, 1975.

Baker, Jonathan, Ethiopia's Road to Perestroika, in Search of the End of the Rainbow, Current African Issues, Scandinavian Institute of African Studies, Sweden, 1990.

Bates, Darrel, The Abyssinian Difficulty, the Emperor Tewodros and the Maqdela Campaign 1867–68; Oxford 1979.

Bender, Gerald J. and Others, Africa Crisis Area and USA Foreign Policy, Berkeley and London, University of California Press, 1985.

Berkley, G. F. H., The Campaign of Adwa and the Rise of Menilek, London, 1902

Booth, J. A., The End and the Beginning: The Nicaraguan Revolution, Westview, Boulder, 1985.

Briton, Crane, The Anatomy of Revolution, New York: Random House, 1938.

Calvert, Peter, A Study of Revolution, Oxford: Clarendon Press, 1970.

Chaliand, Gerard, Revolution in the Third World: Myths and Prospects, New York: Viking Press, 1977.

Chege, M., The Revolution Betrayed: Ethiopia 1974–1979, *Journal of Modern African Studies*, vol. 17 Part iv, London, 1979.

331

Clapham, Christopher, Transformation and Continuity in Revolutionary Ethiopia, Cambridge: Cambridge University Press.

Coffey, Thomas M., The Lion by the Tail: The Story of the Italian-Ethiopian War, London: Hamish Hamilton, 1974.

Cohen, John J. and Kohen, Peter H., Ethiopian Provincial and Municipal Government, East Lancing, Michigan: African Studies Centre, 1980.

Darkwah, R. H. Kofi, Shewa, Menilek and the Ethiopian Empire, London: Heinemann, 1975.

Derby, R., Revolution in the Revolution, Harmondsworth: Penguin, 1968.

Eden, Sir Anthony, Facing the Dictators, Boston: Houghton Mifflin, 1962.

Eisenstadt, S. N., The Political System of Empires, London: Free Press Glencoe, 1972.

Fikre Tolossa, The Amhara Contribution to the Civilisation of Ethiopia, *Ethiopia Review*, Los Angeles, April 1993.

Getahew Haile, The Unity and Territorial Integrity of Ethiopia, *Journal of Modern African Studies*, vol. 24, No. 3, London, 1986.

Gilkes, Patrick, The Dying Lion of Feudalism and Modernisation in Ethiopia, London, 1975.

Graffin, Keith, The Ethiopian Economy, New York: St Martini Press, 1992.

Greene, H., Comparative Revolutionary Movements, New Jersey: Prentice-Hall, 1984.

Greenfield, Richard, Ethiopia a New Political History, London: Pall Mall Press, 1965.

Haile Selassie I, My Life and Ethiopia's Progress, London: Oxford University Press, 1976.

Halliday, Fred, Molyneux, Maxine, The Ethiopian Revolution, London: Verso, 1981.

Harold, Irving, Kaplan and Nelson, Ethiopia: A Country Study, Washington DC, American University, 1981.

Harris, Michael, Jansson, Kurt, and Penrose, Angela, The Ethiopian Famine, London: Zed Books Ltd., 1990.

Hartslet, Sir E., The Map of Africa by Treaty, Frank Cass & Co. Ltd., London, 1967.

Hoare, Sir Samuel, Ourselves and the World Peace, National Union of Conservative Associations, Facts and Leaflets, No. 3363–3486, London, 1933–35.

Hobens, Allen, Land Tenure System among the Amhara of Ethiopia, Chicago: Chicago University Press, 1973.

Hrbek, I., General History of Africa III: Africa from the Seventh to the Eleventh Century, California, UNESCO, 1992.

Human Rights Watch, Evil Days: Thirty Years of War and Famine in Ethiopia, An African Watch Report, USA, 1991.

Huntingdon, S. P., Political Order in Changing Societies, Newhaven: Yale University Press, 1968.

Jones, A. H. M., and Monroe, Elizabeth, A History of Abyssinia, New York: Negro University Press, 1969.

Keller, J. Edmund, Revolutionary Ethiopia: From Empire to People's Republic, Bloomington and Indianapolis: Indiana University Press, 1988.

Khalid, Mansur, Nimerie and the Revolution in Dismay, London, 1985.

Korn, David, Ethiopia, the United States and the Soviet Union, London: Croom Helm, 1986.

Korten, David C., Planned Change in a Traditional Society, New York: Praeger, 1972.

Lappiso Delebo, Ye Ethiopia Hizb Ena Ye Mengist Tarik, Addis Ababa: Commercial Printing Press, 1982.

Laval, Josee, The Unpublished Diary of Pierre Laval, London: The Falcon Press, 1948.

Lefort, R., Ethiopia: A Heretical Revolution, London: Zed Books Ltd., 1983.

Legum, C., Ethiopia: The Fall of Haile Selassie's Empire, London: Collings, 1975.

Levine, Donald N., Greater Ethiopia: The Evolution of a Multiethnic Society, London: The University of Chicago Press Ltd., 1974.

Lewis, I. M., Nationalism and Self-determination, London; Ithaca Press, 1983.

Lockot, H. W., The Mission, London: Hurst and Company, 1989.

Longrigg, S. H., A Short History of Eritrea, Oxford: Clarendon Press, 1945.

Marcus, Harold G., The Life and Times of Menilek II: Ethiopia 1844–1913, Lawrenceville, New Jersey: Red Sea Press, 1995.

—— Haile Selassie I the Formative Years, 1892–1936 Lawrenceville, New Jersey: Red Sea Press, 1995.

—— Ethiopia, Great Britain, and the United States: 1941–1974. The Politics of Empire, Los Angeles, Berkeley and London: University of California Press, 1983.

Markakis, John, Anatomy of a Traditional Polity, Oxford, 1974.

Markakis, John and Nega Ayele, Class and Revolution in Ethiopia, London: Spokesman, 1978.

Matthew, David, Ethiopia: The Study of A Polity, 1540–1935, London: Eyre and Spottiswoode, 1947.

Menasse Haile, Legality of Secessions: The Case of Eritrea, *International Law Review*, vol. 8, No. 2, Fall, 1994.

Mesfin Wolde Mariam, The Background of the Ethio-Somalia Boundary Dispute, Addis Ababa: Berhanena Selam Printing Press, 1964.

Meter, Karl Van, Ray, Ellen, Schaap, William, and Wolf, Louis, Dirty Work: CIA in Africa, London: Zed Books Ltd., 1980.

Michael, Joel S., Peasants, Politics and Revolutions: Pressure Towards Political and Social Changes in the World, Princeton: Princeton University Press, 1970.

Moore, Jr. Barrington, Social Origin of Dictatorship and Democracy: Lord and Peasant in the Making of the Modern World, Boston: Beacon Press, 1966.

Murno-Hay, Stuart, Aksum: An African Civilisation of Late Antiquity, Edinburgh: Edinburgh University Press, 1991.

Norberg, V. H., The Swedes in Haile Selassie's Ethiopia, 1924–1952, Uppsala, 1977.

O'Kane, Rosemary, The Revolutionary Reign of Terror, Edward Elgar Publishing Company, 1991.

Ottaway, David and Marina, Ethiopia: Empire in Revolution, New York: Holmes and Meir, 1978.

—— Afro-communism, New York: African Publishing Company, 1988.

Ottaway, Marina, Social Class and Corporate Interests, *Journal of Modern African Studies*, vol. 17, 1979.

—— Superpower Competition and Regional Conflicts in the Horn of Africa. The Soviet Impact in Africa. C. Nation and M. V. Kauppi (eds), Lexington, Massachusetts and Toronto, 1984.

Pankhurst, Richard, State and Land in Ethiopian History, Addis Ababa and Oxford University Press, 1966.

Pankhurst, Richard, Taddesse Beyene and Taddesse Tamrat, The Centenary of Dogali: Proceedings of the International Symposium, Addis Ababa, Asmara, January 24–25, 1987, Institute of Ethiopian Studies, Addis Ababa University, 1988.

Pawlos Gnogno, Atse Menilek, Addis Ababa: Bole Printing Press, 1984 (EC).

Perham, Margery, The Government of Ethiopia, London: Faber and Faber, 1948.

Petrides, S. Pierre, The Boundary Question between Ethiopia and Somalia: New Delhi People's Publishing House, 1983.

Pool, David, Eritrea–Africa's Longest War, Anti-Slavery Society Human Rights Series Report No. 3, 1980, London, 1982.

Prouty, Christe, Empress Tayetu and Menilek II of Ethiopia: 1883–1910, Trenton, New Jersey, Red Sea Press, 1986.

Ray, Ellen, Schapp, William, van Meter, Karl, and Wolf, Louis, Dirty Work: The CIA in Africa, London: Zed Books Press Ltd., 1980.

Rubenson, Sven, The Survival of Ethiopian Independence, London: Heinemann, 1976.

—— King of Kings Tewodros of Ethiopia, Addis Ababa: Oxford University Press, 1966.

Sbacchi, Alberto, Ethiopia Under Mussolini, London: Zed Books Ltd., 1985.

Scheer, R., and Zeitlin, M., Cuba: An American Tragedy, Harmondsworth, 1964.

Schwab, Peter, Ethiopia: Politics, Economics and Society, London: Frances Printers, 1985.

Searle, Chris, A Blindfold Removed: Ethiopia's Struggle for Literacy, London: Karia Press, 1991.

Sergew Habte Selassie, Ancient and Medieval Ethiopian History to 1270.

Skocpol, T., States and Social Revolutions, Cambridge University Press, 1979.

Spencer, John, Ethiopia at Bay: a Personal Account of the Haile Selassie Years, Algonac, Michigan, 1984.

Taddesse Tamrat, Church and State in Ethiopia, London: Oxford University Press, 1972.

Bibliography

Tekeste Negash, Italian Colonialism in Eritrea, 1882 to 1941, Policies, Praxis and Impact, Uppsala, 1987.

Tekle Tsadiq Mekuria, Atse Tewodros Ena Ye Ethiopia Andnet, Addis Ababa: Kuraz Printing Press, 1981 (EC).

—— Atse Yohannis Ena Ye Ethiopia Andnet, Addis Ababa Kuraz Printing Press, 1982 (EC).

—— Ye Gragn Ahmed Werera, Addis Ababa, Berhanena Selam Printing Press, 1966 (EC).

Tesfatsion Madhane, Eritrea: Dynamics of a National Question, Amesterdam, 1986.

Tesfaye Mekonnen, Yedrese Lebaletariku, Addis Ababa: Artistic Printing Press, 1985 (EC).

Thomson, Blair, Ethiopia the Country that Cut off Its Head, London, 1975.

Tilly, Charles, From Mobilisation to Revolution, Reading, Massachusetts: Addison-Wesley, 1978.

Tirmingham, J. Spencer, Islam in Ethiopia, London, New York, Toronto: Oxford University Press, 1952.

Tocqueville, A. de, The *Ancien Regime* of the French Revolution, London: Fontana, 1966.

Trevaskis, Sir Gerald, Eritrea: A Colony in Transition, 1941–1952, London, New Yok: Oxford University Press, 1960.

Ullendorf, E., The Ethiopians, London, 1960.

—— Ethiopia and the Bible, London: Oxford University Press, 1968.

United Nations, Report of the United Nations Commission for Eritrea, General Assembly Fifth Session, Supplement No. 8 (A/1285), Lake Success, New York, 1950.

Vansittart, Lord Robert, Lessons of My Life, New York: Knopf, 1943.

Work, Ernest, Ethiopia: a Pawn in European Diplomacy, New York: Macmillan, 1935.

Zewde Gebre-Selassie, A Political Biography of Yohannis IV, London: Oxford University Press, 1975.

II. Government and Party Publications

Central Planning Committee, Ten-Year Development Plan (1977–1985 EC) of the Provisional Military Government of Ethiopia, Addis Ababa, 1985.

Central Statistical Office, Statistical Abstract, Addis Ababa, 1982.

—— Major Statistical Information of Ethiopia, Addis Ababa, 1984.

—— Peoples Democratic Republic of Ethiopia: Facts and Figures, Addis Ababa, 1987.

Commission for Organising the Workers, Party of Ethiopia, Decisions and Documents of the Second Congress of COPWE, Addis Ababa, 1982.

—— *Meskerem: A Marxist-Leninist Ideological Journal,* vol. No. 5, June, 1981.

335

Ethiopian Revolutionary Information Centre, Class Struggle and the Problem in Eritrea, Addis Ababa, 1979.

Ethiopian Tourist Commission, Ethiopia's Historic Route, Addis Ababa, 1984.

The First Extraordinary Congress of the National Shengo, The Fundamental Ideas in the New Peace Initiative of the People's Democratic Republic of Ethiopia to Solve the Problem in Eritrea Peacefully, Addis Ababa, June 1989.

Imperial Ethiopian Government, Third Five-Year Development Plan, Addis Ababa, 1968.

Mengistu Haile Mariam, Report to the Founding Congress of COPWE, Addis Ababa, 1983.

—— Report to the Founding Congress of the Workers' Party of Ethiopia Addis Ababa, 1984.

—— Central Report to the Third Session of the Central Committee of the Workers' Party of Ethiopia, Addis Ababa, Meskerem, 1978.

—— Central Report to the Fourth Session of the Central Committee of the Workers' Party of Ethiopia, No. 77–02–04/78, Addis Ababa, 1985.

—— Central Report to the Fifth Session of the Central Committee of the Workers' Party of Ethiopia, No. 77–02–04/78, Addis Ababa, 1986.

—— Central Report to the Sixth Session of the Central Committee of the Workers' Party of Ethiopia, No. 77–02–04/79, Addis Ababa, 1986.

—— Central Report to the Ninth Session of the Central Committee of the Workers' Party of Ethiopia, Vols. 1 and 2, No. 77–02–04/81, Addis Ababa, 1989.

—— Central Report to the Tenth Session of the Central Committee of the Workers' Party of Ethiopia, No. 77–02–04/81, Addis Ababa, 1989.

—— Central Report to the Eleventh Session of the Central Committee of the Workers' Party of Ethiopia, No. 77–02–04/82, Addis Ababa, 1990.

—— Report to the Third Congress of the National Shengo of the People's Democratic Republic of Ethiopia, Addis Ababa, 1988.

—— Report to the First Extraordinary Congress of the National Shengo, Addis Ababa, 1989.

—— Interview Granted to *The New York Times*, Addis Ababa, 26 November, 1988.

Ministry of Education, Education Sector Review Report, Addis Ababa, 1974.

—— Responding to International Media: Press Conference, Addis Ababa, 28 May, 1988.

Ministry of Foreign Affairs, Ethiopia's Policy of Peace and Co-operation in the Horn, Addis Ababa, 1988.

—— Press Conference on the New Peace Initiative, the Attempted *Coup D'état* and Other Issues, Addis Ababa, 6 June, 1989.

Ministry of Information, Ethiopia: Laying the Foundation for a Sustained Socio-economic Development, Addis Ababa, 1988.

—— Ethiopia the Cradle of History, Addis Ababa, 1989.

—— Eritrea a Multinational Component of the Ethiopian Polity, Addis Ababa, 1988.

—— Ethiopia from Feudal Autocracy to People's Democracy, Addis Ababa, 1987.

336

—— Peace Initiative and the Problem in Eritrea, Addis Ababa, 1988.

—— *The Ethiopian Herald* from 1974–1991, Addis Ababa.

—— Three-Years Development Plan (1979–1981 EC), Addis Ababa, 1979.

Planning Commission of the Imperial Ethiopian Government, Third Five-Year Plan, 1968–1973.

Preparatory Committee for the Founding of the Peoples' Democratic Republic of Ethiopia, Ensuring the Rights of Nationalities, Addis Ababa, 1987.

Propaganda and Culture Committee, Ethiopia: a Decade of Revolutionary Transformation, 1974–1984, Addis Ababa, 1984.

—— Ethiopia Ye Rejim Zemene Tarik Ena Ye Hidree Misreta, Addis Ababa, 1980 (EC).

Provisional Office of Mass Organisational Affairs, The New Democratic Revolution and Ethiopia's National Democratic Programme, Addis Ababa, 1969 (EC).

The Workers' Party of Ethiopia, Programme, Serial No. 77–01—01/77, Addis Ababa, 1984.

III. Proclamations

Proclamation No. 1 of 1975.

Proclamation No. 2 of 1975.

Labour Proclamation No. 64 of 1975.

Public Ownership of Rural Lands Proclamation No. 31 of 1975.

Government Ownership of Urban Lands and Extra Houses Proclamation, No. 47 of 1974.

The Constitutions of the People's Democratic Republic of Ethiopia, Proclamation No. 1 of 1987.

IV. Miscellaneous Sources

Cohen, Herman, Statements on the London Peace Talks, London, 27 and 28 May, 1991.

Ethiopian Government Delegation to the London Peace Talks, Counter-Proposal on the US Government's London Accord, London, 27 May, 1991.

—— Press Statements of the Ethiopian Government Delegation, London, 27 and 28 May, 1991.

EPDRF, EPLF and OLF, Joint Statement, London 28 May, 1991.

European Parliament, A Resolution on the Situation in Ethiopia, Strasburg, 13 June, 1991.

Henze, Paul, The United States and the Horn of Africa: History and Current Prospects, A Paper Presented to the Conference on International Relations in the Horn of Africa, Cairo, 27–30 May, 1990.

—— Address to the Symposium Sponsored by Eritrean for Peace and Democracy, Crystal City Arlington, Virginia, 10 March, 1990.

337

Independent Committee for Peaceful Transition to Democracy in Ethiopia, London, 6 June 1991.

Isayas Afeworki, Statement at a Press Conference, London, 29 May, 1991.

Melese Zenawi, Statement at a Press Conference, London, 28 May, 1991.

Mengistu Haile Mariam, I had to Break Silence, *Ethiopia Review*, Vol. 4, No. 3, Los Angeles, March, 1994.

—— Confession From Harare, *Amiro*, vol. 8, No. 11, Addis Ababa, Tahsas, 1986 (EC).

Mesfin Wolde Mariam, Speech Delivered to the XI International Conference on Ethiopian Studies, Addis Ababa, 1–6 April, 1991.

Peace and Reconciliation Committee, Letters to the President and Friends of Ethiopia, Addis Ababa, April, 1991.

Public Records Office, FO 371/27518, London, 1941.

—— FO 371/35634, London, 1943.

Rasoon Yebetene Serawitu (The Army Disbanded Itself), *Tobya* vol. 2, No. 5, Addis Ababa, Nehasse, 1985 (EC).

US Government, The London Accord, London, 28 May, 1991.

Index

Mahdists, 22
recognised Menilek as king of
   Shewa, 23
rescuing an Egyptian garrison, 22

Za Dengle, King, 11
Zagwe Dynasty, 5–6
Zara Yaqob, King, 9

Zeila, 4, 38
Zemecha, 149–52
Zemene Mesafint, 14–16
Zerai Dresse, 244
Zewde Gebre-Selassie, Dejazmach, 24,
   123, 129
Zewditu, Empress, 23, 36–7
Zimbabwe, 312